THE P

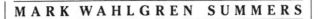

MARK WAHLGREN SUMMERS

THE PRESS GANG

Newspapers and Politics,

1865–1878

The University of North Carolina Press

Chapel Hill & London

© 1994 The University of
North Carolina Press
All rights reserved
Manufactured in the
United States of America

The paper in this book meets the guidelines for permanence and durability of the
Committee on Production Guidelines for Book Longevity of the Council on
Library Resources.

Library of Congress Cataloging-in-Publication Data
Summers, Mark W. (Mark Wahlgren), 1951–
The press gang : newspapers and politics, 1865–1878 /
by Mark Wahlgren Summers.
p. cm.
Includes bibliographical references and index.
ISBN 0-8078-2140-3 (cloth : alk. paper). —
ISBN 0-8078-4446-2 (pbk. : alk. paper)
1. Journalism—United States—History—19th century. 2. Press and politics—
United States—History—19th century. 3. United States—Politics and
government—1865–1883.   I. Title.
PN4864.S86 1994
071'.3'09034—dc20   93-36489
CIP

Mark Wahlgren Summers, professor of history at the University of Kentucky, is
author of many books, including *The Era of Good Stealings*.

98 97 96 95 94   5 4 3 2 1

This book is dedicated to my most beloved Susan,

and to my parents,

Clyde and Evelyn Summers,

whose passion for justice would rival

Henry V. Boynton's.

Contents

Illustrations

Acknowledgments

In tendering thanks, let me begin by rounding up the usual suspects: libraries whose courtesy and friends whose unsparing kindness made this book better than it could have been otherwise. In every archive, the staff worked diligently and energetically to roust out materials that I needed, though, as ever, those running the manuscripts division in the Library of Congress did the most, and with patience and humor. As usual, my chums at the University of Kentucky were trumps. Among those who pored over the chapters and red-penciled purple prose were Jeremy Popkin, Thomas Cogswell, David Hamilton, and David Olster. Besides some shrewd suggestions for ways that the manuscript might expand its focus, Jeremy did what he could to shorten the final work substantially. William R. Childs, at Ohio State, made more sense in his comments than much of the writing he was criticizing, and out at Arizona State, Brooks Simpson applied his expertise on General Grant's career to that particular chapter. Still more let me hail Donald Ritchie, whose book on a similar subject might have made him incline to behave as a competitor. Instead, he welcomed the company; many short hours we spent swapping stories about the "press gang" and treating the reporters with all the cynicism they bestowed on public officials. His glance at the manuscript left it improved in quite significant ways. My appreciation for the painstaking copyediting of Stevie Champion goes beyond words.

A very different debt I owe to my dear wife, Susan Liddle, who let me rant about whole mobs of journalists as if they really existed, and to Ariel, who more than once reorganized the whole work by pushing the pile of pages onto the floor, a summary judgment which some critics may think the best of any. And finally, of course, my thanks go to my parents, Clyde and Evelyn Summers, the smartest, most thorough, and best editors of all. Their mark lies on every page of the finished manuscript.

Reporters' Initials & Pseudonyms

"Agate"   Whitelaw Reid, Cincinnati *Gazette*

"Creighton"   R. W. C. Mitchell, Danbury *News*

"Data"   W. W. Warden, Baltimore *Sun* and New York *Times*

"Dixon" Sidney Andrews, Boston *Daily Advertiser*

"D. P."   Donn Piatt, Cincinnati *Commercial* and *Enquirer*

"Gath"   George Alfred Townsend, Chicago *Tribune*
and New York *Graphic*

"G. G."   Grace Greenwood, New York *Tribune*

"Gideon"   W. S. Walker, Chicago *Times*

"H. J. R."   Hiram J. Ramsdell, Cincinnati *Commercial*

"H. V. B."   Henry Van Ness Boynton, Cincinnati *Gazette*

"H. V. N. B." Henry Van Ness Boynton

"H. V. R."   Horace V. Redfield, Cincinnati *Commercial*

"Laertes"   George Alfred Townsend, New York *Graphic*

"M. C. A."   Mary Clemmer Ames, New York *Independent*

"Mack"   Joseph B. McCullagh, Cincinnati *Commercial*

"Mrs. Grundy"   Austine Snead, Washington *Sunday Capital*

"Nestor"   William B. Shaw, Boston *Transcript*

"Observer"   R. J. Hinton, Worcester *Spy*

"Occasional"   John Wien Forney, Washington *Chronicle*

"Olivia"   Emily Edson Briggs, Philadelphia *Press*

"Perley"   Ben: Perley Poore, Boston *Morning Journal*

"Warrington"   W. S. Robinson, Springfield *Republican*

"Z. L. W."   Zebulon L. White, New York *Tribune*

THE PRESS GANG

Introduction

You are they
That search into the secrets of the time,
And under feign'd names, on the stage
present
Actions not to be touch'd at; and traduce
Persons of rank and quality of both
sexes,
And, with satirical and bitter jests,
Make even the senators ridiculous
To the plebeians.

Philip Massinger,
"The Roman Actor," 1630

The Third-Term Panic
(Thomas Nast, *Harper's Weekly*,
November 7, 1874).

The cartoon from late 1874 is one of Thomas Nast's most famous: barely concealed in a lion's skin called "Caesarism," a donkey brays and panics the animals of the woods—a monocled unicorn, a frantic giraffe, an owl, and most conspicuously, in its first appearance as a symbol, a Republican elephant stampeding into the political abyss.[1] Any blockhead can understand the point—or can he? The more closely the picture is examined, the more puzzling it appears. The donkey, it turns out, is not a symbol for the Democratic party, but for a newspaper, and so is much of the rest of the menagerie. The cartoonist has made the jackass a virtual stock symbol for editorial idiots.[2] But why make the New York *Times* a unicorn? Or the New York *Tribune* a giraffe, or the *World* an owl dropping an arithmetic book?

Nast's cartoon, in fact, is a comment on the so-called press gang of his age, and his better-read readers might have grasped the point of his symbols at once. They would have known that the *Times* was edited by the Englishman Louis J. Jennings; what better beast than one from the British coat of arms? Anyone familiar with Nast's caricatures would connect *World* proprietor Manton Marble's nose and the beak of a bird of prey; anyone familiar with Marble's editorials would appreciate his reliance on statistics to make his points for free trade or to change a setback for Democratic candidates into a victory.[3] As for the *Tribune*, the so-called tall tower of its unfinished office building was as conspicuous on Printing-House Square as a giraffe's neck, and it just may have been Nast's inspiration.

The fact that all these allusions might be second nature to Nast's audience and not to later historians should give us pause. Rare is the artist today who would feature a newspaper, much less an editor's face, in his cartoon, but in the 1870s the caricaturist poked fun at journalists on a regular basis. Even in cartoons where politicians took center stage, newspapermen often showed up in the background, observing, commenting, or just swelling a crowd.[4] Nast's penchant for making journalists his subject was typical of cartoonists in the nineteenth century.[5] Clearly, something was significantly different about the role that the press played in politics, different perhaps from earlier times and certainly from our own.

This book is about that difference and its consequences for the making of policy. It is a study of professional journalism fresh out of the eggshell, just as it is discovering itself as a profession and before it has established standards of conduct and freed itself from the legacy of the past, a legacy

"A Live Jackass Kicking a Dead Lion."
And such a Lion! and such a Jackass!
(Thomas Nast, *Harper's Weekly*, January 15, 1870).

of political engagement. It is the story of the independents' attempt to turn that legacy to new ends: the political engagement of the outsider, with editors playing the role of Thersites, commenting on the flawed nature of the generals. And it is, in the end, a story of failure, a war with the politicians that the politicians, or at least politics, won.

Does the story really need telling? No scholar can fail to be daunted by the heaps of books already written about journalism, the magisterial overview by Frank Luther Mott, the biographies of editors, the works popular and scholarly about Civil War reporters, and the pathbreaking study of Washington correspondents up to 1932 by Donald Ritchie.[6] And yet our first glance at the materials can be as illusory as our quick look at Nast's cartoon of the Republican elephant. We know everything about a few editors during Reconstruction, but much less about reporters, and practically nothing about those outside of the capital. We also may not know the right things. The younger James Gordon Bennett cuts a delightful figure as he quails beneath the horsewhip swung by his former fiancée's brother; but it was his jackass, the New York *Herald*, that did the braying in Nast's 1874 cartoon, and the bray goes unheard by the biographer.[7] Many an authoritative book on journalism seems to leave no stone unturned, and apparently no newspaper consulted. The omission is understandable. To read through ten years of one journal, much less several dozen journals, is tedious work, and the scraps of information often are scattered widely.

There is much that only exhaustive study would turn up, and on some matters, however reticent the press later became about its own habits, it loved discussing no topic more than itself. We know what position editors took on page four—but what about page one? What happened when the same man sat behind an editorial desk and in the legendary smoke-filled room with the politicians? We need to scrutinize a process as neglected as it is obvious: how reporters and editors gathered the news and how they slanted it. But *how* only leads to *why*. What was their relationship with those in the government, and how did officials try to control what the press said about them? What did patronage and personal influence mean for the way the news was reported? Precisely what role in party politics did the editors and correspondents play, and how well did this fit with their duty to inform the public?

This book is a beginning in answering those questions, a study of the way policy, political power, and press coverage merged and clashed between the end of the Civil War in 1865 and the end of Reconstruction a dozen years later. As readers will soon discover, the way the metropolitan newspapers transformed, to meet their readers' demand for information and to pay for the soaring expenses of efficient news gathering, had a powerful effect on their role as partisan tubs, thumped to the rhythm that political organizers set. At the same time, a growing sense of professionalism among reporters and the need to provide facts that the wire services had missed created a very different kind of Washington correspondence, where competition and cooperation together allowed readers to learn more about how their government worked and much more about what went on behind the scenes. In all these changes, the public was the gainer. Yet "independence" among editors, a sense of themselves as a profession among correspondents, did not do away with distortion and the ancient tradition of power brokering right away. Old habits outlived old conditions; professionalization came haltingly. Newspapers might not toe the party line (though most did, and even independents did not venture far from it), but they drew lines all their own. By the questions they asked, the information they chose to consider relevant, and the stereotypes they accepted, the new journalists could shape public discussion, and not always in the public interest. The inability of Southern Republicans to make themselves heard in a press establishment of their own or in the leading papers of the North, for example, would give a powerful impetus to the nation's abandonment of its commitment to Reconstruction. Some of the manipulation, indeed, was deliberate, the determination to make news fit an ideological line. The "press gang" had set itself free, not just to report events, but to make them; journalists held government jobs, took favors, hired themselves out as lobbyists, acted as advisers, errand runners, and campaign organizers for politicians they liked, and attended political conventions to pull the wires against those they detested.

What developed was an uncomfortable misfit between officeholders and journalists. It ranged from "kept" correspondents passing on puffery to self-appointed advocates of the public interest pursuing blind vendettas. From the first, many politicians found ways of shaping news their way, but their control was always tentative and got more so as the adversarial way of thinking strengthened among denizens of the press gallery. They still had partisan editors willing to do their bidding, but they found this support less satisfactory than before. Even self-proclaimed party organs chose to speak with their own voices and went jangling out of tune. Beset by a journalism that had changed its character in ways they did not understand, others, notably President Ulysses S. Grant, made a botch of news management from the first and paid dearly for it.

By 1872, politicians and much of the "independent" press had taken on a poisonous quality. That year, some of the more ambitious editors grew so restive that they sought for political alternatives to the two-party system that once they had served so faithfully. Two years later, the midterm elections turned into a shindy, with journalists trying to persuade the public that the republic and a free press were in danger. The press gang scored one last victory, but changes in how public figures handled the press and how the press interpreted its professional responsibilities helped bring an end to the fighting. So did new commercial realities, which forced many of the independents back into the parties. Changed conditions did not turn them into the old-fashioned organs again. Professionalization and commercialization had gone too far for that. Instead, the changes helped remove the adversarial relationship and opened the way for a new kind of independence, where news and editorials each stood on their own.

Obviously, a monumental study of newspapers in the Gilded Age needs to be done.[8] Clearly, this book is not it. Foreign policy, local crime reporting, society columns and the way class biases affected major metropolitan journals' accounts, the methods and working conditions of city reporters all need coverage. A dozen reporters need biographies, a dozen editors need studies that concentrate more on what they said on the news page than in the lead editorial. With thousands of different newspapers extant and hundreds of correspondents covering Washington, D.C., alone, this book necessarily must be selective in both the journals and issues it covers, even within the narrow bounds of the relationship between the press and politics in the Reconstruction years. But a start must be made somewhere, and if a host of obscure figures—Donn Piatt, "Deacon" Smith, and "Gath" among them—are tugged out of the shadows, it will be a down payment on the reward that their energy and merits deserve.

The book has another aim as well. Historians use newspapers to document the events of the past, and well they should. They can do no other. For every limit and lapse, many a journal compares favorably for coverage of domestic events with its descendant today. But papers are sources with underappreciated risks, and not just those posed by the most obvious prejudices of race, class, and partisan affiliation. Distortions stem from the very definition of news itself. The biases are not just ideological, but occupational (what is defined as news? and does the ephemeral reflect or distort a larger and less newsworthy reality?) and institutional (what does it suit the financial and personal political fortunes of the paper's owner to see published?). It is well to study the messenger carefully when the message he carries comes in his own handwriting.

PART ONE

THE LORDS OF
THE LINOTYPE

"Red Hot!"
(Thomas Nast, *Harper's Weekly*,
July 13, 1872).

CHAPTER 1

Wonderful! Wonderful!

Traveling down the Mississippi on a steamboat in 1871, a journalist watched a yawl shoot out from the bank. If he thought that the two passengers were coming to board or trade, he was quickly set right. "Throw me a paper!" one of them shouted, "throw me a paper!" Visiting America just after the Civil War, Scotsman David Macrae found newspapers as necessary as money but much more plentiful. Even some prisons supplied prisoners with the morning edition. To do otherwise, a warden informed one visitor, would be cruel and unusual punishment. By Macrae's count, more dailies were published in New York City in 1868 than in England, Scotland, and Ireland combined.[1]

Americans going abroad were impressed in just the opposite way. They returned aware that the press at home was something special. Anglophiles at the *Nation*, America's foremost journal of opinion, had to admit that while European journals beat American ones for editorial writing, they came nowhere close at news gathering. For all the wit and eloquence in their political essays, French newspapers struck travelers as sensational claptrap;

not even the New York *Herald* could match them. "To be in France is to be excluded from news of France," a reporter for the Springfield *Republican* complained from Nantes, as he tried to find the latest news of the Franco-Prussian War. His first word about the fall of Paris came from New York; stories from Paris or Bordeaux "seem to arrive by snail carriers," and the "innumerable childish *on dits* from the English newspapers" left confusion worse confounded. Staffed by young men reading law and graduates from Oxford and Cambridge, the great English journals put out essays as bulky and painstakingly prepared as a plum pudding; but fine phrases could not make up for a lack of up-to-date reports or factual accuracy in all but the best of them. Bemused Yankees traveling abroad could read that former Confederate president Jefferson Davis was now a Georgia congressman, that the American holiday Thanksgiving celebrated the end of the Revolutionary War, and that the ever-grasping United States was marshaling troops to annex Utah, which one newspaper put down as a British colony. A few hours dozing over the London *Times* would make anyone appreciate the American journalist, " 'cute', lean, yellow-whiskered, . . . one leg thrown over the other, body bent, the nervous, rapid hand flinging ink now on the paper, now on the wall," with an output as direct, energetic, and effective as himself.[2]

Macrae's figures were wrong,[3] but he got the essentials right. By 1870, New York City had over 150 newspapers. Most of them were weeklies, of course, just like most papers were published outside city limits, but rare was that community with no press at all. Any place with more than five thousand people could support a daily, and many supported two or more: one for Democrats, the other for Republicans. A middle-sized city like Cincinnati began the 1870s with eight dailies, plus forty weeklies.[4] All told, the country in 1870 had over 5,000 different newspapers and periodicals, one-tenth of them published every day, 258 German-language papers, 48 in French, and 15 in Scandinavian languages. (In Michigan, Hollanders could choose between the *De Wachter* and *Vrijheids Banier* [Republican], *De Hollander* [Democratic], and *De Hope* [Dutch Reformed church].) The greatest increase had come in the last ten years, as the number of dailies rose by 40 percent and their circulation by over 70 percent. The pace would only quicken over the decade to come. By 1880, 971 dailies served the public.[5]

How well they served it depended very much on how big a public read them; the most marked trait of the press was its uneven quality, between

North and South, city and county seat, partisan organ and independent. Most papers were partisan, blatantly and deceptively so, in the way they slanted news and in what events they considered fit for their readers. Making good Democrats or Republicans mattered more than making a good profit. Beyond that, most journalists had little to say and precious little space in which to say it, even if their imaginations had run wild. Readers fared worst in small towns across the North and in nearly every place south of Louisville. The Little Rock *Arkansas Gazette* was the most important and richest newspaper in the state. Yet a glance at its contents in the late winter of 1870 would discourage any reader anxious to know what went on in the world. It was four pages long. Of its thirty-two columns, news rarely took up more than eight, and sometimes as little as five. Most of that was national. On February 24, the *Gazette* had thirteen *lines* of local and state events, on the following day two columns, and on the next two days only one. As for events beyond the United States, the ten days starting on March 4 were typical:

> March 4, 18 lines
> March 5, none
> March 6, 12 lines
> March 7, no newspaper at all (it being a Monday)
> March 8, no news from abroad
> March 9, 62 lines, 54 of them a dispatch from Cuba
> March 10, 35 lines
> March 11, no news from abroad
> March 12, 30 lines
> March 13, no news from abroad[6]

Compared to the hinterland, Little Rock's papers looked downright informative. "Viator," a correspondent of the Chicago *Times* visiting the resort at Hot Springs, Arkansas, looked through the newspapers available to residents and found plenty of advertisements, some tirades in the editorial column at the extravagance of federal officeholders, but not a jot of local news. Even a robbery less than one hundred feet from the newspaper office went unmentioned. "The productions . . . denominated here as newspapers, are the most wretched sheets I have ever seen," "Viator" summed up, "and are a disgrace to a civilized community."[7]

Yet the inadequacies of so much of the press establishment should not obscure the excellence of the few dozen newspapers that towered over the others in scope and influence, nearly all of them in the great cities of the North. Indeed, readers in New York, Boston, Chicago, Philadelphia, and Cincinnati could choose between rival eight-pagers of national consequence and extensive coverage.

Some 150 journals in metropolitan centers had circulations over 10,000. Only since the 1840s had technology made it possible to serve that many customers, with the spread of railroad lines and the improvement of printing machinery. Instead of 1,000 copies daily, the horizontal cylinder of the rotary Hoe press turned out 20,000 an hour.[8] The Philadelphia *Public Ledger* building covered a third of an acre; lumber mills had to process fourteen tons of raw materials for a day's publication, read by 400,000 people. So great was the demand by 1870 that no self-respecting city paper limited itself to one appearance a day. The Philadelphia *Evening City Item*'s first edition came out at 10:30 in the morning. The last, which might be its twelfth, hit the streets at 7:00 that evening.[9]

Journalism in the metropolis, obviously, was transforming from a printer's shop into a big business, different in size, character, and financial backing from the establishments that had been publishing since the early 1700s. In small towns, the one-man operation persisted. A few thousand dollars could endow the would-be editor and publisher with office space, blank paper, and a well-worn flatbed press. Printing handbills, calling cards, and anything else that the community wanted, he could scrape by. Still, the sum called for there was in the thousands. No longer could any partisan hope to start the way "Viator's" boss, Wilbur F. Storey, did in 1838 in Laporte, Indiana, on two hundred dollars. "A young friend of ours wants to know a remedy for love sickness," a Georgia editor wrote. "We advise him to start a newspaper, and if that don't take the starch out of his hifalutin ideas of worldly felicity, we'll cave."[10]

The sums called for in major cities made the old ways of raising money out of the question. Just to replace the type and buy a faster press cost the Memphis *Appeal* $10,000 in 1872, and had it bought one of the Hoe presses, the cost easily would have been double that figure.[11] In the late 1840s, as the potential of telegraph lines for the speedy transmission of news was just being discovered, New York's most prominent newspapers set up the Associated Press (AP) to share the advantages at lower cost. Lower cost was a relative term. Regular members paid $14,000 a year for the service; together with other cable expenses in 1880, a metropolitan newspaper could pay Western Union some $70,000 annually. Naturally,

AP's sponsors only used their shared dispatches as a starting point. The more a journal aspired to publish the news, rather than merely editorial opinions, the more it laid out for its own telegraphic reports from Washington, D.C., and overseas. When the New York *Tribune* needed to cover the Franco-Prussian War in 1870, it put some of its best reporters on the job, including George W. Smalley. Their supplements to the Associated Press provided special prestige, but at a dear rate. Four days of Smalley's cable bills from France totaled $4,000, and the whole war cost the *Tribune* $125,507 in telegraph costs.[12] The New York *Tribune*'s calculation of expenses just after the Civil War may offer a suggestion of how costly the whole enterprise could be:

Printing paper	$315,163
Compositors	73,770
Editorial expenses	51,884
Correspondence	41,074
Pressmen, repairing presses, etc.	35,255
Mailing, counting, and packing papers	35,088
News by wire	22,045
Publishing office, salaries	19,721
Ink	8,420
Postage	6,184
Harbor news	1,875
Glue and molasses for rollers	869
Total	$646,107[13]

Gradually, then, big newspapers had to take on the characteristics of corporations just to carry on their business. They might be financed by a dozen partners or, if they sold stock, by thousands of shareholders.[14] Instead of relying on a few dozen news agents to sell the paper just to subscribers, they marketed their product wherever space was available. For the daily, news vendors mattered far more than subscription lists. Every hotel had its newsstand, and salesboys ran down the aisles of railroad cars hawking the latest copies of the New York *Tribune* or Cincinnati *Commercial*. Advertising, almost all of it for local firms, usually merchants announcing their wares, had grown important enough as a source of funds for newspaper offices to set up separate departments to handle it. Indeed, the expansion and specialization of the city journals' staff were as impressive as the growth in cost. In 1840, editors worked as reporters, compositors, and general custodians. Those in New York, at the top of the profession, could afford only three assistants. No major daily in New York had less than one hundred employees thirty years later, and some had five times as many occasional contributors. In place of one printer, eight to ten were required. Forty people worked in one city paper's Editorial Department, which split into eight specialties: Writing, City, European, Exchange, and Ship News editors among the most important.[15] Different qualifications brought a wider span of wages between the ranks. Thus, a managing editor, paid as much as $10,000, would supervise editorial writers making $50 a week, subeditors earning $40, experienced reporters taking in $20, and novices beginning at $12 to $15.[16]

In the most essential sense, then, the *Tribune*, "New York's most honest newspaper," was no longer the one Horace Greeley had founded in 1841. Raising a few thousand dollars, taking a partner who tended strictly to the business, the editor had begun by doing everything. In time, he had taken on special correspondents (including Karl Marx and Thomas Hughes, author of *Tom Brown's School Days*), editorial assistants (among them Henry Jarvis Raymond, who would found the New York *Times*), and managing editors like Charles A. Dana, who by 1866 was running a newspaper of his own in Chicago and would soon turn the New York *Sun* into a dangerous rival to Greeley's *Tribune*. Gradually, the founder's own role receded in everything but popular reputation. By 1866, stockholders owned the *Tribune*. Though he still headed the concern, Greeley was too busy to write more than an occasional editorial, much less a news report, and went to the city only on Fridays. Instead, he collected a crowd of earnest, capable reporters, including James R. Young, Zebulon L. White, and Hiram J. Ramsdell. Two managing editors gave the *Tribune* its zest and thoroughness, first the brilliant, unscrupulous John Russell Young and then in 1869 Whitelaw Reid ("Agate"), star correspondent for the Cincinnati *Gazette*. With more manners and a tighter grip on day-to-day business than Greeley, Reid brought new talent and expanded coverage in all areas.[17]

More newsmen meant more news, but there was more to it than that. Along with specialization, a change in how journalists saw themselves, a professional ethic, was beginning to emerge.

Before the Civil War, only a humorist would have described reporting as a profession. As a class, newsmen were as disreputable as drunkards, if somewhat less regular in their habits. It was only in slight deprecation that New York reporters took the sobriquet *Bohemians*, a term suggesting artistic pretensions less than personal irresponsibility.[18] *Correspondents* were different. Many were contributors, paid for their letters, but were not regular employees. Their time, naturally, was their own, and they had discretion over how much opinion and rhetorical polish they put into the essays they sent. A few were literary men supplementing their incomes. Others were editors on tour. But neither group owed its reputation to its news gathering, if, indeed, the long ruminations and fulminations sent home could be classified as news at all. Only in the nation's capital might the designation *professional reporter* seem more than a contradiction in terms, and then only in a few exceptional cases. Nor did reporters seem all that necessary. One could put together a very informative newspaper on clippings from the "exchanges" and the stenographic reports from House and Senate.[19]

Yet even before the war, a change was visible, though mostly on the metropolitan papers.[20] The war accelerated it by calling forth a public demand for eyewitness reports, graphic ones, in-depth, and everyday. From every city special emissaries hastened to the front—more than 150 in all and 40 from the New York *Herald* alone. War impelled newsmen to be more enterprising than before and drove them to a fierce competition to press ahead of all rivals.[21]

To journalists, the war seemed the moment when their craft came into its own. Before the war, men became editors because their party needed a reliable voice. After it, a journalist had a good chance of taking the editorial chair himself, and some editors treated service as Washington correspondent for a big-city press as if it were a promotion. By 1866, historian James Parton could extol the ascendancy of the news gatherer as the latest step toward modern journalism. "For the majority of readers it is the reporter, and not the editor who is the ruling genius of the newspaper," agreed another essayist some years later. If the way that many of the leading editors were made is any indication, the two professions led to each other.[22] Many a city publisher seemed intent, as one critic gibed, on giving "the name and age of every dog that dies within a hundred miles of the city, with the color of his hair and the quality of his bark."[23]

For well or ill, there seemed no getting away from journalists by the 1870s. Waiting on death row in the Tombs, twelve prisoners were interviewed on their views of capital punishment by a New York *Herald* reporter. (All but two of those responding disapproved of it, and the two ardent defenders had just received commuted sentences!) Foreign guests found the press gang waiting for them before their ocean liner had docked. Woe be to that stranger who made his way into some Western town short on copy! He might find himself cornered in an Omaha hotel and quizzed about where he was going, where he had been, what he thought of leading English politicians and California demagogues, his views on the projected canal across Central America, a flexible money supply, and a third presidential term for General Grant. One such victim discovered that the only way to rid himself of reporters' presence was to recite the first chapter of Samuel Johnson's romance, *Rasselas: Prince of Abyssinia*, from memory.[24]

Two postwar examples showed journalism at its news-gathering best: the New York *Herald* and the Chicago *Times*. Founded by James Gordon Bennett, Sr., in 1835, the *Herald* was, a French traveler declared, "one of the most eccentric, the most intelligent, and most influential organs of the American press. No one has any idea what it stands for; to tell the truth, one suspects it doesn't have any fixed principles. . . . it knows only that it is for the winning side."[25]

So it was, but in the war for circulation the *Herald* knew that the winning side was the one with the best news and the most. Special correspondents from Austria to Asheville brought the freshest information, whether it was about the Battle of Sadowa or the latest depredations by half-breed Indian gangs in North Carolina. Its letters on French politics were so good, the *Herald* boasted, that even the French could make sense of them. Those lost in the wilds of Africa could not escape the Bennetts' emissaries. There one of the paper's correspondents, Henry M. Stanley, tracked down an elusive explorer in 1871 and obtained a fame greater than the man he met when he uttered the words, "Dr. Livingstone, I presume." With a circulation as high as 150,000 in the 1870s, the *Herald* would remain unsurpassed until Joseph Pulitzer took over the New York *World* in the following decade and revolutionized New York journalism.[26]

The Chicago *Times* was an even more astonishing success because it improved so rapidly. A poverty-stricken Democratic organ at the start of the Civil War, it was transformed by Wilbur F. Storey into one of the most thorough and raciest papers outside of Manhattan. Its Sunday edition, full of feature articles, ran sixteen pages, and Monday's carried summaries of the leading sermons. That way, the *Times* boasted, readers could get the benefits of attending church at the bargain rate of a mere nickel. Or, if

J. G. B. Jun. [James Gordon Bennett, Jr.], in His Property Room
(Thomas Nast, *Harper's Weekly*, December 25, 1875).

their tastes ran in other directions, they could read the regular feature, "Nymphs du Pave," on Chicago's prostitutes. By 1876, thirty or forty columns of "specials" by its journalists in the field were commonplace, to the amazement of even New York's reporters. "Does the Chicago Times do this every day?" one of them asked in amazement; on being told that it did, he could only shake his head and murmur, "Wonderful! wonderful!"[27]

Chicago had room for a *Tribune* every bit as wonderful as the *Times*, and the *Herald* found its match in three other New York dailies. This was so not because papers offered the same basic services, but because their wares were sharply different. In New York City, an unflinching Republican might subscribe to the short-lived New York *Standard*, though he would be content with the coverage and biases of the New York *Times*. If he wanted free-trade argument and liberal reform, he might prefer the New York *Evening Post*; if he inclined to high-tariff ideas and humanitarian reform, nothing would do but Greeley's *Tribune*.[28] And those were just some, not all, of the Republican alternatives.

The alternatives afforded more than a choice between distortions put on the same news stories. They allowed very different news, delivered in different ways. Separated from the daily routine though he was, Greeley's own utopian vision continued to define the *Tribune*'s strength in news gathering until he died in 1872. Whether it was a conference of old abolitionists or a convention of temperance reformers, the newspaper most likely to report it fully and most sympathetically would be Greeley's, just as the most friendly and thorough coverage of laborers' doings and union meetings appeared in Charles A. Dana's New York *Sun*.[29] Readers could gather nearly all the news from one paper and then pick up another to get the rest. The comparative strengths of New York's most important dailies became clear to "Seymour," the Mobile *Register*'s local correspondent, during the adultery trial of the Reverend Henry Ward Beecher, foremost minister of his day: The *Tribune* and *Times* provided verbatim reports of the proceedings, the *Sun* gave "the kernel of the testimony without superfluous husks and chaff," and the *Herald* specialized in trenchant courtroom sketches. Ask a journalist which newspaper he would pick to get his news of the world, a Charleston correspondent wrote in 1881, and he would choose the New York *Times*; but ask which paper he would most like to read if he had an hour to pass on a train ride, and very likely it would be Dana's *Sun*.[30]

Clearly the metropolitan press, individually, even more collectively, provided a marked contrast to the general mediocrity of provincial four-pagers. They were more: a potential rival to any and all of them on their own ground. Their clients stretched far beyond their own borders and did what they could to get more. In Hot Springs, "Viator" could go to a book stand and buy the Chicago *Times* (if he got there quickly enough; they sold out almost at once). Thanks to early morning trains, booksellers in Birmingham had the Louisville *Courier-Journal* in twenty-four hours. From Chicago, the big journals spread their readership and special news coverage across seven states. In 1876, newsdealers outside of Chicago sold over 14,000 copies of the *Times* every day in Illinois, more than 4,000 each in Iowa and Wisconsin, nearly 3,000 in Michigan and Indiana, and 66 as far away as New Orleans. In an age when a small-town newspaper had a circulation of around 500, it was a significant conquest when over 700 residents of Springfield and Peoria, over 400 in Joliet, Decatur, and Milwaukee, and over 200 in Quincy, Galesburg, and Pekin took the *Times*. Even by its own figures, hundreds more bought retail copies of its two rivals, the *Inter-Ocean* and the *Tribune*. That was just the impact of the daily. Most prominent metropolitan journals published a weekly, distilled from six dailies' articles, for the countryside, where mail service was less regular. Farmers from upstate New York to Iowa read the New York *Tribune*'s weekly edition appreciatively and thought that there was none better. Indeed, for many newspapers, the *Tribune* among them, the weekly outsold the daily several times over.[31]

This was just the beginning of the larger presses' influence, however. Thanks to their control of the Associated Press, New York's leading newspapers made themselves the news distributors for presses nationwide. The system was far from perfect. Every bias, political, personal, and local, interfered with objective coverage. Returns from upstate New York, for example, became national news; but even Tennessee papers were in the dark about election results from the Volunteer state if they left official tallies up to AP. "Every day almost a fresh lie," growled a former senator of its political coverage. The desperate effort of L. A. ("Father") Gobright, the AP bureau chief at the capital, to make the Washington wire service fair infuriated those who wanted zest and scandal. "There is no 'go' in him, and he is not 'bright,'" sneered one critic, who accused the big dailies in charge of AP of keeping Gobright on hand as a way of making the syndicated news gathering so inferior that their own special reports (which they were paid for) would be in demand. Mormons complained that after the

AP manager had a personal difficulty in Salt Lake City, he repaid scores in every dispatch about Utah affairs. Members roared lustily at the fees, especially those for foreign reports. Still, the association made news more readily available to over two hundred dailies, and just after the war, other consolidations rivaled AP. Exasperated at the financial costs and the New York bias, a host of major journals in Boston, Philadelphia, Chicago, and New Orleans formed a "United States and European News Association" and forced AP to give them better terms. There was a Western, a Southern, a New England, and a Texas Associated Press. The participants of each consortium would share the costs and scoops of far-flung correspondents. With each local agent paid per dispatch, the incentive to gather and send in news was immense.[32]

Supplementing the commercial venture of press services was the established custom of taking and using anything good that appeared in print elsewhere. Large newspapers could afford a stable of reporters; if small presses could afford few or none, their editors could afford printers' devils, scissors, and paste, and the material that metropolitan correspondents gathered, both editorial and news, was clipped out and fitted into the weekly columns of their lesser competitors (sometimes it was pared so skillfully that the original source would reprint it and imagine that it was getting something original). As any respectable paper received fifty to one hundred other sheets nationwide in exchange for copies of its own publication (and the New York *Tribune* got at least 2,500 on "exchange"), that gave the country publisher a broad array of news items from which to choose, but it also meant that whatever topic interested the major presses would have a national impact.[33]

The important newspapers were not necessarily those with the largest circulation, but those with the best reporting and the most effective voices on policy. Among New York dailies, for example, the *News* outsold any rival locally. Beyond city limits, it had barely any impact. It was almost never quoted, nor even noted. The New York *Evening Post*, with one-seventh the circulation, gained more national attention; in that sense, *it* was more a major newspaper than the *News*.[34]

Americans thus had reason for priding themselves on a press as diverse, as energetic, and as interesting as its people. The columnist Donn Piatt told a joke that took to extremes a faith rather widely held in Greeley's newspaper. A Bible salesman traveling Ohio's Western Reserve, it seemed, had tried to sell his wares to a Yankee farmer by leaving a sample copy with him for a week. To his distress, the Bible was returned, with thanks. "Well, I declare, there's a deal of good readin' in it," the farmer admitted, "but I've subscribed for the [New York] *Weekly Tribune*, you see, an' there's readin' enough in it for my family." [35]

Whether it was worth reading is another matter. While journalism at its best delivered a prodigious supply of information, the quality of that information varied. One English critic suggested a connection between the declining importance of subscribers and the rise of misleading and sensational stories. As long as news vendors did the selling, they needed to excite and inspire prospective readers with "extras," outlandish headlines, short paragraphs that sacrificed good writing for quick reading, and eye-catching stories, no matter how dubious. [36]

The Civil War, for example, had shown the limits in the correspondents' craft plainly. At their best, of course, wartime reporters were magnificent, and some were downright lyrical. No war had such speedy, thorough, and generally accurate coverage, with such attention to detail. But error was common and deception almost habitual. Still miserably paid, reporters pocketed bribes for the favorable mention of certain officers and filled their reports with every bias. If editors had denounced each others' reporters as liars beforehand, at least now they had good cause for it. Only in print did Confederate general Sterling Price capture St. Louis, Union general George McClellan die at the second Battle of Manassas, Union general Nathaniel Banks surrender his army to General Dick Taylor, and General William Tecumseh Sherman, having burned Atlanta, *retreat* south toward the sea to escape a Confederate army. Every triumph became a Glorious Victory, every retreat a Shameful Rout, and the most inventive Bohemians never had a whiff of the gunpowder from the fray they described in such graphic detail. At a banquet after the war, Mark Twain toasted "the journalist's truest friend—the late 'Reliable Contraband,' " as former slaves had come to be called—and who deserved it more?:

> When armies fled in panic . . . and the great cause seemed lost beyond all hope of succor, who was it that turned the tide of war and gave victory to the vanquished?
> The Reliable Contraband.
> Who took Richmond the first time? the Reliable Contraband.

Who took it *every* time until the last? The Reliable Contraband.

When we needed a bloodless victory, to whom did we look to win it? The Reliable Contraband.

Thunder and lightning never stopped him; annihilated railroads never delayed him; the telegraph never overtook him; military secrecy never crippled his knowledge.

No journalist among us can lay his hand on his heart and say he ever lied with such pathos, such unction, such exquisite symmetry, such sublimity of conception and such fidelity of execution, as when he did it through and by the inspiration of this regally gifted marvel of mendacity, the lamented Reliable Contraband.

Such was the natural result of sending "police reporters to do the work of historians," as one newspaper put it.[37]

Factual error at the reporters' level was matched by idiosyncrasy and bias in the main office. Many a four-pager was published by promoters with either dyspepsia or delusions of magniloquence. For all its completeness of coverage, the compulsive alliterative whimsy in the headlines of "Viator's" own paper had a kind of mechanical persistence that must have left doubts in some readers' minds about what the articles referred to, and certainties in many about Wilbur F. Storey's lunacy (which would soon be medically confirmed).[38] In just one issue, articles were entitled "Public Papers," "Lots of Lucre," "The Ruin of Rome" (which had nothing to do with Rome), "District Debauchery," "John's Jaw" (about Senator John A. Logan's chances of reelection), "Tragic Testimony," "Fitchette Fixed," "Seeking Salvation," "The Commodore's Clay" (an obituary on railroad magnate Cornelius "Commodore" Vanderbilt), "Laid Out by Lawyers," "Fish or Famish," and, for what remained, "Nubs of News." Even for rhetoric, it is hard to respect an editor who declared of the opposing party that "Democracy runs in their blood *like wooden legs*," or who shrieked at "those base-born, blood-besprinkled blisters on the body politic" and called for "the iron heel of power" to grind them "to atoms so infinitesimal that the winds of heaven might blow them into interminable space."[39]

Because news, in the end, was what the newspapers said it was, the power of an editor both to extend the boundaries of what merited reporting and to confine it was made for abuse. Storey's articles exposing the private lives of ministers and couples suing for divorce won the Chicago *Times* a particular ill-fame. Proudly, the city editor praised his staff as ready-made for the task Storey set them. "Two of my men are ex-convicts," he explained, "ten are divorced husbands, and not a single one of them is living with his own wife." Not surprisingly, by the spring of 1875, the *Times* was fending off three criminal indictments for obscenity and twenty-one civil suits for libel. So bitterly did the Boston *Daily Advertiser*'s editor detest one Republican politician that he forbade the offender's name anywhere except under the notice of "Deaths" and stripped mention of his appearance from otherwise full coverage of campaign rallies. "The *Daily Adverti*—we beg pardon! the *Daily Suppresser*," jeered a rival. And every city had its *Suppresser*.[40]

Still, as an Englishman pointed out of the New York *Herald*, papers throve not because of their outrageous opinions and low moral tone, but in spite of them.[41] In the long run, reliable reporting and a reputation for temperate utterance gave journalists their power. No better illustration of quality's importance could be found than the influence of the Springfield (Mass.) *Republican*, edited and published by Samuel Bowles. Its weekly readership approached 15,000, which was half again as much as its daily circulation. Yet only the New York *Tribune* could match its high reputation among Republicans in the late 1860s, and it merited Horace Greeley's description as "the best and ablest country newspaper ever published on the continent."[42]

Bowles was one of reform's strongest voices. Brusque on entering the *Republican* offices in the morning, quick to let an underling know of failures, slow to praise work well done, he was at his worst when depression, dyspepsia, or sciatica was upon him. But if he kept his employees under pressure, the training was such that young men from across the country flocked to Springfield for the chance of a job. It was his boast that the *Republican* made politics interesting to women and millinery interesting to men, perhaps by wasting no words in discussing either. Its extensive local coverage would explain its prominence in the Connecticut River Valley, but the editorials free of cant and slangwhanging made it nationally respected, and its Boston and Washington correspondents were regularly cited.[43]

Journalism just after the Civil War, then, had an ambiguous character, caught precisely in the praise it got from two of its great practitioners. "We surpass the English in journalism as the English surpass us in fiction," Henry Watterson, editor of the Louisville *Courier-Journal*, boasted. "The born journalist is a Yankee product." All the literary talent in Watterson's hometown went into the press, Washington correspondent Hiram J. Ramsdell agreed. "Louisville literature means her newspapers."[44] Perhaps it did, but journalism required talents beyond those making successful literary men, among them a scrupulous attention to fact and a restraint that professional standards and training alone could impose. How unformed those other talents were becomes a crucial part of the story of the way in which politics shaped and was shaped by the press gang in the years just after the Civil War.

CHAPTER 2

I Want to Give Those Fellows Hell!

For all their limitations, journalists of the 1860s had a talent worth admiring, but was it also a talent worth fearing? What kind of power did the press wield over public attention and affairs, and what kind of power could be wielded over the press?

Certainly the editors themselves deemed their power immense. The newly discovered honesty of Wall Street speculators, wrote "Pink," the Charleston *Courier*'s New York correspondent in late 1869, came from journalists' exposures of the recent conspiracy to corner the gold supply. "I sometimes think that if New York were made of glass its morality would rise 50 per cent in a single year," the Reverend Henry Ward Beecher confessed. Barring such a miracle, he added, the journalists' pursuit of stories produced very nearly the same effect.[1]

It was in politics that journalists claimed their greatest influence, and reasonably, since political coverage provided much of the news and most of the amusement. Less commonly than a generation before, but still as a general rule, most editors saw themselves as distributors of political information rather than general purveyors of news. What was said in Congress mattered. Many papers, especially in the larger cities, republished a summation of the daily debate and with a more scrupulous accuracy than the official record. A campaign speech might receive two columns. If lengthy, it merited the full front page or a special supplement. Appeals and exhortations, the proceedings of partisan clubs, and fragmentary returns from insignificant towns all got space.

The emphasis on politics meant that, more than at a later day, readers were inspired to care about what happened in Washington and to spy larger significance for the republic in every party contest. Indeed, as the nature of politics began to change in the decade after the Civil War, newspapers' influence in stirring partisan enthusiasm may actually have increased. The hoopla, the banners, the great speeches continued and would persist well into the last decade of the nineteenth century. But already by the Centennial Year, at least according to editors (who had the most to gain from their claims being believed), attention was slipping away from the extravaganzas. Whatever did win elections, the Indianapolis *News* commented, as the canvass of Indiana closed in 1876, the recent campaign showed that stump speeches, "enthusiastic meetings," and "tremendous outpourings" did not."[2]

Newspapers were more than echoes of party organizers, much less objective reporters of political affairs. They proclaimed themselves a power in their own right. "Here generals and admirals and statesmen have been set up and overthrown through the potent power of the press," wrote a visitor to the reporters' offices on Newspaper Row in Washington. More pompously, the Memphis *Appeal* spoke for all, and in a refrain all too common: "The newspaper press of the United States is the true standing army of the republic."[3]

Newspapers singing their own praises should never be wholly trusted. Still, from the attention that politicians paid the press and the energy with which they threw themselves into replying to editors, or into winning them over, and from the regularity with which the press appeared in diaries and was commented on, journalists made quite an impact. Even in the northeastern corner of Ohio, grumbled a political sidekick, "the politics of the people in a measure are based on the *N.Y. Tribune*."[4] As the newspapers spread their influence wider, the self-proclaimed court of public opinion found the number of appellants increasing dramatically, especially among politicians. A damaging story could not be ignored. Congressmen

rose on points of personal privilege or rushed to their special friends in **the** press corps to clear up reporters' misconstruction of the facts.[5]

Yet influence on and by the press remain tricky things to measure. Newspapers found their ability to shape opinion confined by all sorts of conditions, not the least important of which was the reputation they already had for reliability, both factual and partisan.[6] Instead of making up readers' minds for them, editors might find public demand making up theirs, especially when patrons had a satisfactory rival paper to turn to. Leading articles on page four lost their impact when reporters' accounts on page one contradicted them, and reporters, too, had ideas of which way politics needed to be directed.

All the limitations and conflicts stand out in the shaping of Reconstruction and in the failed presidency of Abraham Lincoln's successor, Andrew Johnson. Though Confederate armies surrendered in the spring of 1865, peace could not restore the country half slave, half free that had taken up arms in 1861. To beat a slave-holding rebellion, the North had emancipated slaves across the Confederacy. With the Thirteenth Amendment in 1865, it abolished slavery everywhere else. But how far did freedom go? Should the reconstructed South be allowed to have the same old unreconstructed Confederates running it?[7]

Northern Democrats were willing to take the risks in a peace settlement that brought the country as close to a restoration as possible: "the Union as it was and the Constitution as it is," as they put it. A generous peace, they argued, was the only one sure to last; and what could be more generous than a settlement that would give Democrats a solid South at the next election and put the national government back in their hands? As for the former slaves, freed from what Democrats protested were the most comfortable of chains, emancipation was more than they deserved and punishment enough for the South. Let white Southern authorities, not egalitarian Northern cranks, decide what rights the Negro had coming. States' rights, rather than the decrees of a Republican Congress, must define the peace terms that the North was permitted to dictate to the South.[8]

As members of the party that ran the federal government and just about every Northern state, Republicans were the ones whose opinions mattered, and they wanted firmer guarantees for a meaningful kind of freedom and an unbreakable Union. Those included steps to exclude most prominent Confederates from office and open the witness box for blacks, but beyond protecting the most basic civil rights, moderates and radicals could not agree. Radicals hoped for Negro suffrage, certainly. Most of them wanted broader disfranchisement of rebels, and a paltry few even dreamed of taking planters' estates away and making former slaves into freeholders.[9]

Radicals lacked the votes to shove a Republican Congress far from the center, but Andrew Johnson did the next best thing. He helped shove the center closer to where radicals had been standing. Slaveholder and Democrat though he was, his staunch support for the Union in its moment of crisis had made him a hero to the North and the ideal running mate on the Republican ticket in 1864. Then, barely a month into Lincoln's second term, an assassin's bullet made him president.[10] The choice was catastrophic. Johnson had the courage of his convictions and the cunning not to let the Republicans know just what those convictions were until he had set up new state governments across the defeated South. At first relieved to find him no radical, the moderates in Congress soon suffered a shock: Johnson was no moderate, either. Not only did his program withhold the vote from blacks. It left their most basic rights at the mercy of their old masters, too fond of liberty to share it indiscriminately. Measures to protect black Southerners met a presidential veto, and when a constitutional amendment setting the peace terms for the South went through Congress, Johnson did all he could to keep Southern legislatures from accepting it. By the middle of 1866, the president was trying to build his own political party, courting Democrats and even hinting that Congress, still without any Southern representatives readmitted, might be illegal. "His character is certainly a singular one," wrote Ohio's governor, who had stood by Johnson long after other Republicans had lost faith in him. "He is always worse than you expect."[11]

Johnson failed to convince Northern voters. The midterm elections sent back a more radical Congress than before, and the Reconstruction that the South ended up with went further than moderates had planned. By the time the process was complete, ten states had written new state constitutions permitting Negro suffrage, ratified the Fourteenth Amendment, and elected Republican governors. After a series of clashes with Congress and attempts to thwart the Reconstruction laws, Johnson himself was impeached, escaping conviction by a single vote. Seeking an explanation for Johnson's ruin, one historian, Howard K. Beale, gave the press a considerable share of the blame. Republican newspapers, he argued, all took the radical side. Distorting the news, keeping their readers from learning the truth, they shoved the voters into the arms of Northern extremists. Worst of all, the disaster was aggravated by the president failing to use government spoils properly: radical editors snapped at the administration hands that fed them.[12]

Northern newspapers did twist events to fit their partisan biases. They did affect the course of public policy. But Beale's diagnosis of how things went wrong and what would have set them right rested on five very dubious assumptions: first, that radicals ran the Republican media; second, that the president's critics carried the day by deception and distortion of the evidence; third, that they were able to produce a news blackout about Johnson's side; fourth, that using patronage more cleverly might have neutralized the radicals' power; and finally, that if Johnson had actually been able to carry his case directly to the people, the administration might have triumphed. In its own way, each assumption misunderstands the limits that the political culture put on the press and on press manipulators.

Whatever Johnson's problems were, they did not include a press establishment dominated by radicals, implacably hostile and secure in their monopoly of the public attention. When his Reconstruction program got under way in mid-1865, it floated on a tide of almost universal goodwill among the newspapers of the North. Just about every Northern city had a Democratic daily singing its praises, and even radical Republican papers credited Johnson with the policy's achievements and cleared him of blame for its failures.[13]

One paper was not as good as another, to be sure. Democratic newspapers did Johnson no good among Republican readers. Time and again, for example, his friends chafed at the lack of a reliable voice in the capital. They were right, though in fact they had three journals eager to act as spokesman: the *National Intelligencer*, the *Constitutional Union*, and the *National Republican*. What was lacking was not a voice, but anyone prepared to listen. Edited by an old antiwar Democratic hack, former congressman Tom Florence of Pennsylvania, the *Union* had been, as one reporter put it, "a McClellan hurdy-gurdy [in the 1864 presidential campaign], which dragged out a moribund existence until [given] some official advertising." (The president's friends, embarrassed by such backing, swore that Florence copied the government advertising free of charge to make it seem as if he had White House support.)[14] Once a leader in news gathering, the *Intelligencer* had fallen on hard times and straight into

Democratic politics during the war. By 1865, its Confederate sympathies had made it worthless for winning over Republican congressmen to the administration. "Stupid and anile," "edited by men whose intellects are so obfuscated that none of them can write a clear English sentence," it came as close to accusing congressmen of treason as any paper could.[15] Yet it was there that Johnson let forth his semiofficial statements. When a bill was to be vetoed, congressmen learned it from editorials printed in the *Intelligencer* and written in the White House. One might as well hope to win Republicans through the appeals in the Chicago *Times*, which was urging Johnson to arrest leading senators and make himself military dictator until Reconstruction was complete.[16]

Indeed, the wrong sort of support did the president positive harm. True lovers of the Union remembered their enemies. When New York lawyer George Templeton Strong heard the New York *Daily News* prate about patriotism, it was enough to make him sick: well he knew that Ben Wood, the proprietor, got a $25,000 check "from the treason fund of rebel refugees and plotters in Canada." By spring of 1866, his faith in Johnson was shaken, not, as he admitted, by any logic so much as the journalistic company the president kept, Wood's paper in particular. Having supporters like that, the New York *Times* complained, was "the most formidable obstacle" that conservative Republicans "have yet been called to encounter."[17]

For nearly a year, Johnson also had the bulk of the Republican press behind him. Radicals left him sooner, but there were just not that many radical papers of consequence, and those in the big Northern cities always had to compete for Republican readers with moderate journals.[18] Displeased with the Cincinnati *Gazette*, Chicago *Tribune*, or Boston *Commonwealth*, subscribers could take the *Commercial*, *Republican*, or *Daily Advertiser* instead. If they disliked radical General Carl Schurz's "Observer" letters to Horace Greeley's paper, with their emphasis on Southern disloyalty and bigotry, they could simply pick up the *Times* and get a different version of the truth from the president's own emissary, Ben C. Truman, who, allegedly, got his pay from the Secret Service fund.[19] By the fall of 1866, to be sure, the balance had changed, though in every city, the president could still rely on Democratic newspapers for his defense, and most of the big Republican journals stood as far from the radical end of the party as ever, as unwilling to let blacks vote as they had been the year before.[20]

Nor, when Republican newspapers turned more critical, did they actually shut Johnson out. His opinions may have been offensive, but they were still news. His veto messages appeared in full on page one, regardless of the dailies' affiliation. When the president needed an outlet in early 1868, with impeachment under way, he found it on the Cincinnati *Commercial*, a conservative Republican paper with an even more conservative Washington correspondent, Joseph B. McCullagh ("Mack").

Still a young man, "Mack" had already made a sensational career. An apprentice printer by the time he was eleven, he covered Missouri legislative sessions and the 1860 presidential campaign before he was old enough to vote, but he reached national fame as a war correspondent. When the army banished him for revealing military positions in late 1863, he went to Washington, but not to peer down from the press gallery. Combining news gathering with a job as Senate stenographer, he sat on the chamber floor. That made him no more open to control.[21]

Now McCullagh was summoned to the White House for the first formal presidential interview. Lincoln had spoken to journalists frequently but had kept his words off the record. This time would be different. "The damn newspapers are as bad as the politicians in misrepresenting me," Johnson told "Mack." "I don't want you to take my side. I can fight these fellows single-handed; but put me down correctly." McCullagh did, or at least as well as he could remember when he got back to the office, since he had taken no notes. Even so, the result pleased the president so much that he called "Mack" in for an encore performance. Waving toward Capitol Hill he explained, "I want to give those fellows hell, and I think I can do it better through your paper than through a message, because the people read the papers more than they do messages."[22]

McCullagh got a taste of vintage Johnson. Bred in the democratic rough and tumble of Tennessee party politics, he put all his faith in the people's judgment. On the stump, in the governor's mansion, he had appealed to them directly and usually with success. Long before he hit upon McCullagh, he had determined to run his administration in the same way. Shut-mouthed when senators came to consult him, the real Andrew Johnson emerged clearest only when he opened his mouth in front of a crowd, and that was at every opportunity. There were speeches to supporters serenading him on Washington's Birthday, to delegations from Montana and Virginia, to blacks celebrating the anniversary of slavery's end in the District of Columbia. There were interviews, deliberately leaked by the White House, and cabinet meetings, whose confidential minutes the

president immediately passed to the *Intelligencer* after altering some secretaries' remarks to put them in an awkward position.[23] The culmination
came late in the summer of 1866, when Johnson took his "Swing Around
the Circle," speaking wherever crowds would listen, from Washington to
Chicago and St. Louis, and back again.[24]

The president thus could make himself heard and had plenty of journalists willing to listen. That was, in fact, precisely the problem. Instead of
failing because he could not take his case to the people, he hastened his
destruction by doing just that.

What Johnson said, in a way, was less material than his saying it at all.
However useful the bully pulpit might be to executives in an age when
their leadership of government was taken for granted, it worked less well
in a time when their main purpose was to preside. Political etiquette forbade presidential candidates to take to the stump before an election, much
less after it.[25] "The test to which Mr. Johnson has been subjected by in-
cessant reporting and telegraphing has been unprecedented," one of his
apologists noted mournfully, "and we never have had many public men
who would not have been damaged by it. Add to the extraordinary publicity of every thing said, the extraordinary quantity of the sayings, and to
say nothing of the quality, it is inevitable that the public becomes wearied
and disgusted."[26]

Those Republicans who read his speeches were often converted—the
wrong way. When the president used an address to accuse members of
Congress of plotting his assassination or to brand two of the most prominent Republicans on Capitol Hill traitors, when he compared himself to
Christ or, in the presence of disabled veterans, posed the rhetorical question of who had suffered for the Union more than himself, he did himself
more damage than the most hostile editorial that radical partisans could
have penned. It did the president less than no good at all when newspapers across the land published, faithfully, his snarling response midway
through a speech in Cleveland to one heckler: "I wish I could see you. I
will bet now, if there could be a light reflected upon your face, that cow-
ardice and treachery could be seen in it. Show yourself! Come out here
where I can see you. If you ever shoot a man, you will stand in the dark
and pull your trigger. I understand traitors. I have been fighting them
for five years. We fought it out on the southern end of the line; now we
are fighting it out in the other direction. And these men—such a one as
insulted me tonight—you may say has ceased to be a man, and . . . has

shrunk into the denomination of a reptile, and having so shrunken, as an honest man, I tread upon him." [27]

The Washington's Birthday speech, mourned one supporter, cost the president 200,000 votes in ten days. It was "the most disgraceful thing that ever emanated from the Presidential lips," another backer wrote. [28] Days before the "Swing Around the Circle" had swung back into Washington, friends were running for cover or into Republican ranks and assuring each other that *they* at least were not to blame: *they* had warned the president in advance not to give satisfaction to the hundred reporters hanging on his every word. "Is there no way of inducing the President to believe that *everybody* in America now knows that he 'has filled every station' from Prest down to tailor?" an ally complained. "Does [Secretary of State William] Seward *mean* to kill him off by this tour—and are we to stand by & see him kill us off too?" [29] By acting as his own defense counsel, Johnson convinced most Republicans that he had taken on a fool for a client.

The closer journalists came to the president, the less they liked him. At first Charles Nordhoff, editor on the New York *Evening Post*, gave him credit for worthy principles. That was before he visited Washington in early 1867 and watched Johnson in action. Slowly it dawned on him that the Republican Congress was right after all, because it had known the facts: a clear argument for the *Post* hiring its own Washington correspondent. Fascinated, he watched as the president lured moderate Republicans into making concessions on their Reconstruction bill by giving the impression that he would agree to a compromise; then, when the time came to do his part, Johnson dropped the conciliatory pose. Excited, he raged to Nordhoff against the measure from start to finish. White Southerners, "poor, quiet, unoffending, powerless, were to be trodden under foot 'to protect niggers,'" it seemed. Nordhoff tried arguing but had to give it up, the brave Tennessean he admired shown up for "a pig-headed man, with only one idea, . . . bitter opposition to universal suffrage, & a determination to secure the political ascendancy of the old Southern leaders." Time only deepened the newsman's disgust. "He is really vile, vulgar, coarse, mean, bad in every way, & not least in a kind of low cunning, [which] always defeats itself," he wrote two years later. [30]

Spreading patronage to one's friends in the press was a far more orthodox means of news management in the 1860s. In an era when political issues raged with less intensity, it might have worked better; but for Johnson it did not work at all. Dismissing the growing list of critics in early

1866 as disappointed office seekers, not just blinded partisans, allowed Johnson's defenders a comforting explanation, certainly. When Johnson vetoed the civil rights bill, "Mack" tallied the president's enemies: "such patriotic journals as the Chicago *Republican*, whose editor begged a collectorship, and didn't get it; the [St. Louis] *Missouri Democrat*, whose proprietor wanted the St. Louis post-office for his brother, and was disappointed; and the Washington *Chronicle*, the services of whose editor as chief scullion in the White House kitchen, have recently been dispensed with."[31] But who, in fact, dispensed with whose services, and why? The issue is of critical importance. It suggests how far spoils could actually override political issues just after the Civil War.

No one ever accused the "chief scullion," John Wien Forney, of fair-mindedness. Forty years a journalist, he had come a long way since the days when he and his wife set type for a little press in Lancaster, Pennsylvania—and quite a distance from the Democratic party for which he had served as defender, patronage broker, campaign fund-raiser, and possibly election stealer. By 1865, he owned two newspapers, the *Chronicle* and the Philadelphia *Press*, took a salary as secretary to the Senate, and still found time to churn out two to five columns of material every day. Pacing the floor of his capitol office, dictating to a stenographer, offering opinions and Washington news as "Occasional," he knew more about the inner workings of Congress than his position allowed him to tell. Quite possibly a concern for the personal contacts and government contracts on which his newspapers fattened made him discreet about his employers, and lobbyists paid good money to keep the *Chronicle*'s discretion on other matters.[32] The paper's goodwill was worth paying for; Forney could play the blackguard as easily as the sycophant. When he accused Johnson of having made a drunken spectacle of himself at Lincoln's second inauguration, the charge was strictly true, but, after all, Forney had poured the liquor.[33]

Forney was always asking favors. Surely he would have been the perfect subject for a test on how well presidential patronage could keep its friends. But Johnson never tried to buy the *Chronicle*'s goodwill. Driving to the White House on official business in mid-February 1866, Forney found the door shut in his face. The president was "engaged," a personal secretary explained. When the door was opened, Forney found out with whom: Johnson had been going over editorial proofs with John F. Coyle of a rival newspaper, the Washington *National Intelligencer*! Within days, the

Chronicle had swung from paeans to pejoratives on the administration. Johnson made the breach irreparable. Addressing a crowd of serenaders on Washington's Birthday, the president refused to extend his personal attacks and "give it to Forney" as well: "I do not waste my ammunition upon dead ducks."[34]

If the president had "given it to Forney" in a more positive sense, however, the result most likely would have been the same. However mercenary the *Chronicle* might be on smaller issues, the publisher was unbribable on big ones. (President James Buchanan had tried.) Neither snubs nor spoils made the *Chronicle* the administration's enemy. Johnson's veto of a bill essential for the protection of former slaves did that.[35] Indeed, it was only after the *Chronicle* broke with the administration that it began losing government advertising; as one wit explained, "a 'dead duck' should not be allowed to insert his 'bill' into the Treasury." Operating the paper at "a very heavy loss," as Forney admitted, the *Chronicle* stood fast, with its owner even organizing welcoming banquets for Republican congressmen and stumping Pennsylvania against the president.[36]

Losing patronage did not turn newspapers against Johnson. Keeping it did not hold them loyal. Across the North, complaints poured into the White House about editors who took the administration's coin and repaid it in diatribes. Critics missed the point. Republican journalists could afford to lose spoils more than they could their subscribers, and that was the choice before them.

The story of Johnson's press management therefore needs to be reconsidered with these points in mind. The real problem did not lie in the newspapers' inherent radicalism, cupidity, or ability to conceal essential news. It lay in Johnson's failure to control the flow of news that directly contradicted the assumptions on which his Reconstruction was based, and to recognize that the leading Republican papers themselves were as much made by opinion as makers of it.

The real alternative never lay between Republican propaganda and presidential truth. In an era when partisan papers made an art of shaping, even distorting the news, the president's friends did this as spectacularly as any radical. Only a feverish imagination could brand Republicans the "torch-and-turpentine party," out to spread arson, anarchy, and a new civil war across the whole nation, as the New York *World* did, or to declare that the Democratic party understood the Northern heart better than those in power or, apparently, those who turned out to vote. Blessed

A Brace of Dead Ducks. Forney, D. D., to Andy: "How do you like it yourself—
eh?" (Thomas Nast, *Harper's Weekly*, March 14, 1868). Nast celebrates the
House vote to impeach Andrew Johnson by showing the president and editor
John W. Forney equally dead—which proved to be the case.

in George W. Adams with one of Washington's best and most popular reporters, the editors marred his talent and badly tried his good nature by sticking partisan remarks into the news dispatches he sent them.[37]

There was no need to do so with McCullagh's work. Rather than overcoming the biased press coverage, his writing typified it. Set against the professional standard of his rivals on the Cincinnati *Gazette*, "Mack" looked like a throwback to the party press scribblers before the war. Publishing a story he disbelieved because it would "raise a fuss," as he once did, said more for his pugnacity than his desire to be accurate; and in this case, his story was pure fabrication: a radical secret plan, which simply did not exist, to launch an investigation that would discredit General Ulysses S. Grant as well as President Johnson and keep the war hero from being nominated for president in 1868.[38]

Reading conversations that "Mack" reported and invented—*verbatim*, the congressmen accused were furious. They had reason to suspect the worst intentions: this canard came at the end of more than a year of misstatements, each of them made to help President Johnson's cause. From the time Congress went into session in December 1865, "Mack" had declared that the radicals ran the show (they did not), that they were disunionists (they were not), that the Joint Committee on Reconstruction that was given the task of shaping peace terms was run by Thaddeus Stevens (it was not), and that the party was determined to humiliate or break the president (when precisely the opposite was true). Contemptuous of blacks north or south and baffled that any honest politician could believe that the rights of former slaves were worth federal protection, the *Commercial*'s reporter was soon spying revolutionary plots on Capitol Hill and offering defenses in advance for a presidential coup d'état against Congress. Time and again, he predicted what Congress would do; time and again, he was wholly wrong. When he insisted that the Civil Rights Act of 1866 would compel white women to marry blacks against their will or white theater owners to seat Negroes in the opera boxes, even the *Commercial*, conservative though it was, had to issue an embarrassed correction.[39]

Instead of looking for bias, therefore, the historian would do better to consider the intensity and kind. Incontestably, when reporters fanned out across the South in 1865, trying to catch the public mood and see how well free labor worked, they wrote to please their sponsors. Democrats described a South humble, conciliatory, and advancing as fast as meddlesome Yankee army officers and lazy Negroes would let it. Republicans glimpsed the truculence of unrepentant rebels and the atmosphere of violence and intimidation to anyone, white or black, who failed to fit the role permitted to them by the onetime lords of the lash. "Why, Mr. Smith," a North Carolina justice of the peace protested to one reporter, to illustrate the reason for keeping blacks from testifying in court, "I can go upon my plantation and hire for fifty cents apiece, five of my niggers to murder and bury you, and swear they saw somebody else do it, and they are pretty good niggers, too."[40] The example may have been meant as a veiled threat; others were not so veiled, for Southern editors in particular blamed Northern delusions on the traveling correspondents. "You made negroes your companions," one of them raged, "negro quarters your principal theme, mentioning gentlemen's names with them only for their shame; negro is on your brain, the devil in your heart, and negro is your God."[41]

The bias in Republicans' accounts needs closer inspection, however. For one thing, it extended beyond the conclusions they reached, to the questions they asked to begin with. Those questions mattered; their premises leaned to the conservative side, supporting a moderate Reconstruction much better than they would the one that Congress ultimately enacted. What Northern readers wanted to know was: were the Confederates loyal? had they given up secession and state sovereignty heresies in good faith? Were they mistreating their black workers? Could Negroes support themselves in freedom? The responses that Republican journalists sent back might support civil rights bills, loyalty oaths for Southern officeholders, and constitutional guarantees that the national debt would be paid. Giving blacks political power, on the other hand, would be another matter. Even Republican columnists drew the color line in their accounts of the freed millions. Blacks would work, could feed themselves, wanted to marry, worship, and attend school. But they were still far from being able to take care of themselves without Northern guidance. Their words rendered in dialect, they remained faintly comic and strongly alien, fittest as field hands. "V. H." of the Cincinnati *Commercial* turned up his nose at Montgomery quite literally. "The several stinks of Cologne are all numbered here, and, in addition, that particular *otar* to the perspiring Ethiopian cuticle," he wrote.[42]

More important, for many months, reporters failed to write to fit the party line; it was not clear just what that line was. As one correspondent complained, attacking presidential Reconstruction might be read as an attack on Andrew Johnson, which in 1865 few Republican newspapers cared to do.[43] So reporters for the same paper disagreed about how well the South was reconstructing, how well free labor was turning out, how far the violence against Union men was orchestrated. Even the New York *Tribune*, as radical a daily as that city could boast, published letters that fit the conservative view, and quite a number of correspondents went away despising the Southern Unionists they had gone south to glorify.[44]

At their most propagandistic, those letters and the packaged "outrages" still carried less decisive weight than other information about events, relayed through the Associated Press and available in newspapers of all partisan creeds. Reporters' accounts of Southern gasconade had plenty of corroboration from Southern editorial writers and politicians, oblivious to the effect their remarks would have on Northern readers. When South Carolina Governor Benjamin Perry prefaced his message to the legislature with a rebuke at Republicans for forgetting that "this is a white man's Government, and intended for white men only," he did what no partisan columnist could have done, and when his state and others put through black codes offering the former slaves only a limited freedom, Northern misstatements of what the laws included were rather beside the point: a fair statement of their provisions left the same general impression.[45] Even from reading the Democratic *World*, one could see the discrimination against blacks and the reluctance with which white Southerners relinquished the right of secession. It was a plain fact available to all that instead of facing the gallows or prison, former Confederate leaders took seats in Congress, the legislatures, and the governors' mansions, even if far more of them were reluctant secessionists than Republican journals made out.[46]

The availability of conflicting accounts, the richness of evidence, rather than its suppression, gave editors the opportunity to hold firm to their original beliefs, but among moderate Republicans, it worked rather differently. As the reports grew ever less promising, their own views on Reconstruction began to harden. By December 1865, moderate Republican papers had made up their minds about Johnson's policy and waited for the president to make up his. But Johnson had already made up his mind. Gradually over the course of the next nine months press news from the South and pronouncements from the White House had less and less connection with each other in any way that Republicans committed to the protection of blacks' basic rights could appreciate.[47]

By the fall of 1866, readers had no doubts left. What discretion editors

may have had was gone, and with it the basis for any newspaper outside
the Democratic party to stand by the president. In New York, Johnson had
begun the year with a tremendous advantage. Among the dailies, only the
Tribune voiced criticisms of his policy. Nobody needed to prove his Republican credentials with backers like the *Evening Post* and the *Times*.[48]
He lost them both.

As a congressman, Henry J. Raymond of the *Times* gave Johnson backing of the most personal kind. Six months changed him from the most
promising freshman in the House to a man with a brilliant future *behind*
him. Again and again, Raymond looked for common ground between the
president and the party that had elected them both. Over and over, Johnson cut the ground from under them and forced the editor to retreat, voting to sustain the veto of bills that he had voted to pass only days before.
Instead of starring as the polished orator and political manager of House
moderates, Raymond turned into the unwelcome onlooker in party caucuses, his name synonymous with political trimming. One critic dubbed
him a "boomerang" statesman: "Launch him out of the front door, . . . and
the next moment, crash he comes, flying through the back windows. If
he was pointed at the White House, we should expect he would land in
[the radicals'] back yard."[49] Raymond did not journey as far as that, but
by September 1866, he had gone as far as the *Times* could stand. Instead
of converting its readers, the readers converted the paper. Rather than
follow Raymond out of the Republican party, they switched to the *Tribune*
by the thousands. Disillusioned with Johnson and unwilling to abandon his
last connection with the party he had helped create and hold a deathwatch
over the newspaper he had founded, the editor swung the *Times* back onto
a solid Republican basis.[50]

What made losses like Raymond's so damaging to the president was not
in the way they biased news coverage against him. Especially in small
towns where the weekly four-pager still distilled news down into editorial
squibs, unfriendly papers did real harm. By contrast, the most conspicuous change in the *Times* came on the editorial page. Raymond continued
to speak for those Republicans most willing to give Johnson the benefit
of the doubt. Instead, the editor's abandonment of the president's cause
mattered in having happened at all. Like every other paper's change of
base, it showed what the people were thinking: press opinion reflected
the community's views far more than it made them. When former senator
William Bigler of Pennsylvania reached New York, he found the presi-

dent's friends utterly demoralized by Raymond's defection; the news even dampened Democratic spirits in Green Bay, Wisconsin.[51]

The assumption that newspapers spoke as their constituencies decreed was one of the strongest reasons that Republicans found it so hard to take Democratic newspapers' praise for the president. The *Daily News* did not lead its readers; it represented their views. The Richmond *Enquirer* spoke for Richmond, not to it, just as the ranting language of Robert Barnwell Rhett's Charleston *Mercury* revealed the true character of white Southerners. Conceivably, then, the most damaging evidence against the former Confederate states to appear in Northern papers came out of Southern editorial offices.

The same assumption explains why moderate newspapers, less easily predictable in their responses, less driven by ideological considerations, held so much weight in political discourse. Losing the *Tribune* said very little about Johnson's popularity. Horace Greeley was notoriously hard to please, and the *Tribune*'s radical reputation defined its public constituency. But James Gordon Bennett's *Herald* said whole volumes. Vituperative toward blacks, Southern Unionists, and Republicans, and read widely enough to have a wide discretion in the causes it endorsed, the New York *Herald* could stick by the president longer than any other independent newspaper in the city could. Yet Bennett, who had been bombarding Johnson with political advice and hectoring him to create his own political party, left the president a week before Raymond did. "While he is naturally disposed to change with the changing tide, or when he believes the tide is going to change," an editor wrote the president apologetically, "he makes this subservient to his business interests. His business is in the midst of an . . . excitable people."[52]

So, too, in 1868, when the House voted for impeachment, the real forces legitimating it did not come from radical newspapers. When Greeley's New York *Tribune* demanded Johnson's conviction, it probably changed few minds; radicalism and the *Tribune* were synonymous. (In fact, Greeley, who had been away, was a reluctant impeacher, at least at first. As he put it, "Why hang a man who is bent on hanging himself?")[53] Nor, when Johnson got off, did anyone ascribe it to McCullagh's interview. Instead, if journalists deserved any credit at all, it belonged to the men running moderate Republican newspapers like the Springfield *Republican* and the Chicago *Tribune*, whose support for impeachment seemed to reflect the movement's broad base in the Republican party, and whose firmness in making clear that a vote to acquit would not be held against any Republican assured the seven holdouts a fair hearing.[54]

Press support and political management of the press, then, were more tricky than they appeared and less practicable, given the constraints built into the system of Johnson's day. Neither spoils nor speeches would be enough to tame the newspaper fraternity, and in many cases, the rewards were as modest as "Mack's" contributions turned out to be.

Perception, however, lies far from reality. So the politicians did what they could to have the papers on their side. As the 1868 presidential campaign got under way, Democratic leaders knew that they could rely on the party press, but that hireling editors were not enough to sway public opinion outside of the ranks of the true believers. What if the New York *Herald* could be swung round? Once editor of Andrew Jackson's Washington organ and now father of the vice-presidential candidate, old Francis P. Blair had ideas for converting the great independent daily. No one doubted the prize worth capturing. From another solon came advice for exploiting the Associated Press dispatches to best advantage. Most ambitious was Congressman R. W. Latham's proposal for carrying the Washington correspondents. The Republican leaders "have declined to pay them any money, but offer *largely in case of success!* This don't suit." For $3,000 to $3,500 a month, some thirty reporters could be secured through election day, and even $10,000 a month, Latham reminded his superiors, would be dirt cheap. It was crazy advice; even journalists peddling their columns to a railroad lobby would balk at selling out their party. Still, it showed how seriously insiders took a press that served their ends.[55]

Out of that search for power over the press and the press's search for influence on government decisions came a series of alliances, clashes, and frustrations. At best, the relationship could lead to more incisive news coverage and a sharper glance at government's workings than Americans had ever enjoyed before. It could strengthen the hand of reformers in office or hasten on changes in the way politics was run. At worst, the meeting of politicians and journalists fostered distortion, deception, corruption, and misrepresentation. Then news management became a contradiction in terms.

CHAPTER 3

Organs
out of Tune

The 1868 presidential campaign was beyond all question the most venomous, scurrilous, and misleading—since the last one. A dispassionate observer would have seen merits in both parties' nominees. On the Republican side stood General Ulysses S. Grant, defender of the Union; on the Democratic, former governor Horatio Seymour of New York, defender of civil liberty.

Finding a dispassionate observer would have been virtually impossible. "We must have the victory, or the country is lost," a senator wrote. So thought thousands less highly placed. Great issues were at stake: should the Republican effort to remake the South on the basis of equal rights be abandoned? how liberally, how literally, should Congress and president interpret their powers under the Constitution? on what terms should onetime Confederates share political power? Lit by flaring torchlights, the procession banners caught the mood: "We Go for Seymour as We Went for Lee," "U. S. G.—the Tanner of Rebels," "Let all good men vote no nigger," "Our Symbol is Peace, not the Sword."[1]

Muddling the debate was an incredible array of insults and conjectures propagated by the partisan press on either side. Seymour had called Negro-butchering rioters "my friends" during the war; his chums were traitors or fellow travelers, his cabinet would look like a rebel reunion, his Southern policy the prelude to a second Civil War; so Republican newspapers said. Republicans widely believed that the Democratic running mate, General Frank Blair, Jr., coveted a dictator's power to settle Reconstruction matters once and for all. That made all the more alarming the news reports spread about Seymour's health, so delicate that the shock of inauguration would pass him into the grave and Blair into the office. One correspondent saw "an uneasy wildness of the eyes" and recalled "the misfortune of his parents, both insane." Indeed, if Republicans were right, Seymour's whole family had died in a madhouse or by their own hands. Election would be more than his overtaxed brain could stand.[2]

What about "Useless" Grant? It was not enough for Democratic organs to brand him tyrant, embezzler, hater of Jews, and butcher of soldiers. Had voters heard about his *other* wife, that Indian squaw out west and their three children? No doubt the wedding occurred while Grant was drunk, apparently his normal condition. One story that Democratic editors delighted in had Grant celebrating the Sabbath in Washington by a drunkard's dance in front of a church.[3]

Sensible people had foreseen the abuse beforehand. In the dog days, when family pets went mad with the heat, so would Republican editors, a Democratic journalist warned. The average reader would have a treat in store if he scanned their columns:

> He will learn therefrom many things about Horatio Seymour that no one ever learned before.
>
> He will learn that Horatio Seymour was born with double rows of teeth; and that his first lively performance was to bite off the nurse's little finger because she had a brother in the army.
>
> That he grew up a deceitful young rascal, who bamboozled "good little boys" into the belief that swallows might be caught by putting Onondaga salt on their tails.
>
> That he cut the throats of six school-fellows, extracted their livers, and sold them to a sausage-maker.
>
> That he studied law because lawyers succeed better at rascality than any other people, excepting those who get war-contracts, or places in the revenue service.

That he joined the church in order to gratify a personal grudge against the worthy rector, whom he afterward drowned in the Herkimer river, by tying a large stone to his neck.

A proper rebuke! and it would have been more so if the offended editor had taken his own plea to heart when talking about General Grant.[4] But that would have been out of character for a party press.

If voters had taken every charge seriously, they would no more have gone to the polls than into a smallpox ward. But the turnout that November that put Grant into office was immense. Indeed, hardly anyone in either party had been converted by the other's allegations.[5] For that willingness to vote, just as for the spreading of false charges, the party press deserves special credit.

Though an independent press was on the rise, though reporters' search for news would shape discourse increasingly in the years to follow, the 1868 campaign fit squarely in the Golden Age of partisan journalism. Never again would party organs monopolize debate (much less first publication of the president's annual message), but to the century's end they would play prominent roles.[6] That persistence, as well as the organs' continued hold on rural subscribers, needs to be stressed, for it was an influence that the metropolitan, independent papers could temper but not entirely supplant. Outside of the subscribers to the large metropolitan dailies, most Americans who read political news still got their information from the party press, and that press depended on party coffers and official funding. Congressmen might speak of the rural weeklies as the true voice of public opinion. In fact, they generally were the most partisan of papers, the most likely to be controlled by "court-house rings," the most dependent on officeholders' generosity and the subsidies of official advertising.[7]

Partisanship was no disgrace just after the war—or at any rate not so great a disgrace that newspaper proprietors did not try to win subscribers by flaunting their loyalties: "a wool-dyed Democratic weekly journal," say, or "the universal center of light to both Democrats and the 'balance of the world.'"[8] A single glance at the masthead often told the whole story. One did not have to ask the politics of the Hudson *True Republican* or the Linn *Unterrified Democrat*.[9] It was a safe bet that the McGregor (Iowa) *Progressive Age*, the Pittsfield (Ill.) *Old Flag*, the Estherville *Northern Vindicator*, and Altoona's *Blair County Radical* would be Republican, just as that the *Conservative* (whether in Hopkinsville, Kentucky, or Independence, Iowa), the *Jacksonian*, or the *Constitution* (whether Atlanta, Keokuk, or Warren, Ohio) would be Democratic. One could be a little less certain with a name like the *Union*, since both sides embraced the cause across the North, though below the Ohio River nearly every *Union* was Republican, and above it, the odds were slightly in Republicans' favor.[10]

Acting as a party shill may seem distasteful today, and in the postwar years the practice faced mounting challenge. Still, the protests rest on two assumptions, neither of which good Democrats or Republicans shared: first, that the purpose of newspapers was to provide news more than to guide public opinion, and second, that one could be partisan or objective, not both. Not even the organs' critics would have gone as far as that. Independent newspapers provided news with the hope of steering public opinion; they differed only in believing that the right direction followed no specific party line. The assumption did not go unchallenged. In an age when Republicans saw Democratic spokesmen as the front men for traitors and terrorists (which, in a sense, they were) and were themselves seen as plotters out to stretch strict constitutional provisions like India rubber and endow unschooled Negroes with political rights for which they lacked training (which also had some modest connection to the truth), partisanship and patriotism were easy to confuse. So party presses went out of their way to make clear what a party label meant: "the Organ of the People against corruption in politics, &c.," or the voice of white men everywhere.[11]

Most readers probably would have had it no other way. "Our opponents here, as elsewhere, are . . . so stubborn that they will not read anything unless it bears the impress of democracy or is recommended by [its] leaders," a New Hampshire Republican explained. Advertisers, therefore, paid special attention to the political affiliation of the area in which they were selling; there was no sense in patronizing a Democratic newspaper, for example, in much of Vermont, where democracy and typhoid were equally popular, equally uncommon, and responded with equal lack of success to treatment. But in other places, where a minority party had a substantial following, businessmen might pay heed to the underdog's newspaper voice; ill-matched at the polls, its readers made up a fair share of the market and could be reached through no other medium. Thus the Centralia *Democrat* may have been "one of the best advertising mediums" in the southern Illinois counties, even though its Republican rival, the *Sentinel*, had "the largest circulation in city, county, or Congressional District."[12]

If partisanship could be seen as good for the country, a partisan press was certainly good for the parties. "A party without an outspoken fearless advocate and defender, in short an *'organ'* will soon 'go where the wood-bine twineth,'" one Democrat wrote another. "We should *start a new paper at once.*"[13] He was not exaggerating. Recent scholars have shown how useful the party press was for whipping up sentiment or for shaping unpalatable truths into palpable untruths. However significant the historian might find the brutal overthrow of Republican government in Mississippi in 1875, all the stories about it combined would not have amounted to the coverage Northern journals gave to one day of the Ohio race for governor. Partisan journals helped make eligible voters define the world of public events in terms of competitive politics, and news in terms of who won what. The organs may not have converted masses from one side to the other, but they reinforced loyalties already present, reassured readers that the differences between the parties were deep, irreconcilable ones, and catered to some of the meanest of ethnic and sectional prejudices conceivable, with striking effect.[14]

The demand from rank and file, the needs of party managers combined to ensure the establishment of organs everywhere that resources permitted, and the demand for resources went on incessantly, sometimes across very long distances. Thus John Forsyth, editor of the Mobile *Register*, called on his New York Democratic allies to contribute $4,000 to the cause, and New Orleans editors wanted them to provide incalculable sums.[15] Buying and converting established organs was nothing unusual, nor was harboring fears that without a fresh dose of funds, this publisher or that might put his purse before his principles; a party organ that had to be bought, after all, was really only rented. Most editors would let their paper die before deserting, of course, but without regular supplies of cash, death was a real possibility.[16]

Where did the money to keep an organ going come from? Advertising revenues mattered everywhere, and in the city news vendors' sales to occasional customers, but subscriptions remained absolutely essential. In upstate New York, the Democratic executive committee even offered prizes to those workers who raised the largest number of subscribers.[17] Party and official funds made a useful, even a vital supplement. During a political campaign, publishers might dun the national party treasury, sometimes successfully.[18] More often, government revenues were applied to sustaining the newspapers that sustained the party in power.[19] Editors lined up for appointments, some of which paid better than the title might indicate. As clerk to the Ohio senate, the editor of the Columbus *Ohio Statesman* passed in vouchers that did some violence to the traditional calendar: he was paid for 462 days of work in one year and 383 in the next. Perhaps he only prided himself on his self-restraint, as the house clerk drew pay for more than 1,100 days' labor in the same period.[20] Most editors settled for a $1,200 postmastership, which let them send their newspapers free under the official frank and harass rival presses: confiscating circulars, finding out their subscribers' names and convincing them to cancel, or fostering newspaper-subscribing clubs.[21]

When the government wanted order forms, official stationery, and even labels printed up, they looked to their friends; to inform the public, they paid the local party press to publish General Assembly acts on page one. Public money also helped publishers generate private funding. Outside major cities, status as an official organ made a newspaper somewhat more enticing to advertisers. The paper would live, at least while the party reigned. So when editors sought business patronage, they stressed the status that a government connection had given them—"The official paper of the City and County of Leavenworth, and the only paper in Kansas that publishes the *Advertisements of the War Department*," the Leavenworth *Times* boasted.[22]

With state, local, and federal authorities all disposing of contracts, patronage spread widely. As of 1867, fifty-four newspapers received money for printing the laws of the United States. There were always supplicants left out and demanding some other means of income. New York's Republican papers fought over the contract to print revenue stamps for the Treasury Department and denounced each other as liars and blackmailers when not endowed. State legislatures opened with battles between rival newspapers wanting to act as public printer.[23]

What exactly taxpayers got for their money was less clear than it seemed. One could draw two very different, equally plausible conclusions about the partisan press. On the one hand, one might argue, it defined news so narrowly as to leave the public ill-informed and interpreted events with such a deadening uniformity as to stifle real choices; in that case, the coming of an independent press was a positive blessing. Alternatively, the party press fired the public to share the pleasures of politics; in that case, the coming of a less politically oriented independent press did democracy a real injury. Both are true but misleading by themselves. However efficiently the press worked for the party organizations in theory, in practice it took constant management and repaid with constant worry. Not even patronage could control the wagging tongues and ravening ambitions of editors who thought of themselves as power brokers and as fitter voices for the rank and file than were its leaders. Even at their most obliging and influential, those in the larger cities could not suppress the truth or make the party membership march in lockstep.

Loyal journals did more than enlighten the people. They educated the politicians about what people wanted. If farmers grumbled over high railroad charges and government extravagance, Senator William Allison of Iowa could find it out from the editor of the Ottumwa *Daily Courier*. Republicans heard plenty from Joseph Medill of the Chicago *Tribune* about how to run the 1868 campaign and which issues to stress.[24] Now and then, officeholders owned the establishment outright. On the Democratic side, the Indianapolis *Sentinel* owed its rescue from foreclosure and the auction block to a joint stock company organized with party committee funding. Heading the stockholders' list were the secretary of state, the state auditor, the treasurer, and one of the most prominent Democratic congressmen.[25]

Under the circumstances, editors became political forces to be reckoned with in their own right. Many congressmen began their careers behind an editor's desk: Democratic House floor leader James Brooks of New York, for example. Other editors wrote party platforms, served on state executive committees, took charge of fund-raising, or distributed the campaign literature. They recommended men for office, especially themselves. Above all, party papers proclaimed themselves the authoritative voice of the organization and denounced all public figures failing to share the same opinions.[26]

Among Democrats in 1868, that role fell to Manton Marble's New York *World*. "James Buchanan," a country partisan was said to have admonished his son, "you must go to college and be able to read this 'ere sterling paper." Good news gathering made it worth reading, to be sure; but very likely the senators and congressmen who subscribed did not cull it for the sparkling society columns of Mrs. Grundy or the witty barbs that "Parsee Merchant" leveled at the high-tariff men. They did so for the true Democratic gospel. "Lord, Lord," mourned one Republican, "how this *World* is given to lying!!"[27]

Marble was no mere lead singer in the chorus, descanting the sheet music that his superiors presented him with. He helped write the music himself. Politicians did not direct him; they appealed, consulted, and informed. Nothing happened in party councils without Marble learning of it. Even August Belmont, national chairman, had to find out what his underlings were doing by turning to the *World*'s proprietor. How could it have been otherwise when other editors read and took their cues from the *World*, when President Andrew Johnson balked at helping the party in the 1868 campaign as long as the *World* failed to award him all the credit he thought was his due, and when the negative tone of the canvass was set on Printing-House Square?[28] Attacked though he might be inside the party and out, Marble remained a power to reckon with as long as he owned the *World* and was an insider of considerable influence long after.

Marble was not the only Democratic editor whose influence was worth cultivating. He had rivals, even in New York, speaking with an entirely different voice. Anyone reading the brimstone-laden columns of the New York *Daily Democrat* expected to see Marble's opposite in its proprietor, the notorious Mark ("Brick") Pomeroy: a "Copperhead" Democrat straight out of a Nast cartoon, red-nosed, rough-looking, and rough-tongued. They were not disappointed, though one Republican editor was surprised in certain respects: "Unlike most Democrats, he neither drinks whiskey nor wears a dirty shirt." Energetic and combative, with a mean streak that showed itself in sadistic practical jokes and may have explained his three divorces, Pomeroy knew how to make money by making enemies. Going to Wisconsin in 1860 with five dollars in his pocket, he turned the LaCrosse *Democrat* into a four-pager nationally read, enjoyed, and damned.[29]

When he arrived in New York in 1868, it was as a celebrity, his latest newspaper project offering an appeal to laboring-class Democrats, with a rough, masculine style quite unlike the *World*'s. "Damn It! Damn It!" "Damn it, if you will," his circular for the organ read, "—but read it first." Outside the rooms rented in the New York *Sun* building swung the vermilion sign, "Red Hot!" And it *was* red hot. Objective reporting appeared never, news only fleetingly. But Democrats could read attacks rich in hyperbole that perhaps reflected more on the writer's gifts than on his subject: how Lincoln was assassinated for having broken his promise to John Wilkes Booth, that paragon of chivalry and honor, how Secretary

Wilkes Booth the Second (Thomas Nast, *Harper's Weekly*, November 7, 1868).
Brick Pomeroy, with vice-presidential candidate Frank Blair, Jr., backing him
up, prepares to dispatch General Grant. Blair had warned that Grant, if elected,
would never leave the White House alive, a statement that, taken out of context,
sounded like an assassination threat.

of War Edwin Stanton's death was actually the suicide of a guilt-ridden
butcher of those two innocents: Booth's coconspirator, Mrs. Surratt, and
the Goddess of Liberty.[30]

In principles, too, the *World* and the *Democrat* stood at opposite ends
of the party. The *World* really only spoke for the upper-class "Swallowtail" faction of the city party, to whom the Manhattan Club was as much
a headquarters as was Tammany Hall to laborers. Well-to-do Democrats,
convinced that rule by their class was crucial to good government, knew

editor Marble stood at their side. So did bankers distrustful of paper currency. His newspaper was among the first to urge the party away from its Negrophobia and toward economic issues, and one of the first organs to decry the Tweed Ring (as well as one of the first to abandon the fight).[31]

Pomeroy, by contrast, never made his peace with any part of the postwar order. His view of the struggle as "but a murderous crusade for cotton and plunder" lasted lifelong. Reconstruction would only sharpen his tongue. It was the *Democrat* that urged that President Lincoln's second term be abbreviated with an assassin's knife and that fastened the nickname "Spoons" to General Benjamin F. Butler, whom it claimed had stolen silverware from New Orleans aristocrats. Glimpsing a plot of bankers and speculators to thrust Americans into commercial and political bondage, he turned his wrath on the Democrats of Broadway and Wall Street, the Money-Power that would wrest the party from its ancient heritage.[32]

The existence of party organs, therefore, did not necessarily rule out alternative views of public policy within the party. Far from forcing members into a specific orthodoxy, the newspapers fostered the inclination within party lines to differ on issues. On topics like the tariff, money supply, temperance, and Bible reading in the schools, Republicans quarreled angrily, and when Kentucky Democrats discussed an inflated currency, they wasted no energy in civility.[33]

Besides the editor's sense of his own opinion's importance and ideological rifts in the ranks, a third force impelled party presses to undermine unity. Many of them were the personal voices of individual politicians. The Chicago *Inter-Ocean* spoke for Senator "Black Jack" Logan, the Indianapolis *Journal* for Senator Oliver P. Morton. As contemporaries noted, however able the latter paper might be, it "must spit when [Morton] snarls."[34] When lead articles followed the leader, a journal could move to the outskirts of the organization, just as the *Times* did with Henry J. Raymond in 1866.[35]

Whatever the reasons—ambition, disappointment, idealism, or personal fealty—the parties found that organs were not easily kept in tune, even with the lubrications of patronage. How could they be, when each party faction had its own idea of what the proper tune was? Blessed with *World* and *Democrat*, New York City's Democrats railed at them both. In early 1870, dissidents from Tammany Hall, christening themselves the "Young Democracy," launched an attack on William "Boss" Tweed and a paper to deliver it, the *Daily Free Press*. Tweed himself invested heavily in Pomeroy's *Democrat* and, when it failed to satisfy him, funded other alternatives that folded almost instantly. His successor as boss, John Kelly, imagined that $50,000 in cash and $200,000 in stock would buy him the New York *Express* as the organ for Tammany Democracy. So it did, briefly; all it needed then was somebody willing to read it.[36]

New York provided an extraordinarily rich soil for factional journals to grow in or, to change metaphor, an extraordinarily large graveyard for them, one after the other, to be interred in. But the sense of disgruntlement with what organs a party had could be found everywhere. New Hampshire Republicans could not help feeling that their failures at the polls stemmed from their failures in the press.[37] In Philadelphia, Democrats were "literally at the mercy of the dishonest and treacherous *Times*."[38] One year, Indianapolis Democrats actually put through resolutions to exclude anyone connected with their *Sentinel* from the coming state party convention as a delegate. It was on such papers that the blame fell when voters were "confused"—that is, when they began to believe the opposition's argument.[39]

Party organs, then, often seemed nearly more trouble than they were worth. The more influential a paper was, the more damage it had the potential to wreak. The *World* taught Democrats that lesson in 1868. State committee members complained at how little was said on behalf of the party's financial plank; did Marble want to make Western partisans think that the bankers would run the next Democratic administration? Even more mischievous was Marble's action scarcely three weeks before Election Day. Never enamored of the ticket, he abandoned hope altogether when state returns from Pennsylvania and Ohio went against the Democrats in mid-October and called for changing vice-presidential candidates. General Blair must go.[40]

Invigorated by the *World*'s appeal, others in the party took up the cry. The Chicago *Times* demanded an entirely new ticket. Many Democrats mistakenly thought that Marble spoke for the national committee; when they found otherwise, bewilderment turned to rage. "A leading Democrat has just said to me 'the *World* is *bought*,'" one reader wrote Marble. Other subscribers branded their editor "a miserable pander" to bondholders, despots, and other Republicans. Grant was momentarily forgotten as all the old rivalries between would-be candidates resurfaced. Even Democratic insiders who had been plotting some change in the ticket were forced to retreat. By the time the *World* had made amends, the party's morale had suffered almost as damaging a blow as another speech by the vice-presidential candidate would have been.[41]

When politicians endowed faithful newspapers, they did so not simply out of gratitude, but from fear of the consequences of doing otherwise. Hell had no wrath like an editor scorned. Journals not endowed as generously as their proprietors thought their merits deserved were all the more likely to break loose and stir up havoc.

If party organs fell so far short of the politicians' desires and caused so much trouble in the ranks, the outcry against them grew still more from those for whom party success mattered less than the triumph of reform. By 1868, the complaint against hireling editors was growing; so was the pressure for some alternative, freeing the public purse from hungry partisan supplicants.

One could excuse the printing of legislative proceedings as a public good, to be sure. Only by a daily official report of debates could the people catch swindles and frauds, the *Illinois State Register* explained. It was those who desired as little notice as possible—insurance, railroad and warehouse companies, and other thieves—who wanted silence.[42] But the argument was a specious one. The patronage system necessarily meant high prices and superfluous printing. When the Illinois legislature wanted to endow Springfield newspapers, it ordered them to publish the official proceedings. That would have been all very well had those newspapers a statewide circulation (which they did not) or had other presses not done the same work daily as part of their normal reporting of the news (which they did). The St. Louis *Missouri Republican* charged that it had ten times the Illinois circulation of both the Springfield dailies put together (which, since neither could have had a circulation much larger than two thousand, seems possible). There was no real public need to print every bill offered in the Missouri senate, when nine-tenths would never leave the committee to which they were referred and only one in fifty would pass the chamber in the same shape as it had been introduced. Nor was there a good reason to print documents that had no repository except the capitol basement, where vast piles of them moldered and afforded bedding for rats. But such projects kept the party presses going.[43]

The costs were also exorbitant. New York City authorities would not have paid a dollar a line to publish advertisements, when the going rate was less than forty cents, had it not been buying influence as well.[44]

There is no question, then, that the connection between government and the press meant financial corruption and conflict of interest. Did it also corrupt the responsibility of the press to spread the news? "Like the Romans of old," the Milwaukee *News* charged, "the people are to be crushed with the treasures stolen from them by their captors."[45]

Certainly partisanship defined political news in the most personal and often the most scurrilous terms. To hear Democratic editors tell it, Lincoln had been "the patron saint of niggerism, *who owes so much to John Wilkes Booth.*" Republicans would soon make the same allegation against Andrew Johnson, and both parties, at different times, came to the original discovery that he was a habitual drunkard. If Democrats were not offended enough by the civil rights notions of Congressman Thaddeus Stevens of Pennsylvania and Senator Charles Sumner of Massachusetts, they could take delicious horror in the revelation that Stevens kept a black housekeeper as his mistress and Sumner found it impossible to satisfy his wife's connubial needs. As for Governor Oliver P. Morton of Indiana, the ferocious enemy of wartime disloyalty, readers of the Democratic press knew for a fact that his patriotism paid. The paralytic stroke that left him chair-ridden came from syphilis, an inevitable result of his habits with every young lady seeking official favors. "Governor Morton sleeps with your ma!" one urchin was reported to have shouted at another. "Shucks, that's nothing!" the other replied. "Governor Morton sleeps with everybody's ma!"[46]

Yet as Johnson's Reconstruction experience showed, there were limits to how far a government-fed press could conceal, suppress, or mangle the news. North of the Ohio, each small-town party press was matched by its counterpart in the opposition. Gettysburg had scarcely three thousand residents, but they could learn the Democratic version of the truth from the *Compiler* and balance it with the Republican *Star and Sentinel.* A party organ might fail to cover a scandal that reflected badly on men it supported, but readers would at least know something was going on, by reflection, in the editorial replies to the opposition newspaper's charges.[47]

When a party was divided, different party organs representing either faction could force the other to exposure. That division was no rare occurrence. Rhode Island politics were peculiarly corrupt and personal.[48] By 1870 Republican disputes had turned into a fracas between the rival financial houses of Sprague & Company and Brown & Ives. Both had textile factories, banking investments, and a senator. Wartime governor and speculator William Sprague held one Senate seat and cast baleful glares at Henry B. Anthony, who held the other. Neither could drive his rival from power, but they could show their muscle in other ways. In 1870 they squared off over one of Anthony's allies, the reform-minded Congressman Thomas Jenckes. In the filthy five-man contest that followed, Jenckes was bested by Sprague's man and money.[49]

Usually, partisans kept their internal disagreements within the family, but the faction's organs made that impossible. The Providence *Journal* remained Anthony's property and spoke with his voice, while the Providence *Press* became the mouthpiece for Sprague. When Republicans fell out, investigative reporting got its due. Thus one might learn how local primaries were packed with Democrats paid at one hundred dollars a head, how Sprague got rich running guns to the Confederates in wartime and smuggling out cotton for his mills, and how Jenckes endorsed notes that he could not redeem. When five-dollar Republicans were arrested for fraud and marched into the counting room of Sprague's factory, it was the *Journal* that published the story.[50]

This diversity of reporting, however, was more available to historians poring through archives than to people at the time. If they wanted to know the truth all the time, readers would have had to look at several newspapers, not one.[51] The truth was not suppressed. It was simply hard to get in any one place; for no matter how much any one organ exposed wrongdoing, there would always be matters on which it preferred to be silent. When a Providence alderman some years later detailed the enormous increase in city expenses, his remarks received a deafening neglect from the local newspapers. None of them would publish a word. In the end, he had to print his allegations at his own expense and distribute them through the mail.[52] Least of all would newspapers scrutinize the steals they shared in. With petty pilfering everywhere in the Indiana legislature, "Pickaway" wrote, the state press glossed over it all. What more could be expected? "They are all sucking pap from the public teat, and the moment they open their mouths . . . the teat will drop."[53]

All too often a publisher had to lay down his lie for his party, even when it meant, as in the *World*'s case, that it would hawk a gambler, saloon keeper, bruiser, and former prize-fighter as a congressional statesman. "From the hour I first occupied the position of editor to the present time," a retiring journalist confessed, "I have been solicited to lie on every given subject, and can't remember ever having told a wholesome truth without diminishing the subscription list or making an enemy. Under these circumstances of trial, and having a thorough contempt for myself, I retire in order to recruit my moral constitution."[54]

There was, therefore, some reason for even politicians to hold their newspaper tools in contempt. Increasingly, even faithful party shills did their best to distance themselves from hireling status. The alternative was to be deemed "the Barnacle Organ," unworthy of credence. When the *National Republican*, widely seen as the administration's mouthpiece, published an editorial entitled, "Who Shall Be Believed?," the St. Louis *Republican* had a ready answer: "Anybody who disagrees with the Washington *Republican*."[55] As one of the sages of the New York press and its first serious historian, Frederic Hudson, summed up, "No great journal can be a party organ."[56]

Nor could it if greatness was defined by news coverage. Each year, this became more the case, and with it, the organs felt the pressure at the very least to relegate politics to the sidelines and expand the alternative entertainments open to their readers. Let editors look to Brick Pomeroy if they ever imagined otherwise. He began his New York career with plenty of advantages, including the advance publicity as editor of a paper "famous for its entire disregard both of grammar and propriety." Ten thousand dollars were spent just to prepare for the first issue. A splendid Bullock press was bought for $15,000 to do the printing. Special local sketches were provided by correspondents at high cost, and the price of two cents rivaled the low cost of the *Star*. Over 20,000 copies sold on the first day of publication. But the novelty of unmodulated vituperation wore off quickly. By the following day, sales were in decline. Before the presidential campaign had reached its midpoint, Pomeroy was selling 5,000 or less. In a year, he had lost over $100,000. In two years, Pomeroy had sold the daily and restricted himself to a Saturday edition called *Pomeroy's Democrat*; another six months and the daily expired, its relict bought by the New York *Star*. Perhaps New Yorkers bridled at Brick's venom; more likely, they noticed that in news gathering, Pomeroy's journal lacked the redeeming qualities of the *World*. There was something to be said for society columnists and "scoops" after all.[57]

This point opens up the obvious division of loyalties that could take an organ out of tune over time: was the editor's first loyalty to the party or to the paper? It might well be the former; after all, most party editors were not in the job for the money (however much they welcomed it), but for the cause. That was one reason they dared disagree with their leaders: the party's good mattered more than any politician's weal. But if the account books came to matter more, the editor might temper his doctrines to suit the climate of the surrounding community, not just in politics but in the subordination of views to news. Then he might act as did the owners of the Boston *Post*, a Democratic newspaper reliant on Republican advertisers. The *Post* was a good paper in its own right—"very frisky," in fact, according to "Warrington," the keen-eyed reporter for the Springfield *Republican*. It was too frisky to lead a forlorn hope and lose patrons in a Republican state. When public opinion was clearly against the *Post*, it would admit its opponents "more than half right" and "curtail expenses and gibes at the same time, and half the day you don't know whether the paper is for the administration or against it." [58]

The tug to independence only got stronger when the patronage dried up. Then the partisan editor had no choice but to scramble for readers and advertisers where he would. As Forney's break with President Johnson showed, patronage could not ensure a docile party press, nor an effective one. But take the spoils away, and one more argument for taking the partisan line at a financial cost was wiped out.

To assume that an editor like Wilbur F. Storey of the Chicago *Times* let his ledger dictate his loyalties would be rashness itself. In an age of eccentric editors, he held a special place. In wartime, his rage at Republican methods led to government suppression of the *Times*, and by late 1866, there were even some Democrats who wished heartily that the suppression had been permanent. Still, it is not impossible that late in 1868, he considered how little his paper needed, much less could expect, a subsidy from the authorities running a Republican Chicago and a Republican Illinois. So when the state Democratic leaders called him to Springfield to chastise his digression from uncritical loyalty to the national platform, Storey was no longer the meek disciple. After listening to his accusers for several hours, he stood up and shoved on his hat. "Gentlemen," he snorted, "I thought that I owned the Times! I think so still. Good night, gentlemen." [59]

CHAPTER 4

I Am the Paper!

The Independents

In 1875, a magnificent building front-
ing New York's Printing-House Square
opened for business. Designed by Richard
Morris Hunt, it featured a Florentine
campanile that gave one of the best views
of the city; only the Trinity Church spire
rose higher. Visitors might admire its
safety: there was not a single wooden
beam or lath partition in the place, and
even the floorboards were set on a cement
foundation. Or they might admire its
almost palatial grandeur, from the counting rooms to the roof of slate and iron.
Entering on the ground floor, they would
gaze beneath their feet on inlaid Mettlach
mosaic, specially prepared in Germany
and "so hard that they will cut glass." In
the entry, bronze chandeliers with special
designs cast light beneath vaulting arches
and between two seventeen-foot columns
of dark Quincy marble. Small wonder that
the new building sold some of the city's
most desirable commercial space; in its
cellar, a saloon did a brisk business (too
brisk: police arrested the proprietor for
doing business on the Sabbath).[1]

Descriptions of the structure sounded
regal, and rightly so, for this was the
palace of the New York *Tribune*, which

one reporter called "the best newspaper in this country" and another, "the best paper in the world."[2] What made it best was not just its coverage of events but its independence of outside dictation. The two qualities actually complemented each other. Not just at the *Tribune*, but in the press offices of a dozen other Northern cities, the transformation of the newspapers' purposes and account books had dramatic effects on their politics.

Vast profits beckoned those with the circulation of the *Tribune*. Common report put the personal fortune of the New York *Herald* publisher, James Gordon Bennett, at $6.25 million and lesser New York publishers at more than a quarter of a million dollars each.[3] Proudly, George Jones showed off the New York *Times'* ledgers to a visiting correspondent. Of $820,000 brought in over one year, $154,000 had been pure profit. "At no time during the last fifteen years has the paper paid a less dividend than 80 per cent on the original capital," the New York *Times* boasted in 1876, "and in some cases the dividend has been 100 per cent."[4]

Even failed enterprises now required prodigious sums. In St. Louis, the *Evening Dispatch* began in 1862 with high hopes. By the time it was sold sixteen years later, all it had to show for the effort was high losses. Over a quarter of a million dollars had gone to keep it alive, $100,000 in its last four years. More than bare survival that amount of money could not deliver. By 1878, only a couple of reporters remained in the office and the books showed less than a thousand subscribers. News gathering depended on theft from the columns of rival papers. Its flatbed press was worn down, its type practically worthless. What killed the *Evening Dispatch* was not extravagance but penury. No paper could prosper "on the cheap and nasty plan," the St. Louis *Post* explained cheerfully, having just bought up the remains. "The history of journalism in this country shows that while a cheap newspaper always loses money, a newspaper which spends money for news succeeds."[5]

Outside of the big cities, the patronage that partisans could throw an editor's way still made the difference between bare solvency and pauperism. F. P. Baker of the Topeka *Kansas State Record* discovered the cost of acting alone. Already feared and honored for a weekly whose editorials enriched some Topekans and empowered others, he had begun publishing a daily edition on the promise that Republican officers would give it a share of the spoils. He collected nothing but promises. When the legislature handed out state printing, it devised a new organ in Topeka simply to have a paper to endow. Disgusted, Baker sold out with a valedictory:

"I would advise no young man to enter the editorial profession. If he does so, and expects to make a living by it, . . . I would advise him to avoid the luxury of independence; to cringe at the feet of power; to always help the strong and kick the weak; to avoid indulging any opinion where results are doubtful; and thus avoid the misfortunes of F. P. Baker." But by 1865 the story was different in most of the major cities of the North and, indeed, in much of the Northern countryside, where, according to the Cincinnati *Commercial*, nine defunct papers in every ten "have died of too much politics." Those that did the best could dispense with the $1,200 of county printing as long as they could give readers good local reporting. "Who cares for a party organ?" jeered the Chicago *Times*, with all the scorn of a late convert. "Who can endure its monotonous music? Of what consequence is it on the earth?"[6]

Where news had become the crucial selling point of a paper, the old-fashioned organ was of less consequence all the time. It was all very well to denounce the New York *Sun* for "telling the most infamous falsehoods about the gold ring and the gold clique," though, as one journalist had to admit, the falsehoods increased its circulation dramatically. The proper question was, why did the revelations appear in the *Sun* and not in the *Times*? The answer was self-evident: no Republican spokesman would delve into matters that did the Grant administration an injury.[7]

Even when information was given, it became suspect. If the administration really thought it could benefit from an organ in New York, David Ross Locke commented, "then the Administration is a d–d fool. . . . D–n these little machines that praise everything, right or wrong! If I was President, and had one of them about me, I'd turn round to it and say: 'For God's sake, stop and find some fault, or you'll kill me!'"[8] Lickspittle service was more likely to slay the papers.

Certainly it limited the quality of the staff. The more news a journal offered, the more readers it had, and, consequently, the more it attracted businesses wanting a medium in which to sell their wares.[9] But while a brilliant editor could thrive at a party newspaper, a good reporter could not. Because of the limited freedom allowed him, he would rarely stay long. The pressure even applied to the metropolitan editor of more than partisan credentials. He would seek to own the newspaper himself or move elsewhere to establish an independent voice.[10] Where news gathering was concerned, then, independence was not just good business but virtually indispensable.

The posture of independence did not just sell papers. It entailed less risk than it had in the past for those editors inclined in that direction. No longer did those in well-established journals need to fear a new-made rival, ready to toe the party line that they had abandoned. The prosperity of the metropolitan press and the growth in expense both tended in the same direction: they made it harder to set up a competitor.

Of course party organs could still be set up in major cities, though at nearly prohibitive cost. They could even survive for a few generations, as the Chicago *Inter-Ocean* did, though as critics joked, the initials "I. O." told everything that needed to be known about it. The concern was practically shingled with promissory notes. It lost money even with a growing circulation, trimmed expenses, a new printing press, and the privilege of publishing the tax lists.[11] Not all of Tammany Hall's largess could breathe much life into the New York *Star* or the New York *Leader*. Both of them ended up so dependent on municipal moneys, and so unable to sustain a clientele of readers, that when the Tweed Ring shattered, they both put up their shutters.[12] A few Republicans must have sympathized. They, too, had tried to set up a reliable New York organ, the *Standard*, with equally dismal results. A low price helped to raise its circulation to 12,000 and administration funding kept the presses rolling for two years. When subsidies were cut back, the *Standard* suspended publication.[13] The Brooklyn *Union* went through four Republican chief editors in six months; city officials loaded it with government advertising, but in the end it slid into bankruptcy. "If we depended upon the patronage of this city, *no paper* could live here," a Cincinnati editor summed up.[14]

The rise of the most famous new recruit to the independents provided a salutary contrast. The last thing the prominent Republicans bankrolling Charles A. Dana's purchase of the New York *Sun* expected was waywardness. Dana had impressive party credentials. He had served as assistant secretary of war during Lincoln's administration, had run the Chicago *Republican*, and had put in over fifteen years of service as editor on Greeley's *Tribune*. Within a year, he turned a straggling sheet into the best-written, best-edited four-page paper in New York. "The New York *Sun* is to journalism what the can-can is to dancing," a critic remarked—which, in view of the excitement and popularity of the cancan, fit Dana's paper exactly.[15]

Circulation doubled in two years and more than tripled in six. At two cents, the *Sun*'s price was half the *Tribune*'s or the *Herald*'s, but that alone did not explain its success. The brief, lively notes on its first page, the em-

Every Public Question with an Eye Only to the Public Good: "Let He Who Is Without Sin Cast the First Stone" (Thomas Nast, *Harper's Weekly*, March 15, 1873). Horace White (Chicago *Tribune*), James Gordon Bennett, Jr. (New York *Herald*), Whitelaw Reid (New York *Tribune*), Ben Wood (New York *Daily News*), Charles A. Dana (New York *Sun*), Mark ("Brick") Pomeroy (New York *Democrat*), Theodore Tilton (New York *Independent*), and Manton Marble (New York *World*).

phasis on the doings of the working class, and the high quality of the prose explained far more. As one joke playing off the *Evening Post*'s stodgy respectability put it, "the *Sun* makes vice attractive in the morning, and the *Post* makes virtue unattractive in the evening."[16]

Its sponsors could not have been content, however. Dana spoke his own mind, not Republicans'. "Judge [Edwards] Pierrepont is in mortal danger," the Washington *Chronicle* later gibed. "He is actually being flattered by the New York *Sun*. Like an unnatural cat, the *Sun* always licks its off-spring before it eats them." President Ulysses Grant could attest to that. The paper veered from his cautious supporter in 1868 to his most savage critic a year later. "It is announced that 'Mrs. Grant will receive every Tuesday afternoon during the winter, beginning with Jan. 10,'" one gibe ran. "President Grant will receive anytime and anything whenever anything is offered." Tammany Hall ward heelers, Manhattan Club swells, and genteel reformers all winced under Dana's blows. Such independence was not incidental to the *Sun*'s success. It was crucial to it. Appealing to a working-class audience, most of whom inclined to the Democrats, the paper would have ended as quickly as the *Standard* did if it swore the same party allegiances and limited itself to those enemies that the administration or the silk-stocking respectable classes approved.[17]

Opportunity and financial advantage explain much about why journalists chose to go it alone without party support, but there were other, more personal reasons. Like Dana, many an editor had risen through attention to journalism, rather than through party fealty. A few had begun as reporters, whose first concern had been collecting the news rather than writing political propaganda. Witness the shift in the Chicago *Tribune*, until 1865 one of the most reliable Republican papers in the West. Then Horace White took control. Hailed as "unquestionably the best national editor" in American history, White built on the *Tribune*'s strengths in commercial news with a new emphasis on news of every other kind, from gold strikes in Dakota Territory to "strikers'" gold in Springfield.[18]

That was to be expected. Before the war, he had had a sterling Republican record, but it was as a reporter that he won national fame. White was, as one friend put it, "a charming man to meet . . . in a quiet sort of way, for he does his conversing with his ears and eyes," and high-ranking sources loved nothing so much as a good listener. From a partisan perspective, however, the new editor could hardly have proven worse. Judicious in judgment and, as one admirer said, happier to be correct than consistent, White strayed with increasing and irritating frequency from Republican orthodoxy. It was one thing to oppose the protective tariff (most Republican papers west of the Appalachians did), but the *Tribune* marked how far from radicalism it had gone in the latitude it gave reporters to send in impartial or even sympathetic coverage on senators inclined to acquit President Johnson. That same readiness to seek news whomever it hurt meant an increasing number of stories centering on Republican corruptionists in city and state offices. Where the reporters went, White himself followed. By 1871, the *Tribune* had virtually read itself out of the regular Republican organization.[19]

So, too, one might notice the rise of Murat Halstead from reporter to editor, and the transformation of the Cincinnati *Commercial*. Beginning his career as a writer of Western stories for a weekly literary magazine, Halstead achieved national recognition with his reports on the execution of John Brown in 1859. His eyewitness accounts of the presidential conventions in 1860 were so good that a Columbus publisher compiled them into a book, and the following winter he was sent to Washington. There it became clear that news mattered more to him than political apologia. So corrosive was his attack on military blunderers in wartime that rivals dubbed him "Field Marshal" Murat, though his being named for one of Napoleon's generals made the choice a natural one. He returned to Cincinnati as assistant editor, but not for long. In 1866, with the death of the *Commercial*'s original owner, Halstead assumed command and made the paper one of the leading news gatherers in the land. Separating the news services from the editorial page, he set reporters free to record information rather than echo the opinions of the leading articles.[20]

Financial realities allowed editors to adopt independence, professional journalism backgrounds made them think differently of news than party shills might, but the personal pride of self-made men inclined them to go their own way in any case. They were public figures, quoted and appealed to; they owned not just a printing press but a prospering business, the success of which owed much to their management and felicity with words. All these qualities hardly inclined them to defer to hack politicians. So far were many newspapers imbued with their proprietors' personality that outsiders could not dictate policy without robbing the journals of something vital. With understandable surprise, a rustic greeted the news that an acquaintance of his was still employed on the New York *Tribune* in 1873: "Does it print yet? I thought Greeley was dead!"[21] Independence suited such an outlook exactly.

For all these reasons, newspapers made their detachment from orthodoxy a selling point wherever readers wanted news. "Independent in Everything, Neutral in Nothing," the Philadelphia *Evening Mail* declared itself, in a boast so common as to become cliché. "Independent of all Species of Political Rings, Monied Monopolists and Other Enemies to the Public Good," the Utica *Daily Bee* promised fearless advocacy of "butchers, bakers, candlestick makers," and "honest folks" in general. Increasingly, even the party organs tried to distance themselves from the loyalties of the past. When the Selma *Times* advertised itself as "Democratic in sentiment" but "strictly independent in its course," it joined a legion of papers that put a qualifier just ahead of their party label.[22]

What made this attitude new was how independence showed itself. Before the war, many journals, especially those in the penny press, had proclaimed their detachment from political battles. They lived on their daily sales quite happily. With a few exceptions like the New York *Herald*, however, theirs was a detachment based on neutrality and a dread of party brawls. Such newspapers still survived. A few, notably the Philadelphia *Public Ledger*, throve.[23] But by 1870, "independence" meant something rather different from neutrality. It meant political engagement and a strong commitment on public issues. The Springfield *Republican* was typical: "as full of opinions as an old cheese of maggots."[24] All that was lacking was an adamant party allegiance.

To some extent, this was a matter of degree and widely recognized as such.[25] Each of the great independents leaned to one side or the other, and quite a few, the *World* and Cincinnati *Enquirer* particularly, declared their freedom from dictation more often than they demonstrated it. However much the *Enquirer* might pitch into Democrats it disliked, it returned to regularity in plenty of time to set the tone for the campaign. The *Herald* might seem an exception, swerving as it did from one position to its opposite, "for everybody and nobody," as another paper gibed. But generally, the *Herald* could be depended on to mock blacks, humanitarian reformers, and Republican officeholders and, after a number of sly digs, to line up with the Democratic party.[26]

At the same time, "independence" was more than a pose. Even reliability at election time might not make up for the dissension that the paper had raised in the ranks until then. Maintaining a tenuous party tie may have restricted the editor a little, but it made him more dangerous to the political managers. If he threw off the last vestige of allegiance, party rank and file might dismiss his arguments. If he claimed to share their party affiliation, his complaints at least received a hearing.

When independence meant a readiness to criticize one's own party, it could be troublesome enough, but by 1870, many of the leading Republican "independents" were going further still. They had begun to question the very basis of politics, and, worse, the right of politicians to define the issues at all. "It is time that venal congressmen should be made to understand that although states may be reconstructed, state rights usurped, and the public treasury emptied into the pockets of Grant's speculators and army parasites, the press is not subject to congressional jurisdiction," the Chicago *Times* warned in 1870.[27]

A suspicion of those in power was nothing new. Well before the Revolution, newspapers had voiced the widespread suspicion that those who took office would use it to take anything else, from the people's taxes to the country's liberty. Candidates had mingled their requests for official position with warnings against ambitious men, and jeremiads against the corrupting effect of party were a staple of party oratory. The expansion and increased sophistication of party organization in the nineteenth century, combined with the press establishment that Whigs and Democrats erected to advocate their claims, muted this rhetoric but never silenced it entirely. Once a generation, the outcry about selfish politicians got louder, usually just at the point when the original issues on which the party system had been founded began to lose their resonance. Then editors began to wonder if politics, instead of serving high goals, might be nothing more than a grab game for those holding places of trust.

Now such a time had come around again. The issues of the Civil War certainly had not vanished by 1868. Generations would pass before would-be officeholders stopped flaunting their uniforms, empty sleeves, and combat records. Well into the 1880s, orators invoked that mingling of nostalgia and resentment that the war and the issues surrounding it had raised and that, when it stirred Northern anger against the South, earned the derisive phrase, "waving the bloody shirt." But the original causes on which the Republican party had come into being and over which the war was fought, slavery and disunion, became more irrelevant every year. Not all those who rallied around the flag could persuade themselves that ensuring black political equality, whatever the cost, mattered as much as saving the Union. Increasingly, they wondered whether the new issues were being slighted in favor of the old because the old were to the advantage of men in power.[28] Had the people's trust been betrayed once more?

Reporters from Springfield, Albany, Boston, and Washington all found evidence to turn doubts into certainties. There by 1869, they had sensed in corruption a new and pressing issue and an explanation for why politicians dared not let the old cause die away. Before Grant could be sworn in as president, editorials in Cincinnati and New York already were warning him not to concentrate his attention on the Reconstruction of the South. With some tinkering, the national policy was completed and only needed time to fulfill its purposes. Instead, he must turn against the free-spending congressmen and the interests clamoring for a handout from the Treasury. "The Railroad lobby . . . is one of the strongest which has begun here since I came," reporter Henry V. Boynton wrote to Whitelaw Reid, editor on the New York *Tribune*. "It don't like the Tribune editorials. Honest men, do, however."[29]

The corruption story was all the more appealing to the independent editors because so many of them, like Reid, had served as capital correspondents themselves. Halstead's stint in Washington just before the war had impressed him not with the patriotism of public officials, but with the army of contractors and self-seekers already entrenched. Soon his columns began uncovering the grafters and suppliers of shoddy goods that preyed on the Union soldier. Horace White knew all about the whiskey and gold speculators, and not just from personal experience as one of them. For others, very possibly, the corruption issue's appeal was much more opportunistic. It was a good story, made all the better because it undermined the legitimacy of placemen and the journals they subsidized. Politics, Reid informed Dartmouth's graduating class, was a "vulgar struggle of vulgar men through vulgar means for petty offices and plethoric but questionable gains."[30] Such a crowd had no right to speak for the people.

Who should speak in their place? On this, of course, the editors had no doubt. The one true friend on which the public could rely were their *Tribunes*, *Enquirers*, and *Watchmen*, whose very names suggested their role as protector and investigator. Investigate they did. They did not just permit their correspondents a free rein to look into abuses—they encouraged it.[31] Not surprisingly, to the politicians, a press so untrammeled by party all too often seemed like one untrammeled by responsibility. In one partisan's apt metaphor, the independents were "jolly bachelors of politics, who refuse to wed, but are by no means above flirtations with doubtful characters."[32]

For this uneasiness, plenty of evidence can be found: charges that amounted to nothing, distortions of the public record to make a point, and an utter unwillingness to print both sides of any issue. "Independence" did not mean that Greeley would play fair with tariff reformers, any more than it would make the Cincinnati *Commercial* drop false allegations about Democratic gubernatorial candidate "Gentleman George" Pendleton. Halstead's business was journalism, after all, Pendleton explained to a *Sun* interviewer. "He makes his papers like the razorstrap man did his razors, to sell."[33]

The "independent press" establishment of the early 1870s should not be so lightly dismissed. However venomous, venal, or unfair it might be, it was no worse than the party organs, and in news gathering and readiness to deal with a broad array of issues, its wealth and circulation made it far better.[34] To sell papers, editors encouraged their reporters to become professionals and set an example (rhetorically, at least) for journalists to put their responsibility to the profession ahead of their obligation to politics. The principle it called for, but never really carried out, of newspapers separate from the parties, would serve as the model for the second wave of independents yet to come. Yet the transition to independence was incomplete, and it had costs of its own, which affected the editorial policy and the news itself that the papers would print.

Independence obviously was a complicated blend of self-serving and idealism, just as the corruption issue was a mix of real concerns and political manipulation. To denounce the political connection cost a journal unendowed with patronage nothing, and reform might well remove undesirable rivals. The press must be purified, Murat Halstead told Kentucky's editors, and there was only one way. It must make "the submission of the Press to the base uses of the ring . . . an intolerable disgrace." The patronage-free system that the editor blessed, of course, would have eliminated many of those voices that party organs had managed to raise against that of larger newspapers like Halstead's.[35]

In a larger sense, the editors' drive to supplant politicians as leaders of public opinion suggested an even more serious limit to the independent press. Having freed itself from a commitment to party, it had kept the old assumptions from the age of the party press, that editors had the right, even the duty, to take office, involve themselves in caucuses, offer private political advice to senators and congressmen who made alliance with them, and even deign to take patronage if it were offered with no explicit conditions attached. They were not simply interested in commenting on politics, but participating in it as full players.

Charles A. Dana was a particularly disturbing case. As editor of the Chicago *Republican*, he had given Andrew Johnson loyal support, at least until March 12, 1866. That morning, readers spotted a squib in the journal's columns: "The scheme to buy up the present managers of *The Chicago Republican* by the government collectorships is very smart, but it won't win." It sounded as though the administration had tried to buy Dana's friendship. Exactly the opposite was true. Dana had asked Johnson to make him collector of the Port of New York, the country's fattest patronage post. It was the president who made the refusal. From then on, he had no friend in Dana.[36]

Not all editors sought office as avidly as he, but there were other ways in which they involved themselves in politics. Some engaged in lobbying efforts against the protective tariff by caucusing with like-minded congressmen. One such conference in Washington in the spring of 1870 must have looked like a convention of editorial men; Charles Nordhoff of the New York *Evening Post* was there. So were Halstead, Horace White, E. L. Godkin of the *Nation*, Colonel W. M. Grosvenor of the St. Louis *Democrat*, and Joseph Hawley of the Hartford *Courant*. What they discussed was not simply the best means of publicizing their cause, but how to remake party lines along the tariff issue. Late that fall, they held another meeting in New York.[37]

Between shaping opinion and wielding political power, distinctions were blurry, but they were ones that the independents might have done well to ponder. Their strictures against ambitious officeholders lost much of their force the moment newspaper readers spotted ambition and self-seeking in the editor making the charges. Dana's attacks were easier to ignore after his aspiration to office became public knowledge, just as Joseph B. McCullagh's criticisms stung less when their source could be explained as the unrequited yearning for a postmastership.[38]

Even when they divorced themselves completely from politics, how independent, indeed, were the independents? It was true that the great metropolitan journal might need patronage no longer, but its freedom from party trammels was being replaced by new constraints that the dependence on private patronage ensured.

Those biases could be as obvious as a cautiousness about straying too far from the party fold in which so many of its readers still remained (it would have been suicidal, say, for the Louisville *Courier-Journal* to endorse Republican candidates) and as general as a booster's loyalty to his community. A paper in St. Paul could not be expected to let its independence extend as far as criticism of the Northern Pacific Railroad even if the company placed advertising elsewhere. The line so benefited the city that it would have been as impossible to treat the Northern Pacific dispassionately as it would have been to weigh fairly the merits of Wisconsin cities that rivaled Duluth as a terminal point for the Western trade.[39] Nor was such an inclination anything new.

More disturbing to observers was how the backing of big business made the big-city presses timid in expressing an opinion to which its sponsors might take offense. "Half the great newspapers in our cities are bought up by some political *or other great interest*," "Carlfried" wrote from New York in 1871.[40]

Had he written two years later, he would have found an ideal example in the maneuvers used to save the *Tribune*'s "independence." After Greeley's death late in 1872, Republican politicians applied their exertions to making the paper a loyal voice again. A few, led by Congressman Benjamin F. Butler, wanted to put its old managing editor, John Russell Young, in charge. Young's career had been cut short by scandal in 1869, when he was caught having filched Associated Press dispatches for a Philadelphia newspaper that paid nothing for the wire services and that he happened to own.[41] Perhaps it was this record, or more possibly his disastrous failure in running the *Standard*, that inclined other partisans to favor retiring Vice-President Schuyler Colfax instead. As onetime editor of a South Bend paper and a contributor of unsigned editorials to the *Tribune*, Colfax had slim newspaper credentials, but excellent political ones, or would have if he had not been accused of corruption in the Credit Mobilier scandal.[42]

With their own autonomy threatened, the paper's reporters reacted with dismay. Managing editor Whitelaw Reid had been a Washington correspondent himself and had given them leeway to send what news they pleased. If the *Tribune* meant to stand by that policy, the bureau head in Washington wrote, well and good, "but we can not without losing our self respect say that the black spots in the Administration are white— and what is more, we will not. So you see that if we can remain, we don't know that we shall wish to." Friends of administrative reform offered to buy shares in the paper just "to keep up the high standard." Dissidents like William Sprague of Rhode Island opened their checkbooks, too. In the end, it was Reid himself who won control. He would dominate the *Tribune* well into the next century. "After a few weeks' experience with it," the new owner wrote a friend, "my conviction is that the purchase of one half of the Tribune, at a trifle over half a million of dollars, was the cheapest bargain of my life."[43]

Cheap it may have been, but where did Reid raise so much money? Then and later, reports circulated that Wall Street speculator and rail- road manager Jay Gould had put up Reid's stake. A majority interest had already been bought by William Orton, a regular Republican who also ran the Western Union Telegraph Company. At first, Orton had made Colfax an offer, but within a day it had been rescinded and Orton's shares sold to Reid. Possibly Gould induced that change of heart as well, since his involvement in Western Union forced Orton to be on good terms with him. Nothing more than circumstantial evidence survives. Reid's heirs saw to that by culling his private papers for any material touching on Gould. Still, contemporaries were suspicious, and the paper's reporting over the next nine years turned their conjectures into conviction. Gone was the *Tribune*'s free denunciation of Gould's manipulations. Now he got outright support or silence. So strongly did members of the stock exchange believe that the journal spoke with Gould's voice that they once cuffed and kicked its financial editor and turned him out of the building.[44]

Reid's takeover bid was only an extreme case among many. By the mid- 1870s, the *Tribune* and the *Herald* shared the same uncritical judgment when it concerned the merchants whose advertisements kept New York papers in the black. If such men acted corruptly, it could not reflect on them—but on how badly government was run that such good men should be forced to apply such regrettable means.[45] Conceivably, business patron- age also affected the attitude of larger newspapers to labor, as well. With one exception, the independent presses grew increasingly suspicious of the so-called dangerous classes in general and unions in particular. By 1876, they were united in their denunciation of workers' right to organize and to strike and in their demands for state intervention to preserve order when strikes did occur.

The one exception was Dana's *Sun*. Mocked as the paper "read by horse car drivers," it kept readers like those by taking their side. Working-class amusements and local trade union activities got extensive coverage. While Dana's favorite solution for the workers' troubles was self-help, he neither berated those who joined unions nor muted his attacks on monopoly for paying starvation wages. When, in the wake of the panic of 1873, hungry New Yorkers rallied at Tompkins Square, where mounted policemen charged them, only the *Sun* put the blame for the melee on city authorities and on the law enforcement forces; all Dana's contemporaries palliated for the brutality by accusing the workers of being communists bent on violence. It may have been more than coincidence that the *Sun*, a four-pager throughout the 1870s, made its money through mass circulation and needed businessmen's patronage less than any other paper; or that patrons often found their advertisements returned or derided in the editorial columns, or that news copy replaced commercial squibs whenever the editors needed extra space.[46]

The business orientation did not just affect the city newspapers' views of who was worthy, but of what was newsworthy, as well. Increasingly, reform organizations and labor movements found themselves shut out of coverage. At no time was this clearer than during early 1874, as Congress considered the so-called Inflation Bill to halt contraction of the money supply. Where bankers and "respectable" professional opinion stood, no one could doubt, not after reading the metropolitan press. From the protest rallies, one might assume that the people's will stood for "sound money"—that is, no more greenback paper dollars than gold coin could redeem. But from New York City, "Broadway" wrote his Cincinnati readers an important correction:

> The so-called "great dailies"—Tribune, Times, World, Post and such —have neither sentiments nor interests of the working laboring people, who constitute five-sixths of the population of the city. They oppose them in regard to every matter which concerns them, and invariably take the side of the classes from which their own patronage is derived. They make the mistake of supposing that these hard-handed multitudes are more selfish, or more thick-headed, or more wicked than the rest of us, and the idea that such people actually have opinions of their own, seems to them quite ridiculous. . . . A few days ago all the papers here struggled to get up a great anti-inflationist demonstration, and yet they

were unable to assemble one-half as many people as attended a working-men's meeting on the same night, which was hardly mentioned in any paper, and at which inflationist speeches were delivered. The one meeting was made up of rich men, and the other of poor men; but the poor man counts on election day, as well as the rich man. I have been present at scores of workingmen's meetings within a few weeks, at which inflationist speeches were made or resolutions passed—and mind you, this correspondent is an anti-inflationist—and you'd never have known, by reading the papers, that they were held. Why, this very week there is an "Industrial Congress" sitting at Rochester, in this State, at which delegates from every State in the Union are present, representing societies which number hundreds of thousands of voters, and which has adopted a series of inflationist resolutions, and yet it is a fact that but one daily paper in this city has even mentioned it, and that only in a dispatch five lines long. I repeat it, that the "leading" daily papers here do not, in any way, speak for the multitude, or represent their interests; but rather boast that they stand up for what they are pleased to call the "more intelligent sentiment"—more properly called the advertising sentiment.[47]

In the end, then, the independents may have traded one master for another. The editors' loss of autonomy was not immediately visible. Those men associated with the paper's founding might have a certain amount of latitude, because personality defined the journal's appeal. But as the news columns gained in importance, and the editorial page declined, the editor in chief lost his old significance and with it some of his discretionary power. Now the board of directors might well rein him in and, with each newspaper still read largely by one party's rank and file, might decide that orthodox partisanship in editorial policy was a business matter.

So it proved on the New York *Evening Post*. For a generation, William Cullen Bryant and Parke Godwin had tried to reconcile Republican loyalty with an intense dissatisfaction with the party's views on tariffs, civil service reform, and Reconstruction. By 1876, a host of scandals made that impossible. When the Democrats chose a reformer for president, Godwin tried to bring the paper to his support. He soon found how little power he had and how much rested with business manager Isaac Henderson. Fearing that profits and dividends would suffer, Henderson put the paper behind the Republicans again and exploited Civil War issues to the utmost.[48]

The *Post* foreshadowed things to come. Within four years, Bryant had passed into his grave and the paper into the hands of railroad promoter Henry Villard. Horace White and E. L. Godkin would revive the *Evening Post*'s reputation for independent thought and leave distinct marks on both the style and substance of editorials, but they were a vanishing breed. Within two generations, editors no longer experienced the same popular fame they had had in the 1870s. Nor did they deserve it, for they no longer enjoyed the same control. Independence marked the beginning of the transformation of newspapers into corporate enterprises, over which no one person had the authority that Dana and Greeley had commanded in their heyday. There would continue to be exceptions (Joseph Pulitzer and William Randolph Hearst among them), but the rise of the "independent press" augured the beginning of the detachment of the editor from the game of politics.[49]

PART TWO

ALL THE NEWS
THAT FITS

Diogenes Still Looking—
"We Are the Gentlemen You Are in Search Of"
(Thomas Nast, *Harper's Weekly*,
April 15, 1876).

CHAPTER 5

Despotism Tempered by Assassination

Visitors to Washington saw a changed capitol at the end of the Civil War, from the dome newly installed to the space newly expanded. Contemporaries might have thought it only fitting: government power had advanced by giant strides in wartime, and those who wielded it needed palaces suited to their new importance.

Those tourists preferring the obscure attractions, however, might have spied another symbol of how significant doings in the capital had become. Across the way from Willard's Hotel on Fourteenth Street stood the "rookeries" of Newspaper Row, where the representatives of a nation's press did business well past midnight.[1] The outward appearance of those dingy suites of offices might be nondescript, but that a Newspaper Row existed at all showed how important Washington had become as a source for news.

It also said plenty about how important the reporter's job had become. Even before the war had ended, some of the brightest (and, to military authorities, the most troublesome) reporters had shifted from battlefield accounts to Washington reporting: "Mack" of the Cincinnati *Commercial*, Whitelaw Reid ("Agate") of the Cincinnati *Gazette*, and George Adams of the New York *World*. A host of others would join them, trading on their wartime fame and their military acquaintances.[2]

Washington was no deserted outpost for the "Bohemian Brigade" to occupy. The Bohemians simply sent reinforcements to a swelling host of journalists. Admittedly, within living memory the press corps in the capital mustered no more than a corporal's guard. Before the war, most newspapers might credit a letter to "our occasional correspondent" in Washington, and when the occasion passed, so did the journalist's occupation.[3] Congress arranged for special press galleries only in 1857 (though newsmen had been given reserved seats in existing galleries in 1841).[4] There had been no need before.

That the press gallery had come into being four years before the Civil War needs to be stressed, however. Already by the late 1850s, the number of Washington reporters was growing and by 1860, there were three score. Before the war few newspapers had sent permanent correspondents, whose professionalism would serve as a model for generations to come. Boston correspondents Ben: Perley Poore and William B. Shaw could date their arrival from the early 1850s (Ben: was Poore's own preferred punctuation and one generally followed by his press associates in their reports on him). Poore's career actually had begun as an eighteen-year-old in 1838, when his father, a Massachusetts dry-goods merchant, bought him the Athens *Southern Whig* down in Georgia. By the time he started his "Waifs from Washington" column in 1853, "Perley" ranked as an old-timer: he had written foreign correspondence for some Boston papers, edited and owned a few others, written novels and biographies, and held office as a diplomatic attaché. Experience, not age, earned Shaw the pen name "Nestor" by the 1860s. By the time they reached their forties, he and Poore had become the acknowledged custodians of a past that nobody could recall (except perhaps James Brooks, a New York congressman and Shaw's close friend; he first appeared as a reporter in the 1830s). "He is a perambulating encyclopedia on newspaper matters," one correspondent wrote admiringly of Shaw. "If anybody wants to know anything in this line since the days of *The Federalist*, let him go to Shaw."[5] The New York *Tribune* had kept a staff on hand for twenty years before the war. One of them, William E. ("Richelieu") Robinson, sat in the House afterward and must have relished the irony, having been expelled from it as a reporter for expounding on the crude eating habits of a congressman thereafter known as "Sausage Sawyer" in 1846.[6]

The war simply quickened the process of building a permanent, respected press corps in the capital. By 1870, the *Congressional Directory* listed twice as many holders of press gallery privileges as ten years before; by 1880, three times as many. Though some of the new crowd just after the war were battle- and bottle-hardened Bohemians, others had come to report on the government stirred into life by war's demands. Many of them never got much closer to the war than the War Department. When the conflict was over, other journalists without wartime experience went to Washington to swell the numbers. It was not the war that made Washington so important for reporters, then, but its consequences: a government with more responsibilities and able to take actions with broader consequences.[7]

Finally, there were a few special reasons why the Washington "beat" grew in importance, public affairs aside. Under the rules governing the Associated Press, all national news gathered by its member newspapers had to be shared freely, with two exceptions: reports from Albany and from Washington.[8] For a New York newspaper that was determined to outstrip its rivals in the city, the incentive to put two or even four correspondents in the nation's capital was immense. The fall of telegraphy rates between New York and Washington made it more so: between 1861 and 1886, the charge per word fell from six cents to a quarter of a penny. Instead of just one train a day chuffing in from the capital with a "special's" letter, there would be nine.[9]

Whatever the reasons, the role of the Washington reporter had altered dramatically by 1870. Newspapers might change the personnel, but the job of capital correspondent was there to stay. Major metropolitan newspapers knew that telegraphic communications alone would not satisfy the demand for news from Washington or set them ahead of their local rivals. They needed a special, distinctive voice, the best at their command; and so to the capital they sent journalistic veterans celebrated for wartime letters or editorial experience.[10]

Understandably, correspondents in Washington had a clearer sense of their own importance than anybody else. Many of them were cocksure to the point of hubris. They took pride in pseudonyms that readers might know even better than the real names of their local congressman. Their proper names, too, were ones to be noted, and it was one symbol of their status that the *Congressional Directory* by the war's end listed not just lawmakers but accredited representatives of the press. "Truly it is better at this juncture for a curious man to wear the humble raiment of a reporter than to be clad in purple and fine linen," a Washington correspondent would boast.[11]

Diverse in background, Washington correspondence was of a rather motley quality, as well. Journalism everywhere had a hierarchy both of responsibility and talent, embracing such worthies as the author of "Maryland, My Maryland" (who bitterly rued having written it and spent most of his time cadging free dinners on his reputation), a sodden defamer nicknamed "the Awful Squid," Henry M. Stanley, and the popular raconteur Joseph Howard, whose columns so improved on the facts that a newspaper canard was rechristened a "joehowardism."[12] So, too, in the capital, the range went from professionals like Whitelaw Reid, Joseph B. McCullagh, and Mary Clemmer Ames to writers of cheap fiction. One journalist likened his associates to insects in their variety: busy bees, stinging wasps, mosquitoes, worthless butterflies, and, of course, humbugs. Classifying the head of the *Herald*'s Washington bureau was easy under that system. Dissatisfied with the latest cabinet change, he made up a slate infinitely better and published it instead.[13]

Responsibility was partly a matter of job description. Leaders of the fraternity distinguished between *reporters*, the news gatherers who did nothing beyond wiring the freshest information daily, and the *correspondents*, whose supplementary longer reflections might evaluate the significance of what was going on in Washington, as well as give an edited version of events. Most of the first group were young, new to Washington, and with hopes of rising to a better-paying position in the home office. Looking on the reporter's gallery at the capitol, one of the greatest of the correspondents described it as "a set of upper school boys in appearance and general manners—the graver chaps hardly noticed; the hilarious, only, popular." Many had been government clerks, others printers and proofreaders, though the latter class often produced the most reliable information. The correspondents could generate many of poor capacity, to be sure. When George Alfred Townsend ("Gath") went to the capital in 1868, he found "gowks and clodhoppers, with no ear above scandal." Still, higher wages attracted a higher level of talent.[14]

Among the correspondents, a small elite earned national recognition.

Powerful, widely reprinted, influential, their columns were clipped and republished by impecunious country editors from coast to coast. When "Mack" lost his temper at a surly hotel clerk and whipped off his cloak to mete out a thrashing, he made national news. When women correspondents, Ames (M. C. A.), "Fay," and Emily Edson Briggs ("Olivia") in particular, attended high official receptions, they went as guests, and their attire and manners were as remarked on as any cabinet officer's wife. Journalists of the highest prominence were welcome guests at officials' homes and the confidants of even the most aristocratic politicians. Everyone knew "Major" Poore, the "plump, sunny, and happy" correspondent for the Boston *Morning Journal*. Let there be a dinner at the British legation or a banquet to honor Hawaii's King Kalakua, and "Perley" had an honored seat. As an old friend, he was with Senator Charles Sumner at the statesman's deathbed.[15]

Two political correspondents rank foremost: Townsend and Henry V. Boynton. Possibly the most famous of his day, Townsend was undoubtedly the most literate. A tall, light-haired man with blue eyes and a thin face, he took an interest in everything and wrote about it with humor and pungent description. He was, thought Mark Twain and Oliver Wendell Holmes, the best journalist of his time, and editor John Hay complained that if he printed only "Gath's" best copy, there would be room in the paper for nothing else.[16]

If any man was born to the profession, Townsend was. The son of a poor minister, he learned good writing from Bible reading and good editing from a stint on the Philadelphia *Inquirer*. Barely twenty when the war began, he enlisted as a special correspondent for the New York *Herald*. Townsend wrote quickly—a column and a half of leaded nonpareil in an hour on one occasion—but with a clarity and wit that made him a sensation. When General George B. McClellan's Peninsular campaign began, Townsend went along, witnessing some of the march from the basket of a balloon. Asked whether he had visited a certain spot, President Lincoln assured his questioner that there was no need to: "George Alfred Townsend has been there."[17]

So ubiquitous a journalist was sure to make his mark not just on the news gathering, but on the high society of Washington. Dictating to three stenographers at once, turning out reams of material at thirty dollars a column, "Gath" managed to satisfy newspapers of both parties simultaneously and wrote so much that he adopted a second pseudonym

George Alfred Townsend ("Gath") (Library of Congress)

("Laertes") just for variety. "Did anybody ever see anything from the pen of 'Gath' that was not readable?" an admirer wrote. No one ever did. It was equally true, as an editor gibed, that the correspondent wrote "a good letter from almost any stand-point," though his views shifted less from mercenary inclinations than from his own remorse at giving offense and from the haste with which the victims of his columns rushed to get back in his good graces.[18]

The correspondent as a litterateur of politics was one model in that day; quite a different brand, and as highly esteemed as Townsend, found its greatest personal exemplification in Henry Van Ness Boynton ("H. V. B.") of the Cincinnati *Gazette*. A runaway Ohio boy who had joined the circus as a teenager and clerked in Washington before the war, in which he served, he would return to Washington as correspondent in 1865 and stay there until 1891. Even in his first years on the job, however, he was generally accepted as the dean of the capital's Bohemians and "one of the two or three really honest, independent, well-informed newspaper correspondents who write from Washington."[19]

Boynton had neither the lyricism nor the cynicism of his contemporaries. His columns were dignified, unrelievedly solemn, and often pedantic. His righteousness, a virtue he received from his clerical father, could have a nagging quality. The interview never interested him, nor did legislative prognostication and broader considerations of political thought. Sometimes his columns would devote themselves to one subject for a month, and that one remote from the government's main concerns. What redeemed them was Boynton's thoroughness. Disputed on an allegation, he would republish reams of official documents culled from department archives to make his case. Rarely did he stray far from the truth or get the worst of an argument; and from his first days in Washington, he made it a point to admit his mistakes. ("Mack," of the Cincinnati *Commercial*, mastered the art of admitting error by coupling it with personal abuse of the person done wrong in the first place. In one case, having been proven wrong on the evidence of J. M. Comly, editor of the Columbus *Ohio State Journal*, he stuck to his original story, insisting not only that there was no such person as Comly, but that the very name should have tipped off critics that they were the victims of a hoax!)

As a result, Boynton's influence spread beyond the *Gazette* and the three other newspapers for which he did anonymous work. His knowledge of lobbyists and intriguers was so great that congressmen consulted him rather than the chairmen of their investigating committees.[20] Colleagues honored his fearlessness and integrity. He was, wrote Francis A. Richardson of the Baltimore *Sun*, "the highest type of manhood." It was a manhood quickest to act on reporters' behalf. In 1883, when the Speaker of the House breached the privileges of capitol correspondents by opening their gallery to public seating, Boynton mustered his colleagues, arrayed them under military discipline, and used force to keep trespassers out. Other journalists copied his leads and benefited from the leaks he gave them.[21]

Boynton and Townsend set the style for the best of Washington journalists, the pundit and the muckraker, and had plenty of imitators. But what the whole press gang had in common may matter more than the contrasts in quality. The reporters were hungry for the latest and the most they could find. "I don't think he ever sleeps," a colleague said of E. B. Wight of the Chicago *Tribune*. "At least, I never saw him sleep. Instead of 'How'd'ye do' when he meets you, it's 'What's new,' or 'D'ye know anything?' And if you happen to know anything, and give him all you have, he will quietly remark at the close of your recital, 'S'more!' and look at you as hard as a lobbyist's cheek."[22] Washington had dozens of Wights.

It was no easy discipline in which reporters had put themselves. Associated Press dispatches covered the easiest news to gather. To find the rest, a capital correspondent had to bustle in all directions. As "Perley" explained, the good journalist needed to visit the White House every day, make a run of the departments and the leading hotels, pass the time with "communicative Congressmen at their rooms, dine with diplomats, chat with promenaders on the Avenue, listen to the conversation of those who may be his fellow-passengers in the street cars—in short . . . ever be on the *qui vive* for 'items.'" That search was at its most challenging in late spring and summer, when Congress and legislatures alike were out of session and the president and cabinet were relaxing along the shores of Long Branch. "In the winter so much of consequence is happening that if anything is not obtained, it is not missed," Hiram J. Ramsdell wrote in 1871; but in summertime, even the most strenuous cultivation of bureau officers, strangers, special committees, and capitol contacts might amount at day's end to "half a dozen items not worth the telegraph tolls."[23]

Not surprisingly, then, it was a young person's profession just after the war, for the job was an enervating one.[24] The first to feel the strain were those whose work was all transmission rather than a collection of news. The daily routine drained their originality and vim, a correspondent wrote, until they became "mere machines that will some time break down with an almost noiseless thug, and be at once replaced by other machines that will run to the same race." In time, that same wearing quality affected their more highly placed colleagues, too. Tireless, sleepless in following stories, by 1878 Zebulon L. White of the New York *Tribune* was a haggard shadow of the youth who had arrived in Washington eight years before. When he fainted in a streetcar and was carried home barely conscious, his colleague Ramsdell thought the situation serious enough to bring to his superiors' attention. "[A]ltho' he has been about," he confided, "he has looked more like a dead man than anything else."[25]

White's debility, like Wight's persistence, only testified to the energy with which the press corps threw itself into its task. By 1870, nothing seemed beyond its capacity to discover. In the process, it carried the definition of news beyond what government officers chose to tell. The more dogged reporters unearthed confidential matters and exposed public officers at their most offensive.

Their inability to collect enough news therefore was not for lack of trying, nor for lack of government sources. There was always an "honest man in the Treasury Department" if reporters looked hard enough, and with the classification of documents in its most rudimentary stages, it was easy enough to get anything even without that honest man putting in an appearance. Department clerks let journalists riffle through their files and copy any document they fancied. When Boynton called at the Treasury, he was actually allowed to take the relevant papers home with him. Even politicians using the telegraph lines of the city might find their secret wires printed on page one the next day. As one official complained, the Western Union office was notoriously "*leaky* on all political matters."[26]

Able to find just about anything, reporters had difficulty resisting the temptation to publish it posthaste. Those who had sources to protect sometimes knew how to keep a secret. To editors, Washington reporters would send confidential memoranda on the inside workings of politics on condition that none of it be published—or that the exclusive copy of that report on the "gold corner" investigation not reach readers before it reached the floor of the House (the condition was violated).[27] Yet too often the desire for news was so consuming, the need to be first with an exposé so impelling, that reporters lacked all discretion. Even before the special commissioner on revenue had finished his report to Congress, early drafts of it somehow reached the press. The preliminary copies might be "of no more value . . . than *last year's almanac*," as he protested to irritated solons, but there was nothing he could do to keep any version confidential.[28]

Reporters could hardly have afforded to do otherwise when the demand for news was so great, but it meant stories ill-founded and rumor dressed up as fact. "Mr. Greeley is going to lecture on the Byron scandal," Mark Twain wrote in a satire of press gossip. "We have no authority for making this statement, but then it makes an interesting item of news, and the inexorable business of a newspaper is to collect interesting news."[29]

A reporter sent to cover the summer pleasures of Saratoga might run out of things to say. Then he or she concocted scandals or described the decor of gambling palaces with egregious fantasy.[30] More often than politicians liked, their speeches were set down in language that, as a senator put it, was "conspicuously inexact." So desperate was one New York newspaper for something to fill its columns when Congress was out of session that it published two long bits of correspondence as fresh news; both had been published half a dozen times in the three years since they first appeared. The same morning edition contained a Washington dispatch describing a bank robbery in Selma, Alabama; it appeared in the same words elsewhere in the paper, there credited to the Selma "exchange."[31]

That same indiscriminate search for news helped develop the interview. The first one formally given may well have taken place before the war, though there is some debate about this, but the use of interviews became far more popular in the 1870s.[32] By the start of the decade, indeed, one of its special practitioners was complaining that the interview had been used to death. So it had, unless one counted only the *genuine* interviews given. It was positively miraculous how well Governor John L. Beveridge's voice must have carried when the Chicago *Times* reporter calling at the Briggs Hotel in Chicago interviewed him in 1874; for the governor was working at his desk in Springfield that day. Reporters, for lack of other means of access, would express what they believed were a celebrity's views and print them as if they were the result of a conversation. President-elect Grant, Congressman Thaddeus Stevens, and Senator Roscoe Conkling were only three in an army of mortified public officials who had to deny having spoken at all. Alternatively, an enterprising journalist could embarrass officeholders by asking for an interview and printing in detail the conversation in which the latter refused to grant one. It was a craft easily abused, even when interviews faithfully recorded attitudes that the subject held and found impolitic to proclaim, as he often did.[33]

In a city full of young, eager reporters pressed to find the last scrap of news, no matter where they had to look, and of public officers ready to make the best case for themselves that they could, nothing could remain hidden for long. That may have been one of the reasons that the big story in the years after the war increasingly was one of skullduggery and corruption. Many journalists sent balanced reports, and a few like "Perley" and the New York *Times* correspondents did their best to overlook any sensational story based on less than irrefutable proof. But news at its worst became a catalog of things rich, strange, and peripheral to the everyday workings of government. When the emperor of Brazil arrived on America's shores in 1876, "Laertes" predicted, he would find in any major newspaper the following view of the Great Republic:

> Three columns interview with Burglar Miles.
> Five telegraphic columns on sutlers [robbing the West].
> Eleven noble detectives' remarks on the science of justice.
> One hundred titbit items from apprentice detectives.
> Article on the President's high salary.
> Article on the President's penurious dinner to the Emperor.
> Ragout of innuendo.
> Reform page served with horse pepper.
> Triple sheet of denials of yesterday's reports.
> Abuse of a subscriber who says the license of the press makes hard times.
> Five lofty articles on the "unbridled press" and uncurried.
> Eleven attacks on the opposite newspaper.
> Congratulations on our circulation.[34]

To those under attack, Newspaper Row was "Rotten Row," and the search for scandal was not simply immediately degrading but in the long run dangerous to American faith in republican institutions. One correspondent wrote Congressman Benjamin Butler for remedy against

> the dirty torrent . . . covering the country with poisonous sediment. We are lower in the eyes of the world, Republic though we be, than any other nation, through the impressions created by these bad men, and the Republican thought even among ourselves is black & frost-bitten by them & the Great Dailies they represent. The crying reform of the hour is reform of American sentiment respecting ourselves. The mistake of the correspondents is that they mistake spying information for attempted

reformation, & what is worse they vainly imagine that healthful reform can come from such as they who represent only the vagabond and
Bohemian principle in ephemeral literature.[35]

If by "the vagabond and Bohemian principle," the complainer meant the
hunger for a lively story, he gave the offenders too much credit. The search
for news was not merely a sort of scavenger hunt. It was a still-hunt for
rascals.

Every report was tempered by a point of view. Even "Gath" was not
immune. "It is sad to have written so much at twenty-five, and yet to have
only drifting convictions," he confessed. It was in fact one of his strengths.
His writing style was tempered by doubt and a search for evidence from
the start, and he became increasingly skeptical of those who professed
to know one simple truth.[36] But that drift in his convictions had limits.
Wherever his journalistic home, he remained a reform Republican, and it
showed in his arguments, still more in the political topics that he considered newsworthy. Others were franker still in their partisanship. "I wish
[A. M.] Gibson [of the New York *Sun*] was back," wrote one Democratic
leader to another. "He could serve you signally, and color many dispatches
besides his own. He has been doing good work for you indirectly from
N. O. but his blows would be heavier from Washington."[37]

Gibson was more than a hack or a hired shill. He was a tough investigative reporter, who, as one defender put it, was "too ugly a writer to
be answered with ink, and too big a man to lick. Perhaps he just enjoyed
starting a row. Once, a policeman, sent to quell a brawl in a whorehouse
and convinced that he could not do it alone, asked Gibson's help. Gibson
pitched in willingly and, by one witness's account, seized one tenant by
neck and heels and threw him in the street as easily as most men would
adjust their neckties. Many a profiteer learned to fear "this most terrible
detective of political evil-doers": the Northern Pacific Railroad lobby, the
contractors who milked the District of Columbia's treasury, the grafters
in the War Department, and the "Star Route" thieves in the Post Office.[38]

Yet it is hard to tell where the muckraker left off and the partisan began. With one exception, Gibson was interested exclusively in Republican
scandals, and even that exception was illuminating. In 1875, he turned
his fire on the "Treasury Ring" that controlled Pennsylvania politics and
belabored its Democratic adjunct, led by Senator William Wallace. Moral
laxity there certainly was; embarrassed treasurers, convicted embez-

zlers, and absconding officers all testified to that. Undoubtedly Gibson relished bringing malefactors to justice, but his zeal was whetted by his connection to one of Pennsylvania's most prominent Democrats and one of Wallace's most bitter foes, Congressman Samuel J. Randall. Breaking the ring would give Randall control of the Keystone state, a reformer's reputation, and perhaps even the Speakership of the House. Publishing a forged letter by one of Randall's rivals, countering slanders circulated by other newspapermen, using his contacts to bring the railroad lobbyists' conspiracy against Randall to light, Gibson continued to use his columns on the Pennsylvanian's behalf for the next two years.[39]

A journalist who felt his passion for muckraking stir on a friend's behalf could feel it quicken still more against an enemy, and with still less regard for the merits on his side. In that respect, Boynton himself provides the most disturbing example in his campaign against General Oliver O. Howard, head of the Freedmen's Bureau. Since its founding in the last days of the war, the bureau had faced constant abuse from Democrats, north and south. This was not surprising. White Southerners resented its efforts on blacks' behalf, particularly when those interfered with the civil courts and the planters' power to dictate the terms of work contracts. Correctly, Democrats claimed that many bureau employees turned into Republican organizers and used their official rank to advance themselves into political office. None of these charges amounted to much of a scandal.

Boynton's did. In early 1869, the Cincinnati *Gazette* began publishing revelations about the building of Howard University, in which bureau officials played a leading role. A series of accidents had slowed the construction—quite avoidable accidents. As the foremost member of the university board of trustees, Howard had persuaded the other members to give a brick contract to the Washington Block Company. It was a costly mistake. The bricks were made of white sand and lime, a combination unable to bear even as much pressure as blocks of chalk. Treasury architect A. B. Mullett washed one such brick to pieces in two minutes by plunging it into a bucket of water.[40] The results were as might be imagined. Buildings were no sooner completed then repairs had to begin. A schoolroom wall fell down, iron pillars had to be put in to prop up the chapel, and roof timbers crushed the west end of a building.[41]

How could Howard have made such a mistake? Boynton had a ready answer. The general had helped organize the Washington Building Block Company. On its staff were Howard and other leading bureau officials and

prominent public figures in the District of Columbia. They had seen to
it that the university, which subsisted on bureau funds, should buy from
them. The general himself had such faith in the bricks that he had his own
home made of them, which attested more to his sincerity than his sense:
part of the back wall tumbled down, bricks cracked, and sills and caps on
windows had to be replaced. Howard had sold his interest in the company
before the contract went through and, far from profiting, was out $5,000,
but the whole transaction had a sinister look, all the more so because,
according to Boynton, bureau commissioners had also used government
money to buy land that they sold to the university at a tidy profit.

Democrats demanded an investigation. A Republican majority exonerated Howard of anything worse than misjudgment, though the evidence
showed him lax and liberal in his use of bureau funds and cavalier in his
interpretation of law. Prepared to condemn the general from the start,
the minority came to more harsh conclusions. They found enough shreds
of circumstantial evidence to pronounce Howard the recipient of two salaries at a time, a corruptionist who had loaded the university board of
trustees with his army cronies and a land speculator with government
funds. Though a military court-martial exonerated him completely four
years later, Howard never escaped a sullied reputation. Like other political generals, he became one more piece of evidence that Republican military heroism cloaked theft in office.[42]

Boynton had not cooked a scandal from nothing, to be sure, but his letters showed more than a newshound's quest for truth. A year before, his
father, the Reverend Charles Boynton, another founder and first president
of the university, had quarreled with Howard over admitting blacks into
his church, a church built in part with the bureau's educational funds. Before the fight closed, Dr. Boynton had accused Howard of misusing public
money and conflict of interest. Howard drove Boynton from the presidency and pulpit. Now the son had a score to settle by putting a dismaying
gloss on the evidence.[43]

Correspondents' prejudices were deplored then, as they would be today.
For all the partisanship of so much of the American press, the ideal of
objectivity remained one that journalists professed to believe in. But
Boynton, "Gath," even Gibson would have argued that they *were* being
objective, that the responsibility to be objective did not deprive them of
the right to make judgments, but only to make unfair ones. Indeed, as
observers, they were obligated to give their professional opinion of right

and wrong. When a Columbus correspondent accused Ohio lawmakers of "a fearful amount of demagogism," described the discussion of a tax bill as "sickening," or pronounced one member's argument a "stale falsehood," he was doing his duty as an "objective" commentator. "Don't you know that I am a privileged person, and really the sixth member from S.C.?" the correspondent for the Charleston *News and Courier* joked. "I am entirely independent of every representative here and am sent for just that purpose—to criticise whatever seems worthy of criticism."[44]

There was, therefore, a second layer of ideology shared by many of the leading correspondents in the early years of the Gilded Age. It was a prejudice more professional than partisan: the belief that the important story was what took place in cloakrooms and on backstairs beyond the AP's observation, and that a real reporter had the duty to expose it. Boynton seems to have seen himself not just as a Republican champion, but as a crusader against wrong. It was with this white-hot indignation that he took on General William Tecumseh Sherman for having slighted so many other veterans in his memoirs. Letter on letter to the Cincinnati *Gazette* exposed the falsity in Sherman's every claim (even when there was no falsity to expose), to the war hero's fury.[45]

The most serious charge, rarely voiced against the press, was that by the nature of its business, it emphasized the extraordinary rather than the commonplace. Readers readily assumed from what they read that the Boss Tweeds and "Subsidy" Samuel S. Pomeroys of Kansas were the main forces in politics. Far from driving around in gilded landaus, living on stolen wealth, the average beneficiary of the spoils system was a department clerk, poorly paid, working from nine to four and supping at his boardinghouse. In place of hypocrites and heroes battling it out in the House or threading their way through halls thronged with buxom lobbyists, the visitor to Washington would see overworked, commonplace men serving their constituencies by a daily round of petty errands, shepherding trivial bills through committee, and wondering more how they might pay their board than how to plunder the republic. These were the plain realities of Washington, but they were not news, and in light of newspaper revelations, they would not have been believed.

Against this misleading array of information, public officials had no real protection, at least in the years just after the war. The New York *Times* correspondent might make a career out of exploding false tales, but it was thankless work when, as a colleague explained, nine times out of ten

readers would believe the liar and dismiss the correction. Several prominent women correspondents, notably Mary Clemmer Ames and Emily
Edson Briggs, did much to highlight the more commonplace everyday life
of Washington, and to put public figures in a more sympathetic light.[46]
Theirs were scattered voices against a chorus of critical ones; as custom
prevented ladies of the press from doing investigative reporting and rele-
gated them as far as possible to society events, their insights were easier
to dismiss as womanly sentimentalism.

As "privileged communications," newspapers claimed a special latitude
in reporting public affairs, even when that meant personal attacks and
accusations of officeholders' motives. Since the 1850s, many court decisions had sided with the press. Statements could be wrong, damaging,
and yet not libelous, said judges. The plaintiff must prove malice on the
editor's part. "Good faith"—a belief that the facts were true—was enough
to clear a newspaper of liability in Texas. Even when the law went against
them, newspapers could have faith in juries to see facts their way. With
jurors so unpredictable, laypersons dreaded instituting a suit at all: an
acquittal, even on technical grounds, would damage the plaintiff's reputation as badly as the original libel—or worse if the newspaper, as was
usually the case, published the result as a vindication of its side. Often
juries awarded damages, but of such an insultingly small amount that
they gave the paper an effective right to libel as it pleased. With odds so
weighted in journalists' favor, a French visitor concluded, America was
press-run, a "despotism tempered by assassination."[47]

Power newly achieved, newly discovered often has a raw quality, just as
that of the Washington correspondents had. The youthfulness of the press
corps and its recent arrival at the capital helped explain the temper of
journalism as well. Time would remedy both defects; by the 1880s, most
of the early ebullience and aggressiveness would be gone. But for the moment, Washington reporters stood at a crossroads, their ability to wreak
damage already clear to them, their need for professional standards defining what was news and how far journalists should involve themselves in
their stories not yet apparent. Used to the editors' power to inflict damage, politicians had just begun to find means of mastering the reporters.
It was a struggle that would never be fully resolved.

CHAPTER 6

A General System of Exchange, or, A D–d Bad Beat

As the joint high commissioners from Britain and the United States finished work on the *Alabama* treaty in late April 1871, every report agreed that the results would be far-reaching. Covering not just the claims Americans demanded for depredations committed by the British-built Confederate privateer, the *Alabama*, but disputes in the Pacific Northwest, along the Canadian border, and among fishermen off the Atlantic coast, the document's provisions would remove every excuse for war between the two great English-speaking powers. It should have been a time for celebration.[1]

For some it was, but not for journalists. They had been shut out of the negotiations. Correspondents hounded the English commissioners from the moment their steamer had reached Jersey City, chased after their carriages, pursued them into the hotel washrooms, pumped the secretaries and valets for information, and even tried to coax tidbits of evidence from the diplomats' wives. None of it did any good. The English commissioners politely declined to be interviewed, as did the Americans, not so politely. Reporters desperate for information invented material, all backed up by "undoubted authority," that Great Britain would be compensated for its subjects' slaves, or that it would receive more in damages from America than America from it (neither was true, and since British law forbade citizens to own slaves, the "undoubted authority" must have been a New York *Herald* correspondent). Now, with the work complete and the general outlines of the agreement public knowledge, readers wanted to know the treaty's precise wording, but that would remain confidential until the Senate had gone over it in executive session.[2]

So custom dictated. But on May 11, senators were thunderstruck to discover the document, the Treaty of Washington, printed in full on page one of the New York *Tribune*. Somehow a copy had fallen into journalists' hands, and apparently before most senators got a chance to see one themselves. How could such a breach of security have happened? Correspondents were summoned to divulge their sources. If they refused, a senator swore, he would "shut them up, put a guard over them, and feed them on bread and water until they were glad to answer!"[3]

The journalists did refuse and they were locked up for it. They were quite willing to reassure their inquisitors that no senator had peddled the document. More they could not say or, in the case of the two men most clearly responsible, Zebulon L. White and Hiram J. Ramsdell of the *Tribune*, would not say. In a rage, the Senate arrested both White and Ramsdell.[4]

The world has worse punishments. The two offenders were lodged in the chamber for the Senate Committee on Pacific Railroads, with its fine, large parlor, refreshingly cool in the late spring heat, plus a room for them to sleep in with all the modern improvements. Mrs. White dropped in for a few hours every day, as she explained with a touch of sarcasm, "improving the opportunity to get acquainted with her husband." Ramsdell was even allowed to keep his parrot. They ate spring chicken, strawberries, lamb, and green peas from the Senate dining hall and pocketed salaries doubled for the duration. Most ironically, lawmakers no longer had to troop to the *Tribune* offices to leak information. They just slipped down the hall.[5]

The Senate quickly tired of the farce. Storming at the recalcitrants, Matthew Carpenter of Wisconsin declared that if he had his way, they would get "forty years in the common jail." Of course the Senate could only hold them as long as it was in session, but Carpenter knew how to turn a few days' lockup into months: let the investigating committee be permitted to remain formally in session throughout the summer. Senator William Windom of Minnesota agreed, as long as the committee members stayed in Washington, too, as jailers. That was too high a price to pay for senatorial dignity, especially with orders to suspend an investigation coming from the White House itself. When the members went home, so did the two journalists, and charges against them in the police court were dismissed.[6]

The incident can illustrate any number of points: the battle over the confidentiality of reporters' sources, the antagonism of politicians and members of the press, even the resourcefulness of the *Tribune*. But the story holds another insight. It demonstrates how Washington journalists working both with each other and against each other managed to uncover and deliver the news.

That complex relationship between reporters would be most clearly revealed every day by a visit to Newspaper Row. The location had its disadvantages: exorbitant rents and cramped quarters, in particular. A few papers such as the Boston *Journal* preferred to pay one-fourth the cost for rooms a few blocks away. But the advantages were considerable. If a source wanted to tell his story to journalists, he knew just where to go. One might pass down the halls—for example, to a door labeled "Cincinnati Commercial"—and step into a suite of carpeted rooms furnished with sofas, chairs, desks, tables, and newspaper files. Was the *Commercial* unreceptive? Its rivals were only a door away, and rivals' work was nearer still: on the *Commercial* office tables sat the latest issues of the New York *Sun* and Cincinnati *Gazette*, full of potential leads to follow up.

In a peculiar blend of rivalry and alliance, Newspaper Row reflected its inhabitants' profession. Competition was strong: the search for exclusive news inspired reporters with special resourcefulness. One strong metropolitan paper almost certainly encouraged others in the same city to imitate its success. The excellence of the Cincinnati *Commercial* spurred the *Enquirer* to overhaul its columns and hire away its rival's talent, while the Chicago *Tribune* and *Times* consistently tried to outdo each other's Washington letters, advancing a "Gideon" for a "Gath."[7]

Reporters battled each other for advantage in getting Washington news first or keeping rivals from finding it out at all. At the very least, if they were scooped, their editors would demand an explanation. "It was a humiliating beat—the worst I have ever had," a chagrined "Perley" confessed after other papers had broken the story of corruption in the War

Department in 1876, "yet I don't see how we could have divined what was so secretly done. The Associated Press, which we are told looks after congressional matters—the three Washington dailies—the Balt. Sun—N.Y. Tribune—and lots of other papers were as badly beaten as we were. . . . Those who had the news wouldn't tell—and the committee was closemouthed. When we got it out we did the best we could. But it was a beat—a d–d bad beat."[8]

At its worst, such a competition could breed suspicion and outright ill will. Clashing egos meant that two star reporters for the same journal would chafe at sharing the duties of Washington correspondence. "Newspaper men are like wolves," wrote "Gath," "—when one of them is wounded the others eat him up." George Alfred Townsend should know. His hatred for Uriah Painter of the Philadelphia *Inquirer* and for "Gideon," the "gipsy journalist" and alleged sneak thief from the Chicago *Times*, was well known, and others in the newspaper fraternity won a general dislike among their fraternity brothers. "Eli, why are you so unpopular with the newspaper people?" an editor asked journalist "Eli Perkins." "They all seem to hate you worse than an emetic." When Perkins intimated that it came from his refusal to mingle with them, the editor shook his head. "No, that can't be it," he said, "because, if you went around with the boys they'd hate you worse."[9] Editors, too, took after each other with hammer and tongs. "The *Dispatch* wants the state to build an asylum for the partially insane," editor McCullagh noted, in a dig at another rival. "We think the State has quite enough to do without taking care of the editorial staff of the *Dispatch*."[10]

This was comparatively polite. In an age of "personal journalism," debate degenerated into invective quickly. It was not enough for the Cincinnati *Enquirer* that its rival at the *Commercial* was wrong. Editor Murat Halstead was a toady to the rich, it insisted, "a cowardly bully of the poor," a plunderer of widows and orphans, a blackmailer of society figures, a forger, and an "old dog [who] in his cups boasts of his prowess and his conquests among the wives of his acquaintances." What Halstead deserved was not rebuke, but a long prison sentence, which the *Enquirer* had no doubt would come to him ere long. Some newsmen went beyond words, especially in the rural South, where genteel canings often gave way to knives, rawhide whips, and pistols. In West Point, Mississippi, one editor was so pleased at having shot his rival through the head that he sent a full report to metropolitan journals.[11]

Yet the quarrels within the press gang only set in bolder relief the readiness with which members helped one another. Some of it came from the shared excitement and toil of a common occupation and often of a common employer, for journalists moved easily from one paper to the next.[12] Washington reporters held social receptions, sat by each other in the press galleries, drank at the same hotels, complained of the same snubs by public officials, shared the same miserable pay, and read each other's work. Quite naturally many of them struck up strong intimacies. So the manager of the Rutland *Herald* sent maple sugar to his friend, the Washington correspondent of the New York *Times*, Boston reporters welcomed a long-departed colleague back to town even though he returned as an invalid, Cincinnati journalists rushed to congratulate their associate when he was nominated for a city office, and like-minded editors found time to finish off a fish dinner together. Let a reporter wander far from home after a story, and he could expect hospitality and advice from the editor of the local newspaper. Did a New York *Tribune* man need expert information about Illinois politics? However little his paper shared the opinions of the Chicago *Republican* and *Times*, it could always share their inside knowledge.[13]

A growing sense of their professional status added to the journalists' readiness to work together. Already in the 1860s, the first signs were available as they began to form journalist clubs. Most attempts failed. This was, according to one member, because those that allowed in local reporters had no place for the correspondents, and those open to correspondents had no place for the local reporters. Still, the attempt was made, and some efforts did take hold. City reporters in Richmond, Pittsburgh, Washington, and New York formed lasting societies for themselves. In Washington, led by Uriah H. Painter, a group of journalists from out-of-town papers set up the Correspondents' Club in 1867. It met for annual dinners, at least, during its brief survival. Far more common than brotherhoods of reporters were the editorial associations. Nearly every state had one, and when its members took an excursion to Washington, politicians put on the best show possible for so much concentrated verbal power.[14]

The trend toward professional alliance and with it professional courtesy had not come close to completion by 1880; still, real effects were discernible. Observers thought that they spotted a shift away from the abuse that editors had heaped on each other before. There were more newspapers than before like the Memphis *Appeal*, which refused to publish a communication because of its personal remarks against a rival. "We have no war to make upon journals or journalists," it explained, "and shall not permit correspondents to do so." [15]

Indeed, it sometimes seemed as though the one business journalists most cherished was the bestowing of benisons on each other, accolades that the beneficiaries could then print in their columns as testimonials to their own excellence. [16] They were "among the most respectable, lively and enterprising of our afternoon papers," "neat, wondrous neat, and well gotten up," or even "the livest, red-hottest, hit-everybody paper" in town. "Children cry for it, mothers won't have any other, and ministers carry it to Church Sunday mornings." Let the editor come to town, and the local paper would plug "his popular and original weekly." Let a journal be established, and the encomiums on the first issue would presage all the excellence of years to come. [17]

All of this was more than flattery. Small-town newspapers in particular could use advertising revenue from city businesses. A testimonial helped, especially from the city newspaper that took their weekly regularly in exchange for its own daily. So it meant money in the bank for the flattered journal when the "Personals" column in the Memphis *Appeal* declaimed on the "excellent" Brownsvile *Bee* and described its use for advertisement as offering "unusual inducements to our merchants. It is the busiest *Bee* in the State, and its hum is welcomed by the thousands." (The first claim was truer than the second, since it was the only *Bee* in the state and its circulation stood below 1,300.) [18]

The same search for mutual benefit explains the proliferation of the smaller associated presses in the postwar years. With the arrival of telegraphic communication at Austin and San Antonio and its extension east from Shreveport to Jackson, Mississippi, the trans-Mississippi South was suddenly thrown open to national news services. The only problem was the expense: Texas newspapers could hardly afford to gather local stories, much less pay for what came over the wires. So the Galveston *News* joined hands with the Galveston *Telegraph* and *Flake's Bulletin* and the San Antonio *Herald* to set up the Texas Associated Press, to share expenses and provide news by cooperation. They modeled it on the New Orleans Associated Press and sent a correspondent of their own to Jackson to relay those stories suited to Texas papers. [19]

Cooperation, then, came about not just from a sense of unselfishness, but of self-interest, and the same sense of the craft's necessity that brought editors and publishers to help one another pressed the news gatherers of Washington to pool their resources. They could hardly help doing so when they worked in such close contact with one another. Some of them shared offices, and all of them called on each other regularly to find out the latest information. Good news gathering demanded such tactics: no good reporter could work alone, no good press could survive without connections beyond its own staff. The scramble whenever a tidbit of news hit the Row reminded former reporter Horace White of the Chicago *Tribune* of a flock of blackbirds, clustering after whichever "lucky songster had found a bug or worm."[20]

At times, reporters did not even need to be asked to share their scoops. For one reason or another, the news they had unearthed might not be suitable to the paper for which they worked. The paper's editorial position might make the information inconvenient, for example. A story might fit the newspaper's politics exactly—which would make it the wrong place for the news to be sent. Let a Republican paper like the Cincinnati *Gazette* expose a Democratic cover-up in a scandal involving Gentleman George Pendleton's collection of a claim on the War Department, and readers might dismiss it as just one more partisan attack, even if Henry V. Boynton himself had assembled the evidence. But if it were given to an independent newspaper and then reprinted in the *Gazette*, the tale would win a national audience. So Boynton passed along his charges against Pendleton to Charles Nordhoff, Washington correspondent for the New York *Herald*. Indeed, as one critic joked, Boynton had spread the story far and wide, "like a man liberal with the smallpox." As a result, every single paper in Cincinnati published allegations against Pendleton—except Boynton's, which demurely declined to mention him by name.[21]

Even when neither the concern for credibility nor the desire to ensure an item's publication affected their judgment, journalists shared material with each other readily, and for the most obvious reason. If they had no time to follow up on clues, they still hated to see their work go for nothing. Besides, in the long run, they were not volunteering information—they were trading it. Courtesy repaid courtesy.[22]

There were also financial reasons why no newspaper could expect an "exclusive" from its Washington correspondent. Necessity virtually ruled it out when reporters earned so little and wages often depended not on the number of hours worked, but on the amount of space a journalist's work filled. If the editor trimmed the dispatches liberally, he also slashed his reporter's income, no matter how much effort had gone into a story. That income was paltry enough at best. At fifty dollars a week, Washington reporters were among the aristocracy. Still, costs in the District of Columbia were high, and many journalists found themselves living more frugally than they would have liked.[23]

Many reporters, to make ends meet, took on several employers and a few furnished the same "special" letter to fifty rural papers every week. The practice was far more widespread than readers imagined, as an incident at the closing session of the Tennessee legislature showed. An offended lawmaker rose to move that the legislature tender thanks to the reporter for the Nashville *Banner*, but not to the *Union and American*'s man. They were, however, the same person. For reporters, the arrangement could bring in $7,000 a year and if folklore meant anything, as much as $20,000.[24]

Necessarily, the practice made confidentiality almost impossible. If "Perley" found something good for the Boston *Morning Journal*, he could hardly keep it from his coworker, E. B. Wight. But Wight worked for the New York *Times* and later for the Chicago *Tribune* as well. What he knew might at once become common knowledge for others involved with the *Tribune* like Boynton. It took a special effort for any reporter to stop the flow, though he might do so if the scoop was big enough.[25]

Cooperation, indeed, had only one relatively unbreachable limitation: when newspapers from the same city and in open rivalry for circulation were involved. To oblige the Cincinnati *Commercial*, the New York *Tribune* would share its news items liberally, but when *Tribune* and *Times* correspondents met in Alabama in 1874 and pooled their information, there was hell to pay in the home office.[26]

Finally, there were also sound pocketbook reasons for journalists working together, if not in common cause, then at least in rival coalitions. Sending news over the wires could be a costly business. Editors might complain less if several papers footed the bill. But collecting news too had its expenses. Journals vying to be first in publishing an official report needed inside contacts or an entente with reporters who had some. A newspaperman holding government office had a special advantage and often an irresistible one. Cabinet officers might wonder how Andrew Johnson's annual message got out in late 1867, but not reporters, not when W. W. Warden, private secretary to the president, moonlighted as a representative for the Baltimore *Sun*.[27]

When responsible officials would not produce the documents on their own, reporters bought someone who would. However much congressmen deplored it, journalists failed to see anything wrong with buying clerks. News was "as much an article of merchandise as beeves, stoves, or grain," one reporter explained, and "a live paper always has an open door, and, in the inner office, well-filled money bags with which to pay liberally for the commodity." Newspapers readily spent $100 to $250 in telegraphing costs and in transportation expenses such as for special locomotives to carry a major speech to their offices. If the story was worth paying to transmit, why was it wrong to pay for acquiring it?[28] The trouble was, reports might cost more than people in the home office were willing to pay. If shared, the expense could be lessened considerably. So the rivalry of newspapers became a spur for cooperation as alliance pitted its resources against alliance.[29]

Professionalism, friendship, and competition all brought newsmen together in networks and leagues and fostered rivalries in confusing array. It was into such a tangle that in 1870 Zebulon L. White arrived to manage the New York *Tribune*'s Washington offices. White's talents were considerable and his college degree was an unusual pedigree for a journalist. He had all the drive that the job demanded and plenty of crusading zeal.[30] But White was just beginning to learn about journalistic method. "I find, as you supposed, that there is a general system of exchange of news in the Row which seems only to be limited by the rivalries of papers published in the same vicinity," he wrote managing editor Whitelaw Reid. Being on top of the latest stories depended not on resourcefulness alone, but on contacts, and that, in turn, seemed to rely on two men: Henry V. Boynton and the second man at the *Tribune* office, Hiram Ramsdell.[31] Both men had connections up and down Newspaper Row and with the administration. Ideally, White could have drawn on both for information—at least, if the two men had not been rival reporters for Cincinnati's two Republican newspapers. In the end, White decided to stick with Ramsdell. He never had cause to regret it.

A native of upstate New York and editor of a small Pennsylvania newspaper at the start of the Civil War, Ramsdell dropped his pen to shoulder a musket, served three years in the field, and took a bad wound at Antietam. With peacetime, he entered the Washington office of the *Tribune*, though he found duties light enough to vary them with a job as special postal agent and to run a post office in Pennsylvania while Congress was in recess, and he collected a salary as committee clerk while it was in session. Working for the Cincinnati *Commercial* and taken on as extra staff for a time by "Perley" at the Boston *Morning Journal*, he managed to live up to or beyond whatever income he brought in.[32]

All of these entangling alliances sat ill with members of the *Tribune*. White, with only one salary to live on, resented his subordinate's earning higher pay than himself. Reid grumbled about the clerkship and complained that very often the best items went to the *Commercial* alone. In time, he managed to force Ramsdell to drop his other newspaper ties, though he could never keep him from hunting up government jobs. Still, the inconvenience of divided time and loyalties was worth it to the *Tribune*. No one could get the news better than Ramsdell or find the same stories. "He is painfully quiet," an observer wrote, "and takes in an item that would make many gyrate with delight without the slightest emotion, as he demurringly and evenly drawls, 'Yes-s, I thought so.'"[33]

Ramsdell's strengths came from his inside contacts. Attorney General George Williams talked freely with him, affording the *Tribune* special insights into administration policy; certain Southern senators traded confidential information for protection from damaging dispatches leaked to the paper by their enemies; but most of all, Ramsdell joined in the pool of reporters who shared the costs of buying government documents in advance of their appearance, or, indeed, any information. When an Interior Department's report got to the public a week before it reached Congress, a rival reporter was "mad as the devil" and the secretary "was on his high horse," but they could not keep secret what a $200 bribe could bring out. White quickly adopted the same methods. As a House committee summoned witnesses in the Credit Mobilier scandal, he sought an exclusive copy of the testimony and offered the official reporter "any liberal price within reason." With other New York journalists making bids, the officer had no intention of letting their money go untaken, but he did let the *Tribune* have the first copy. So slowly did the telegraph office transmit it that White's purchase was the only one to reach New York in time for the morning edition.[34] When the two *Tribune* correspondents were hauled up for their part in leaking the Treaty of Washington, then, they had not been caught in a sudden excess of zeal. The two men were hardened offenders.

They were no worse than the rest of the press gang, however. The story of the treaty needs to be examined in more detail, for it reveals clearly that complicated mixture of competition and cooperation among Washington correspondents that assured the document's premature publication, if not by the *Tribune,* then somewhere. In a confidential letter to the home office, White explained how he had managed it:

> On Monday night I heard that the State Department had sent to the [Washington] *Chronicle* and [Washington *National*] *Republican* an abstract and immediately 'went for it.'—or Ramsdell did. After considerable trouble we got the promise of a slip and were assured that no one else but the [New York] *Times* would have it. Before our slip was ready, however, [Lawrence A.] Gobright [of the Associated Press] heard of it and by promising to have it credited to the *Republican* all over the country obtained a copy. On learning this, of course, I did not send it. That same night a man who claimed to know where he could get a full copy went to [George W.] Adams [of the New York *World*] to sell it. Adams *knowing what Gobright had already sent off* immediately offered $750. It was not accepted and the treaty was then offered to the *Herald.* McFarland (Anderson was away) immediately made the *Herald*'s standing offer of $1000. The price was set at $1500 and McFarland telegraphed to New-York about [it] and received an order to pay $1500. The price was then placed at $2000 and as it was too late to get further instructions from New-York, the matter was lost.

It was just as well. By the next morning, the price had fallen; by Wednesday, May 10, no one was offering to pay more than $200. Journalists assumed that copies were easier to get: mistakenly, they believed that each of the senators had been given a copy of the treaty. When they discovered otherwise, they began offering more, and before the *Herald* could pay the $500 required for a copy, White managed to get one on his own for the same price and split the cost with the Cincinnati *Commercial.* That night, hustling out visitors, turning out the gas in the *Tribune*'s front office, and closeting himself in the small back room, he and his colleagues spent two hours copying it out in longhand at record speed for transmission across the wires.[35]

What insider produced White's copy? Government clerks were peddling summaries of its contents or pretending to have friends with drafts, but the Senate investigators very nearly hit on a prime suspect when they grilled Senate secretary Willard Tisdell, present at the *Tribune* office on the climactic evening. He let slip the name of another of the guests present that night: Ben: Perley Poore, the Senate Printing Committee clerk, who, as usual, was in debt and had made a hobby of abstracting original documents for his personal collection.[36] Perhaps rightly, the senators disregarded the hint. Means, motive, and opportunity could hardly outweigh the long, friendly relationship that so many officeholders had with Poore, who deplored modern innovations like the interview and the purchase of inside information. Yet it is just as possible that Ramsdell went to his old employer and friend to make a financial proposition and found him receptive.

Cooperation and competition alike made the journalists' profession more effective than it would have been otherwise. With a network of newspeople, allied and affiliated with presses of every major city on the continent, no story could be suppressed or easily hidden. Rumors got instant, nationwide circulation, and disparate strands of information—often unrelated—could be followed back to their original sources for new material or spun together from a dozen correspondents' sources into a fabric of dubious inference. Boynton might not know all the facts about the way the Pacific Mail Steamship Company bought its subsidy through the House, but he could share notes with the reporter from the Boston *Daily Advertiser* and pass on what he knew to the *Tribune*. Inevitably, the rumors of corruption spread so wide that Congress had to investigate, snaring among the lobbyists a few members of the newspaper fraternity in the process.[37]

But if competition and cooperation enhanced news gathering, each had serious drawbacks. That very drive to outdo one's rivals pushed reporters beyond the bounds of responsibility. Having to supply at least as much material as their rivals, every journalist was compelled to seek news and not discriminate between fact and rumor. Not stopping to verify became standard practice, as one member of the press gallery explained, "because to lose a lie by one day is a greater crime in newspaper 'enterprise' than to correct a dozen the next day." As a result, newspaper reporting, in the *Nation*'s words, was "about as demoralizing a business as a young man can engage in."[38]

The practice of paying per column made it more so. A journalist compensated by the bulk of his dispatches and in constant competition with the Associated Press for news most easily obtained and with rival newspapers for fresh items just beneath the surface of events would produce anything and ask no questions. "Five, six, *seven* daily papers in a city of less than a hundred thousand inhabitants" ensured "a daily miracle of calumnious inanity," the historian James Parton charged. "Falsehood and folly in daily papers are . . . not so much an evidence of depravity, as of poverty. Intelligence and character are costly; frivolity and reckless-ness are cheap." What would do the art of journalism the most good, he concluded, would be to wipe out half the daily papers in the land.[39]

Cooperation, too, could lead to misleading and unreliable assumptions. Reporters might not believe what an official told them, but they trusted to their confidants on Newspaper Row, and uncritically. One man's hearsay built on another's:

> Nordhoff knows that Storrs
> Got from Pierrepont dimes;
> This was sure, becors
> 'Twas in the Chicago *Times*!
>
> .   .   .   .   .   .
>
> Boynton, Nordhoff, me
> And the Keyhole party
> Laid at Grant's last night
> Under the piano-forte![40]

If politicians looked with increasing uneasiness on Newspaper Row, they had good reason to do so.

There was a final way in which journalists' cooperation seems to have added to the peril that seemed to face public officials in the years just after the war. Out of that sense of common purpose that bound journalists together came an aggressive, often arrogant spirit, ready to administer rebuke to congressmen but not willing to take it. When White and Rams-dell were confined for their silence about the leaking of the Treaty of Washington, newspapers regardless of party rushed to their defense; it was none of the Senate's business from where or how reporters got their information, editors exclaimed, as long as no senator acted as accomplice. Denounced by a Pennsylvania congressman, members of the press corps knew that they could rely on their editors to repay the abuse in kind. "I pity any one, possessed of a grievance, who appeals to the whip in News-paper Row," one correspondent wrote. "He stands not only a chance to be shot, but a certainty of being reported and pitched into by the pen-driving hornets on all sides."[41]

What had emerged by the 1870s, then, was a peculiar, unstable balance. Washington reporters had just begun to see themselves as professionals. Their power and their sense of a common interest were already plain enough to them; their sense of responsibility still remained obscure.

CHAPTER 7

Mr. Striker Goes to Washington

Slouched, and surly, and sallow-faced,
With a look as if something were sore
misplaced,
The young man Striker was seen
to stride
Up the Capitol stairs at high noontide.
And as though at the head of a
viewless mob—
Who could look in his eye and
distrust it?—
He quoth: "They must let me into
that job
Or I'll bust it!

"*Gath,*" *Cincinnati* Enquirer,
April 27, 1877[1]

Striker's real name was Uriah Hunt
Painter. Colleagues who knew him well
enough to dislike him called him "Uriah
Heep," "this singed rat," or "that persistent falsifier."[2] As reporter for the Philadelphia *Inquirer* and New York *Sun,* his
undeniable abilities were applied in the
lobby, not just the press gallery, and it
was in the former that he was known
as the fugleman for the Western Union
telegraph, the Pacific railroads, and the
patent lobby "and as a general agent for
all sorts of jobs. Painter does this busi-

ness by wholesale," another Washington correspondent wrote, "and he keeps a lot of subordinates in tow."[3]

He also kept his news columns in tow. Did Painter's clients need favorable publicity? slurs on his enemies? a well-timed silence about their operations? All could be arranged for a fee. Furiously, banker Jay Cooke read a dispatch in the Philadelphia *Inquirer* harmful to his firm's reputation as the special agent of the federal government. Painter must be reminded that where the Cookes' interests were concerned, a man on their payroll must "find out from us what the truth is . . . and what we want said!" If he insisted on printing news releases just because they were news, without clearing them with his sponsors, "he must count on the loss of our friendship." Painter made quick amends.[4]

The interest that dared leave him out of its plans paid for its mistakes. Reportedly, when House officers charged him for a copy of the *Congressional Globe*, he threatened to "bust it." Enraged at Senator Simon Cameron, he cooked up false accusations against the senator's son-in-law. In all, George Alfred Townsend declared, he could summon at least fifty victims of Painter's extortion racket in Washington alone. It was for that reason that the poet-correspondent pronounced him the archetypical "striker," the lobbyist as shakedown artist:[5]

> What it was that troubled him so
> How shall we innocent visitors know?
> Perhaps a scheme of subsidy great,
> Or perhaps a mightier project of state;
> A plot, perhaps, some widow to rob—
> Whatever, whoever discussed it,
> Unless Mr. Striker was "let in the job,"
> He would "bust it."

In late 1868, reports began to circulate that the appropriation to purchase Alaska had gone to buy leading House members instead. Allegedly, Congressman Nathaniel P. Banks of Massachusetts had taken a $250,000 bribe; his colleague Benjamin Butler and one of the leading House Democrats, Samuel J. Randall of Pennsylvania, were purchased as well. R. J. Hinton, a Washington correspondent who dabbled in lobbying, put together a series of rumors for a scandalous article in the Worcester *Spy* that implicated the banking firm of George W. Riggs, former secretary of the Treasury Robert Walker (who had acted as the most prominent lobbyist for the Alaska appropriation in tandem with Frederick P. Stanton, his past ally in the territorial government of Kansas), and a number of others, including newspapermen. Reportedly, the daughters of an Ohio congressman took $10,000 apiece and Walker, $25,000 in gold; to the correspondents of the Philadelphia *Press*, Chicago *Tribune*, Boston *Daily Advertiser*, and New York *Times, World,* and *Evening Post* bribes of $2,500 or more had been promised, though in many cases, never paid: "Of the $7,200,000 in gold for Alaska, the amount, it is now reported, Russia actually got was $5,000,000 in gold—about one million pounds sterling. This leaves $2,200,000 to be accounted for. How much of this went to pay for the collection, preparation, and publication of documents and reports of a favorable character, published in all sorts of ways and by all sorts of persons, is more than can ever be guessed—doubtless a good round sum."[6] In all these allegations, there was not a scrap of demonstrable truth, or so a House committee concluded. The $2.2 million figure was a case in point. It had been calculated by a correspondent, when he read a wire service dispatch stating that $5 million in gold was being sent to Russia. His powers of subtraction outdid those of deduction: the $5 million had nothing to do with the Alaska purchase price. English financiers raised it to invest in Russian railroad enterprises.

That correspondent was Painter. He had been spreading whoppers for half a year, including many of those that Hinton picked up and added to others flying around the capital. He just may have believed them. Possibly, when he demanded a cut from the Alaska lobby and made threats if his wishes were not granted, it was to smoke the rascals out. That, at any rate, was the story he told on the stand when his machinations were revealed.[7] Still, it would have been slightly out of character for Painter, whose interest in exposing corruption worked only fitfully and whose interest in being cut in on lobbying deals had been intense. It had been especially intense in the summer of 1868, perhaps because he was so out of pocket from having used his inside knowledge to place bets on the conviction of President Andrew Johnson during the impeachment trial—a conviction that his dispatches to the Philadelphia *Inquirer* had worked in vain to ensure. At the very time that he later proclaimed himself on the trail of an Alaska scandal, he was at work for railroad, insurance, banking, and telegraphic interests.[8]

Conceivably, then, Painter's righteous indignation came to life only when his chance of buying into the Alaska lobby was killed. His colleagues

in the press corps knew him all too well. The only wonder was that he
had not been caught "in various matters of *business* before," Boynton
remarked.[9]

> Wonderful youth! such power to keep
> In a land where Justice ne'er is asleep;
> To stagger the councils of state with fear,
> Or stop the growth of a hemisphere;
> The time-piece of law to crush in the fob,
> Or by violence re-adjust it,
> And, lest he be "let" into this or that job,
>   He can "bust it."

Painter reflected quite a common condition among Washington reporters. "I know—everybody knows—that there are professional correspondents in this city who attack projects that are before Congress for no other
purpose than to get paid for silence in the future," one observer wrote. "I
believe—everybody believes—that there are agents of newspapers here
who bargain for the opinions of the journals they represent."[10]

> Striker! in thee no specie rare
> We see ascending the Capitol stair,
> All the ages and States of eld
> Some similar hound or highwayman held;
> Some Herod, who ere Heaven's babe might throb,
> In the cradle, would strangle or thrust it,
> And, unless he were "let in" the holiest "job,"
>   He would "bust it."

By no means were all or even most journalists as venal. Historian James
Parton calculated that of the sixty reporters covering Washington when
he was there in 1869, no more than five were corrupt; in the most fla-
grant sense, Parton's figures may have hit close to the mark, though,
like Painter, information sharing and serving a dozen newspapers at once
magnified their power. But that would exclude two classes, journalists
lobbying as a sideline and those speculating on inside information. A far
larger crowd of newsmen stood in that ambivalent ethical limbo, including "Gath" himself, George W. Adams, and others who held Painter in
scorn. "The innocent public suppose that the Washington correspondents
are paid to gather news for their respective journals," a correspondent

gibed. "That is only an incident in the career of a genuine Washington 'special,' one who has got his 'eye-teeth cut.' His real business is to dabble in stocks, speculate in gold, or use his paper for lobby interests, either on his own behalf or some one else's. News-gathering is only a convenient pretext for more profitable employment." [11]

Why would journalists lend themselves to the lobby? Why would supplicants for government aid think them worth buying? For newsmen, the answer must be largely conjectural. The professional status of reporters was still very new. Standards of conduct remained vague. For editors accustomed to a system where newspaper establishments were bought or sold to take a political position, being bought or sold to support a commercial one may not have seemed indefensible. For reporters to whom independent attitudes meant passing judgment, overt advocacy may not have seemed unethical at all. If, for example, they thought that a land grant was a steal, it made sense to say so. And if that put them in alliance with, or even on the payrolls of, the lobby working against that bill, the public interest was none the worse off for it. [12]

Reporters also needed the money. The same force driving Washington correspondents to sell their wares to several editors at once encouraged them to moonlight as lobbyists. There was only one legal limit: before the Speaker gave out press gallery privileges, a journalist had to sign a pledge not to involve himself in private claims. With so many alternative ways of cashing in, that restriction was like a locked door without a house around it. Newsmen speculated in gold and whiskey on their inside knowledge during the Civil War and afterward. They were not ashamed of doing so. One reporter even admitted the widespread speculation to vindicate his colleagues of getting rich by corrupt means! [13]

For the lobbyist, the reasons why journalists were so useful was still plainer. First, no one was better versed in what government officials intended to do, nor with readier access to insiders who might need convincing or persuasion; an experienced journalist knew not just who held which offices, but where the real power in any department or committee actually resided—at least, that was what he prided himself on. Like Painter, he might even know what other lobbies were up to and keep them from interfering with each other. [14]

Second, with the power that newspapers wielded over public opinion, they needed squaring if any lobby wanted to make its case effectively. "*Shut* up Phila. correspondent of Times if you have to lynch him," a London member of the Cookes' banking firm pleaded. Lynching was not usually necessary, nor was purchase, for that matter. Hungry for information, journalists often would welcome leaks and transmit stories dutifully. Not just individual reporters, but the Associated Press wire services opened their cables to corporate explanations passed as Washington dispatches.[15]

Of course, if it took money to make reporters report, the money was available. Taking a Columbus reporter on a carriage ride, a local lobbyist chaffed him badly for taking the wrong side in a fight over a bill shifting a county seat, but worse for not making cash out of it. Itinerant reporters like Ben C. Truman earned extra money writing books on resources for railroad baron Collis Huntington and shoved sketches of the landscape into the New York *Tribune*'s weekly.[16] Other journalists tendered their friendship for free passage over railroad and steamship lines.[17]

Finally, reporters could use their inside knowledge to act as lobbyists themselves and their influence over columns to bring refractory legislators to terms. As long as a journalist's accounts could make or break a public official, his advice on a measure would be heeded with some courtesy.

How many active lobbyists were there among the reporters? Though reputation put Painter foremost, with "the credit of controlling one third of the members of the House," he found trusty allies in Joseph Mac-farland of the New York *Herald* and Philadelphia *Telegraph*, Lorenzo L. Crounse of the New York *Times*, and Erastus P. Brooks. As clerk to the Committee on Banks and Currency, Crounse also had a chance to speculate on inside knowledge about the progress of funding legislation; for $150 a month, he passed on the information to the Cookes as well. According to Boynton, Crounse was also "a very active member of the [Post Office] ring." [18]

None of them could compare with W. B. Shaw, "Nestor" of the Boston *Transcript*. Reporters admired his "handsome residence on Vermont Avenue" and appreciated his tips on the gold market; belied by that "stiff hedge of bristles, red in color" that surrounded his face, the *Transcript* correspondent had a generous heart and, wrote one colleague, "is kind to all of his friends." Those who knew him calculated his worth at $50,000. His press gallery privileges enhanced his fortune in two ways. First, Shaw used inside knowledge of financial legislation to speculate in stocks; he would leak his information to New York banker Henry Clews, who used it to their mutual benefit (and probably to the benefit of New York's Congressman James Brooks, who acted as the original source). Second, he and Painter allegedly "[hunted] in couples." As clerk for the House Committee on Post Offices and Post Roads, Painter made any supplicant "consult" him. "If they don't 'come down' liberally they are approached by Shaw and gently reminded that they had better do so," another journalist wrote, "and are informed that they can 'go through easy enough' if they 'fix Painter.' The result generally is that Painter is fixed." So was Shaw: *well* fixed—$15,000 worth by promoters of a subsidy for the Pacific Mail Steamship line.[19]

News columns were only the beginning of the alliance between press and lobby. Editors, especially those in charge of the financial page, must be accommodated. A friend at headquarters could allow promoters to insert ready-made articles to publicize anything, from Alaska to a pension bill. This, too, often occurred without money changing hands. Certain newspapers had so close a rapport with prominent politicians that to make a friend of one was to make a partisan of the other. Editors could be convinced of the merits of an enterprise and, given a little attention, become earnest in their advocacy. But all too often, even with the prestigious metropolitan independent press, businessmen were met with itching palms. "Nothing is being done for any of [our newspaper friends]," an alarmed banker wrote, "& they will not work without pay. We know that some of them are pirates & unprincipled, but we must manage to keep them sweet."[20]

One sweetener worked best because it had the added advantage of sparing the giver legal trouble later on, should charges of corruption arise. As a journalist gibed: "a New York Banking house does not pay in a vulgar way for having some thing disagreeable printed in a paper. It usually sends a good '*refresher*' in the shape of a fat financial advertisement." Those who received advertising, of course, were more likely to reprint articles from other publications supportive of the patron. From one banking house alone, advertising in New York newspapers cost $9,500, but then, the firm was buying goodwill, with one dollar in four "subsidising the money editors."[21]

Other arrangements were more open. Businessmen valued a newspaper's high reputation for probity—at top market rates when buying went on. But others with a lower reputation managed to come in for regular shares of whatever funds were being handed out. For $2,500, the Pacific Mail Steamship line was able to acquire the correspondent for the Washington *Chronicle*, and for $1,500 more its former editor. However

wrong Painter may have been about the Alaska lobby buying congressmen, his allegations were right on the money where the *Chronicle* was
concerned, and two years later when the governor of Georgia needed supportive legislation, he bought the *Chronicle* too.[22] With Dana's *Sun*, one
journalist charged, "blackmailing has become a science."[23]

Estimates on the going rate varied. Metropolitan editors reportedly
would sell out for less than $15,000; $8,000 was a figure commonly bruited
about.[24] Sometimes editors simply needed help to keep their enterprise
afloat. No specific quid pro quo was mentioned, but the relevant columns
would be colored in the future in their benefactors' favor. Perhaps, as in
the case of the Richmond *Enquirer*, they needed $5,000 to shore up a
losing concern and turned to the Richmond & Danville Railroad to make
up the difference. (The railroad refused the appeal; perhaps it simply did
not want to take up paying the *Enquirer*'s bills that Tom Scott of the
Pennsylvania Railroad had previously footed.)[25]

A managed press, full of "puffery" and abuse compensated for, was
nothing new. But the process added to the unreliability of news coverage, not just of business but of politics and public policy where a firm's
interests were at stake. It was widely believed, though not proven, that
railroad titan Tom Scott pulled the strings at the New York *World* and
that the New York press in general left its pages open to misstatements
that would drive down the value of the Baltimore & Ohio's stock at the
very moment that outside interests were trying to buy into it.[26]

The campaign launched by Jay Cooke's banking firm to renew and expand a land grant for the Northern Pacific Railroad in 1870 serves as a
model for how lobbyists could put the press to their own use. It was a
monumental task. Not only must Congress confirm one more in a series of
increasingly unpopular subsidies, this one was for a road going from Lake
Superior to Puget Sound ("from Nowhere to No-Man's-Land to No Place,"
in one critic's words). Then the railroad would have to sell its bonds and
entice settlers to buy the land Congress had given it, land that General
William Tecumseh Sherman rightly called "as bad as God ever made, or
any one could scare up this side of Africa." Obviously, a national publicity
campaign was required. All this the Philadelphia banking house must do
against the rival schemes of a Southern transcontinental railroad company
and the active hostility of the rival banking house of Drexel, Morgan, &
Company.[27]

Nothing therefore could be left to chance. Buying silence from some newspapers, the Cookes bought favorable mention from others. "You have no idea how much we are obliged to ride our money editors on the Superior subject," a member of the New York branch complained.[28] In Philadelphia, some newspapers (Painter's *Inquirer*, say) could be relied on. To bring John W. Forney's *Press* into line, Henry D. Cooke gave him a generous stock option plus "financial inspiration" for the paper; as a bonus, Forney promised to keep the Washington *Chronicle* friendly. Building up another rival to the *Public Ledger* had added benefits: the *Ledger* had a larger daily circulation than any other paper in the city and opened its columns to attacks engineered through Drexel, Morgan, & Company.[29] Elsewhere, newspapers also felt the benefactions of the Cookes. Some editors wanted money to purchase a larger interest in the paper, as the head of the Toledo *Blade* did; occasionally, a journal in a crucial spot was bought outright, as the *Minnesotian* was. The new editor on the latter, a friend assured Jay Cooke, "has sense enough to know what to say and when to say it."[30]

New York *Tribune* veteran John Russell Young mattered still more. In wartime, he had taken off time from his newspaper duties to found the Cookes' publicity bureau in New York. Now, just embarked on making the New York *Standard* into the city's official administration organ and needing all the cash he could get, he was glad to use his influence to screen all AP telegrams before they got out and could cause damage.[31] Young even offered to visit Washington and lobby congressmen himself.[32]

That was hardly necessary. Cooke already had two newspapermen doing that on Capitol Hill: Painter and Samuel Wilkeson, himself an old hand in the Cookes' bond-selling campaigns and Civil War correspondent for the *Tribune*. "Why, Sam, you are a Bohemian!" a friend exclaimed. He did not mean it as a compliment. "A Bohemian is a man who refuses fifty dollars a week for a thousand dollars now and then." Wilkeson did not see the humor; but he did see the money and was very likely worth it, for he knew the subtleties of lobbying, not just the basics.[33] His influence in part came from the well-founded belief businessmen had that, when needed, he could give enemies "a blast in [the] Tribune." Now he tried to pass off as exclusive tidbits of leaked information that would advance the railroad's interest. (To Horace Greeley's credit, he refused certain such "scoops.")[34] By May 1870, Painter was stalking the House floor, rallying the bankers' forces, while Wilkeson kept a close tally of heads. As the vote in the House approached, Wilkeson's efforts intensified, pausing only when the Cookes had won a complete victory. "I have seen great battles in

Congress in my experience of nine years," he wrote. "None of them *began* to compare with this contest in difficulty, peril, obstinacy and sharpness— *none whatever.*"[35]

Having sold the Congress on Northern Pacific, the Cookes had to sell the country on its possibilities. Besides lending his pen to the Northern Pacific with laudatory articles, J. Russell Young found time while in England on a confidential government mission to tout the Cookes' bonds there. Again, Wilkeson and Painter were on hand, Wilkeson even suggesting his ally as the proper man to head a bureau spreading the glad tidings and bring newspapers around (instead, General A. B. Nettleton, who ran the Chicago *Advance*, a religious publication, got the job).[36] To his old friends on the *Tribune* Wilkeson offered twenty weeks of articles made to order: "a dramatic *but strictly faithful* description of the country from Puget Sound to Lake Superior," with special attention to the wealth of salmon and bison, the minerals, and the Indian tribes. "*It will be good,*" he assured editor Whitelaw Reid. "What do you say?" It *would* have been good—for the Northern Pacific Railroad, projected across that very route.[37]

Nettleton sent out articles for extensive publication, one of them appearing in nearly four hundred newspapers, including the leading dailies of Milwaukee and Chicago. Some of the most fulsome were Vice-President Schuyler Colfax's pious exaltations, for which he earned a dollar a line. Among other places, they appeared in Henry C. Bowen's religious weekly, the New York *Independent*. Bowen actually printed an extra 75,000 copies for national distribution, but then he was hardly doing the Lord's work. By written contract, the Cookes had promised him, for his good offices, a percentage of all the securities sold. That amounted to $60,000 in bonds and $460,000 in stock.[38] No pay induced Charles Nordhoff, editor of the New York *Evening Post*, to reprint a ready-made squib as an editorial. He acted willingly, and his support was particularly valuable for two reasons: the *Evening Post* was famed for its honesty and for its hatred of land grants. In Washington, the close alliance between Henry D. Cooke and "all the leading correspondents" continued. "So far, I have only given them the assurance that they will be liberally treated, if they do good work for us," he wrote his brother. ". . . It will cost something, but I know of no *cheaper* advertising, and none, on the whole, so efficient." (Among those "seen" was Henry V. Boynton, though precisely what the "understanding" was that made him "all right" was left tantalizingly unclear.) Even the London *Times* was brought around, though not for cash. Instead, its editor asked the Cookes' influence against the railway manipulations of Jim Fisk of the Erie Railroad.[39]

The press campaign spread wider than the number of newspapers backing the Northern Pacific subsidy might indicate. The Chicago *Times* branded the aid bill a swindle, except in the crucial two months between the time that the House began to consider the measure and the moment the president's signature put it into law. On this legislation, its Washington correspondent had nothing to say. Meanwhile, other articles appeared in the *Times*, extravagant in their praise of the railroad's prospects. Whatever the Springfield *Republican* thought of the grant, and editor Samuel Bowles spurned the Cookes' offer of a special stock deal, it carried descriptions sure to boost the Northern Pacific's bond sales. Apparently, the roads would bring in $300 million in trade from China yearly, at the very least. Readers learned that snowfall on the Northern prairies was "extremely light." Cattle needed no fodder in wintertime. Idaho's herds grazed the range and emerged "fat in March." As for cherries, pears, peaches, and plums, the Pacific Northwest could grow them all.[40]

A well-mounted lobby, then, could work wonders on the kind of news many Americans read. Observers may not have seen every working of Jay Cooke's press staff, but they spotted enough in a general way to suspect the honesty of journalists in general. Businessmen, in particular, suspected a desire for plunder wherever they looked, even when it was not really present. By early 1873, a few newsmen were beginning to question the bright write-ups that the Northern Pacific had enjoyed. One of them was H. V. Redfield of the Cincinnati *Commercial.* In a series of devastating articles, he visited the wonderland of the Northern prairies and found exactly what he would have anticipated. The land was barren, winters were long and severe, commercial possibilities were much exaggerated, the advertising was a lie, and the correspondents who sent back glowing reports were deluded by visits in springtime and jollied along with free passes and royal treatment. The railroad itself was being built negligently; its debt was so great and its prospects of making it up in business growth so modest that bondholders were likely to lose their investment. Redfield was right, pending bankruptcy included; but to Sam Wilkeson and no doubt to the Cookes, telling such unpalatable truths could have but two motives: blackmail or a design to break down the company's credit.[41]

Assumptions like that were self-fulfilling. Once financiers concluded that journalists were in the market, they felt less scruple about buying them. To the Cookes, the unfriendly articles in the New York *Express* and *World* were easily explained. Jealous rival businessmen had used their contacts to feed the reporters damaging information. Drexel, Morgan, & Company reportedly had originated the money article damaging the Cookes' interest in the New York *Herald*. "They dine and wine people here and get articles written and arrangements made," Jay Cooke wrote, apparently not considering imitation in this case the sincerest form of flattery. His indignation did not last long. Within the week, one of his friends had dined and wined the leading editor of the *Herald* himself and got all he could wish "by adopting a certain course, which from its importance, I dare not mention by this medium." [42]

If that were so, how many of its dispatches could be trusted or explained as honestly felt? Sentiment in favor of American intervention to set Cuba free from Spanish rule may have been sincere, but perhaps former attorney general Caleb Cushing was right when he attributed it to " 'hordes' of penny-a-liners, bribed with bonds of the Cuban Junta." "You don't know, as I do, how it destroys men to go into the Lobby," Sam Wilkeson warned his employers. *"It uses them up quite as effectually as it uses up women."* [43] This applied just as much to journalists as to others, and to Wilkeson and Painter themselves as trustworthy sources. There was nothing absurd in surmising, as the *Nation* advised readers to do, that whenever any financial editor urged an enterprise, moneyed influence made him do it. [44]

When Hugh J. Hastings of the New York *Commercial Advertiser* flayed one of his political foes for buying a Senate seat, other editors hardly knew whether to laugh or fall into a fit of apoplexy. "For, what rottenness was ever revealed in the recent political history of our State that Hastings was not implicated in," the *Tribune* demanded. "Who has a bad reputation for jobbery if he has not?" [45] The seediness of so many members of the press was precisely what made the politicians most contemptuous of their preachments on ethical issues. A Washington correspondent objected indignantly to one officeholder's insistence that only one among the newsmongering tribe could not be bought (and that one Boynton). Still, he could not deny the ubiquity of the sentiment. [46]

Of course, the politicians' dismissal of even the reforming journalists as hirelings was mistaken. As has already been made clear, reporters were genuinely excited by scandalous news stories and many of them unfeignedly indignant at what they found. Most took no retainer but the newspaper's, and others who lobbied or provided information did not compromise their integrity in what they put into their columns. They kept the two occupations separate. Yet whatever the realities, their reputation was not an enviable one. By the mid-1870s, movements were under way to repair the damage. When the House itself in 1875 ordered the expulsion of journalists who did lobbying, it was posturing. Even Painter and Shaw continued to enjoy press gallery privileges. Far more significant were the negotiations that several leading journalists, among them Boynton and George Adams, started with Speaker Samuel J. Randall in late 1877 to set up an organization that would let newsmen police themselves. Two years later, reporters gathered in the New York *Times* offices on Newspaper Row and set up a list of rules, enforced by a Standing Committee of Correspondents. The system, accepted by House and Senate, remains in effect to the present day.[47]

Not all the rules covered conflict of interest. Some of them defined the qualifications for press gallery privileges. The requirement that the correspondent send telegraphic dispatches to daily newspapers had the ugly side effect of barring blacks and women, most of whom either sent letters or corresponded with weeklies. Other conditions were more to the point: journalists' main source of income must come from their newspaper work; they could not act as lobbyists nor serve as clerks in the executive branch. The loopholes were large enough to let Ben: Perley Poore keep on as a Senate clerk, and, thanks to an incumbency exception, to leave gallery passes in the hands of those who already had them, even Painter's. As late as 1882, a South Carolina journalist complained that a majority of his colleagues in Washington sold their influence regularly and that one reporter made $150,000 "by this kind of dirty work." Nevertheless, a change had begun that within a generation would wipe out the most flagrant abuses.[48]

The overt corruption of the press was relatively easily handled. Less blatant influences remained: the free pass over the railroads, the manufacture of apparent public opinion for a measure that could then be brought to newspapers' attention, the generous ad campaign. And there were still more subtle ways in which the marketplace manipulated the news, and against them editors and reporters made no headway at all. The mildest of these was the "reading notice," an advertisement inserted in news columns without special warning to unwary readers. More pervasive, if arguably less worthy of the label corruption, was that determination to advance "progress," which for most publishers meant advancing the material interests of their community, whatever the cost to truth or to employees' rights. News insisting on the excellent prospects of this railroad line or that canal, or the comparative benefits of Port Royal's harbor over Charleston's, was so commonplace as to excite no remark. Yet it was advertisement itself and often entailed a corruption of the truth. "I have generally found that the Editors and Reporters of the New York journals are influenced fully as much by their own pecuniary interest as by their duty to the country," Secretary of the Treasury Hugh McCulloch commented.[49] Very likely he was thinking only of the open payoff in the palm; instead, the payoffs were everywhere. They were essential to the newspaper business.

CHAPTER 8

The Capital Offenses of Donn Piatt

Those who met William McGarrahan liked
him, and no one who spent much time
around the capitol could help meeting him.
For more than thirty years, the dogged
little Irishman stalked the lobbies and
waited in his hotel room for a decision in
favor of his claim. The decision would be
worth waiting for; McGarrahan wanted
title to a vast tract of land in California, the so-called Panoche Grande, which
Mexican authorities had settled on one
Gomez, who deeded it to him. What made
the land all the more valuable was the vein
of quicksilver that ran through its hills, a
vein that interlopers, calling themselves
the New Idria Mining Company, had been
tapping since the 1850s without government title.[1]

Year on year, McGarrahan had fought
for possession. Courts ruled in his favor
and then turned against him on the basis
of forged documents and perjured testimony. House committees had sustained
his cause, only to report so late in the session that no final action could be taken.
Indeed, when McGarrahan died in 1894,
it was generally agreed that the govern-

ment owed him relief. But that relief was as far away as ever.[2]

Momentarily in 1879, it looked as if some justice might be done, if not to him, then to the government's right to property still in the national domain. A bill was offered to send the New Idria company's claim to the court of claims. Since the company was extracting the mineral wealth in the ground without the formality or expense of buying it from the government, the motion was bitterly opposed by those already enjoying the advantages with none of the costs.

The company had a strong ally. Donn Piatt's *Sunday Capital* never missed a chance to expose the "full-stomached Orangeman's" methods and morals in unsparing terms. Piatt had even hired Bret Harte to write "Romance of a Mine," based on the editor's version of the McGarrahan claim. Allegedly, $6 million in stock in his project had been used to buy government officials; 100,000 shares went to purchase a prominent congressman, 50,000 bought another. Mountains of "crisp, new paper" had done its work before. If Congress caved in now, it would prove that the members had sold themselves again.[3]

Congress never got around to caving in. To come up for consideration in the last days of the session, the bill had to be advanced on the calendar, and just one senator's objection could prevent action—and did. It was then that McGarrahan, pacing in the hallway outside of the chamber, smarting from his latest setback, spotted the offending editor himself, there to orchestrate further obstructions. In a rage, the victim strode up to his accuser, to promise a future reckoning "for the dirty manner in which you have vilified myself and my friends in your dirty newspaper!" As Piatt stared at him, the hot-tempered little Irishman changed his mind. "D–n it," he exclaimed, "I'll do it now. I don't know when I may have a better opportunity." Before Piatt could do more than knock McGarrahan's hat off, McGarrahan had given him one blow that shunted him against the wall and a second that dropped him to his knees. Thereupon, as the claimant put it, "I gave it to him good." He would have given it to him better if respect for the decorum of Senate proceedings had not kept him from dragging Piatt down the steps and giving him such a pounding that "he wouldn't have been worth two cents." Senators trotted out to see what was going on, capitol employees stayed McGarrahan's hand, and Piatt was taken into another room to have his bruises sponged and from there was carried home by carriage.[4]

The attack surprised Piatt, but McGarrahan was given a surprise, too.

"I never in all my life received such attention," he marveled. "When the affair was over, page boys and messengers got me towels and water, picked up my hat, and came and showed me every courtesy." Returning to the scene of his triumphs the next day, the claimant found himself lionized. Someone even sent him a large bouquet by way of McGarrahan's attorney.[5]

The fact was that no matter how far McGarrahan's cause was distrusted, no one sympathized with Piatt. As the victim noted bitterly, the whole fight was watched with interest and with some delight by former congressmen, all of whom—according to Piatt—were bribed with stock. One New York congressman, known for his wit (very likely Samuel "Sunset" Cox), joked some days after the fracas that since it occurred, he had offered to give $100, a bottle of wine, "and a chromo" to anyone who felt for Piatt, "but up to this time nobody has appeared to claim the prizes." Senator-elect Zachariah Chandler commented that he had never realized that there was so much good in McGarrahan's claim before, and perhaps he had better look into it again![6]

It is Donn Piatt himself who should be looked at again. Ranked while alive as "the most sensitive, provoking, genial satirist in America" and "the most successful correspondent of the age," he has long since faded into obscurity and, indeed, had done so by the time he died at his mansion in Mac-o-Chee in 1891. Even the New York *Times* misspelled his first name in its obituary; later historians, mentioning him tangentially to their real subject, did not even come that close. Biographers of Bret Harte confused him with his relative, the poet J. J. Piatt (though they had no confusion about the fact that whichever Piatt it was, having promised Harte a generous sum to write the serial, welshed on the deal).[7]

Piatt, however, is worth a little extra trouble, and not only because he gave a little extra trouble. In him appeared many of the strengths and weaknesses of journalism in his time. Indeed, the personal style and the cynical "inside look" that he did so much to promote provided inspiration for a dozen other reporters, and his columns were widely quoted and commented upon nationwide. Few correspondents were so imitated and admired. None was so hated and feared. Like "Gath," Piatt had real literary gifts; like Boynton, ideals intensely held. Both he used lavishly, and both, in their own ways, distorted the news that came out of Washington. It was only right that he should be struck down in the lobby; for on more than one occasion he involved himself so deeply in the making of policy that his role as reporter was compromised fatally.

Donn Piatt was not the natural curmudgeon that his talent for making enemies suggests, though he had an aggressive streak. As a youthful correspondent he fought a duel outside Columbus. (No one was hurt, the seconds having surreptitiously loaded cork pellets into the pistols.) But the warm-bloodedness that made Piatt a good hater also made him a liberal benefactor and a generous friend. Even journalists who found his writing provoking loved him. He was, Hiram J. Ramsdell declared, "one of the most charitable and tender hearted men in the community." He was also one of the richest, though not from his legal practice nor his sparkling impromptu speeches. Marrying an heiress and then, upon her death, her sister helped his household finances.[8]

By 1870, his age should have given him the status of elder statesman among the Bohemians, though his black hair and brown whiskers might deceive the casual acquaintance. Twenty years before the Civil War, he had drunk juleps with Martin Van Buren's vice-president, Richard M. Johnson, and edited a Democratic newspaper on Van Buren's behalf in the "Hard Cider" campaign. He had served on the staff of General Robert Schenck during the war and done his best as a member of the Ohio legislature to send Schenck to the Senate afterward. But on the whole, he left no mark on public life worthy of his talents until middle age. In the General Assembly, as he joked, his opposition to a measure was desperately courted by members wanting it to pass. As proprietor of the *Mac-o-cheek Press*, he turned a losing concern into a bankrupt one. By 1867, he was groping for some new way of affecting public events. "The great work of regeneration must be done through the press," a friend advised him. What if Piatt turned his energy to contributions to one of the leading dailies?[9]

Piatt did just that. In 1868, Murat Halstead of the Cincinnati *Commercial* sent him as special correspondent to Washington at $25 per letter. In view of the aggressive temper on both sides, it is surprising that the two men were able to work together at all. On at least one occasion, Piatt threatened to resign when his work was not published, and by the summer of 1871, Halstead had lost patience and dismissed him, a mistake that, Piatt later wrote, foreshadowed the *Commercial*'s decline.[10]

Three years was time enough for Piatt to make an indelible mark on Washington correspondence. His news-gathering abilities, to be sure, were barely adequate. Through the first half of 1870, the big stories on Capitol Hill included the final Reconstruction of Georgia and Virginia, railroad subsidies, and plans to annex Santo Domingo. On none of them did Piatt utter a word. Tariff reform alone interested him, but on that he offered nothing beyond opinion and aspersion. Later, he would take credit for forcing the House to look into the link between high-placed administration figures and the plot of those cunning speculators, Jay Gould and Jim Fisk, to corner the gold market; in fact, he simply repeated charges that the New York *Sun* was spreading far and wide. When he did track down a scoop, it was usually wrong. From Piatt's evidence, readers could see plainly that there was no chance of President Grant putting so detested an enemy as former secretary of war Edwin M. Stanton on the Supreme Court; looking a column or two away, they could see just as plainly that Grant had done just that and that the Senate had confirmed the name at once.[11]

News gathering, while of increasing importance to a special correspondent's reputation, was not the secret of Piatt's success, however. A personal, lively style was. Most particularly, he indulged in what a contemporary called the "amusing but risky custom of epithet slinging." Secretary of State Hamilton Fish received mention as "the old sardine," Senator Lyman Trumbull became "Old Specks," Senator Cornelius Cole of California was "the fiery Cole," and the president appeared as "Utter Silence" Grant.[12] The frivolous style held a serious message: the powerful were unworthy of deference. What Piatt was doing was tearing the mantle of respectability from them and revealing them in all their littleness. It worked. Thanks to him, for a generation the House would be called the "Cave of Winds," the upper chamber the "Senatorial Fogbank." Cutting statesmen down to size was only part of his main purpose. More than ever before, what Piatt offered readers was the story behind official events, the sordid inside workings of politics, the things *done* while congressmen spoke.[13]

That purpose became all the more apparent in 1871. Long ambitious to own a major metropolitan paper, he joined forces with his friend and rival George Alfred Townsend to create a weekly, the Washington *Sunday Capital*, "aggressively independent in politics and neutral in religion and morals." When Townsend retired after a few weeks' work, it became pretty much a one-man operation, though Piatt later would hire a stable of able correspondents, including Austine Snead, who as "Mrs. Grundy" had become the most famous social correspondent of her day, and Congressman Benjamin Butler's dissolute nephew, whose drunken brawls proved him an expert on "wine, women and song."[14]

The *Capital* throve. Its independence of the administration provided a sharp contrast to other District newspapers, and its flippancy put it in a class by itself. Washington correspondents' only complaint was that it came so infrequently. Within a year it was publishing a Saturday edition for subscribers outside of the District. Later, Piatt would boast that he had sold an interest in it for $10,000 in cash and that even in the hardest times, it yielded him $3,000 to $5,000 a year.[15]

Readers laughed; politicians trembled, and not just with fury. Aptly, the Chicago *Times* referred to the editor as "Donn Piute, the savage scalptaker," and many officials resented having their scalps taken. His descriptive term for Vice-President Schuyler Colfax ("Smiler") was one of his most apt plays on words: Colfax's oozy combination of sanctimony, benevolence, and affability looked all too much like an ambitious politician's hypocrisy. But the term cut the vice-president to the quick, coming as it did after Piatt had been his guest.[16] Local police confiscated a special edition publishing a satire on the president's inaugural address, the Italian minister reportedly thought of challenging him to a duel, and federal authorities were only too happy to swear out a writ seizing all his property, press included, to settle the debts of a defaulting paymaster for whom Piatt had given bond (the writ lacked jurisdiction).[17]

It would be easy to dismiss Piatt as a clown. That was often how he passed himself off. "Had we sought to instruct, instead of amuse, we would have accomplished a failure in little cash and less thanks," he wrote on his retirement. When Baron Catacazy of the Russian mission quarreled with the State Department of Hamilton Fish, Piatt dubbed the disagreement the "Cat-Fish War." Among Catacazy's many offenses (among which was an ability to manipulate press leaks better than Fish did), the State Department had objected to the chasseur that the Russian envoys brought with them, a dignitary dressed in a feathered hat of white and red and gold lace, who preceded the minister "carrying a huge sword that was dreadful to behold." But it was not the secretary's negotiations that brought about his retirement, Piatt would boast; it was the *Capital*, which poked such fun that the minion was pelted with rotten eggs the moment he showed his face.[18]

That sense of mischief did exist. In fact, it had kept Piatt from a place on Greeley's *Tribune*, or so Piatt remembered, though the story he told differed from time to time. In one version the old editor grumbled at the applicant's excess of talent. "A certain amount of dullness is necessary to make a newspaper please the masses," Greeley explained. "The editor of a newspaper can less well afford to be brilliant than stupid." "I solemnly assure you, that if occasion requires, I can be as stupid as yourself," Piatt said. In another version, Greeley offered Piatt the job of agricultural editor and asked if he knew anything about pumpkins and squashes. "No," said the Ohioan, "but I can soon learn all about them through a study of your editorial corps." [19]

In fact, the last thing observers should have taken seriously was Piatt's occasional plea not to be taken seriously, a journalist "pungent without principles." [20] Just as with his newspaper columns, the *Sunday Capital* chose its targets to make a point, the pettiness and self-seeking of politics. His idea that the secretary of state should be replaced with a machine that, when visitors turned the crank, would say, "Yes, sir" and "No, sir" might be mere whimsy (still more the suggestion that the change be made, to save taxpayers money). But there was really nothing all that whimsical about his main point, that the government could do without a State Department building entirely. All it had to do was transfer business to the Spanish legation, "where all our foreign relations have been conducted for the last two years":

> Scarcely beneath the stars and stripes
> Beats there a heart so lost, so low,
> That struggling Freedom's cause will fail
> To light with sympathetic glow.
> Alas! could hope itself expect
> More than Spain's myrmidons can wish
> When a misguided nation's pulse
> Throbs through the cold heart of a Fish? [21]

What a world it was if Piatt was right! A visit to the Supreme Court showed not just dim lighting—perhaps, Piatt joked, because when justice was supposed to be blind, illumination was uncalled for—but dim intellects. As arguments went on before the judges, the journalist spotted one reading a newspaper, another browsing through legal documents, two more in conversation, and a fifth dozing. [22] Tourists might prefer Congress, "a machine run by wind." Through Piatt's eyes, one would see self-interested and mediocre men stacking the most prominent committees ("when a senator is placed at the head of a committee, it is rather conclusive evidence that he knows less about the subject . . . than any other of the dominant party in the chamber"), from the "fanatical" Horace Maynard of Tennessee to Congressman Oliver James Dickey of Pennsylvania, "a lock of hair or the toe-nail paring" of his predecessor, radical Republican leader Thaddeus Stevens. Then there was Ben Butler of Massachusetts, who resembled nothing so much as "an animated bundle of sky-rockets."[23]

Who public figures were mattered less than how they reached their decisions, and on this point, Piatt had the simplest answer: incompetence and corruption.[24] Corruption did not stalk the capitol, as one bad bit of doggerel suggested. It rushed down the aisles pell-mell, touching as many lawmakers as it could. Around Washington clustered the attorneys and lobbyists, looking for cheap politicians. If, as Piatt contended, fifty-two congressmen went on sale at a thousand dollars apiece, it showed what price the market would bear. With such personnel, government had to be one large steal. Corruption, Piatt insisted, was not just common. It was *everywhere*, and the mainspring on which everything ran. In 1876, the *Capital* spotted a swindle in the way that military graves had been filled in the national cemeteries. The more corpses the contractors found to bury, the more money they got, and to government disbursers, one bone looked much like another. As a result, many a mule was reincarnated into one of the honored dead, and civilian cemeteries became excavation sites for raw materials.[25]

Most efforts toward reform earned little beyond Piatt's impatience and scorn. Supposedly competitive examinations for Patent Office positions only put the gloss of civil service principles on the selection of favorites; some applicants got jobs without being tested, others were chosen long before they were submitted for examination. Assessments on federal officers were frowned upon and winked at. In the Interior Department, the contributions were avowedly voluntary, but since workers who failed to give were fired, one might as well make the department's motto "Your money or your desk."[26]

Piatt did not dismiss all reform as cant—only that coming out of a Republican administration. The *Capital* had solutions, some of them ingenious. Just as Parliament did, why not license attorneys to solicit before congressional committees? "Such a law would at once elevate and purify the business." Better still, the editor advised removing congressmen's desks. Forced to stand, the solons could neither read newspapers nor open mail. They would be forced to listen to debates and committee reports and find out just what the lobbyists were up to.[27]

These were stopgap remedies; the *Capital* had others, not far from the Jacksonian ideology that Piatt had held in his youth. A government made of such base materials could be trusted neither with power nor with money; a lobby filled with so many powerful financial interests could not be trusted to define America's political economy by dictating a program of bounties, subsidies, and protective tariffs. Certainly no one in Washington could be relied on to ensure justice in the states, especially when it meant protecting the vote of people whose color and intelligence Piatt despised. "Death to the carpet-bagger," the *Capital* cried. "Death to a paternal government. Death to the thieves."[28]

The cry may not have been meant figuratively. Government of the people had fallen so far out of fashion, Piatt argued, that its restoration could only come through outright revolution. This held truest in the South, where Republicans faced open insurrection and midnight violence. "These political miscreants and ignorant plunderers of the regular army want war," the *Capital* snarled. "Well, we hope they will get it. We hope that not only will the White Leagues of Texas and Louisiana continue their organizations, but that such organizations will continue until it will require a regiment to keep one carpetbagger in place."[29]

Piatt's views had at least some basis. Railroad lobbyists did indeed try to buy friends in Congress with legal retainers and easy credit on stock purchases, cabinet officers did endow their relatives with government contracts for which no work was done, and President Grant's own private secretary shared in the hush money that tax-evading whiskey distillers doled out.[30] But Piatt's vision of debased government was deeply flawed, however sincerely held. That a man could honestly believe in a high tariff or in Reconstruction the journalist thought impossible. That an abolitionist could be anything but a lunatic or a sentimentalist was more than he could accept. For all the major scandals, most legislation that passed Congress owed more to public pressure than to some sinister lobby, and more to political realities than to the clandestine chink of coin. For all the abuses of the spoils system, the civil service reformers were winning a few victories, even under President Grant. Any outlook that blamed the drawbacks to governance on thieving, imbecility, personal ambition, and illicit influence and substituted the conspiratorial for the obvious explanation for why things happened did worse than mislead its readers. It made them grasp simple explanations where complicated analysis was necessary— and consequently, grasp simple solutions.

As for the men whom Piatt took to task, not all of them were rascals. Partisan Republicans though they were, Congressmen Henry Dawes of Massachusetts and Charles Foster of Ohio and Senator John Sherman stood with the reformers on many issues. Dawes's record of exposing swindles in his own party dated to the first days of the Civil War, when he went after grafting contractors and shoddy military merchandise. The Grant administration had no love for Dawes, whose attacks on it for extravagance were as damaging as anything that Piatt wrote. A future secretary of the Treasury, Foster assailed the different means by which Custom House and Internal Revenue officials raked in extortionate profits. As head of the Senate Finance Committee, Sherman acted cautiously, even with calculation, but no one ever made a serious challenge to his honesty or ability. Yet to Piatt, Dawes was "the little dodger," "a prostitute . . . by nature"; Sherman was a political craven possessed of "all the cunning of Mephistopheles without any of his intellect"; and Foster, if he were made Speaker, would inaugurate "a carnival of rogues."[31]

When it came to black officials, Piatt's readiness to believe the worst made his distortions all the more palpable. Reporting for the Cincinnati *Commercial*, Piatt chronicled the arrival of the first black U.S. senator, Hiram Rhodes Revels of Mississippi, with barely concealed distaste. Unable to keep his eyes off "the decided brunette," nor his pen from referring to "the saddle tinted Senator," the journalist sneered at senators who deigned to shake hands with their new colleague. Revels had served in the pulpit and then in municipal office, but Piatt looked further back in his career and described the seat once occupied by Jefferson Davis as turned now "into a barber's chair"—rather like describing Lincoln's election as turning the ship of state into a flatboat. There was demeaning gossip, to the bargain: Revels could not have written his maiden speech personally, he had turned away all visitors because of a desire to spend his every minute contemplating the Constitution and Senator Sumner, and Sumner, whose marriage had failed, meant to bring Revels into his own domestic circle "to restore the lost happiness felt there so long"—a comment that may possibly have been meant to back up the hints of homosexuality that underlay gossip about the Massachusetts senator's private fiascoes.[32] Other blacks fared still worse. The Washington *New National*

Era was quite correct when it called the *Capital* "tolerably trustworthy as a representative of stupid prejudices and negro-hating isms."[33]

Piatt's attacks therefore were not just powerful but intensely unfair. There were two reasons why he went so far wrong as an observer of public events, and each might be called a corruption of judgment, the first stylistic and the second personal.

Piatt's literary cleverness was strength and weakness both. It was a mighty power to be able to sum up anyone in an epithet, but the merit of a mot juste comes in just how *juste* it is. Even at its most apt, a term may distort the man as a whole. Piatt hit close to the mark when he called Congressman William D. Kelley "Pig-Iron." The Pennsylvania protectionist actually liked the name, and when Piatt tried to explain himself, waved away any apologies: "when I die, I want that title engraved on my tomb." The name did Kelley's reputation more injustice than he thought. It conjured up monomania, cynicism, possibly even corruption. In fact, Kelley held as deep a compassion for blacks, laborers, and debtors as he felt for the beneficiaries of protective tariffs. He neither invested in ironworks nor speculated himself into wealth. Bribe givers were thrown out of his office bodily, and at one point, he grew so tired of the office seekers' clamor that he tried to retire from politics (admittedly, it took little convincing to make him change his mind).[34]

The more carelessly Piatt flung his epithets, the more damage was done not just to his victim, but to himself as a person worthy of credence. When he sued the commissioner of pensions for slander, the Chicago *Times* correspondent professed amazement: "Donn has belted the just and the unjust alike, and has pelted fact and fiction so gaily at all possible targets that the town is agog to learn he objects to being lied about."[35]

The second corruption, that of personality, stemmed from the fact that Piatt refused to remain as an observer. He was a political participant and had been for some time. As a journalist he had joined conferences with the politicians to coordinate the fight against high tariffs. As an editor, he could hardly escape the partisan rough-and-tumble and did nothing to escape the donations of conniving politicos like Senator Reuben Fenton of New York. There were political strings attached, and Piatt wore them proudly, soliciting his political patrons to do "something for the Capital so that the Capital can do some thing for the cause."[36] But what happened to the journalist's ability to keep a close watch on those doing "something for the Capital"? What happened to that scrutiny when political friends were concerned? Piatt's choice of targets was not random, and not just from the way he felt about political issues. Loyalties, personal and financial, played a great role.

One of those was his loyalty to his wartime superior, Robert Schenck, who went from the battlefield to the House to the Court of St. James. Piatt's faith in him never wavered, nor did his bitterness over the 1866 Senate race in which Sherman beat "as gallant a gentleman as ever the Lord endowed with human locomotion." From this came a readiness to abuse Sherman at every opportunity as corrupt, and a resolute refusal to believe that Schenck could have done wrong. A better case could have been made against Schenck's honesty than Sherman's. Jay Cooke's banking house found the Ohio congressman a faithful mercenary; that was why, after Schenck lost his bid for reelection in 1870, the Cookes used their influence to make him minister to Great Britain, where confidential information helpful to the bankers' speculations could be leaked. While he was there, Schenck augmented his salary by acting as front man for sellers of stock in a worthless silver mine. As the story came out, it proved quite a scandal—but not in Piatt's hands.[37]

Piatt never forgot a personal injury. Rival Ohio journalists, like the young Whitelaw Reid, fell afoul of Piatt early and felt his stings from then on. "Geiger & co. pushed on that case to a judgment against me," he wrote of some litigants, "and have thereby entered up a judgment against themselves which I will see is satisfied." Piatt disdained to refute aspersions against himself in the Cincinnati *Chronicle*—not when he could do the proprietors more damage with "some choice material."[38] The settling of scores was one of Piatt's greatest delights, but it was something of a luxury in a journalist wanting the public trust.

That same personal bias goes far to explain why Piatt turned against Carl Schurz in 1877. The former senator was pretty much the same man he had been when Piatt had hymned his praises three years before: proud, ambitious, and flintily honest. He had been among the earliest supporters of a civil service based on merit and one of the most faithful spokesmen for what enemies of paper currency liked to call "honest money" principles. Now as secretary of the interior, he warred on the very grafters and wastrels that Piatt had fulminated against. "I doubt my own convictions when Carl Schurz argues against them," a fellow Republican confessed. Yet Piatt now saw only a mercenary who demanded cash for campaign appearances and decided weighty matters from a hunger for social acceptance. The cause was personal: McGarrahan's friend was Piatt's foe, and Schurz had just declined to award the New Idria Mining Company a patent to the disputed land.[39] Piatt honestly believed that McGarrahan was perpetrating a fraud. When a cohort of McGarrahan's approached one of Piatt's close friends in 1870 to offer him stock to act as lobbyist with his old friend Jacob D. Cox, then secretary of the interior, Piatt really may have believed that it was an attempt to bribe the secretary himself. It was no such thing, but that is what he told Cox.[40]

Piatt left one essential fact out of his story then and later. He was on the payroll of the New Idria company and remained there up to the time that McGarrahan confronted him in the hallways of the capitol and knocked him down. The money for Bret Harte's roman à clef on McGarrahan was to have come from men connected with the New Idria who guaranteed Piatt pay for capturing the famous story writer. Could his misunderstanding of McGarrahan's friends' overtures have been more than accidental? That is at least possible.[41]

Nor was this the only time when Piatt's scrutiny lapsed on matters where money was at stake. Through his influence, the firm of Cowles & Brega won War Department approval for its contract to mothproof army clothing. His advocacy helped convince the House Appropriations Committee, which Piatt's friend James A. Garfield headed. Very likely it was just coincidence that Piatt discovered the worthlessness of the chemical preventative only after the firm rejected his demand for a larger lobbying fee than originally arranged. Righteousness rather than vindictiveness may explain why he went to the secretary of war to expose the fraud and have the contract annulled. "I do so hate to be beaten by these rascals—eaten as it were by my own dogs," he wrote. But the suspicion that there was some connection between events was one Piatt himself would have proclaimed absolute fact had he been writing up a like scandal for the *Capital*.[42]

Piatt's paper also could justify support of the Board of Public Works for the District of Columbia and its "boss," Alexander R. Shepherd, even after the Washington ring's incompetence, if not outright thieving, was common knowledge. When Murat Halstead came to town, Piatt had the boss invite the Cincinnati editor to dinner and abused Halstead as an ingrate when a good meal did not result in a good press write-up. When Zebulon White of the *Tribune* made the first exposure of the frauds, Shepherd and Piatt both exerted pressure on his employer to compel a retraction.[43] Perhaps Piatt's

Hang Yourself for a Pastime (Thomas Nast, *Harper's Weekly*, March 17, 1877).
Having urged the lynching of Republicans, Donn Piatt is offered a chance to try
it himself. The remarks about mothproofing allude to his lobbying on behalf of
Cowles & Brega's formula. The Cincinnati *Enquirer*, which employed him,
professed delight with the attention. "It is glory enough for a man to be a regular
correspondent of the *Enquirer*," the editors explained, "but when the first page
of *Harper's* is assigned to him, even with lamp-posts and ropes, it strikes us that
the cup is full" (March 10, 1877).

fidelity was one more example of how friendship could overrule judgment, though another explanation is just as tempting. "I have always admired the brilliant editor of the *Capital*, and could forgive his injustice for his wit," Congressman Robert B. Roosevelt protested when he was abused for his criticisms of District misgovernment; but he wondered if wit had any connection with the thousands of dollars in advertising bestowed on the weekly by local authorities. He might have wondered further about the fact that the paper's business manager held the sinecure of secretary to Boss Shepherd and that Shepherd had deeded property to Piatt's wife.[44]

A ring subsidy would not have made Piatt unique. Every other newspaper in the District got public funding. When a congressional investigation in 1874 began to look into charges of malfeasance and incompetence, for example, other papers printed the testimony as news; the *National Republican* published it as advertising matter, which the Board of Public Works paid for at the usual rates. The board also paid the paper's reporter. W. B. Murtagh, as owner of the *Republican*, had special reasons for not wanting a full investigation. Evidence showed that he had used his influence to bestow building contracts on firms that never applied in return for a share of the profits. When the books of one of the biggest paving companies were opened, investigators found Murtagh set down for twenty-five shares, none of which he had paid for, while the Washington *Evening Star*'s editor and business manager each had a like amount.[45] The *Chronicle* and even the *New Era*, Washington's black newspaper, lived off the advertising that Shepherd bestowed.

Other journalists lobbied; still others involved themselves in relations that gave their columns' motivations some ambiguity, if not worse. What makes Piatt's behavior more disturbing was its contrast with his public claim to act as moral censor for everyone else in politics. No one expected better things of Murtagh, but Piatt's newspaper was the only one in Washington that made plausible claims of independence; it was one that based its credibility on its commitment to reform and its hatred of corruption. A generous interpretation of what motivated his writings is possible, but how difficult it is to give to one whose interpretation of public officials' actions was so lacking in that same understanding!

Readers may not have known how far Piatt held politicians up to a moral standard to which he could not hold himself, but politicians knew. That was one reason that, more than any other journalist, his diatribes provoked not just anger but violent assaults like McGarrahan's. One of the

House officers read with outrage an attack on a corrupt congressman in the *Capital*. What incensed him most was his knowledge that the moralizers were "fed & clothed in fine linen by the District Ring to write this vile stuff." "You are handsome and you are fascinating, D. P.," jeered the Washington *Post*, "but you are afflicted with calculus in the gall."[46]

Piatt's deficiencies and strengths are worth considering, for they included several common ones. The word pictures that he gave were a characteristic of the time, when photography was unavailable for a daily's publication and most public figures had to be described.[47] Observational reporting extended far beyond political letters. By the 1870s, the sensationalism of the elder James Gordon Bennett's *Herald* also had begun to give way to a more graphic, not to say, horrific descriptiveness of murders, and the detailed accounts of life in a madhouse or the stench of the slums in Five Points were aimed to give readers the chance to feel as if they themselves crept through the alleys or stood in the basement over the putrefying corpse.[48]

In Washington, the observational report became something of a specialty of women correspondents, some of whom gave Washington society the glamour and gilding of Paris under the Second Empire and invested descriptions of the mansion at Arlington with the tragic poetry that the surrounding cemetery required. That specialty may not have been wholly by choice. " 'Our own' gentlemen reporters find it not difficult to attain to the 'dignity of dullness,' with their political platitudes, and perpetual items of Congress and war," Mary Clemmer Ames complained. "But the great Mogul 'We' in the editorial chair, warns the lady 'Own' to keep clear of 'current events.' He wants nothing of her but 'pictures' and 'personal gossip.' And as the literary and art-life of Washington is nowhere, and its intellectual life so purely nomadic, what can she, poor soul, do, but begin her letter as she usually does, with:—'Last evening, the most brilliant affair of the season came off at the house of Secretary—,' or, 'the magnificent hop at the National last night was a decided success.' " Ames stretched the bounds further than most, but ladylike conduct ruled out even her doing much investigative reporting, and even political analysis had to be couched in the diffident language of an observer entitled to hold opinions. That Ames's columns were entitled "A Woman's View of Washington," while her colleague on the New York *Independent* wrote one headed "Washington News," only typified the limitations.[49] No man would have sullied his columns with hymns to the latest bloom of springtime or gushed about clothing, and not many of them would have the lasting attraction of Ames's columns after the day-to-day wrangles lost their interest.

Applied to public life, such reporting by the Piatts, "Gaths," and "Olivias" meant descriptions in the capitol that came to life: the yellow kid gloves of the ladies in the gallery, Illinois Senator John A. Logan, "black and ominous as an Indian," and Senator Roscoe Conkling, of New York, striding the streets of his hometown "like a young god." To most readers Senator Matthew Carpenter of Wisconsin was just a name, but one that took on substance when he appeared, at least in print, restless, stalking the Senate, coat buttoned a little too tightly, hands in his pockets. A form solidified in the mind, as "Gath" depicted him at a Washington reception, "a bullock of flesh and force." The picture sharpened as a correspondent limned the massive head, covered with shaggy iron-gray hair, and an eloquent mouth, concealed by a heavy mustache. And here is "Gath," watching Carpenter argue a case in court: "greasy olive skin," "puffy chops," "over-fed dimensions," "plausible tongue." Beyond that, others could capture the spirit that makes this voluptuous, swaggering politician a creation as real as anything from Dickens.[50]

In an age that took politics seriously, such reporting gave a welcome artistry to commonplace events. If readers were to keep their interest in public affairs, there was no better way than to bring them into familiarity with the leading players. Still, as Piatt's comments made clear, the vehement and colorful description of public life had a second aim. Just as sensationalism was occasionally wielded to make a moral point, so reporters' visual description was used to illustrate the essence of a politician's character. Its closest equivalent may not have been literature but Thomas Nast, whose caricatures in *Harper's Weekly* turned the cartoon into a political force more powerful than any leading article. "He travestied Tammany into ruin, bastard liberalism into oblivion, and will sketch the death of paper currency," the Chicago *Times* promised. In equally fervent testimonial, one of Ben Butler's constituents raged against the "infamously libellous caricature that Nast-ies the first page of 'Harper's Weekly'" and urged him to take legal action. Nast was a pioneer in many ways, but among the most important was the same technique in drawing that Piatt was applying to writing. For the first time in American history, an artist was able to use exaggeration not simply to make a public figure look ridiculous, but to expose his soul to public view—at least, his soul as Nast interpreted it. "It is a slander and a libel to insinuate that I ever caricatured Mr. Schurz," the cartoonist protested, "as it is an utter impossibility to do so."[51] The truest equivalent in correspondence to Nast at his best may well have been "Gath," perhaps because he had more poet in his composition than the others (perhaps it was no coincidence that other outstanding practitioners of the descriptive style like Ames and Piatt also wrote poetry). One member of the House was "a Gradgrind with traditions," a senator was "a great benevolent Pumblechook to every modest Pip in Vermont."[52]

Description for moral effect, like caricature, was an art dangerously easy to abuse. Style for its own sake, like irreverence, made politics meaningless, concentrating attention on the writer rather than the subject. When a column described one senator as "the Pied Piper playing the tune of himself" and "a small bank-account god," say, the author obscured every point he was trying to make except his own cleverness.[53] Much of the description, too, verged on vituperation, just as Nast's drawings did. Like so many other observers, Mary Clemmer Ames saw what she wanted to see in the faces of public men. It was, after all, unlikely that every man "of rather demonish aspect, gesticulating violently, and throwing himself into attitudes of ferocity" was by nature a Democrat, and every calm speaker "throwing back his head, as if he saw in mid-air the immortal gods, and was going to meet them" was a radical Republican; and very possibly the cultured face of editor Henry J. Raymond only suggested to one out of sympathy with him a countenance that "might be kind, . . . might be cruel, but . . . could never be trusted utterly when you needed it the most." Others using the same technique concentrated on stammers, physical deformities, exaggeration of regional accents, and japes at attire.[54] The style was calculated not only to give offense, but also to shift public attention from politics as a process, or from the principles on which policy was based, to the ephemeral and the personal.

From that point, it took only a small step to make political analysis that pinned credit or blame for what happened to individual men. In doing so, journalists obscured the deeper forces in public life: a widespread mania for railroad construction, for example, or a broad commitment to the transformation of sectional and race relations and to the traditional values and scope of government action that undercut all the new ambitions. As the best correspondents saw, the real source of debased government lay in a partisan enthusiasm that in the name of country and Constitution would permit vote fraud, rigged judicial decisions, and the bestowal of offices on men who were amateurs at everything except political activity. It was certainly true that President Grant gave reform less help than it needed; but to assume that the defeat of Grant would deal corruption a mortal blow— or that the misrule of the South was the fault of wicked carpetbaggers, come south to steal—was to simplify problems and solutions dangerously.

Piatt's propensity to see conspiracies, to portray political life in the darkest of colors, helped set a fashion in Washington correspondence. Though never universal, that cynicism about the possibilities for substantial change in the behavior of those governing spread far beyond the pages of the *Capital*. For some years, it served as the stock-in-trade of "Gath," of "Gideon," of A. M. Gibson, and, with more responsibility and far better research, of Henry V. Boynton as well. It even affected Mary Clemmer Ames.[55] A healthy skepticism certainly would serve voters better than blind acceptance of their rulers' foibles, the kind so often instilled through the old party press. But it meant a diminishing faith in the power of government to remedy abuses or even to act at all. Along with other influences, the Piatts helped discredit the activism that the Civil War years had brought to government. Reform increasingly meant retrenchment, frugality was increasingly confused with public morality. William McGarrahan was not the only claimant turned into a monster of corruption in the press, nor was his lobbying effort the only one misread as a conspiracy of bribe takers stretching all the way into the White House itself.

Piatt should not be judged by his writings alone. Looking to a reconciliation late in life, he wrote George Alfred Townsend a most revealing letter. "While you fail to sympathize with my political views, I have always been amused at yours," Piatt commented, "—suppose either of us has any, which I doubt. While you believe in the masses you don't know, and condemn the few you are acquainted with, I on the contrary have a contempt for the many and cherish and believe in my friends and associates." That may well have been so, but it made the plea that followed all the more disreputable. "We have both shaped our wares to suit the market," Piatt reminded Townsend, "and I question whether you or I would care to be held to a responsibility for what we have laid upon."[56] Piatt sold himself short. His own past actions as legislator at least had shown the sincerity of his desire for reform.[57] But even if it had been true, *could* Piatt dismiss his own responsibility for what he wrote? One could suggest that just as manufacturers should be held responsible for the damage their products do, if correctly used, so should journalists be held accountable for the work they set in motion.

PART THREE

NEWS MANAGEMENT MADE EASY

"Still Another Outrage"
(Thomas Nast, *Harper's Weekly*,
February 6, 1875).

CHAPTER 9

A Beautiful Smiler Came in Our Midst

News Management

As the quarrel of North and South reached its climax in the "secession winter" of 1860, Indiana politico Richard W. Thompson sent his son a warning from the capital that later generations would echo. No news from Washington was good news, he wrote; at least, none of it was fit to be trusted. "The 'correspondents' . . . are, as a class, altogether unreliable. They manufacture all sorts of stories—all for the purpose of magnifying their own importance & making their papers sell." How simple life would be if they could be ignored, but that was impossible. No men did more to shape public opinion. "They have such a share of influence over the public mind that they can write a man up or down, just as they think best for their own interest. The politicians are completely subject to them, and the two classes have brought the government to the very verge of ruin."[1]

Politicians had winced beneath the lash of the press gang before the war, and they had made reporters wince on occasion, too. Editor and reporter Horace Greeley got a caning, and one of his subordinates was stripped of press privileges, though neither blow stopped the *Tribune*: visitors on the night of the assault found Greeley scribbling frantically, his head swathed in wet cloths. Still, in retrospect, those in government service must have looked wistfully on the antebellum years. With the coming of the Bohemians, the problem of controlling what reporters said took on a new importance. Sober for once, Senator Richard Yates of Illinois might make a splendid speech to a roaring crowd and then open up the paper to find himself as ill-reported as if he had been drunk. Even the *Tribune*, which "aimed to do the nice thing," botched the job.[2]

To anyone hoping to pursue a long career in public service, the lesson was plain. News was too important to leave to the newsmen. The alert ones were if anything more dangerous than the careless few. Even in Lincoln's day, the *Congressional Globe* was a work of fiction, full of speeches never spoken or elevated versions of vulgar colloquy.[3] In 1876, for example, the few readers of the *Globe*'s successor, the *Record*, might find one of New York congressman Samuel "Sunset" Cox's best speeches replying to the tirade of James G. Blaine. Latin quotations, sarcastic hyperboles, choice puns, parenthetical mentions of "immense applause and uncontrollable bursts of laughter" studded it. But Cox's actual remarks were, "Oh, Blaine! Dry up!" Thanks to the Washington reporters, Americans paying attention knew what he had actually said, and editors were quick to compare the *Record* and the record. On another occasion a freshman congressman uttered a maiden speech better left unspoken. Quick to repent, he hurried to the official reporter to cut it from the *Record*. Later he confided his cleverness to Ohio congressman Job Stevenson. Stevenson simply pointed to the reporters' gallery: how many gentlemen did he see there? "Eighteen, as I count them." "Then," Stevenson told him, "eighteen beautiful youths have sent eighteen different versions of your eloquent utterance to eighteen different cities of the United States, and the same is now in print, and to-morrow it will be spread broadcast to an admiring public."[4]

Hell had no wrath quite like a journalist scorned, as Congressman Hiester Clymer of Pennsylvania learned when he tried to reap the political fruits from his exposure of peculation in the War Department. As the story began to break, journalists clustered around Clymer's committee room door, asking for some kind of lead. "I won't be bothered!" the congressman snapped, his face white with anger. "I shan't have any body here. I won't listen to anybody. Go away, go away, go away!" He slammed his door and posted a servant to guard it from intruders. Reporters were incensed, all the more when Clymer, after pleading the confidentiality of secret sessions, did leak the subcommittee's report to one man on Newspaper Row. The reporters spared no ink in averring Clymer's unfitness for the place he held.[5]

The increased scrutiny of reporters made lawmakers more wary of what they would say, more ready to propitiate journalists. "Twelve years on a newspaper I find to have been the most valuable education for a Congressional career," Speaker James G. Blaine confided in 1873, "—*first* in teaching a fellow what to do—*second* in warning him what not to do—and among the things *not to do* is to quarrel with a newspaper the size of the *Commercial.*"[6]

The power of the press, to be sure, also afforded opportunities, and not just perils, for public men. An aspiring official could turn coverage to his advantage. Journalists eager for new sources were often ready to serve a politician's purposes as long as it meant fresh copy. "I know that breed," Senator Benjamin Wade of Ohio said of the average reporter; "the more you kick them, the more they cling to you." And cling to him they did, for the inside information his allies would feed them during President Andrew Johnson's impeachment trial. Even a man as highly reputed for his idealism as George W. Julian, Indiana's most radical Republican, realized that press publicity could help overcome the strong opposition he faced inside party ranks at home by making him a noticeable figure. When a newspaper gave hostile coverage, he bullied its reporters. Through the years, he wrote paragraphs commending himself in connection with measures that his committee had passed and handed them to friendly correspondents to insert in the paper as their own. It was only when he prepared duplicate copies of those squibs for the Associated Press to run that editors took umbrage and rejected his material.[7]

Properly handled, the interview was even more directly beneficial to politicians. They could attract publicity and at the same time provide reporters with the copy they wanted. Acidly, the *Nation* described the typical exclusive conversation:

> The first surprise was, he is likely to tell us, "when he got off the cars" and enquired where the old senator's residence was situated, for he had been expecting to see a mansion whose appearance should be in pro-

portion to the national fame of its owner. The house was a plain frame structure, a little the worse for wind and weather, with a large barn behind it; near by were two men and a boy at work. The ill-dressed man was the old champion himself, feeding a pig; the boy was his youngest son, sawing wood. The room into which the correspondent was invited was very plainly furnished, without pictures, except a photograph of the Capitol at Washington and a portrait of the Senator. Noticing the absence of a piano, the correspondent was told that the senator "believed in a churn." His wife did her own washing, he said. The dinner was very simple, and the stories about the senator's drinking at Washington and on the cars were not confirmed by the pitcher of remarkably cold and clear water which stood on the table. The first thing he did, the senator said, when he got that lot, was to dig a well. He had always voted for a prohibitory law when in the State Legislature. The well and the cellar he dug in the day-time, and at night did sums on his slate by fire-light. He preferred a rag-carpet, he said. As for a big library, he thought if a man had one or two good books and made himself master of them he was more likely to turn out successful than if he spent his time looking up dead men's thoughts. Past ages were not progressive; and what might do well enough for Europe would not do for this country.[8]

A more mutually beneficial arrangement came from providing a ready access to useful information about the inner workings of politics in Washington. Even those targets of reporters, the senators from Iowa and Kansas, who at heart, thought one man, "would have delighted in hanging them one and all," fed them with tidbits of information.[9]

As a result, a good newspaperman could know what had happened in executive session in the Senate before late-coming senators did. Between the moment that two treaties were read aloud in Senate executive session and the moment that the excluded reporters had verbatim copies of them both, only thirty minutes elapsed. Early in 1876, indignant senators expelled the press from the galleries and in executive session stormed at the way journalists were able to report what went on behind closed doors. To lawmakers' chagrin the following day, they found deposited on their desks the latest issues of the offending papers, with complete details on the fulminations of the day before.[10]

So friendly a relationship did not just cause more news to be published, but some of it to be suppressed. Reformer Carl Schurz might want the

Cincinnati *Commercial* to keep its shorthand reporter from covering his speech, at least until he had given it at enough other spots to fashion it into a polished address. One of the senators from Arkansas might want his friends at the New York *Tribune* to close its columns to embarrassing descriptions of party factionalism back at home. There were any number of ways to oblige politicians.[11]

Where the reporter could not be sweetened, he could be stymied at the home office, and by the same personal blandishments. A shrewd senator like William Boyd Allison of Iowa did himself no damage by buying tickets to a benefit concert to buy the *Nord Iowa Post* a printing press, nor by offering the Chicago *Tribune* proprietors a loan to help them rebuild after a ruinous fire. When one of the New York *Herald*'s leading spirits went to Washington to lobby for a tax bill, it was his relationship to the publisher that most interested prominent Republicans. "[H]e is worth 'cultivating,'" one of them wrote Senator Edwin Morgan of New York, "not socially I don't mean, but personally and is worth obliging where you can. The Herald is a good thing for a public man to have on his side, especially in these days, when we don't know what may turn up."[12]

A kinsman or comrade on the newspaper staff afforded help of a more regular sort. Governor Henry Clay Warmoth of Louisiana could expect a fair hearing, if not favorable coverage, from the Chicago *Tribune* because the brother of one of his allies sat among the editors. Others close to him shaped dispatches to the New York *Times*, *Evening Post*, and Washington *Chronicle*. Governor Richard Oglesby of Illinois worried about sly digs from the Chicago *Tribune*, but not for long, thanks to an insider who talked both editor and publisher around.[13]

Journalists wanting to supplement their salaries with a small public office got the chance as well, whether it was a committee clerkship on Capitol Hill or a sinecure in the Census Office, where duties consisted of appearing every other week to pick up a paycheck.[14] Some journalists made a career out of government jobs, notably Ben: Perley Poore of the Boston *Morning Journal*. From 1865 until his retirement some twenty years later, he put together the *Congressional Directory* (with a list of all the reporters privileged with access to the press gallery, in the bargain). When Congress needed an editor for the transcripts of Johnson's impeachment trial, or, some years later, for the *Congressional Record*, when officials hired help compiling Patent Office reports, "Perley" went on the payroll. His close friendship with the heads of prominent committees ensured him an important clerkship as long as Republicans held the Senate and modest positions even after they were turned out in 1879.[15]

Even when they could not award government places, officials could leave journalists beholden to them by sponsorship. When Hiram J. Ramsdell wanted a spot in the Treasury in 1877, he found the ready support of the vice-president, a Supreme Court judge, and a handful of senators. One of them may have held special usefulness: former Speaker of the House James G. Blaine. Four years later, President James A. Garfield signed Ramsdell's commission as register of deeds for the District of Columbia. It was Garfield's last act before leaving the White House for that fatal rendezvous with Charles Guiteau at the railroad station and quite possibly done to oblige Blaine, now secretary of state.[16]

For all of these kindnesses an unspoken price was extracted. The reporter was put under obligation to one patron, if not a dozen. It was true that the appointments often went to men more competent than the usual political hack; Poore's *Congressional Directory*, as one newspaper remarked, "never fails to be promptly issued and complete in its details."[17] But the appointments remained political. When Congressman George F. Hoar chose R. J. Hinton ("Observer") of the Worcester *Spy* to serve on a government labor commission, he knew that the selection would please workers' organizations throughout New England; but most likely, it crossed his mind that the nomination might just have some effect on what Hinton wrote about Hoar. Journals had no doubt that when the Tammany Hall machine put William H. Hurlbert of the New York *World* on the commission to open Madison Avenue, it was not acquiring his skills as a civil engineer: he had none. The job was a plum to sweeten the tongue of a troublesome Bohemian.[18]

"In the phrase then common among Washington correspondents, every one of them had his own senator, representative or cabinet member," Francis A. Richardson of the Baltimore *Sun* later recalled. Richardson might have pondered further: who really possessed whom? Did not every senator have his own correspondent?[19] Ramsdell repaid Blaine's kindnesses in 1876 by writing his campaign biography, and when Blaine received the presidential nomination eight years later, Ramsdell issued a longer and more formal work. Other correspondents turned into avid "Blainiacs," most usefully the local AP reporters. George Alfred Townsend was all the more ready to find excuses for Secretary of War

William W. Belknap's misdeeds because he ate at Belknap's table and had secured his help in finding a government berth for a worthless stenographer.[20]

The intimacy with politicians carried a real danger of making the journalist their captive. Poore should have served as an object lesson. Contemporaries noticed increasingly that his best days as a correspondent had passed by the 1870s. Some of that had to do with age, more still to do with Poore's reluctance to use new-fangled techniques like interviews and "deep background." But his critical edge may well have been dulled by official station. For Poore by 1871 was not just a plodder. He was to contemporaries "that unctuous correspondent." He wrote speeches, addresses, and even letters for congressmen. Privately, he might protest his contempt for Ben Butler, but his columns were discretion itself and he helped swing local caucuses behind the congressman at election time. Did this have nothing to do with Butler's attentions, including loans that "Perley" was always needing and was hard put to repay?[21]

Henry Boynton was right, then, when he later declared that the most successful public men usually were those who had made a close study of how the press worked and knew how to put it to the best use.[22] But news management had its limits, as politicians quickly found.

One reason was that a system benefiting certain politicians necessarily worked against others. The leak, for example, was ideally suited to smear tactics and baseless charges, hard to refute or even track down, and reflected only on the well-aired mendacity of the press should the person under attack vindicate himself. Journalists knew it. They printed the information given to them but could hardly help resenting the way they were manipulated. Possibly, that resentment explains the growing popularity of the interview format. Then the accuser, not the journalist, would shoulder most of the blame for allegations made.[23]

Editors also found galling the readiness with which a congressman provided them with special copies of speeches for which they had no use. "Mr. Dixon! Oh, Mr. Dixon!" the Norwich *Bulletin* appealed to Connecticut's senior senator. "We have received a sufficient number of copies of your debate with Senator Ferry [Connecticut's junior senator] to last us for the next six months, and give us constant reading. Will you please stop sending them. Hash for fifty or sixty meals will do very well, but after that it palls upon the appetite. Send what you've got left to some other office." Even more coolly, the New York *Herald* responded to the speech one Democratic congressman sent the paper by offering to publish it as an advertisement, at the usual rate: $1,500.[24]

The crusading spirit of the journalist also made news managing less than effective. Those who believed in the natural wickedness of officeholders found it confirmed as they felt themselves worked on. "Pickaway," the Cincinnati *Enquirer*'s correspondent in Indianapolis, was offered a gold watch by the clerks of the state house, which he declined, and received a box of cigars from a legislator who wanted good coverage for a speech on the evils of drink. *Enquirer* readers were informed of both benefactions with all the outraged dignity that "Pickaway" could muster, which, since the cigars were very poor quality, was considerable.[25]

Nor did politicians find satisfaction in the arrangement. Witness the pitiful case of Blaine's predecessor as Speaker of the House, canny Schuyler Colfax. His own experience as editor of a small newspaper in Indiana may have given him special insight, or perhaps it came from his close friendship with Horace Greeley. As long as he wielded the gavel, Colfax paid special attention to the press gang. Subscribing to seventeen daily papers and a host of weeklies, he followed public opinion carefully before making up committee assignments and was ready to oblige editors with words of thanks for favors done, or of gentle correction for mistakes made. Newspaper Row knew him as a regular visitor, always ready to leak information.[26]

A good name took constant upkeep, however. When circumstances changed and Colfax became vice-president, his relations with the press began to deteriorate badly. He never lost the friendship of some of them: Boynton, Scott Smith, Lorenzo Crounse, Zebulon White, and Mary Clemmer Ames stood by him to the end. Many more had never been won over by his charm. Perhaps two-thirds of the Washington correspondents had preferred someone else for vice-president originally, and "Mack" nursed a positive hatred for him. But now the number of antagonists grew. The first jarring notes were sounded in the winter of 1869, when he took advantage of his address to the Correspondents' Club dinner to rebuke the scandalmongers among them. The restiveness increased as the new vice-president dropped his old social ways. A select few journalists still came to dine, but not the ordinary reporters. Could it be that Colfax thought himself too good for them now? That was what the correspondents thought, but they were wholly mistaken. As Speaker, Colfax had enjoyed the free time of a widower. He could call at Newspaper Row because he had no home life. Marriage changed that, and so did his mother's lingering, fatal illness. Under "the shadow of coming death" in the household, dinner parties were out of the question, much less hobnobbing with members of the press.[27]

As a result, when the time came for renomination, Colfax was in terrible trouble, a trouble made worse by a letter of declination that he issued and then thought better of, and by his foremost rival's skills at news management. Senator Henry Wilson of Massachusetts had plenty of good qualities. He also had the press on his side. Nightly, he made it his habit to visit Newspaper Row and, as one reporter recalled, "always spoke of the journalists as . . . 'the boys,' and he was as busy hunting up items as if he were in the profession."[28] Now, the pace was stepped up. Early in the year, Grenville M. Dodge, lobbyist for the Texas & Pacific Railroad, turned his newspaper connections to account to push the New York *Times* behind Wilson, and to get the backing of Uriah Painter and Boynton as well. Not that the senator stood aloof. According to Colfax, Wilson called at Newspaper Row "asking them to telegraph that he was gaining steadily, that I did not care for it, that he had been induced to run by my declination &c. . . . & many newspaper men told me they had to write & telegraph him up, so urgent were his appeals & so much had he set his heart on it." When the convention met, "Mack" was on hand to agitate for Wilson and to take the credit for his victory. Colfax accepted defeat graciously and stepped up to Wilson to congratulate him, but his famous smile, an observer remarked, was "but a whitened skeleton of its former self."[29]

Worse followed. In 1873, the House investigated charges that Credit Mobilier, the railroad construction firm that had built the Union Pacific Railroad, had swindled the government, which was subsidizing the transcontinental line, and had bought influential lawmakers by giving them special stock deals. As twinges of conscience or fears of exposure set in, most of the lawmakers rid themselves of the stock, though not of the phenomenal profits on an investment into which they had paid nothing.[30] Colfax and Wilson still held their shares. Both denied any involvement at all, and both were confronted with evidence that, at least circumstantially, made them look like liars. But with so many friends in the press, the vice-president–elect received the gentlest of treatments.[31] His predecessor fared worse. Denying that he had ever taken shares in that discredited corporation, much less that they were given to him on special terms, he found himself confronted with the memorandum book and shifting memory of Congressman Oakes Ames, of Massachusetts, the alleged bribe giver, determined that if he must fall, he would fall in the best of company. Colfax's denials rang hollow before Ames's certainties and a check endorsed by one "S. C." Though Ames contradicted himself and showed a memory increasingly vague the more questioners pressed him, the vice-president's reputation was pulverized. "A beautiful smiler came in our midst," the New York *Herald* jeered:

> Too lively and fair to remain;
> They stretched him on racks till the soul of Colfax
> Flapped up into Heaven again,
> May the fate of poor Schuyler warn men of a smiler,
> Who dividends gets on the brain! [32]

For all his cultivation of the press, Blaine, too, would find himself discredited and seriously damaged by those he had been unable to win over, though he achieved more success, at least, than Colfax.[33] But both politicians were warnings to their fellows of how fragile and tentative a thing press support could be. They had uncertain protection and knew it.

It was an infuriating situation. When one delegate to the Pennsylvania constitutional convention rose to protest the "men of no character" who had been sullying his name, he let loose a torrent. Member after member got to his feet to brandish lies about himself. "Do you know what I think?" an officeholder exploded. "I think all the damned reporters ought to be drowned dead."[34]

We may well wonder whether the quarrel between politicians and press gang was not more a convenient Punch and Judy show, with neither side hurt, than a reality. Might it not be a working out of a public adversarial relationship advantageous to both? Benjamin Butler, for example, did not let public feuds get in the way of social intimacies. A host knew that one of the best jokes on other guests invited to dinner (and a perfectly safe one) would be to sit the Massachusetts congressman next to a journalistic foe and let everyone else tremble at the prospect of violence.[35]

Still, the evidence of legislative exasperation is too voluminous to ignore. In letters to their families, lawmakers fulminated not at the inaccuracy, but the dishonesty of the journalists around them: "truthlessness and malice," "unjustly and viciously assailed," "great unkindness," "vile & persistent" assaults. Denounced by the Washington *Intelligencer* and New York *Herald,* Johnson's secretary of the Treasury Hugh McCulloch feigned indifference rather unconvincingly. Abuse from a man like the editor of the *Intelligencer,* he insisted, was "more creditable" than getting his praise. No doubt greed to shove into the public crib explained the attacks. As for the New Yorkers, "everybody knows . . . in what manner the 'Herald' can be propitiated."[36]

"Curses, instead of blessings, are falling upon my head this morning," a reporter wrote from the state capitol at Indianapolis. He was lucky nothing worse fell there, as it so often did to offending newsmen. One angry Ohio lawmaker rose to remind reporters of how the bad little boys had taunted the prophet Elijah, and of the bears sent to rend them. "Now," he concluded, ". . . if they don't stop these yere things they may overdo matters, and some day a bear might get after them and hurt some of the little fellows. Their little lead pencils won't be of no use as a defense when the bears get after 'em."[37] It was no idle threat. Lorenzo Crounse of the New York *Times* found his remarks about a notorious lobbyist repaid with her husband's cowhide whip. (Crounse's diminutive frame was deceptive; before the attacker could deal a second blow, he found himself on the floor with a penknife between his ribs and the reporter sitting on his midriff).[38] "Among the more civilized Republicans, when anything disagreeable was said . . . the [reporter] was invited to dinner . . . and the affair was adjusted over a bottle of wine in an amicable way," one victim complained. "But now there is a brutal disposition manifested to punch the journalistic head that ought to be at once discouraged."[39]

Most of the press gang escaped the violence, but they had plenty of other proof of their ill-favor. Irritated at the attacks that W. S. Robinson ("Warrington") meted out, Ben Butler had him fired as clerk of the Massachusetts house and deprived of extra income. Committees set up to look into allegations aired in the press quickly transformed into engines for harassing individual journalists. Called on to reveal their sources, reporters were traduced as rumormongers or fibbers and responded with accusations that the only aim their inquisitors had was the blackening of reputations.[40]

There were still more substantial means of bringing journalists to terms. In New York, the former speaker of the assembly proposed that for every attack a newspaper printed, the victim receive one column to reply in. Any such policy would be sure to wreck the press financially and compel it to withhold all criticism. Enraged California lawmakers made libel a felony punishable by two years in jail and a $5,000 fine, and they discussed a measure compelling every correspondent to sign whatever he or she wrote, so that legal blame could be assigned.[41]

After 1875, some newspapers noticed a change in the way courts reacted to press comment as well. There were more lawsuits for libel and apparently more cases where juries awarded damages. "Liberty in a land of fishwomen is not worth having," one observer explained. Judges worked to define libel in plaintiffs' favor. For years, newspapers had proclaimed a special freedom in public comment that individuals did not share, as "privileged communications." Now a few courts denied any such distinction. In Minnesota, the justices ruled that a charge of incapacity or corruption was equally libelous from whatever source it emanated. Another state court made editors liable for the attacks contained in correspondents' letters, and Louisiana judges extended liability to advertisements abusing public officials, even when malicious intent could not be proven and editorials appeared repudiating the allegations made. In Louisiana, a publisher who retracted false charges was declared still liable for damages; elsewhere, both good intentions and belief in the truth of the charges were ruled out as defenses against a libel suit. When newspaper comment touched a public official's private life or character, even when the charges were true, courts in Pennsylvania, Michigan, Kansas, and Illinois agreed, the publisher was still liable as long as malice could be proven. The truth, said Kansas justices, must be published only "for justifiable ends."[42]

So venomous a relationship showed itself most clearly with Ben Butler, the most notorious congressman from Massachusetts. "Ben Beast Brute Blundering Butchering Blear-eyed Blackguarding Bag Faced Ben Butler," Brick Pomeroy's headlines shrieked. Such treatment was to be expected from a Democratic organ, especially one that stood a small statue of the man outside its office door with the inscription, "Thief Robber and Woman Insulter."[43] But Republican papers vented a hostility nearly as venomous. According to the Boston *Morning Journal*, the assassination of President Lincoln came all too conveniently: it protected Butler from his certain arrest for trading with the enemy. The New York *Tribune* published forgeries, signed with his name, implicating the congressman in nefarious acts.[44] Normally restrained, the Springfield *Republican* lost control when he came to town in 1871. "BUTLER'S BIG BLOW," the headlines ran. "THE GREAT STINK RAISED IN SPRINGFIELD.

THE ESSEX HERO AS A LIAR. GEORGE FRANCIS TRAIN OUT-DONE."[45]

Butler had given them provocation. Coarse-featured and never overly dainty in political practice, "the Beast," as Democrats called him, had won an ugly reputation as occupation governor of wartime New Orleans. Three terms in Congress as spokesman for such disreputable groups as mill hands and onetime slaves had not redeemed it.[46] Yet even this background did not fully explain the unusual intemperance of the *Republican*. Something else did. Butler came spoiling for a fight with his favorite enemies: newspapers in general and Samuel Bowles's in particular. So it was only natural that in the midst of a tirade against the press, he singled out the low morals of one of the editors of the *Republican* for having backed the mad revolutionary John Brown and then, when the scheme to raise a slave rebellion failed, for having fled out the back door, leaving his sister to face officers of the law. When Franklin B. Sanborn, the man accused, rose from the press desk to brand the accusation a falsehood, Butler browbeat him, and the crowd loved it.[47]

The incident reveals one of the reasons that Butler made such intense enemies, but the zest with which the audience turned on Sanborn suggests something else that the congressman had discovered. Goading the press paid off. A newspaper could be read, believed, and still resented for telling distasteful truths. The righteousness a politico put on could not compare with the editor's hollow sanctimony. When Butler ran for the gubernatorial nomination in 1871, he made the most of the fact that every Boston daily but one stood against him. Scarcely a rally was held that the general did not take metropolitan papers to task by quizzing the reporters sitting at the press table just below the podium. Why did the Boston *Advertiser* turn against him? Because, said Butler, he had acted as attorney in a libel suit against the paper for obscene slanders it had committed against a talented young lady. Of course, the Boston *Morning Journal*'s editor had no use for him, said Butler. The man had tried to overcharge the general seven dollars for a political advertisement and never forgot the shame in being caught at it. Or perhaps, he theorized, the *Journal* was opposing him simply to depreciate the market value of its stock so that the paper's managers could buy it cheaply.[48] The hostility was more than campaign rant. In the House, Butler strove to restrict newspapers' mailing privileges and expand the libel laws.

The Power of the Press. Press witches (to Macbeth—Uncle Sam): "Show! show!
show! Show his eyes, and grieve his heart; come like shadows, so depart."
—Shakespeare (Thomas Nast, *Harper's Weekly*, May 9, 1874).
The weird sisters of the press conjure up their latest terror: "Butlerism,"
the spirit of Benjamin F. Butler.

Politicians' antagonism and press abuse, then, fed on each other and
worsened in the early 1870s. Investigative reporting and cheap attacks
alike strengthened the popular impression that politics was by its nature
a dirty trade. That was the barb in one joke by a city reporter for the
Chicago *Times*, who took his friend Joshua into a den of iniquity. Did he
know where he was? "Why, of course I do," the friend exclaimed. "It's
a rat-pit!" "Joshua, Joshua," the journalist rebuked him, "won't you ever
overcome your Milwaukee ignorance? Don't you know that rat-pits are
more respectable places than this?" Informed that he was actually visiting
the city council, Joshua wanted to leave at once: after all, he had twelve
dollars on him.[49]

Captive correspondents and mortal foes: neither relationship boded well
for the accuracy of news gathering in Washington. The latter may well
have had the greater effect by the mid-1870s. So deep did suspicion run,
so convinced of the fell purposes of government officials was the press
corps that it was ready and eager to assume the worst. The big story in

Washington became one of corruption and self-seeking. For it there were grounds enough. It took no grotesque distortion of the evidence to conclude that Schuyler Colfax had taken a bribe from Credit Mobilier, that Speaker Blaine had used his official position to coerce special deals from banks and railroads, that Benjamin F. Butler helped a bevy of rascals pillage the Treasury and shared in the take. But other interpretations were possible, too, and these were dismissed. If the American people doubted the wisdom of letting government exercise its powers or use funds freely, they had strong reasons for feeling so, but they owed that mistrust not just to the readiness to unearth wrongdoing that journalists showed, but to the poisoned atmosphere that sensationalism and the adversarial relationship had helped to raise in Washington.

CHAPTER 10

A Little Attention from James A. Garfield

At the height of their friendship, journalist Donn Piatt spotted the fatal weakness that held James A. Garfield of Ohio back. It was that deplorable good-naturedness that kept him a mere chairman of the House Appropriations Committee. "If you were a shade more aggressive, had a little audacity in your composition, you would be Senator, President anything you pleased," the journalist mused, "—but then you would not be Garfield."[1]

Like so many of Piatt's political judgments, this one missed the mark. Garfield would be senator and president both, and that within seven years. Yet he was Garfield still, the diligent, intelligent partisan of no remarkable merit that he had always been. What made his rise the more astonishing was that it happened in spite of a record tarnished by scandal. Contemporaries who did no worse than he found their careers cut short. How could Garfield have come so far?

There were many reasons, of course. A clumsy Democratic campaign and a united Republican one, "soap" (as Election Day cash was called) to buy voters in Indiana, a deadlocked and desperate convention, and pure luck all put Garfield within range of an assassin's gun. The country could have chosen worse and usually did: few presidents have come to the task with so much experience at governing and so many plodding virtues.[2] But Garfield would never have been nominated, much less elected, without experience of another kind: keeping the press gang at bay. He knew how to read an audience, but as an aspiring politician, he cared just as much that they read *him*. No public figure better serves to show how far the combination of the new journalistic stars and the old, the party press and the independent editors, the reporters and the exchange clippers could be put together to give one of politics' supporting players a faint aura of statesmanship.

In the proper mood, Garfield could belittle the press impact. Who cared what the Cincinnati *Times* said, for example? Its attacks, he wrote, had been carried to such absurd lengths that people generally dismissed them as personal spite. But he could not keep it from worrying him. Constantly, the letters went back and forth between his local fugleman, Charles E. Henry, and himself: how could the *Times* be neutralized? After all, its weekly edition had a large circulation in his district. Disgruntled farmers took it seriously. "I have watched carefully the papers generally read in the 19th District and find the enclosed most likely to do you harm," Henry wrote, enclosing an offending article. "The N.Y. *World* and *Sun* have but little influence whatever they may say. Is there no one in Cincinnati to set you right with the *Times*?"[3] Similarly, when something good was put out about him, Garfield could distribute it throughout his district. Thus, Henry saw to it that one particularly useful issue of the Cleveland *Herald* was spread by the hundreds. Garfield approved heartily. "Order as many *Heralds* as you think best and scatter them wherever you think they are needed," he wrote, "and I will cheerfully pay the bill."[4]

Because a newspaper had such importance, a canny politician could not ignore the internal fights inside a party organ about just who would control it. Bickerings between rival journals were no esoteric events. A congressman's future support hung on the outcome. He had to know who were friends with whom, not only to exploit jealousies, but also to escape the consequences of an exclusive alliance with one side or the other. With two faithful Republican organs in Cleveland, the *Herald* and the *Leader*, both widely read by his constituents, it hardly seemed that Garfield had anything to fear. Nor did he, as long as the two journals worked together. Woe upon him, however, when they threatened to "get by the ears . . . and fight like cats and dogs." The support he gave to one might just turn the other against him.[5] Too close a connection with any one newspaper might be more risk than benefit. Fulsome support itself stirred trouble, as Garfield's enemies, insisting that he owned the newspaper, vowed to raise the money to set up an antagonistic press.[6]

When a friend sold out his stock in a paper or enemies tried to buy in, a congressman had to know it at once. "There was a move made to get the *Niles Record* up to Warren [Ohio] and open out on you," Henry wrote him in early 1873 in one such case, "but after some talk they concluded not to risk the money necessary, as the editor gets drunk and Dyer could not be trusted with money needed to run it. [J. H.] Scofield [of the Painesville *Telegraph*] and Jules Converse told me that the Painesville *Journal* would only do you good in its attacks, as the paper had no character."[7] Then, two years later, Henry relayed more disturbing news. Scofield himself had spoken of leaving the newspaper business. Prospective buyers wished Garfield nothing but ill. "Whether you remain in public life or not," Henry warned, "we don't want the *Telegraph* to fall into hostile hands." Something must be done.[8]

Garfield's letters were full of speculations about newspapers—what they would do, where they stood, who would run them, and how little they could be relied on. If an article in the *Nation* did him honor, that got mention in Garfield's diary. If the "pirates of the Press" opened fire on the congressman's record, he would complain about it to his subordinates.[9] How, then, did a successful politician handle the press? How did he keep on good terms with it? Garfield may have been exceptional in this regard, or the paper trail that he left behind him may be all that was exceptional; but through his letters and diary, the historian can spot a consistent effort to keep the press on his good side.

Most important, to begin with, was to keep on good terms with the reporters and editors personally. This Garfield managed rather well, especially over a good meal. He might share a table at one of Washington's best restaurants with Treasury officers and Ben: Perley Poore or attend a dinner there to honor Murat Halstead of the Cincinnati *Commercial*. "Gath's" sparkling conversation enlivened a Sunday meal at home, and the journalist's prospects of selling a story to the *Atlantic* were enlivened as well by a personal note to the editor. Democratic journalists like William Henry Hurlbert of the New York *World* supped with Garfield and talked finances or, like William H. Roberts of the New Orleans *Times*, explored the possibilities for settling the election disputes of 1876. When General James M. Comly of the Columbus *Ohio State Journal* dined with the governor of the District of Columbia, Garfield attended; when Cowles of the Cleveland *Leader* came to town, the two men supped at a club; when Garfield went to New York, he breakfasted with Manton Marble of the *World* and paid a social call on the editor of the New York *Evening Post.*[10] When editors passed through the capital, they might stay overnight at Garfield's house. Traveling across Ohio, he might stay at theirs. Correspondent E. B. Wight of the Chicago *Tribune* joined him on horseback rides through the park, and Henry V. Boynton shared a carriage drive with him to the Soldiers' Home on a warm summer evening.[11] Going by train, it was only natural that he strike up a conversation with reporters or editors heading the same way.[12]

Access was only the first requirement. Attention must go further. It was not from simple courtesy that the congressman subscribed to the Cleveland *Leader*—or to the New York *Tribune* and *World* and the New York *Nation.*[13] Nor was it an incidental favor when Charles E. Henry sent his friend slips from Cleveland newspapers that might seem to have originated in the Nineteenth Congressional District. It was to Garfield's interest to see that his speeches were published in a form he approved, even if it meant that he had to go over the proofs at the newspaper office personally. Individual correspondents needed to be read with care and their actions monitored. "John was raving about you a few months ago but is strong in your favor now," Henry wrote about a local correspondent from Aurora. "A little attention to such noisy fellows sometimes wins them over; that attention was shown him by R. P. Cannon and myself."[14]

Garfield hardly needed surrogates. Editors who gave him friendly notice earned a letter of thanks, those who failed to notice matters he thought important received a corrective suggestion, and those who did him injury could expect to hear about it, not in indignation but in the plaintive tones of injured innocence. Indeed, Garfield often wrote without the stimulus of personal mention. Editors who stood for sound money or who favored reform and objected to the Grant administration were assured that Garfield shared their sympathies. "I hope you will continue to prick Congressional bubbles and lash 'Blatherskites' as you have so well done hitherto," the congressman wrote the *Nation*'s guiding spirit. "There ought to be a new 'Dunciad' written, each decade."[15] Personal blandishment only began the process. Friendly newspapers could expect copy. A full manuscript version of Garfield's latest speech, government documents otherwise hard to obtain, copies of the *Congressional Globe,* and leaked inside information all were at their service. The gift might have nothing to do with the congressman himself: a slip about a lecture on liberty delivered "in the very shadow of the Tuileries," a memorandum on the coolie trade from the British Foreign Anti-Slavery Society, official documents exposing Democrats for the liars they were. But, of course, a congressman had his own remarks in special abundance. The editor of the Geauga County *Republican* had Garfield to thank for the advance copy of a local address, the New York *Independent* was grateful for an article on financial topics, and other newspaper owners were nonplussed by the offer of a weekly letter from Washington provided for a fee by their congressman.[16]

Naturally, the evidence provided was self-serving. Garfield got publicity for what he said and for his own version of matters relating to himself. Still, his ministrations to the press went beyond advancing his own reputation. Newspapers that kept on the congressman's good side obtained authoritative confirmation of events in Washington. When other editors published material implicating President Grant in the Gold Ring of 1869 and charging Garfield with a cover-up, Frank H. Mason of the Cleveland *Leader* went right to the source for clarification. The odds of the Supreme Court overriding its decision on the Legal Tender law, the president's latest thoughts about the commissioner of internal revenue, the fate of the apportionment bill, the inside workings of a movement to release a swindler—the Ohio congressman was the ideal source on them all.[17]

A powerful politician had more than information to grant. There were any number of more specific favors he could do. Editors who needed a letter of introduction for their reporters to permit them to learn "the pure milk of the word" from other congressmen, or help in digging materials out of the War Department to further a history they were writing, or support in arranging a friend's discharge from the army could depend on Garfield.[18]

From all this, Garfield reaped plenty of advantages, and not just those of shaping the news to serve his own ends and furthering the newspaper "exchange" when it concerned himself. These, to be sure, were the main benefits.[19] But there was another real advantage. Editors were the ideal means of finding out what was actually going on in local politics. They could warn of factional trouble almost before it surfaced, passing on the faint grumbles of constituents to Washington. Press gallery reporters swapped information with their source; even some events in the capital reached Garfield's ears through the journalists. For the latest information on whether Republicans would carry New York, he could rely on Zebulon White; for the presidential prospects of Rutherford B. Hayes, Boynton was particularly well posted and happy to give him the facts as the two friends rode in the cool of the evening to the Soldiers' Home.[20]

An editor's closeness to public opinion was one reason that a congressman should heed his advice, but there was another. Whatever issue was concerned, a journalist might have an expertise that even the chairman of the Appropriations Committee lacked. From his correspondence, one might imagine that Joseph Medill's first thought when he woke in the morning was the money supply and that Samuel Bowles's last before slumbering was civil service reform. Having thought so long about the topics, they might have proposals worth considering. "I should be glad to receive your suggestions at all times," Garfield wrote Medill—in which case he must have been glad on a regular basis.[21]

Even at its most skillful, of course, news management had its limits. With party organs, it reinforced a loyalty already to be expected. With the independents, results were tentative, mixed, and unreliable. Garfield paid special attention to Halstead's Cincinnati *Commercial*, which affected national opinion as much as any journal in Ohio. When he gave a speech in Wilmington, Ohio, in 1872, he noticed that the paper had sent a shorthand reporter to cover his statements. Three years later, when he delivered another address, he provided a manuscript copy to *Commercial* reporters. When there was a dispute over who had won the presidency in 1876, Halstead was on hand to provide inside information for Garfield, and Garfield conferred with him about strategy. It appeared to be a very close relationship.[22]

So it was, but only from time to time. The *Commercial* kept being fractious. Reporters hired on the recommendation of regular Republicans "went off perfectly wild." "The little rascal knows he is lying," the congressman raged at one offender, "and for the first time Crete [Garfield's wife] shows belligerent anger against these people. She thinks I ought to horsewhip this man, but he is not worthy of it." Later in the year, the editorial page made trouble. Calming influences restored good feeling, but by the following summer, the *Commercial* was cutting up again, urging that Garfield be "hooted from the stump" for his views on silver.[23]

Nor was Halstead a unique case. Through Garfield's letters and diaries run fulminations at newspapermen's remarks. One day it might be "a long, stupid, malignant article of four columns" in the Cincinnati *Chronicle*; another day, it was the Cincinnati *Times* that needed fixing. "What do those fellows mean?" C. E. Henry asked him, on reading the Chicago *Tribune*. "It looks like personal spite."[24]

Garfield's relationship with Donn Piatt ranked among his closest. Theirs was a friendship extensively cultivated with visits to Piatt's home, invitations to dinner, personal discussions about the latest political developments, and consultations of the journalist for his views, always treated with grave respect. They went out horseback riding together of an afternoon or shopping of a morning, Piatt sent around theater tickets, and when the chief justice died, the two Ohioans traveled together on the nine o'clock train up to New York for the services there. Garfield even lent his aid in settling a quarrel that Piatt had begun with General Irwin McDowell.[25]

Even with Piatt, however, news management failed in the end. The friendship broke over the disputed presidential returns of 1876. Within months, the editor was denouncing his old ally as a race mixer who attended Negro dances, the apologist for traitors, "insincere as the devil" and an insult to the intellect. Piatt's temper would cool. A year later, he dismissed the very charges of corruption that he had made so much of, but he was not easily controlled, and the warm personal relationship between the two men was at an end.[26]

Yet Garfield should have felt satisfied on the whole, and grateful. At home, there were newspapers that Garfield could rely on whatever trouble he got into politically. Scofield's *Telegraph* was one, the Cleveland *Leader* another.[27] The *Leader* was no mere follower, to be sure. It backed someone else for the Senate in 1871 and on occasion misstated his position; still, it did him good whenever circumstances permitted. In 1879, Garfield balked at a potential movement to nominate him for governor. When the Washington correspondent for the Cleveland *Leader* mentioned the gubernatorial possibility, Garfield urged that it stifle any such dispatches, and his friends acted at once. When Garfield visited Connecticut, his trip was covered in a special to the Cleveland *Leader*, with Henry's approval.[28]

In Washington, Garfield's methods worked especially well. From Boynton came appreciation as one of the rising young men of the party, and from the press gallery notes of commendation when he did especially well. From George Alfred Townsend came word portraits free of all but the gentlest criticism. To hear him tell it, the Ohio congressman was "sweet and gentle in nature, . . . exceptionally well read," the idol of "young men of education," the boon companion of scholarly celebrities. "Gath" even carried his blandishments into verse:

> Regret not now, while meaner pagans play
> Their brief campaigns against the best of men!
> For these spent balls of scandal pass their way,
> And thou shalt see the victory again.
> Modest and faithful, though these broken lines
> Of party reel and thine own honor bleeds,
> That mole is blind which Garfield undermines,
> The dart falls short which hired malice speeds,
> That man will stay whose place the state assigns,
> And whose high mind a mighty people needs.[29]

When the poem appeared in 1874, the people may have needed a reminder, for Garfield faced the roughest challenge of his House career. The Credit Mobilier scandal had broken, and the Ohio congressman was among those exposed as a recipient of special stock deals from Oakes Ames. There were other revelations, less publicized but even more unsavory, about a pavement contract. The DeGolyer firm produced shoddy material, yet Boss Alexander Shepherd of Washington's Board of Public Works had accepted its bid for work after Garfield paid him a visit. Was it for the brief that Garfield filed, critics wondered, that he had earned a lawyer's fee equal to one year of a congressman's pay? Or could it have been for the influence that the head of the House Appropriations Committee knew how to wield with a board dependent on government money? Finally and most controversially, the Forty-second Congress had celebrated its departure with a law raising official salaries, including its own retroactively. It was true that Garfield had opposed the grab and refused to dun the Treasury for his own share of it, but Ohio voters might well have overlooked that fact. After all, he had been on the conference committee that the Speaker had stacked to push the pay increase through. In the end, he had gone along with the rest.

Greater men had been wrecked by revelations less damning. In Ohio, mass meetings called for Garfield to resign. "Good men in various places swing their fists and say they *never will* vote for you again," his old friend Burke Hinsdale wrote. "Ames and Colfax are received by their constituents with ovations," the congressman lamented. "My constituents are hunting for ropes to hang me with."[30] But Garfield survived. Patronage helped; so did a friendly Speaker and a host of other issues to distract the voters, but the press gang's energies also counted heavily.

All across Ohio, a corps of editors leaped to his defense. When the Cincinnati *Chronicle* made trouble, Burke Hinsdale gave him an evaluation of its damage. Thanks to Hinsdale and Henry, the Cleveland *Herald* and *Leader* moved quickly to "set the people right on the Salary Question." Long cultivation of newspapermen made it easy enough to plant articles. Possessed of a "scorcher" on Garfield's behalf, Henry put it in the Cleveland *Leader* and gave the staff pointers on how to "gore" more hostile journalists. "The enclosed has been published in nearly every county paper in Ohio," Henry wrote Garfield in early 1874. "I think the idea is getting into the heads of the people that you are really trying to save something for the Government."[31]

Whatever their later bitterness, Piatt did yeoman's work on his friend's behalf now. He sent a letter to the Cincinnati *Commercial* defending the congressman (and himself) from attacks relating to Credit Mobilier. When Garfield was renominated the following year, the *Sunday Capital* hailed it as vindication. Garfield, Piatt declared, was "a leader of the little band of pure men whose high-toned integrity gives us renewed hope for the republic." Bright, of tremendous attainments, kindhearted to a fault, and well-meaning, Ohio could have no better favorite son.[32]

Trouble with the Andover *Enterprise* needed a more forceful hand. It had no wide circulation, but, as Charles E. Henry noted, it could do "some mischief." After one "absurd and false" attack in its columns that imputed to the Ohio congressman a willingness to raise taxes and described a House vote against such a desire as a rebuke to him, Garfield wrote home in protest. "We can get along with knaves," he grumbled, "but a fool is hard to manage." Not, as it turned out, as hard as all that: the publisher, J. S. Morley, was also postmaster and Republican mayor of Andover. Both positions made him vulnerable to pressure, especially the former, which Garfield had obtained for him. Henry paid him a visit to win, if not his support, at least his silence. "I found his office in bad shape," he wrote Garfield, and "admonished him somewhat sharply, calling his attention to several sections in the Postal Laws that he had violated. After asking him how Genl. Garfield helped him, I put the question: 'How you stood with the people there.' He replied that he was all right but 'some wasent.' I replied that I was glad that he was all right as Genl. Garfield was an able and good man." That was nearly all the inducement Morley needed—that and Henry arranging for a subscription to the *Enterprise* so that a closer eye could be kept on its pronouncements. The publisher's goodwill was augmented by his hope that Garfield would give the post office status as a money order office and increase his revenue. "Little digs" did appear, but on the whole Garfield had every right to be satisfied.[33]

So much for Ohio; what of the national press? Here, too, long cultivation paid off. Boynton was ready to read Garfield's self-defense and make the arguments his own. When dispatches were set to go over the wires, provided by an unfriendly witness on the DeGolyer pavement affair, the New York *Times* correspondent dropped by the capitol to show them to Garfield first and give him a chance to quiz the accuser and obtain a retraction; the correspondent also promised to visit the Associated Press offices and arrange for a correction. Garfield had no need to worry about the New York *Tribune*'s reporter as long as the man covering the House was Eugene V. Smalley, an old friend who owed his job to the congressman's recommendation. Running matters in New York was Whitelaw Reid, whose friendship with Garfield dated back to the Civil War. Many were the times they had dined together in New York or exchanged political confidences. When Reid wanted a speaker for a rally to celebrate the unification of Italy, he thought of Garfield; when he wanted help against a rival editor or suppression of some damaging letters, his friend in the House proved indispensable.[34]

Now Reid was ready to help with advice and support. Would he look over a reply that the congressman had written? "Of course I will be glad to look through anything you may choose to send," Reid assured him, "but if you trust my good will at all you will write nothing for publication. . . . Shut your mouth and keep it shut." (Reid soon changed his mind.) The *Tribune* could hardly afford to whitewash Garfield's role in the "salary grab" or in Credit Mobilier, but it found more than enough extenuation to set him right with its readers. Indeed, after one editorial criticizing his actions, Garfield was offered an exceptional deal: let him write "a communication, not over your own signature, but making the best statement of the case you can" and send it in.[35]

That fall, when Speaker Blaine was listening to advice to throw implicated committee chairmen overboard, he heard louder voices from the reform editors. Long cultivated by Garfield, they now made clear that however much they wanted politics scoured of its rascals, certain statesmen had best be left alone—that is, if the Speaker had any ambitions for higher office. Samuel Bowles of the Springfield *Republican* vowed to tell Blaine that if he dropped Garfield, "he will do the stupidest thing of his life. He won't do it; he can't do it!" Nor did he.[36]

Garfield's success in handling the press therefore showed the limits to which a politician could manage the journalists. He could not suppress stories entirely, nor could he turn editors and correspondents into his uncritical and fawning servitors. Even party papers needed unremitting attention; even personal friends in the Washington press corps could turn more personal and less friendly. But a discreet man could create a temperate enough climate so that those who commented on politics would give him the benefit of the doubt, and those who collected the news about politics would give him a certain amount of prior restraint on coverage. The strategy was not perfect—but it worked. When Garfield ran for the House again in 1874, he did not win by his usual generous margin, but he won. The DeGolyer scandal would come up again, with new detail. Other allegations would be turned against him. None of it made any difference, not even to his more restive allies. "The trouble with Gen. Garfield is not dishonesty or greed, but *greenness* in money matters," Murat Halstead's *Commercial* explained.[37] Halstead was being generous, but then, that was only natural: whatever his other failings, Garfield was far from green when dealing with the press.

CHAPTER 11

The Silent Smoker in the Hands of the Foe

In the columns of his New York *Sun*, at least, editor Charles A. Dana lived a remarkable fantasy life, spotting conspiracy and fraud where none appeared and heeding rumor with creative skill. But even paranoid men have real enemies. Early in 1871, two of them opened up on their old employer in a sensational pamphlet, "The Biter Bit," exposing the blackmail racket that the *Sun* had practiced with the conspirators who tried to corner the gold market in 1869.[1]

The charge could not have been more convenient for President Grant. Dana was among his most savage critics, especially in documenting the president's official incompetence, if not personal complicity, in the Gold Ring. The more the editor thought about it, the more suspicious the attack on his character looked. The pamphlet had been printed in Washington. Reports alleged that Grant's crony Ben Butler had paid the authors' hotel expenses while they prepared the attack. It was said that Secretary of State Hamilton Fish had revised the proofs himself. Why had the journalists been given government sinecures? Who had paid the printing costs? The questions were purely rhetorical. Dana knew that the trail led to the White House itself.[2]

That such ugly suspicions could thrive said as much about the spirit of press relations with the administration as it did about Dana's feverish imagination. Before Grant left office, Henry V. Boynton would recall, only one Washington correspondent out of more than a hundred would even deign to visit the White House. They were full of resentments, and that ill-feeling transferred itself to their reports. "All of Newspaper Row is against him," an insider told Hiram J. Ramsdell in 1871. "With the exception of the New York Times there is no leading journal of the country whose representatives here are with the Administration. That is true, sir, and is a significant truth, too." It was significant, indeed, but not only for the reason Ramsdell imagined, that it showed the president's unfitness to govern. It also suggested that the administration's bad reputation might owe something to its bad press.[3]

The ill will need not have been so strong and so deep. At first, the independent press was eager to say the best about Grant. "The new Cabinet means business emphatically," Horace Greeley wired the New York *Tribune* from Washington. "Each man was chosen . . . expressly to aid [Grant] in carrying out the programme of economy and integrity embodied in the inaugural."[4]

The honeymoon did not last; as reformers fell from the cabinet and mediocrities replaced them, and as scandals on Wall Street and in the Caribbean cast some of Grant's kin and comrades in less attractive roles, the press reaction turned harsh. From the president's cadre rose cries of outrage and injury. As Grant's brother-in-law, New Orleans collector of the port James Casey, told Horace V. Redfield, "the *Commercial* gets mighty wrong sometimes." Another of the president's in-laws was less kind. "That's the paper that's been pitching into us so much," he exclaimed; "it's been giving us fury."[5] Cabinet officers went from exasperation to exasperation at what they read. One story about Attorney General Amos Akerman's ambitions was, as he put it dryly, "in large excess of the degree of lying allowed by usage of democratic journals."[6] There is no record of what Attorney General Ebenezer Rockwood Hoar felt about Donn Piatt's canard that he had subscribed $10,000 to the construction of a leading Boston hotel and had collected $40,000 from the other promoters when it was completed by demanding that it be named for himself ("It would have been so awkward when the trains came in to have a fellow bawling, "Ere's ye'r omnibus for the Hoar House,'" one of his friends purportedly explained), but one could hardly imagine that it improved already chilly relations between himself and its author.[7]

From where did so unpleasant a relationship arise? The most obvious reason why journalists might not be impressed with Grant was that he was not very impressive. "In the Grant atmosphere, masculine or feminine," Mary Clemmer Ames admitted, "there is no hint of intellectual grace, no music, no aesthetic culture, no filtering of thought, no finer aspirations." Though Piatt meant it as a defense, it was one of the weakest sort when he protested that Grant knew nothing and needed to know nothing.[8] But then, Grant's administration provoked widespread disappointment, even among his followers. The settlement of disputes with Great Britain was accomplished without war, but not without years of ham-handed diplomacy. Members of the administration stole or helped their friends do so. They endowed kin with extortionate contracts and grabbed perquisites far beyond what the law allowed. Radicals grieved at how slowly the president moved against the terrorism, intimidation, and fraud that Democrats were using to undermine the Reconstruction governments of the South. Conservatives fumed that he propped up such artificial creations at all. To all outward appearances, Grant presided more than he governed, left domestic affairs to Congress and the cabinet, and applied his energies only in distasteful ways, like his attempt to pass a treaty annexing Santo Domingo. In that he not only failed but also provoked a quarrel with the head of the Senate Foreign Relations Committee, Charles Sumner, that ended in the administration depriving Sumner of his chairmanship. For all these reasons, Grant's eight years rank among the tawdriest of the nineteenth century.[9]

Any defense of Grant, then, will have to be as pallid as Piatt's: his deficiencies were not as great as the press made them out to be. Still, it is a defense worth making. The president was neither a thief nor a fool. With Andrew Johnson's disastrous attempts to make policy fresh in his mind, Grant may actually have shown greater political realism than his later critics in letting Congress take the lead. With a few exceptions, presidents in the nineteenth century presided. Making policy, using the veto power generously, went beyond what tradition expected of them, especially the Whig party tradition to which the Republicans owed so much. Indeed, Grant earned the most infamy when he exerted himself, not alone for what he did, but for not minding his own business. There were plenty of newspapers ready to raise fears of the Union's greatest general becoming dictator and plenty of readers ready to believe it.[10] If anything, the president's historical reputation has suffered most for having done too little in Reconstruction, precisely the area where most of the independent and Democratic press thought he did too much. Grant went as far as Northern public opinion let him; when he advanced further, it cost him dearly.

On Reconstruction, then, the president may well have been more right on the issues than his critics in the press. He was certainly a shrewder politician than they gave him credit for, and a better man. There were ideological reasons why the "independent press" treated his administration so harshly, and those no press management could have controlled. But the attacks on Grant went beyond a disagreement about public issues or even a clear-sighted appreciation of the administration's moral depravity. Much of the venom came from the president's miserable relations with journalists.

When it came to handling editors, admittedly, Grant was no clumsier than his predecessors. Government patronage and ready access to presidential aides gave the administration a largely subservient Washington press. The *National Republican* had eight years' experience in echoing the views of whichever administration happened to be in power, and its ready support was well rewarded. Among other favors, Grant made its editor police commissioner of the District in spite of a pending indictment; Congress had to abolish the whole Police Board to prevent the appointment. The *Chronicle* might have been expected to show more stamina, but three years of fighting one president were enough for John W. Forney, and the rewards for cooperation were too enticing when the president and the proprietor had no vital difference in principle separating them. As one critic put it, the "official atmosphere seemed to settle like a fog and soften and rot every part" of the *Chronicle*. When Grant's onslaught against Charles Sumner began, and Forney had to choose between backing the administration and standing by his friend, he retired from the paper and let others savage the senator's character.[11]

In Elmira, Syracuse, Saratoga, and Niagara Falls, editors became postmasters; those in Canton and Troy, New York, became collectors of the port. New York *Standard* editor John Russell Young took $6,000 for running administration errands to Europe, while a New York *Herald* reporter inspected consulates in the South Seas. No concerted effort was made to win over the metropolitan papers, though Philadelphia's were an exception. There, Forney became collector of the port, another newspaperman was made pension agent, another naval officer, and a fourth solicitor of internal revenue.[12]

Grant's friends had other means of fine-tuning press opinion. They planted articles defending the president or wrote appeals to their friends in the newspaper fraternity. When "Deacon" Richard Smith of the Cincinnati *Gazette* came to town, the secretary of state invited him to a reception. Grant welcomed him for Sunday dinner and several hours of chat in the Blue Room. After months of erratic political support, the *Gazette* became a slightly more faithful backer of the administration.[13]

About the mendacity and malice of the opposition press, there was little that Grant could have done. Like his predecessors, he was accused of everything conceivable, from stealing silverware in wartime to sharing the take of freebooting officeholders in peace.[14] In such an age, not even the best administration could have escaped calumny, though its source made it easy for party loyalists to discount, however pesky the allegations might be.

Two developments that other presidents had not faced made Grant's problems unusually severe: the rise of an independent, and therefore relatively credible and intractable, press in the big cities and the growing significance of the Washington correspondent.

The clash between newshounds and the administration seems to have been almost inevitable. By the time Grant took office, the press gang had a new sense of its own power and, worse, its own right to learn things from administration spokesmen. Journalists were more energetic in suggesting what the administration needed to do and more indignant when it failed to do it. As Johnson's outgoing Attorney General William Evarts grumbled, the press was "giving unmistakeable signs of carrying on the Government *'toutes seules.'*" Before Grant's inauguration, rumors about the cabinet were let loose and bogus interviews published to put the president-elect on the spot and make him reveal his choices. (It did not work.)[15]

Handling newspapers untrammeled by party allegiance would require tools other than well-worn implements of patronage, and those tools Grant never found. Indeed, he never explored ways for managing the reporters, though possibilities did exist. However much they came to dislike him as a president, the reporters admired him as a soldier. When the journalists held a banquet in early 1872, the president was invited and attended, responding to a toast, "To the Sword." Years after his presidency closed, Grant attended press club banquets as the guest of honor.[16] Nor was the president a baby politician where news management was concerned. He knew well enough how to use press leaks to get what he wanted from Congress. In 1874, as the Senate prepared to vote on the so-called inflation bill, the president passed on his own views to reporters, including his readiness to veto any bill as radical as seemed likely to pass. Counting votes, the Senate managers beat a hasty retreat. When the president did veto the final product, their anger was the greater because they felt double-crossed: they had given ground when directed to do so. When a substitute measure went through, Grant intervened again, this time with a public letter to a leading senator. It did more than specify what he would consider acceptable. The letter marshaled the independent press to his side. Again the Senate changed course.[17]

Moments like that, however, came all too rarely. Occasionally responsive to journalism's potential, Grant preferred to leave the reporters alone. The simplest steps were overlooked in cultivating good feeling. As Ramsdell suggested, it would have done the president no harm to invite correspondents to dinner the way Speaker James G. Blaine did, or to hold a picnic beneath the shade trees in front of the White House; it might even have softened "Gath" or Piatt to have received the royal treatment.[18]

Without Grant himself expressing his views of the press, the men around him set the tone. That veered between indifference and hostility, with the indifference perhaps the more insulting. "We don't care a darn what the papers say," sneered the president's brother-in-law, General Louis Dent, "for the people have got this thing to decide." Calling at the Post Office Department, reporters were turned away by the first assistant postmaster general's secretary with a scornful, "Mr. Earle wants no newspaper puffs this morning."[19]

To be shut out of stories was worse than any personal slight. Instead of Johnson's garrulity, Grant gave correspondents silence. Journalists came to take down his remarks and got a whiff of cigar smoke and a few taciturn comments.[20] Reporters protested bitterly when they were turned away from the White House by ushers and told that no one was allowed upstairs on cabinet days or even permitted to send up a card. The journalists complained still more in 1871, when the president invited a delegation of Louisiana Republicans for a personal conference and shut the press corps out. The New York *Sun* gave a clue to why he might have thought it unworthy of recognition; Louisiana politics were run by packed conventions enforced with Gatling guns, and there was "every public reason to believe that the President himself was a party to this atrocious transaction." The less publicity that connection got, the better.[21]

Others kept strictly aloof. Amos Akerman, attorney general for a brief period, kept his own counsel and told the press nothing about his duties, which was one reason that journalists treated him as a cipher. When he quit, a hundred different explanations were given by the press and all of them, at least according to Akerman, were ludicrously wrong. But he never let anyone know what the right one would have been. Other cabinet officers made special efforts to plug up all leaks by specific instructions to bureau heads.[22]

The president's silence meant that the voice of the reputed organ for his administration carried a more personal weight. Any weight was too much for the *National Republican* to bear. As one critic charged, the paper was "pitched from stem to stern with all the filth of Washington." Heading it was W. J. Murtagh, described by one of his foes as "a half educated, unprincipled little Irishman" with a well-practiced talent at blackmail. Rumor said he even plied his trade successfully on Donn Piatt by setting a defamatory article in type, sending him a copy, and then demanding silence on certain issues in return for the essay's suppression. Subsidies from the District Ring and funds from publishing naval contracts and War Department advertisements for the sale of mules kept the newspaper going—just barely. Many a Republican would have wished it had gone under the hammer sooner. It not only spoke with the voice of Congressman Benjamin F. Butler, who provided Murtagh with a personal loan. It opened its columns to the president's private secretary, Orville E. Babcock. On occasion it let him pronounce the foreign policy views of the administration, views that the secretary of state took no part in making. As scandals broke, the *National Republican* affected to speak for the administration in blaming election defeats on the efforts of Congress to economize and reform the civil service. Critics seethed at attacks on them that seemed to have the administration's official imprimatur: Murat Halstead of the *Commercial* as bribe taker, Horace White of the Chicago *Tribune* as front man for the tax-dodging distillers in the Whiskey Ring, Whitelaw Reid as a hireling slanderer of Abraham Lincoln.[23]

This did not mean that the press had no means of finding out what was going on in the Grant administration. Quite the reverse was true.

Every newsman found his own source for information. On close terms with Charles Nordhoff and Whitelaw Reid of the reform Republican New York *Evening Post* and *Tribune,* and equally well situated through his in-law Sidney Webster to curry favor on the Democratic New York *World,* Hamilton Fish could count on both for a fair hearing and gave them plenty to listen to. As for the regular Republicans at the *Times,* they could expect missives clarifying the secretary of state's position and distancing the secretary from the president's Southern policy. When the *Times* wanted to show up the *Herald*'s reporter in Havana, it was able to publish a confidential letter from the acting consul general there, courtesy of the secretary of state.[24] The *Tribune* found a useful source of information in Attorney General George Williams, who leaked materials to Hiram Ramsdell. It was all done in what would later be called deep background; Williams would not permit the information to appear in dispatches. It had to show up obliquely in an editorial comment as long as his own name was not involved. Even Collector Casey was prepared to help the New York *Tribune* with inside information.[25]

These sources had their own serious drawbacks. Solicitor Bluford Wilson was voluble about administration involvement in the Whiskey Ring, and Henry Van Ness Boynton passed on the information to reporters less openly tied to their Treasury Department contacts. Pillage was easy to uncover, generally with the help of what the New York *Sun* called "honest men in the Treasury Department," but smear flowed more readily.[26] Cabinet officers carried out their vendettas against each other, through their special contacts, and built up their own reputations as reformers at the president's expense, while Grant's ever-officious military cronies and in-laws were always ready to leak startling revelations about administration foreign policy—startling, at least, to the president and the secretary of state, always the last to be informed. When Secretary Fish mentioned in one cabinet meeting that a certain congressman was reported to have been "indirectly offered" the State Department, Grant commented dryly, "it must have been in the most indirect way possible, so much so that I could not have been conscious of the question or the offer."[27]

How oblivious to the twaddling press was Grant after all? From journalists' accounts, it would seem that for his breakfast reading he was served the flattering encomiums of the Washington *Chronicle* and *National Republican*; but he closed his evening with the New York *Tribune* and *World,* both of which could be stinging. Horace V. Redfield reported that the president's clerks made daily clippings from the major newspapers to keep abreast of what they said about him. It was quite a collection: "a peck a day, and after business hours he takes a cigar and goes into them as a horse would a feed of oats." (Of course, Redfield could not resist a plug for his own newspaper, which, he maintained, the clerk put in whole, "for if he should clip out everything from it that Grant wanted to see there would be nothing left but the margin.") In view of the newspapers' general level of reliability, all of these reports need to be taken cautiously.[28] But there was no question that the president felt the cut of the journalists' remarks, however little he expressed his feelings in public. One of the few jokes the he was credited with came when he was called upon to dismiss an appointee who had killed a newspaperman: "What! remove a postmaster for shooting an editor? I ought to promote him."[29]

Others in his family expressed the same thinking in a more active form. Louis Dent, Grant's brother-in-law, did not object when the press accused him of being an influence peddler. It was, after all, his profession. Nor did he make a public fuss when the *Sun* called him a liar and a coward. But he lost his temper when the *Sunday Capital* made some personal remarks about the president's wife and daughter. Calling at the newspaper offices, he pounded editor Henry Reed with a club and then spent a night in the city jail.[30] When W. S. Walker ("Gideon") of the Chicago *Times* compared the president's son Fred to the Prince of Wales, the reference was more to debauchery than to royal lineage. Accused of companionship with bawds, drunkards, and blackguards, "a military gem unset in the rich experience of combat," he was described as having spent not a sober day since arriving in Washington and frequenting brothels three nights a week. Any real lady would slap his face, the reporter charged. In three days of hunting with gun and club, Fred never found "Gideon," though a few days later an equally abused "Gath" did and battered him with a gingham umbrella. In 1875 another Chicago *Times* reporter barely escaped a thrashing when he asked Fred for an interview, and a year later the president's son ended up in court for striking a journalist in the face. ("It was only a reporter for an evening paper, however," the Cincinnati *Enquirer* reassured its readers.)[31]

Nor was "The Biter Bit" exceptional. Others around the president engaged in espionage against offending journalists. A minor Treasury official tried to frame Henry Boynton for extortion by having an actor impersonate the reporter and demand a shakedown in front of witnesses.[32] Donn

"Upon What Meat Doth This Our Caesar Feed That He Hath Grown So
Great?"—Daily Press Question (Thomas Nast, *Harper's Weekly*, December 5,
1874). With Hamilton Fish as steward and Secretary of the Navy George
Robeson and Secretary of War William W. Belknap as waiters, Emperor Ulysses
dines on editors: Whitelaw Reid as the peacock, Charles A. Dana as the fish, and
the younger James Gordon Bennett as the calf's head.

Piatt claimed that administration figures employed the Secret Service to
unearth embarrassing facts from his private life and to feed friendly newspapers with "the most infamous lies hot decay ever engendered," including
scurrilous anonymous letters. The president himself turned to Secretary
of State Fish for help in finding damaging information from Piatt's and
George Alfred Townsend's pasts.[33]

More often, Grant responded to newspaper criticism in a more indirect
way. He simply refused to give editors the satisfaction of doing as they
demanded. So it was with the charges against his second secretary of
the interior, Columbus Delano. By 1875, the evidence of mismanagement,
favoritism, and corrupt dealings in the department had mounted too high
for Grant to ignore. The president knew perfectly well that Delano had
to go. Indeed, in mid-April he demanded his resignation. Then newspaper
charges appeared against the secretary, unsubstantiated and slanderous,

and Grant postponed action. When Delano finally offered his resignation that June, the president refused to accept it publicly. For months, the Interior Department remained in Delano's hands. "I did not like the nature of the attack upon him, nor the people who made it," Grant explained later. If Boynton's sources were correct, indeed, Delano played on precisely that presidential obstinacy. Knowing that he would be kept in as long as he was under fire, the secretary used his friends in the Washington press to leak the story that Newspaper Row's journalists were beginning their assaults on him again.[34]

Then there were the snubs. General Dent, who kept watch over the door to the president's private office, treated the press shabbily from the first; he even threatened to throw a few journalists out of the windows. At the official public reception on New Year's Day in 1874, reporters were thrust into the anteroom along with lackeys and valets of foreign ministers. It was the third time this outrage had happened, a Washington correspondent complained, laying the blame on Orville Babcock: "Very few newspapermen, save those connected with the city press, have taken the trouble to visit the White House, in the past year or two, for the purpose of writing accounts of official ceremonies, as the treatment they receive is intolerable."[35]

In so poisoned an atmosphere, reporters were ready to see petty slights, even where none was meant. After the defeat of the Santo Domingo treaty, when the president was allowed the chance to save face by sending a special fact-finding commission to Santo Domingo, newspapers clamored for the chance to accompany the expedition. But permission had to be approved and processed by obliging bureaucrats. These were not so easily found for the New York *Tribune*, which happened to be sharply critical of administration policy and had published much of the evidence that helped defeat the treaty's confirmation the summer before. Secretary of the Navy George Robeson insisted on a letter from editor Horace Greeley himself before he would permit credentials to be issued to its reporter, Hiram J. Ramsdell. Suspicions arose that the delays were meant to bring the *Tribune* to heel or to punish it. Donn Piatt spread the tale (demonstrably false) that Grant had been willing to send a *Tribune* man until he heard Ramsdell mentioned. Actually, Ramsdell ended up among the seven journalists brought on board. So was Henry V. Boynton, another frank critic of the president's Santo Domingo policy. Zebulon L. White, Washington bureau chief for the *Tribune*, blamed the whole affair on excess red tape.

Still, the response of the press was unsettling. All along Newspaper Row, reporters egged on the *Tribune* to repay authorities injury for insult.[36]

From so ill-fated a relationship a host of falsehoods not only developed, but also went unrebuffed. Some of them were the maunderings of ill-informed men. Not all of them were as irresponsible as the *Herald*'s Washington reporter, whose detailed transcription of presidential conversations came as easily as the conversations in Oliver Wendell Holmes's *Autocrat of the Breakfast Table* and from the same source: a fertile imagination. When Donn Piatt predicted that three members of the cabinet were about to retire in early 1871, he gave good, plausible reasons. So did every newspaperman who reported the retirement of Secretary Fish then and after. The only thing missing was the confirmation of fact. Fish stayed on as long as Grant did; Piatt's predictions for a cabinet reshuffle erred in every detail.[37] Several years later, the New York *Tribune* spent much energy announcing at regular intervals the resignation of General Daniel Sickles as minister to Spain. "This is a department of news which it has made peculiarly its own," the rival New York *Times* noted. "How many times has it positively announced the resignation of Secretary [of the Treasury William] Richardson? About fifty, at the very least. Yet Mr. Richardson stands where he did."[38]

Accidents of fact were less significant than misstatements of motivation, and here the press did far more to damage the president. Leading the way among the independent journals was Dana's *Sun*. Where evidence was lacking against presidential appointees, the *Sun* invented what it needed. Objecting to George Butler as consul general to Alexandria, Egypt, it accused him of being a subsidized Spanish agent. The *Sun* even forged a letter in shocking language, fixed his signature to the bottom, and then used the concoction to rebuke him for using profane terms in a family newspaper. Equally devastating was the *Sun*'s list of presidential kin placed in office. It might have been even more so if the list had not included total strangers, appointees chosen before Grant's administration, and former Confederate general James Longstreet.[39]

Another embarrassment was the scandal involving the Seneca Sandstone Company. Its quarries in Maryland produced a red sandstone, but the firm's ease in supplying nearby Washington was not the real source of its attraction. That, the story went, came from the promoters pouring out shares of stock where they would do the most good. "Newspaper Row bought clothes with S.S.S. stock, while the lobby left it in security for drinks at Welcker's." House members sent Seneca certificates home to their wives. Senators and cabinet officers took stock gladly. Most of all, President Grant received a substantial share—$25,000 as a "gift"—in return for which he made Henry D. Cooke, the company president, territorial governor of the District of Columbia. Naturally, the company did a thriving business in Washington and, reportedly, among federal officials. Every walk around the national capital was paved with Seneca stone. So were the national cemeteries. Only a robber could bring down a robber: Benjamin F. Butler, with interests in Massachusetts granite quarries, managed to block the Seneca Sandstone Company's bid to supply the new War Department, Navy Department, and State Department buildings by an indignant exposure of conflicts of interest.[40]

It was a lovely story, seasoned by a light sprinkling of truth. Butler's friends in the Cape Ann Granite Company had made a killing off government contracts. The Seneca company *had* included prominent backers from its start in 1867, among them General Dent, Cooke, and the secretary of state. They were buying into an established concern and each paid $10,000 in cash for a share. The stone, its financiers seem to have believed, was the best building stone in the world. Even before the company's formation, it had been used to make the Smithsonian Institute and the Cookes' dwelling in Georgetown. Private orders poured in, more than the present force could have possibly fulfilled. Certainly the Cookes continued to profit by it, and Henry D. Cooke, as president of the District of Columbia, took good care of his investment. Not yet president, General Grant had bought in on the same terms as the rest. By the time he went to the White House, he had lost interest in his investment; indeed, far from encouraging government contracts in Seneca Sandstone, he positively forbade federal authorities to use it on the grounds of his own conflict of interest.[41]

Grant's failure in this case had been one of omission: the lack of a speedy, well-documented reply. No such excuse can be made for his handling of the resignation of Secretary of the Interior Jacob D. Cox. There, all too many people around the president knew just how the story ought to be managed and did just about everything wrong they possibly could. The scandal was not simply a cautionary tale in White House fumbling and reporters' intrigues. It was one of the defining moments of Grant's administration in reformers' eyes.

It had to be, with a dedicated reformer like Cox at the center. In his battle against spoilsmen and corrupt Indian contractors, the secretary had been one of Grant's happiest choices and by late 1870 had become the rather lonely symbol of the administration's higher-minded side. That loneliness was intensifying as summer ended. The cormorants who clustered around the Indian Bureau, the railroad magnates eyeing public lands reserved for white settlers and native Indian tribes, and the hack politicians clamoring for the right to extort "voluntary" contributions from Interior Department employees all were closing in; finally, there was that "animated sewer," the claim that William McGarrahan made on the Panoche Grande. Cox needed a friend at the White House and, until recently, could have sworn that he had one. Now Grant, too, seemed to be slipping away from him.[42]

Then, on October 3, smarting from one affront too many, Cox sent in a curt if courteous letter of resignation, which he very much hoped would not be accepted. It was, and at once. Not for nearly a fortnight would the public learn what had happened, and when it did, the press was full of questions, all the more so because White House spokesmen at the president's behest had been insisting that there was no resignation. (This was technically true: Cox had deferred his actual departure until the annual report of the department was completed.)[43] From the president came a studied public silence about the reasons for Cox's departure (which, since the secretary left in protest over Grant's failure to back up civil service reform, was understandable just before midterm elections), but privately, neither Grant nor his aides were as circumspect. Friendly editors were assured that Cox was quitting for reasons of such a "purely private character" that they could not "in justice to the Secretary" be made public, though the president listed five of them in specific for two New York journalists,[44] all supposedly drawn from Cox's letter and actually from Grant's imagination. As the questions persisted, other White House sources gave darker hints that Cox had been hastened on his way by the curious way in which he had handled the McGarrahan claim.[45]

Grant was too clever by half. Neither he nor the jobbers had given a thought to the broad paper trail left behind them. Smarting as his friends who knew the truth compared accounts, the secretary grew madder as every new White House leak further obscured the truth. An "official & authoritative dispatch" in the Associated Press was the last straw, and when L. A. Gobright of the AP credited it to the president himself, Cox pulled out several of his letters to supplicating partisans, his own letter of resignation, and Grant's eulogy in reply and handed them over to his friends in the press. They created, as Charles Nordhoff of the New York *Evening Post* told him, "a profound sensation"—especially in the White House, where Cox's discretion had been counted on and a farewell dinner arranged for the very night that the publication occurred. (As it might be imagined, Cox did not attend.) "It seems to me that the President has fatally & finally disgraced himself," the editor added.[46]

At that point, the smartest thing the administration could have done would have been to let bad enough alone. Instead, it set out to discredit Cox by issuing a sheaf of letters of its own, none of them mentioning the resignation and all relating to the McGarrahan case. Suspicious minds could make the proper connection, with a little nudging from Grant's editorial writers, notably those on the Washington *Chronicle*. With John Forney to do the actual writing and Senator Oliver P. Morton of Indiana to advise him, Grant and his friends set to work on an official statement, which, as Cox was warned, would be "some kind of a political hell-broth."[47]

There were only a few drawbacks to the administration's technique, all of them lethal. First, Cox had more documents, putting his relationship with the McGarrahan claim in its true light, and witnesses able to show that something very like a bribe had been offered to Cox's friends to win them over. He was ready to release them, and before the end of November did so. Second and more important, Cox found the ablest members of the Washington press gang on his side. More important than all the rest were "Gath," Donn Piatt, Henry Boynton of the Cincinnati *Gazette*, Scott Smith of the *Evening Post*, and Smith's boss, Charles Nordhoff. Nordhoff listened fascinated as Cox's brother Charles regaled him with the full story.[48] Days before the official statement came out, Boynton knew all about it and was doing his best to undercut it. When Smith needed information about the McGarrahan claim, Boynton knew just where it could be found. When Senator Carl Schurz of Missouri, a reform Republican already badly on the outs with Grant, returned to the capital, it was Boynton who "gave him an inkling of the men mixed up in the McG. fraud." If Schurz "gets at the head of a committee to look into it," the reporter confided, "there will be some blood drawn."[49] Hinting to Morton that Cox had written evidence of bribery attempts, he made the men around Grant hesitate. "It seemed to me that even a day's delay would be a great gain, because it would give time for all papers which had said nothing to speak before they are puzzled by any plausible story from the White House," he wrote the former secretary. Three days later, the official statement was ready. "From newspaper friends *inside politics* I have a positive promise that I shall have a copy *before* it goes off," Boynton assured Cox, "& possibly the only one that will go west. Forney is in charge. . . . I think I can load it down in such a way as to increase its sinking power."[50]

It hardly needed the help, and not just because the White House stuck to a mild denial that the president and his secretary disagreed about the need for civil service reform. Here and there a Republican newspaper found grounds to defend Grant's action—Morton's Indianapolis organ, J. Russell Young's New York *Standard,* and the smaller Philadelphia newspapers— and quite a few of the most prominent avoided any comment at all, at least until after the midterm elections. Some of those taking Cox's side muted their wrath to protect their patronage, as did J. M. Comly of Columbus *Ohio State Journal.* The editor wanted to do right, but "his [was] a Post Office soul—prepaid by the President, as required for all mail matter." Aspirants to office, one of whom, as Boynton put it, had "been rolling over & over, jumping sticks, & going lame for some time" to gain administration favor, might write "authorized" statements, and McGarrahan's cronies published nasty letters about Cox's conduct. Even the New York *Sun* had an editorial exposing the former secretary, written, as it happened, by one of McGarrahan's attorneys.[51]

None of this could counter the tumult raised on the other side. By mid-November, a host of metropolitan newspapers outside of Washington had come out against the administration. The religious press spoke a unanimous condemnation.[52] From the *Evening Post* came an attack on Grant so bold that it even took Cox's brother aback. Influential with reform Republicans nationwide, editor George William Curtis of *Harper's Weekly* published stinging articles on the resignation three weeks in succession. "Mr. Curtis understands the issue exactly," Charles Cox wrote his brother. He should have: Charles was his source.[53]

By the time the affair had run its course, Grant's good name had suffered terrific damage. Loyal Republicans admitted that, on the face of it, the published letters made "judgment by default" against the president. Himself dismissed some months before as part of a political deal on behalf of the Santo Domingo annexation treaty, former attorney general Ebenezer Hoar still admired the president, but he read the correspondence with pain and bewilderment. "I have never known such universal and deep dissatisfaction excited among our best people by your leaving the Cabinet," he wrote Cox. The McGarrahan correspondence made the president's case even more indefensible. How could Grant have allowed it into the open? "He must have been fully taken possession of by those scoundrels, and been induced to believe whatever they chose to tell him," Hoar concluded. "And yet it is perfectly incomprehensible!" Many reformers understood it well enough. Grant was a tool. Only after White House news management did they discover for how many different rotten interests that tool could be used. Not even the president's formal advocacy of civil service reform, which the Cox incident virtually forced upon him, could erase the infamy.[54]

One incident may not have been enough to wreck a reputation, however clumsily White House news management had turned one scandal into two. Grant's presidency survived. For a while, he even convinced Curtis that his support for civil service reform was sincere. There were limits to how much Democratic malice and Piatt's sallies could accomplish. "The specially smart malignity and virulence of the *World* must make friends for Grant every day," a New Yorker wrote in his diary.[55] Yet damage there was, and much of it might have been prevented if the White House had handled the press better. By 1876, the big story about the government was not its foreign policy, nor its pursuit of retrenchment, but the thievery that Democrats and the independent press claimed to have uncovered in every department. If both parties that year made themselves the champions of reform, and defined reform in that most limited sense—budget cuts, improvements in administrative procedure, and a retreat from activism—the ill fame of the Grant administration, as the press had spread it across the front pages, bears a large share of the responsibility.

One last qualifier needs to be made, however. Grant's failure to use the press properly marred his official reputation. It could never quite finish off his personal standing. As the general who won the war, the president remained widely popular. "The people don't seem ready for the agitation of the question of the impeachment of Grant," Daniel Manning of the Albany *Argus* explained to another angry Democrat in late 1873. "His war laurels (how many of them were stolen, or borrowed, or acquired by chance or accident!) although soiled, are yet too green. What a multitude of sins they cover! Our exchanges hesitate and are afraid to discuss the subject."[56] Nor, throughout the Cox imbroglio, could even Cox and Boynton quite believe that Grant himself had orchestrated the smear campaign. Like

Hoar, they saw him as a well-meaning dupe, used by designing men; just conceivably, he really did think that his secretary had resigned for family reasons and was tainted with corruption.[57]

What, in fact, did Grant himself know of the wrongdoing in his administration, and when did he know it? Depending on their partisan slant, reporters could make a guess. It was never more than a guess. Not all their muckraking could assemble the proof that the president had been aware of the Whiskey Ring before its exposure, or of the frauds in Robeson's navy before the House committee brought an army of witnesses to the stand. If keeping his own counsel was Grant's aim, he had beaten the journalists as effectively as if they were a Confederate army. His silence and that mystery continued to the end. It was an elegiac word of praise that "Gath" delivered as Grant left the presidency, but in it, too, was a note of puzzlement at a man he could still not quite figure out: "He is never in a hurry, and never behind; pain and beauty affect him alike; he is next above the mastiff—the King of moral animals. There he walks or sits, substantial, slow, in everlasting equipoise of countenance. . . . Does he ever feel loneliness? Has he our longings, passions, remorses? What supports him in this everlasting human simplicity, who has seen the blood flow in rivers, and heard the sullen roar of public disfavor, and felt the heartfelt homage of whole cities, and then returned to his bashfulness and his cigar?"[58]

PART FOUR

NEWS IN NEED OF RECONSTRUCTION

"Which Means Nothing"—New York Tribune, January 12, 1875. Advertising for an Assassin of the President of the United States (Thomas Nast, *Harper's Weekly*, January 30, 1875). Whitelaw Reid of the *Tribune*, Donn Piatt, and the *Herald*, banditti all, take umbrage over the federal government's intervention in Louisiana.

CHAPTER 12

A Perfect Hell

The Southern Road
to Pike's Pique

Even before his steamboat reached Little
Rock, Horace V. Redfield of the Cincinnati *Commercial* sensed how badly Re
construction was going there. "Well, sir,"
a white passenger told him, "we are in the
d–dest worst fix you ever saw." Thieves
ran the government. "They are stealing
everything we've got, and the war didn't
leave us much." Governor Powell Clayton
himself had pocketed a million, possibly
more. As for the legislators, they were
"mostly a pack of d–d fools," sure to stay
in session until the last nickel was gone
from the Treasury.[1]

The conversation certainly told something about the passenger's hostility toward Republican officeholders, but Redfield did not use it to assign his source
a party label. He took it as proof of an
experiment in biracial politics gone awry.

By 1871, indeed, something did seem
seriously wrong with the new Republican regimes that the Reconstruction Acts
had permitted white and black Southerners to install. For all the governments'
reforms, they had brought neither peace,
order, prosperity, nor honest administra-

tion. The story of that failure was one that a host of reporters, Redfield among them, would detail for Northern readers. On the special correspondents would lie a heavy responsibility for the loss of faith in the Reconstruction experiment in general and in the Negro voter in particular. That responsibility was what made their biases, their political designs, so dangerous.

It took neither the war nor a devastated South to bring the special correspondent into being. For years, the anonymous contributor was a godsend to any paper larger than the four-pager, and not just for news value. Many of the letters had no news value. They could veer from politics to railroad development to scenic exotica, which may explain their appeal. Those in Washington, Henry V. Boynton and "Gath" among them, stuck relatively close to current events, but outside the capital it was different. Paid by the line, and only if the letters were accepted, a writer could be as expansive as caprice permitted. Telegraph costs forced the news reporter to restrain impulses to eloquence and stick to the freshest information. But a correspondent sent his or her work by the three-penny post. There was no restriction on how much to write; indeed, the editors seem to have thought the more, the better. With any news story sure to have been wired in several days before, there was room to talk of the eternal verities of politics, to transcribe interesting conversation, and to study a problem in depth. With a free pass from the railroads, a courtesy journalists often enjoyed, even traveling expenses could be modest.

The Southern story demanded just such roving coverage. Those held in slavery six years before now worked in freedom. The chance to attend schools or form churches, the right to marry or to testify in court—all were newly theirs. Jury box, legislative gallery, and even political office were thrown open regardless of race, though this was not the war's doing. Congress had done it or, rather, virtually compelled the former Confederate states to do it. No one needed to be told that Powell Clayton's rule would have been impossible without the Reconstruction Acts and the federal support for a biracial Republican party to survive against moneyed intimidation and midnight terror. These so-called carpetbag governments were made mostly of native whites, not Northern newcomers—certainly not opportunistic ones lugging carpetbags to haul off the swag—and the term *Negro rule* fit just about nowhere. Still, a correct appreciation of the new ruling class made its effects no less newsworthy. A breathtaking experiment in extended democracy, economic and political, had begun.

Emancipation's effects had been a story all along. Every metropolitan newspaper had sent its emissaries into the defeated Confederate states at one point or another. By the 1870s, the travelers had become a legion. In 1871, for example, the New York *Times* sent its correspondent south toward Atlanta to evaluate carpetbag rule. Not to be outdone, the *Tribune, Herald, Sun,* and *World* sent scribes right after him.[2]

What did the correspondents find? James Shepherd Pike of the New York *Tribune* fit what seems to have been a common pattern. When he boarded the train for Columbia in early 1873, he had a clear picture of South Carolina misgovernment. He had read the official documents and penned his basic indictment. All he really wanted was material to give his story local color, and that of a pitch-black hue, not just morally. Gazing across the state house, he spied "colored men whose types it would be hard to find outside of Congo; whose costume, visages, attitudes, and expression, only befit the forecastle of a buccaneer." Peanut shells cracking, members guffawing and jabbering while the speaker's gavel drummed a futile tattoo for order, barbarians had assumed command—and consumed anything else. Senate seats went up for auction, and ownership of the state railroad went into the stock portfolio of the public officials entrusted to run them. Those whose high position did not allow them to steal state bonds speculated in them instead.[3]

Both as articles and later compiled as the best-selling *Prostrate State,* Pike's accounts certainly stressed the sensational, but however maliciously and mendaciously he shaded his evidence, his accounts squared with those of his colleagues, Charles Nordhoff of the New York *Herald* and H. V. Redfield of the Cincinnati *Commercial.* Nor, as their reports made clear, did South Carolina stand alone in depravity. Louisiana, an Ohio visitor declared, was "a perfect h–l." Without breaking the law, public servants padded payrolls and expense accounts, accepted bribes, held several offices at once, doing the work in none, and took employment with companies seeking legislative support. "It is no more trouble to buy their votes than to buy spring chickens in the Cincinnati market," Redfield charged, and Louisiana's carpetbagger governor, Henry Clay Warmoth, himself would have agreed with him. On a smaller scale, the same conditions could be found in county courthouses and state legislatures from Richmond to Austin.[4]

When it came to exposing the corruption, the correspondents told a story grounded in provable fact. If justice had been done, Southern legislatures would have been emptier and prisons fuller. The story illuminated one of the real reasons why so many Southerners grew increasingly hostile to Republican governments. Yet in three ways, the press's emphasis on misgovernment distorted the larger truth about Reconstruction.

For one thing, many of the charges of wrongdoing rested on evidence as unfounded as the testimony of Redfield's Arkansas traveler. Governor Henry Clay Warmoth of Louisiana might be notorious. Widely condemned as "that *damn thief* Warmoth," he used his powers to enrich himself and empower his friends. He bought state warrants at half their face value and used his inside knowledge to redeem them at par the moment the Treasury had money. But was he a thief and a bribe taker? Common report told how he got $250,000 in one case and $600,000 in another for not vetoing rascally legislation: unbelievable sums, when the going rate for a legislator was $100. No one ever came close to proving either payoff, and plenty of witnesses had seen the governor on the legislative floor bullying members to sustain his veto of other swindles or to keep them from passing in the first place. Thanks to the journalists, everybody knew that Clayton and Governor Rufus Bullock of Georgia had the reputation of thieves—to everybody except the jury that acquitted Bullock and the Senate committee that looked into the charges against Clayton and found nothing but rumor.[5]

Left out, too, was the redemptive leaven among Republican officeholders. Even in depraved South Carolina, looters were challenged and worsted by members of their own party eventually. In Mississippi, Florida, and Texas, honest governors battled the railroad promoters and lobbyists. By the time Nordhoff reached the South in the spring of 1875, the worst excesses were over, even in Louisiana.

Finally, the Pikes were telling only one part of the story. It was an important part, to be sure. No description of Southern Reconstruction would have been complete without it. But it was not the only part, and out of context, it could give a very peculiar interpretation of Reconstruction's impact. Even South Carolina deserved notice for its advances in social welfare, racial equality, and education, but none of these mattered to the special correspondent.

There were several reasons for the distortions in the picture sent north. That which strikes modern readers most forcibly was so common in all reporting in that age that it may have escaped most contemporaries: a deep apprehension of and often a contempt for, freedmen, whether "black or speckled . . . inky or variegated," to use one correspondent's description. Given the racial assumptions that correspondents shared with virtually all their white contemporaries, such a bias was inevitable. Groping for a colorful phrase, they might think nothing of emphasizing support for President Grant's reelection by promising to do the best work possible "if it 'kills every nigger on the river.'" Jokes turning on blacks' ignorance and malapropisms had virtually a universal audience, as did minstrel shows, with their mocking portrayal of the Negro and their wistful portrayal of plantation life.[6] To apply those cultural stereotypes to politics took no conscious thought at all. Indeed, it would have taken an extraordinary act of will to dismiss the image of the plantation "darky" when pondering on the black voter.

It thus came almost naturally for the special correspondent to describe black leaders in contemptuous terms. Even sympathetic witnesses treated them as innocents, passive and taken advantage of by open enemies and supposed friends alike. When James Redpath described Mississippi freedmen as "sheep-like," he meant it kindly, perhaps. So, too, did the journalist who explained a black congressman's intellectual cast of countenance on "the blood of the cavaliers [flowing] in his veins." For others, description only distinguished the Negro as something alien and peculiar: "black as your hat," "black as a tar-bucket, flat nose, thick lips and with about as much intelligence in his face as one would observe in a dead mackerel." Far more often than with whites, the reporter generalized about the character of a race from his impressions of a few. When an account declared the speaker of South Carolina's house "a very good specimen of the typical steamboat barber," or charged that the physique and brains of many state senators "would make more impression in the corn-field," it did not assign jobs idly: those were the customary positions that the journalist thought suited blacks, and, in this case, ones far below those to which many black public officials belonged. Commonly the term *black* was either qualified with the word *ignorant* or the even more generally dismissive modifier, *unusually intelligent.* When the New York *Tribune* described one interviewee as "a negro of rather dull intellect even for a man of his race" in 1875, a Southern editor rightly asked whether the late Horace Greeley would have allowed any such intimation of race inferiority.[7]

From those assumptions, obvious conclusions followed about the experiment in Negro officeholding. Liberal Republican correspondents might show more restrained rhetoric on this point than Democrats, but their difference was stylistic rather than substantial. For all his expressions of sympathy for black aspirations, Redfield never found a black officeholder worthy of his place. Nor did he have faith in blacks as voters, since it took "at least a year to convince the mass of the negroes" on any issue. "As sure as darkness follows day, thirty thousand negro majority will never reform anything."[8]

Possibly what Pike, Redfield, Nordhoff, and "Gath" saw of black Southern life reinforced that conclusion, but what, exactly, did they see? None of them restricted themselves to white witnesses alone, to be sure. Even Pike was willing to set down black comments. If a Negro denounced the Republican leadership, it was even possible that his words would be reported fairly and in standard English; more typically, if he spoke for the regime in power, his comments appeared in dialect, a comic travesty to regale readers with. The less he knew, the more suited his remarks were for inclusion (and of course, black women were not quoted on public affairs at all). He was, in short, not a source, but an object lesson. Such treatment followed naturally from the belief that the "Africans know about as much of the issues involved as a pig does of the Bible."[9]

It was assumed, of course, that whites knew more. From the information they were feeding to the Northern press, that assumption would be hard to sustain. Why was Mississippi a land of negligently cultivated plantations and rickety barns, for example? The New York *Tribune* correspondent's sources blamed emancipation. Negro voting left crops untended, tasks undone. The reporter might have spent his time more profitably reading accounts of antebellum Mississippi. From Frederick Law Olmsted to Hinton Rowan Helper, they all described an identical landscape but blamed slavery itself. Even a few walks across the countryside might have shown the reporter what other wanderers had discovered, that those working in the cotton fields were usually black, and those deploring the decline of the work ethic did so with a drink rather than a hoe in their hands.[10]

Even whites accused of political murders received deferential treatment. When an Alabama Republican was shot from ambush, the New York *Times* correspondent wrote the suspect up in fulsome terms. Rather than looking into the man's past, which included the burning of a Republican doctor's house and the killing of several blacks in broad daylight some years before, the correspondent lauded him as an injured innocent of "more than ordinary intelligence, and . . . refined feeling." (After Reconstruction's close, that "more than ordinary intelligence" earned him five years in jail for horse theft.) [11]

The reference to "refined feeling" brings up a second, less visible bias: that of class. Reporters more comfortable with whites were most comfortable with the "most respectable" ones, professionals and propertied men. When Redfield described the South Carolina legislature as that "riff-raff of carpet-baggers, dead-beats, ignorant negroes and general slush and scum," he meant it not in terms of race alone. His views a New York *Tribune* correspondent made explicit—and with them the Northern parallel. Alabama's sordid politics should have surprised no one, he wrote. Historically, "a rule of ignorance and poverty" always led to "dishonest and profligate" government. Blacks in Alabama confirmed the lesson that whites in Tammany Hall's New York City had taught already. By definition, good government was undemocratic. It relied exclusively on those fit to run matters and with enough of a financial stake in society to care where the money went: the propertied and well educated. [12]

In a sense, Southern reportage was a case of the outs interviewing the outs, and for political ammunition. Pike was a case in point. Long disaffected from the administration, his rage sharpened by Horace Greeley's recent defeat for president, he had a score to repay. More than that, the *Tribune* line blamed President Grant for corruption in states as distant as Louisiana and New York. Pike set out to pin the blame for conditions in South Carolina on Grant as well, and that was precisely the moral he ended up drawing. The Negro, ever imitative, took his moral cue only from the bacchanal in Washington. [13]

To a greater or lesser degree, the other journalists, too, went touring with their minds already made up. Whether it was their adversarial training as newsmen or their liberal prejudices, they arrived with a prejudice against officeholders as by nature suspect, possibly corrupt, and far more self-interested in utterance than those outside of power, even those seeking office. "L. Q. W." did not need to travel to North Carolina to know that government employees were the "vermin of the South, . . . spies, informers, and political wire-pullers." Weeks before he exposed the corruption of Grant's Arkansas backers, "Gath" was writing campaign verse for the Democratic opposition, including one lyric "to fire the Southern heart." In the last days of Louisiana's Republican government, James Redpath sought one last reporter's tour, supposedly to send back news for the *Tribune*. In fact, he meant to write letters that might convince "the antislavery element of the North to acquiesce in white supremacy in Louisiana, *for the sake of the blacks.*"[14]

Sometimes the bias escaped the correspondent himself. When the New York *Herald* sent Charles Nordhoff, its Washington correspondent, into the cotton states in 1875, it sent a man proud of his fact-finding ability and convinced of his own fairness. But anyone who had read his Washington dispatches or remembered his role in organizing a rally against the administration's Louisiana policy knew where he stood. As one critic put it, Nordhoff had shown "a positive incapacity for seeing or hearing anything that did not fall in with his preconceived ideas." Now he turned first and foremost to those opposed to the so-called carpetbagger governments. What they told him allowed a picture with considerable sophistication and insight, but a brief for the prosecution, all the same.[15]

Race, class, and politics: together the three biases could make a hash even of coverage that on first appearance let every side have its say by establishing a hierarchy of reliability. Most trusted were elite whites out of office and out of patience with Southern government. Their words were set down as simple truth, weighed neither for partisan prejudice nor racial bigotry. Dissident Republicans came next. Because they bore witness against their erstwhile allies, their word was implicitly trusted whenever they did so, and only then. Reporters placed far less reliance on the statements Republican officials gave them. These would be checked, matched with contradiction, or dismissed as partisan rant—which they often were, though no more so than the two groups more highly rated. Last of all, of course, came the blacks.

The correspondents' very language took on this loaded, deceptive quality. An "enlightened" or "fair-minded" Republican meant a disaffected one; when a correspondent spoke of "public opinion" or "the general feeling," he meant white conservative feeling. When Redfield insisted that "Southern-born men have had little to do with" the corruption around them, he really meant only the white ones: blacks were always Africans or Negroes, never Southerners, to the newspaperman (and even then, Redfield's assertion was dead wrong).[16]

Ideological biases stare out from the printed page, but other prejudices, though less obvious, had nearly as much importance. One was the bias built into the reporter's very occupation. Free as he might be to pad his letter with descriptive material and human interest features, the roving correspondent had to stick close to topics of national interest, whether it was the story behind a recent news event or an essay pertinent to the larger question of whether Reconstruction was working. Otherwise his letter would be cut, if not rejected entirely. He was not, after all, on salary; there was no obligation by any editor to get the paper's money's worth by publishing whatever got sent. And news still was defined by the exciting, the prurient, and the political. A contested election might set Tweedledum against Tweedledee (as it did in Arkansas in 1872). Still, north or south, it was news. So was a meeting of the legislature. Everyday occurrences in staid hamlets—the erection of a new African Methodist church or the graduation of a class of freedmen's children—may have held greater historical significance in judging what Reconstruction actually meant for the former slaves. But as news, such nonevents were worthless. No editor would pay the travel expenses of a correspondent to track down things like that.[17]

There was another bias so natural to the news business that not even historians have remarked upon it. Traveling correspondents were usually male and almost always so when public events were to be discussed. Victorian codes of conduct allowed female journalists to comment on fashions or impart the picturesque to everyday scenes. But no lady would travel alone; none with any pretense of gentility would partake of the men's world of caucuses and conventions. Politics was, essentially, news for men; Southern events that mattered were political ones. The prejudice was self-reinforcing. How Reconstruction affected everyday life for women, black ones in particular, how, say, the coming of public school systems affected the families of the South, might be matters a woman correspondent would have shown interest in; but they went unreported, because the kind of reporters who would have cared simply did not exist.

The occupational bias restricted more than what the correspondent would look at. He went where he had the best chance of finding a story, which meant state capitals, and where travel took the least inconvenience. For all practical purposes, the uplands of Arkansas were as remote as the Siberian steppes. Railroads might convey riders to Jackson or Vicksburg, but it would take carriages and exhausting travel over back roads to reach the wire-grass region of Mississippi—and then for no apparent story worth telling. The very itinerancy of the correspondent added to his deficiencies. If newsmen had no way to get to the scene where events took place, they were hostages to supposed eyewitnesses, few and sparing. Even if they did visit, as one resident pointed out, the brevity of their stay distorted perspective. To understand a community, one had to be aware of which individuals were worthy of trust and what the day-to-day life was like. That took more than a day or even a week of sojourning. If they stayed longer, reporters might see the greater picture very differently. They would certainly see political confusion, possibly even leadership in the hands of unworthy men. But they would note other things as well, concerns that defined the success or failure of Reconstruction better than governance: the lack of credit facilities and diversified agriculture, for example, or the baneful effect of too much cotton.[18]

In a sense, a person passing through never really left home. The topics a reporter covered were those that interested Northern editors and Northern readers most. In 1865, the issue of Reconstruction was relatively simply put: had the white masses learned their lesson from the war, and would they behave in a docile, loyal fashion hereafter? And what were the chances for the economic recovery of the South?

Those questions remained important well into the early 1870s. Indeed, the one about economic growth never vanished entirely. Special correspondents, to a large extent, were economic boosters, especially when they hailed from the area under study. Redfield's letters put the prospects of the Cincinnati Southern Railroad project in the most glowing terms as construction moved through Kentucky and Tennessee. Others, with florid detail, spoke of the immense mineral wealth of the South, a potential remaining untapped, and the magnificent prospects of cotton as well.[19]

As the bitter memories of the war faded, new questions began to supersede that of white Southerners' loyalty. The most important was, how well was Radical Reconstruction working? It seemed a forthright question. In fact, the answer depended entirely on the criteria used to define the program's success. If one concentrated on the freedmen's adaptation to free labor, for example, or on the growth of the school systems, the development of natural resources, or the new political dispensation in terms of the extension of rights, then the answer was clear: Reconstruction *was* working. If, on the other hand, the question was framed largely in terms of the ethics and efficiency of those put in power, and the qualifications of those permitted to vote, then the answer would be the reverse.[20] Between 1869 and 1874, that is precisely how the criteria changed.

They did not do so from any journalists' conspiracy to discredit Reconstruction, at least among Republican correspondents and editors (Democrats were another matter, and as the race issue lost its impact in the

North, they found the corruption, rather than the color, of Southern office-holders an issue with a broader appeal). What happened, then, was that national events defined what newsmen looked for in the South. Because corruption became the lead story nationally, it became the lead story in the South; when a panic and depression halted development throughout the North, railroad construction and bumper crops in cotton no longer could match the interest that peculating politicians and venal voters had.

Against all of these deficiencies, it would have been difficult for fair-minded journalists to have come to the broad picture that historians would prefer. Nor did they. Their accounts were not simply impressionistic, but wrong on the basics of Reconstruction. Contrary to their picture, the South was not run by Northern interlopers, the so-called carpetbaggers. Southerners who voted Republican were not exclusively "mean whites" and loafers or rich men embracing the party to rob the state.[21] Whatever influence federal marshals used to protect black voters in North Carolina, their activities did not constitute "a reign of terror," any more than Arkansas suffered "an iron despotism." The reporter who insisted that the Ku Klux Klan was simply a defense against "the diabolical teachings to the blacks . . . which lit up the skies . . . with midnight conflagrations, and made every Southern mother press her babe closer to her bosom" spoke pure fantasy. Yet these and many another canard appeared in Republican newspapers, unrefuted.[22]

By accepting local whites' view of black character, a reporter could even explain away the midnight terrorism that conservatives used to overturn Reconstruction. At the very least, he would credit white insistence that blacks shared the blame for every outrage against themselves, and he might well deny that an incident had occurred at all. In the summer of 1874, three young whites returning from a drinking spree near midnight laid seige to the house of Julia Hayden, a black schoolteacher, demanding that she let them in to fulfill their sexual appetites. When Hayden barred the door, one of the assailants shot through it and killed her. The white community furnished an explanation entirely satisfactory to the New York *Tribune*'s man on the scene. The low character of Negroes bore the real responsibility. The overexcited youths would never have given Hayden trouble if it were not common knowledge that black women would sleep with anybody.[23]

The palliation came from Zebulon L. White, head of the paper's Washington bureau, sent south to report on events that autumn. His letters showed how far a relatively fair man's account could stray from the truth. They did not cover the whole cotton South, as Nordhoff's did; most of the time, his beat was Alabama, and that for a few weeks before Congress reassembled and allowed him to return to his regular duties. But their effect was a significant one. Coming just at the end of a campaign where Republicans had been trying to show a white South determined to win by killing as many blacks as necessary, White's account seemed to offer solid proof that no such reign of terror existed. His conclusions were widely republished and endorsed.[24] When the House ordered an investigation of the election, Democrats would call him as a witness to the fairness of the returns, and in the Alabama senate, conservatives would load him with compliments for "his manly and truthful letters during the last campaign."[25] How, then, did White come by his version of the truth?

White was sent with no instructions to find for the *Tribune*'s side in politics. On the contrary, he insisted, the *Tribune* made it a policy to extend more benefit of the doubt to opponents than to allies. Managing editor Jonathan G. Hassard simply wanted an important story covered by the best possible man (and letters by White, he added, "would be read and quoted everywhere"), and Whitelaw Reid thought his paper could "make a hit" by studying race relations. From the moment he reached Alabama, White collected information from all sides. He took tea with the Democratic secretary of the state senate and dinner with W. W. Screws, the Democratic editor of the Montgomery *Advertiser*; he went for a half-dozen rides with the Republican probate judge. He never conversed with the local Republican editor, but only because the latter could not be found.[26]

White's thoroughness provided only the semblance, rather than the substance, of fairness. "Immediately on my arrival in Alabama I was sought by the conservatives," he later admitted. "I received constant and numerous calls from them every day." He was, in fact, wined, dined, flattered, and used. By contrast, the Republicans he interviewed had to be sought out. Nor did all witnesses matter equally to White. Conservatives' names he remembered very well. They were men of great influence, like the president of the national bank at Montgomery. If White's accounts are anything to judge by, however, blacks received no such attention. Instead of seeking out their leaders, he spoke to any he chanced to come across. The only one whose name he could remember was the "very intelligent negro boy, or negro man" sent by the hotel keeper in Livingston to bring him to town by buggy, and even then White only found out his first name.

It scarcely mattered. As White later explained of black passengers he interviewed on the train up to Sumter County, they "seemed to be so ignorant that I got very little information from them."[27]

Was information what he wanted from them in the first place? "If you can get the colored people to talk, it would be well to quote a good deal of their language," Hassard had advised him. It was their dialect, not the the point they were making that readers wanted, and in that respect alone, White's coverage served admirably. Whatever his professions before the House committee, the reporter wrote of blacks with unconcealed contempt. The "very intelligent negro boy" was portrayed as a political imbecile, utterly unfamiliar with the governor's name or even what offices were at stake in the fall election. "The average negro man will steal and the average negro woman knows not what chastity is," White informed readers. Black voters were "impossible to reach by argument" and "kept in line not only by oaths and semi-military organizations, but by the excitement of their fears and the circulation of lies." If White's attitude was as obvious to the blacks he interviewed as to the whites he wrote for, it is not surprising that he elicited no useful information from them. In an area marked by racial and political violence, blacks were not likely to give frank answers about politics to a white stranger.[28]

White's information therefore came almost entirely from whites, and even that was filtered through his political prejudices. Republican officials told their side of the story only so that the correspondent could refute it. No such scrutiny was applied to his main sources, the men of property and status: "a gentleman of this city," "a planter who lives in town," "a physician of Montgomery," "the better classes," "large planters," or "one of the most prominent citizens of Mobile."[29]

White was not simply a careless observer whose assumptions shaped his view of events. He was a political agent. Years later, editor Screws of the Montgomery *Advertiser* revealed that the *Tribune* reporter had fed the Democratic party advance information about troop movements used to guard the polls and protect black voters. Having learned it through his talks with Republicans in Sumter County, White rushed to the railroad depot, boarded the evening train for Montgomery, and told all to Screws himself. The next day, the reporter's scoop covered page one, a daunting warning to Republicans that the enemy was privy to their every plan.[30] More subtle political ends can only be conjectured. Within days of reaching Alabama, White convinced himself that every story of violence against blacks and Republicans was worse than bogus. Its use was directed to poison President Grant's mind, so that he would void the election returns and keep Republicans in power. White's letters made convincing propaganda for the other side, and undoubtedly that was how he designed them.[31]

For propaganda they were, from the by-line to the headline ("The Slandered State" and, heralding Democratic victory, "Alabama Free"). No other term would do for a subtitle, "The End of the Carpetbaggers," when every single Republican state officer was a white native and twenty-two of the twenty-five nominees for state office that fall came from the South. Every atrocity had its exculpation. Thomas Ivey, a murdered black, was "a bad nigger." Democratic intimidation and race-baiting were partisan fabrications, the *Tribune* correspondent insisted. The only provable violence, and it was a common occurrence, came when blacks assaulted those of their own race who deserted the Republican party.[32]

White's reports were worse than misleading. They were full of balderdash, credited because respectable conservatives presented it as fact. New York *Tribune* readers learned that at the end of the war, freed slaves refused to work and, as a result, died of starvation by the thousands; that whites generally were kind to blacks, whereas blacks were "insolent" and "provoking in conduct"; that cotton planting failed to pay simply because blacks stole one-fourth of the crop and every pig or chicken they could lay their hands on; that the Alabama legislature of 1868 was almost entirely composed of "illiterate blacks or white thieves and murderers"; that the state began Reconstruction in healthy financial condition with a light debt, with its bond interest promptly paid, and with no need for onerous taxes; that the race issue in 1874 was raised solely by Republican agitators; that freedom had led to the moral and physical degeneration of the Negro race; that as they drew away from their former masters, the blacks were lapsing into barbarism; that in the black counties of Alabama, marriage was "becoming almost unknown"; that slave children received far better medical care than the master's children, and "the most skillful physicians were employed"; and that the Ku Klux Klan violence was entirely the fault of Republicans for giving blacks the vote in the first place.[33]

A more disinterested observer might have found very different conditions in Alabama. He would note, as White did, that some of the Republican campaigners' specific allegations of terrorism had no basis, but he would have also found a wider level of intimidation in the use of economic pressures by propertied men and in the invocations of white supremacy by the Democratic press. He might also have asked questions that the *Tribune* never did: why did so few blacks hold political office in Alabama? Why were times so hard, and where precisely did tax revenues go? What issues divided Republican from Republican, Democrat from Democrat, and how might these have explained the rise of race-conscious politics in 1874?

The other side did have its voices, as well. Correspondents to the Washington *New National Era* gave blacks the attention and respect that they deserved, and even the independent press had a few correspondents who sent a fairer picture north. From Republican newspapers, like the New York *Times*, readers might glimpse a different picture of the issues at stake in, say, North Carolina, involving not corruption alone, but the expansion of the school system and the completion of the Western North Carolina Railroad. If the *Commercial* relied on Redfield's Negrophobic portrayals of the race issue in Tennessee during the 1874 campaign, it printed an occasional letter from "Stella," a black correspondent who described the malevolence and bullying of the white-liners and exposed some of the worst conservative canards.[34] But the "Stellas" were few and far between, and they confronted a growing multitude of Redfields.

By no means can Nordhoff, White, or Pike take all the responsibility for Reconstruction's fall. Editors did not invent race prejudice; they shared it. Every partisan who stole from the Southern governments stole from their reputation, and a midnight assassin could do more damage to the new order than a journalist with a dozen special letters. There is blame enough to go around, and a share at least should belong to those who reported a misleading version of the news from the South. Republican governments were extraordinarily dependent on federal backing, and that in turn depended on how far Northern voters were prepared to sustain an active policy of support. But who would support "the prostrate state"? Northerners might accept federal intervention against white terrorism, but what if they were assured that the terrorism was no more than a political stunt? Not even radical Republicans found federal intervention in the South a pleasant duty. When correspondents like Charles Nordhoff assured them that the fight no longer set white against black, but honest man against plunderer, that government action itself created the ill feeling that led to violence, that the color line, where it existed, would quickly vanish as both parties bargained for the Negro vote, and that Democratic rule posed no danger to anyone's rights, Northerners found it easy to be convinced. That does not remove all responsibility from those who did the persuading. Political Reconstruction itself would owe its failure in part to the reconstruction of attitudes toward the South that the Nordhoffs and Redfields brought about.

CHAPTER 13

Carpetbagger Chronicles

Horace V. Redfield could find nothing in favor of the press in the Deep South. "The newspapers of Alabama, both Republican and Democratic, are brimful of lies," the Cincinnati *Commercial*'s star reporter wrote. ". . . The Republican papers are filled with grossly exaggerated accounts of 'outrages,' and to get even, the Democratic press blames everything on the negroes. . . . It is useless to try to get at the truth of these disturbances through the press accounts in the Alabama newspapers."[1]

Redfield was right, but he missed the mark in blaming partisanship alone. The problems went far beyond that—straight to the account books, in fact. "A Southern newspaper is generally a dreary sheet," one reporter commented after a vain search for news beyond "the pony telegraph report" and "politics in their most uninteresting form." Editors either scolded or bloviated ("that brilliant statesman and high-toned Southern gentleman, Colonel—, visited us yesterday"). "We do not suppose that a good sensible paper could get a paying subscription in the Southern States," the Cincinnati *Gazette* commented.[2]

The largest cities provided a few exceptions. For local reporting, few newspapers anywhere outdid the New Orleans *Picayune*. Most journals were four-pagers, unable to fill even one with news, but the *Picayune* ran for eight, with seven columns apiece rather than the usual six. New Orleans had other major presses: the *Bee*, which printed one side of each page in French and the other in English, and the *Times*, which on Sundays could afford to put out sixteen pages of material.[3]

Critics were right in the main, however. Not even New Orleans had the equivalent of the North's "independent" press. "Their local departments are miserable, their *news nil*, their markets 'so middling,'" a Chicago editor complained from the Crescent City.[4] Some newspapers proclaimed their freedom from party trammels, and a very few of them meant it, but none of them combined that independence with any news-gathering skills. Outside of New Orleans, almost no journal had the resources to do more than reprint AP dispatches, cover a batch of local incidents, and perhaps issue two regular letters of commentary, one from New York and the other from Washington. No more than a dozen papers from the former Confederate South were represented in the press gallery of Congress in 1870. As for the AP stories, Northern telegraphers knew what the market would bear: news sent west and south went through Buffalo, and with the Southern route via Louisville or Washington. In each city, the telegrams were cut in half and condensed. By the time stories reached New Orleans, there was left "but the mere shadow" of what New England readers received.[5]

The *Commercial* was also correct about the distortion and politically engaged qualities of Southern journalism. Where writing had any life at all, the language was truculent and apocalyptic. Fairness was as strange and unusual as a snowfall in a cotton field. From the Raleigh *Sentinel* came calls for revolution against the party of "leprous, ulcer-eaten Senators" and "a government of thieves and thugs." "Americans! Degenerate sons of patriot sires!" one editorial shrieked. "Behold your country today!" Not an eagle deserved to be its symbol, but "a dingy, skulking, carrion-gorged vulture." Even the *Picayune*, magisterial to the point of dullness, described the Republican party as "revolutionary" and aiming for "centralism." From Washington, the correspondent of the Savannah *Morning News* informed readers that nine-tenths of all federal officeholders lived in "elegant idleness," doing no work for high pay, "sapping the life of the nation." Its editors blamed the poor health of congressmen on the bad ventilation spreading the stench from Negroes in the gallery—a measure of poetic justice to the men who passed the Fifteenth Amendment.[6]

Left to the tender mercies of the conservative correspondents, it was easy enough to make the "carpetbag" legislators look like fools and villains. Their appearance in the columns was not for what they did, but for who they were. "Carraway, the negro representative from Mobile, who dresses his chignon with hair pins, bar's oil and otto of roses, yesterday rose to a personal explanation," one news report for the Mobile *Register* began, concluding with advice that another Republican borrow "Bigamy Harris' jack-knife and cut out Carraway's gizzard." When a white Democrat spoke, his appearance and remarks might be described with respect. No such courtesies were bestowed on views with which the reporter disagreed, and scant effort was made to disclose those views at all.[7]

How, then, could the truth be known, at least the truth as Republicans wanted it spoken? The solution lay in a strong, effective Republican press. But that could not be done from scratch. Starting a new press was not so difficult for anyone with a moderate supply of money, though Republicans usually lacked even that. In as small a town as Lexington, Mississippi, E. M. Main had to go into debt just to buy an old printing press with worn-out type for $2,500. Starting a major newspaper enterprise would have been difficult anywhere, but especially in the South, where Republican newspapers could not depend on commercial advertising or the patronage of conservative businessmen. They could not expect a paying circulation, either. Too many members of their party had little or nothing, and with few large cities in the South, a metropolitan newspaper would have had difficulty surviving long. Even in Louisville, observers estimated that an organ could expect out of some 1,500 Republican voters no more than 300 paying subscribers from within city limits, and then only by setting rates at half those of rival presses and raising a large fund in the hinterlands. Somehow, the Louisville *Commercial* was launched and survived, but this was nearly a miracle, and that in a city with an unusually large propertied white Republican population.[8]

Democrats had no such problems. They had a steady clientele; businessmen gave them advertisements willingly. The New Orleans *Picayune* carried forty to fifty columns of ads in each issue and nearly sixty on Sundays. So endowed, a conservative paper could sell for three or four cents a copy; otherwise, the cost might be as high as the New Orleans *Tribune* at ten cents. Thus, those least able to pay for a daily were forced to pay more or go without.[9]

The businessmen's neglect was not solely political. It was plain sense; many Republicans could not read, which put an upward limit on circulation; and many more could barely afford to buy the newspaper, much less the goods that advertisements offered. There was a sting in the advertisement for the Holly Springs (Mississippi) *Reporter*, which declared its views those of "nine-tenths of the reading men of the county."[10] A newspaper also relied not just on advertisements but on the use of its type and presses for commercial purposes. From stationery to timetables, firms needed printing done and hired the tasks out. The Water Valley *Courier* could afford to publish weekly in Mississippi's black belt because, as it boasted, it did the local printing for the Mississippi Central Railroad.[11] And again, business provided this patronage to the conservative printers, who were well established and politically well connected.

Without any newspapers to their credit, the Republican cause must perish. Political campaigns on occasion became subscription drives for needy newspapers, but there was an alternative solution, and it was one Republicans quickly embraced: funding a press network from the state treasury.[12]

It is often noted with deprecation that the Republicans created and funded official organs with patronage. But that was the case with Democratic ones across the South as well, and it would continue to be the case to the end of the century. Kentucky endowed favored Democratic presses with the right to do public printing and pushed for a bill to publish orders against nonresidents and legal proceedings in rural weeklies, where Democratic editors needed a handout. The Savannah *Morning News* owed its position as one of Georgia's most widely circulated papers to its status as the city's official organ. Thanks to government patronage, it could afford to insert all new advertisements free of charge in its *Tri-Weekly*.[13]

The question was not, therefore, whether the party press would get printing contracts, but *which* party's press would get the most. On such an issue, there could be only one good partisan answer. To leave printing to the lowest bidder was to leave it to the more well-endowed Democratic newspapers. That, as state senator Charles Caldwell of Mississippi argued, was unthinkable, especially when those same journals encouraged their readers to shoot down black officeholders. "These papers have already done enough mischief." Let them stir up revolution on their own money![14]

The press was all the more important because loyalties, recently taken, needed the regular stiffening that a partisan sheet could manage. A party without tradition behind it, with no names to harken to in its past, was one that already lacked much of the root system that a viable opposition would need. But patronage might lead to a permanence of sort for the party, if not for the newspaper.[15]

Many Republican editors were active politicians. The two jobs had to go together just to keep the newspaper going. Mississippi was full of such combinations. M. B. Sullivan ran the Floreyville *Star* while he clerked in Bolivar County's circuit court. The Corinth *News* was bought and funded by a federal marshal and the Lexington *Advertiser* by the local sheriff; a state legislator, asking for the federal district attorney's job, explained that its remuneration would allow him to "control the Greenville paper." In Louisiana, the Homer *Iliad*, "a first-class Democratic paper" before the war and "a first-class Republican paper now," was able to be so because the editor sat in the state house.[16]

This tendency to combine publishing and politicking may have been strongest among the sprinkling of black newspapers across the South. Both the black U.S. senators from Mississippi edited newspapers; so did the secretary of state and the speaker of the house. In South Carolina, no list of the leading black politicians would have omitted Richard ("Big Daddy") Cain, Alonzo Ransier, Congressmen Robert Brown Elliott and Robert Smalls, or William Whipper. All of them set up their own press spokesmen, in one case against each other.[17]

How was the press paid? In Alabama, the legislature left designation of legal advertising to the judges of probate courts but restricted their choice to supporters of Reconstruction—which in Mobile meant none at all until the Mobile *Republican* was founded to take up the lack.[18] Louisiana's patronage came from conflicting sources. The choice of a state printer and the general endowment of patronage to rural newspapers fell to a three-man commission, but legislators designated other rural journals and paid them from the contingent funds. In all, some thirty-five to forty were so selected. Any such system was bound to cost a great deal. In the first three years of Republican rule, Louisiana public printing amounted to $1.5 million, with $100,000 going in one year to several New Orleans papers, excluding the state's official journal, in which Governor Henry Clay Warmoth had a one-quarter share. Reportedly, his four-pager paid a dividend of 110 percent, though Warmoth denied doing so well. In some cases, legislatures also gave gratuities to the reporters, as they did in Louisiana in 1871.[19]

Indeed, a point that Democrats conveniently overlooked was that much of the money for advertising and printing went to Democratic, as well as Republican, newspapers, for items like legal notices simply had to reach the whole public, and some laws mandated advertisement in every daily newspaper regardless of party. Often officials had no Republican alternative to patronize, but even when they did, a sop to the government's enemies might stifle their cries. In 1874, an investigation of printing frauds revealed that the "Negro government" of South Carolina had distributed advertising to twenty-one Democratic newspapers as well as ten Republican ones. The Columbia *Daily Union*'s take of $3,476 was modest compared to the two Democratic organs, the Charleston *News* ($5,070) and Charleston *Courier* ($5,947). *Courier* reporters made six dollars a day as clerks for Republican legislative committees and kept quiet about the specifics of the graft they saw around them. In Mississippi, the Jackson *Clarion* swallowed its conservative scruples and made an alliance with the Republican Jackson *Pilot* for a share of the public printing, and its editor cut dead all those other editors in his party who dared criticize such dealings.[20]

By the standards of Southern states before the war, the sums allotted were stupendous; by any standard, they would have been exorbitant if the legislatures' only aim had been to have the printing and advertising done, and not to prop up press establishments. Iowa spent $121,068 for printing in 1873; Massachusetts the year before had spent $89,766, Pennsylvania $73,378, and Ohio $62,924. Yet all those states together paid out $50,000 less than South Carolina did in 1873.[21]

The process itself could be, often was, an invitation to corruption and overcharging. The worst scandals occurred in South Carolina. There, Josephus Woodruff's Republican Printing Company bribed the governor, state treasurer, comptroller, and members of both houses on a regular basis. The cost of doing so—$36,590 for the House alone in one case— was amply repaid. A $75,000 payment for compiling and printing the General Assembly's report on immigration left a good margin of profit, especially since Woodruff never did the work. Lawmakers were not likely to award some other company without financial recognition. Newspapers took generous subsidies, as well. In less than three years, the Columbia *Union* collected $59,988, when Democratic witnesses claimed that the work could have been done for $33,528 less; the Charleston *Republican* collected $60,982, or more than twice what the work could have been done for. The *Union*'s proprietor, L. Cass Carpenter, did not just overestimate. He cooked the books. An entry for $878 became $1,878, another for $195 became $695, and others were expanded by 300 percent or more. (There was, however, one catch, which may lessen the complicity: Woodruff and Carpenter were not paid in cash, but in state certificates, whose face value was easily twice what they would sell for on the market. How much profit they actually realized is therefore a little unclear.)[22]

By 1872, many Republicans wanted as little to do with printing swindles as possible. In Mississippi, leading radicals joined conservative Democrats to cut printing out of the budget. "I am afraid the rates of the Pilot are too low," admitted A. T. Morgan, who had helped push the measure through, "but, as the bill was purposely delayed until the eleventh hour, believing that the Senate would refuse to concur in the very low rates fixed by the House, and thus go over on old rates, we concluded to put it through."[23]

The ugly scrimmage over public preferment was, to be sure, no Republican monopoly across the South. In North Carolina, railroad presidents did their best to keep their own Democratic journals on Treasury funding and keep the *Sentinel* off of it.[24] But the onus lay on the Republicans; that, at least, was where the publicity came. Nor was all the financing locally arranged. Republican newspapers, like their Democratic counterparts, profited from the federal government's largess and sought it out. Leading Northern senators put their endorsement on appeals for the Atlanta *Whig*. To Edward McPherson, clerk of the U.S. House, came requests for the right to publish federal laws from obscure presses, including the Maysville (Kentucky) *Republican*, the Fort Smith *Arkansas Patriot*, and the Newbern (N.C.) *Times*. Congressmen besieged him on behalf of their own faction's special voice.[25]

With so much manna distributed, Republicans did manage to set up a scattering of newspapers across the Reconstructed South, at least momentarily. Every large city had one paper, and several, like Mobile and New Orleans, sustained a couple. In Calvert, Texas, the *Tribune* offered itself for "the development, improvement and progress of the country." Thanks to the clause in Mississippi's judicial printing bill in 1874 that permitted

Republican judges to choose what organ should do the presswork for their districts, a host of what one hostile rival called "journalistic mushrooms" came into "sickly life." Some of them were not much beyond a heading. Like the Vicksburg *Plain Dealer*, they were printed on the presses of the established journal and were born simply to punish the existing organ for having failed to go along with the newly elected governor's faction in the recent election.[26]

Ideally, the arrangement should have done two things: sustain a strong party and give the newspapers time to find their commercial footing and a local following sufficient to free the journals from patronage's necessity. It did neither, although the promoters promised permanency, ever a few months away. "My position is being sustained better than I expected, much better," wrote one proprietor to Senator Adelbert Ames.[27] But not well enough. By the year's end, his paper had fallen into Democratic hands, and Republicans were forced to establish a new organ. That instability, and the broken promise, was the real story of the Republican press in the South. Hopes withered and died. Fair prospects were invariably dashed. Even in Natchez, strongly Republican, the party organ, the *New South*, had to fend off Democratic purchase offers and constant poverty. Most residents were black, but that clearly was not where the profits came from. They came from white Republicans and from the governor's largess. So within a year of the newspaper's launching, it had become the voice of the more conservative whites in the party. Even that did not suffice. "Our best efforts have always failed to make the paper pay for itself," its manager lamented, "—it has always been an expense to its owners."[28]

Even at its best, how miserable the Republican press actually was! Few of the newspapers could afford Associated Press wire service privileges, and most of them were unable to refurbish their type when it wore out. So the journals that Redfield saw, with the laws printed in them, only excited his disgust. "The one before me is a fair specimen," he wrote, "—small, dirty, badly arranged, old type, thick ink, poor impression, and edited by a jackass. A man could not read the 'laws' in it if he should be inclined."[29]

In Alabama in 1872, only seven of sixty-six newspapers declared themselves Republican, and all but two were weeklies. Arthur Bingham's Montgomery *Alabama State Journal* proudly declared itself the "only daily republican paper in the state." Such pronouncements should have been seen for what they were, confessions of general weakness. If the *Alabama State Journal* claimed a circulation equal to the Democratic *Adver-*

tiser, no other Republican organ could claim the same parity in any other city. Birmingham, Tallapoosa, and Eufaula had no Republican organ at all. "We have no votes or papers to spare in Alabama," a partisan sighed.[30]

The story was not much different anywhere else. Mississippi had fourteen Democratic newspapers that claimed a circulation over 1,000; the Republicans had three, and only one of them had more than 2,500 readers. The other nine in 1872 had circulations of around 500. The Jacksonville *Florida Union* proclaimed itself the "largest in the State; only republican and oldest paper in Jacksonville, a city of 8,000 population." But out of that 8,000, its weekly circulation was 950 and its triweekly 575; no daily was issued at all. For all the patronage that Republicans endowed on party organs in New Orleans in 1871, their circulation never approached that of Democratic papers. Among their upstate organs, perhaps a dozen of them were printed in New Orleans and sent to the parishes that they pretended to represent, just so they could meet the residency requirements for taking local printing patronage. "[U]nless a paper has local support," Attorney General Amos Akerman commented to a Georgia politician seeking Northern funding for his project, "it is not worth much."[31]

Patronage propped up the newspapers. It never made any of them strong. Tennessee Republicans found that to their cost in 1869. They had worked hard to sustain a Republican press establishment. The mainstay of that effort was the Legal Advertising law. By that measure, it was unlawful for any newspaper not designated by the governor to publish gubernatorial proclamations, municipal edicts, administrators' notices, notifications of sheriffs' sales, or any kind of legal publication. Some dozen journals—"little worthless and insignificant sheets," a hostile observer sneered—received the designation and with it monopoly rights. A few of the papers had modest circulations; a few had none at all, not being founded until the need for some source of publication arose. Even a "little nose-rag of a paper" served Republicans better than none at all, though it did not go very far. When Governor DeWitt Senter broke with the party and courted Democratic votes, he was able to smother most of the Republican journals by taking away their patronage. The Memphis *Post* was obliterated when the *Avalanche* and the *Appeal,* both Democratic newspapers and well heeled already, were endowed with the legal advertisements as well. Other newspapers, like the Maryville *Republican,* tacked with the conservative breeze to survive and ended up supporting Democratic presidential nominees.[32]

In Mississippi, cutting off aid meant that the Jackson *Pilot*, the state organ, could no longer publish daily. The publisher, discouraged, set out for New Orleans and left word that the editorial corps must be discharged. "The paper never was so strong, never had so much influence as now," a member of its staff assured Senator Ames. But what did that strength, that influence really mean if the paper after two years could not subsist on its own?[33] In 1875, the legislature wanted to slash court districts' printing, and the *Pilot* was blunt. "Of course nothing but death can follow such treatment." This, after five years of Republican rule, was a bitter confession.[34]

With patronage so important, the struggle for preferment set Republican press against Republican press; with a political voice so necessary, the selection of a press to do the state printing turned into a fracas between Republican factions over which organ would receive recognition.[35] In Mississippi, the struggle became an annual occurrence. Scarcely had the first Reconstruction legislature met before two issues merged: whom to send to the Senate and which newspaper to make state printer. As factions shifted, one press and then another was endowed, with the governor choosing and dismissing editors and the legislature cutting back on payments until it had its own protégés in charge.[36] Even then, patronage was not enough; without advertisers and subscribers, a journal lived on hope, and precious little of that. In 1873, when Republicans split between Senators Adelbert Ames and James Lusk Alcorn, each of them running for governor, the bulk of Republican votes went to Ames; but the white minority of the party, by far the more affluent portion, supported Alcorn, as did most conservatives. For Republican editors, making a choice must have been as painful as it was obvious which side to choose. Like the Vicksburg *Times and Republican*, they came down for Alcorn. As J. G. Patrick, editor of the Greenville *Republican*, explained to Ames, "I was your strongest friend in Washington County. But the *Republican* had to live."[37]

Not all the temptation to break party lines came from conservative pressure. As in the North, it was easier to plan for a party organ than to make one work. Dissident Republicans themselves spoke of corruption in their battles against one another, and in this the editors played a particular role. Freedmen had held lofty visions of a General Assembly where "railroad and bank directors would no longer have it their own way and fill all the chairs in our Legislatures," wrote a South Carolina journalist.

"But money is ahead of us yet." If a railroad aid bill passed, true or not, enemies of subsidies stormed that the lawmakers had been bought, and the press picked up the allegation as a plain fact.[38]

Organs out of tune became, in time, almost as much of a liability as a hostile newspaper would have been. To the North went complaints of this journal or that, subsidized by congressional printing and bristling with traitors to the cause. "He is an unprincipled egotist—a traitor to his party and a *curse* to the Union men in Ga.," the Savannah postmaster wrote of the local Republican editor. "We are at a loss to understand that phase of human nature, that will allow such a hypocrite as the Editor of the Austin Republican to enter the arena with honest men, and with unblushing impudence call himself a Republican," the San Antonio *Express* raged.[39]

There was a final discouragement to a two-party press establishment in the South, of less consequence than the financial problem, but still palpable and influential. A violence never far from the surface of Southern politics meant special trouble for the outspoken Republican editor. Senator Charles E. Furlong of Vicksburg, whose Republicanism had lasted only as long as his power did, took out his resentments at the editorial course of the *Times* by cowhiding the editor on the street. In Louisiana, the official papers of Carrollton were forcibly entered. The type was dumped into the streets and the title headings were carried away. In Alexandria, Louisiana, the Rapides *Gazette* office was destroyed; at Marksville, a mob smashed the *Register*'s type and drove proprietor Amos S. Collins from the parish. All of these may have been unpremeditated incidents, but, as the New Orleans *Republican* noted, it was more than coincidence that they happened almost exclusively to Republican presses.[40]

The end of Reconstruction did not wipe out the two-party press entirely, but it dealt a serious blow and in most states a fatal one. By 1872, Georgia's Republican press had fallen to three establishments, and one of them had to operate out of the offices of another. The largest journal had a circulation of 2,300, no more than half that of any number of Democratic newspapers in the state. In Raleigh, both parties had organs. But by 1872, the *Standard* was gone. There were three Democratic newspapers and only a triweekly to counter them.[41]

Things only got worse. By 1879, the triweekly and the three Georgia newspapers were gone. Nothing replaced them. In the Upper South, several major newspapers survived. German-speaking partisans kept the San Antonio *Freie Presse für Texas* going, and the Dallas *Intelligencer* and

Tallahassee *Florida Union* went on publishing. Beyond that, advertisers' guides listed no journal of consequence. In the Deep South, east of Texas and north of Florida, Republicans had nothing. By contrast, Selma supported a pair of Democratic newspapers. So did Austin, Houston, Mobile, Wilmington, Raleigh, and Richmond. New Orleans had three. Beyond factional disputes, no public debate existed in their columns.[42]

The frustration of Republican hopes had more than a local significance. What party newspapers printed made a difference not just to Southern readers, but to Northern ones as well. The public opinion on which federal support for Negro political power depended relied on reports from the South, and there the strongest presses had a special advantage.

One major reason was that the other side was deliberately suppressed before it could get north. From Republicans came the complaint that telegraph operators did their best to quash or color dispatches sent out. On reaching New Orleans, a reporter for the Chicago *Inter-Ocean* found difficulty in telegraphing anything "not in harmony with the sentiments of the operators. . . . They have altered, omitted, and even suppressed private and press dispatches, and until [recently] it was dangerous to take anything in writing there over your own signature." The head of the local White League instructed the manager of Western Union to submit all dispatches referring to racial disturbances in Louisiana to him in advance; and while a revolutionary Democratic government held the city, it inspected every telegram going out. In another case, an up-country dispatch sent to the New Orleans *Republican* was suppressed in the telegraph office and replaced with another, false in every particular and vouched for with a forged signature. In still another incident, a critical piece of correspondence to the Louisville *Anzeiger* was destroyed by the courier to whom it was entrusted.[43]

Far more pervasive than petty harassment was the way in which the dominance of the conservative press affected what Northerners read on a daily basis. The reason went to the heart of the way that the Associated Press operated.

AP's problems were obvious. As one of the most important news gatherers in the land, certainly the one most used, it had a special responsibility not to make events, but to report those that had taken place and report them accurately. All this depended on the agency's system of telegraphic dispatches, with its local subsidiaries in operation. Southern newspapers subscribing to the Associated Press—that is, those able to afford it, which was more often than not the conservative press—did not simply inform their readers better. They became the conduits for information *from* the South on which the national AP relied. Readers might spot mention of blacks murdered by white-liners in Vicksburg and never know that the crimes happened there; the stories would come out under a New Orleans or Little Rock dateline, with the outrage's location excised. No Vicksburg Democratic editor had any intention of reflecting badly on his party friends. When the dispatches from Columbia were written by an editor who was a member of the white Democratic Rifle Club, one of the leading paramilitary intimidators of blacks, there was sure to be a bias. When the Charleston *News and Courier* sent the information from downstate, its support for the Democratic ticket could not be separated from its reports. Terrible revelations about Democratic intimidation and violence came out of the Louisiana Returning Board's hearings, but they went no further over AP's wires.[44] "I understand the Senator from Connecticut to say that the Associated Press is not under the control of the democratic party in the South," Senator John J. Patterson of South Carolina remarked in 1876. "That may be true; but every agent of the Associated Press in the South is a democrat."[45]

Even Redfield noticed the effect that AP could have when he interviewed Governor Powell Clayton. To his surprise, he found not the corrupt intriguer he had been describing (and would again), but a plainspoken, shrewd, and bold politician, whose worst traits came from his powerful instinct for self-preservation. What could have caused so distorted a reputation as Clayton endured? Redfield suspected that the lack of an official AP agent in Arkansas had something to do with it. The syndicate deliberately refused to hire anyone for Little Rock. Instead, it turned to the Memphis *Avalanche* for all information. The *Avalanche* held its opinions strongly—vehemently hostile ones about anything Republican—and its responsibility to purvey the truth weakly, if at all. The "specials" that came from Arkansas usually were from Powell's foes as well. Then the Associated Press took this information and spread it under its reputation. When Democrats rallied to Governor Elisha Baxter and helped him against a Republican coup engineered by his defeated gubernatorial rival Joseph Brooks in 1874, Little Rock did produce a man to contact the wire services. Unfortunately, he was J. N. Smithee, Baxter's commissioner of immigration, who served as an apologist for his superior in particular and Democrats in general.[46]

The news Northerners read affected not just the credibility but the financial stability of Southern governments. To carry out their plans, Republican authorities had to issue bonds, but they were pathetically dependent on the price that markets on Wall and Lombard streets and on the Bourse were willing to pay. Allegations of fraud or invalidity could sink a security's chances of sale, and Democrats broadcast their accusations freely. Correction lagged far behind. A conservative Arkansas newspaper might accuse the governor of demanding a kickback on any bonds he issued in aid to state railroad construction. At home, the accusations could be refuted with little effort, but not in New York, and the treasury suffered for it.[47]

AP's central office only aggravated the distortion by sifting through and defining what was news. In effect, it could suppress as it chose, condense, and, in abbreviating dispatches, skew their original meaning. With so many agents telegraphing so much local matter, filtering was a necessary part of the syndicate's job. Still, it worked more to Democrats' benefit than Republicans'. "It is a notorious fact that the intelligence from the Southern States in which politics have had any part has been singularly untrustworthy," the New York *Graphic* protested. "Every insignificant offence committed by a negro has been exaggerated into an outrage, if not developed into a bloody and brutal riot, while the telegraph seldom reports the shooting of negroes by whites, even though a score are massacred at a time." Arkansas legislators behaved rowdily as ever, but when black ones showed ill-breeding, AP considered it news.[48]

Beyond the metropolitan papers that could afford to send their own reporters (and virtually none could do it for every story given to them), Republican editors in the North were helpless. They were like gamblers who knew that the roulette wheel they played was fixed and yet kept playing because it was the only game in town. When wire services from New Orleans reported that U.S. soldiers lifted their caps in respect for the White League army that had overthrown the Republican state government, partisans knew in their hearts that the story could not be true. But they had no way of disproving it, and as news it had to be printed. When Southern Republicans held a convention at Chattanooga in 1874, the AP report seethed with hostility. The reason was easy enough to find: just before the convention met, the telegraph office manager had the AP representative replaced with the local Democratic editor. Still, they published the news they were given. "ONE-SIDED," the

Washington *Chronicle* headlined its columns: "WHITE LEAGUE DIS-PATCHES. ELECTIONEERING DOCUMENTS. FEARFUL TALES OF ARRESTS AND TRIALS BY UNITED STATES TROOPS." But it neither countered the stories with alternate reports nor rewrote the material it got to fit its own views. Republican readers could believe the heading or believe the reports.[49]

If the Southern Republican presses had serious disadvantages in spreading their own account of events for Northerners, the black newspapers found their task well nigh impossible. Many of them existed across the South. In Alabama, at least a dozen survived for a year or more. As late as 1880, two were publishing in Huntsville, one in Marion, and one in Montgomery. As far as the Associated Press was concerned, they might as well not have existed at all. They were almost never quoted, not even for the purposes of rebuttal. Their news, such as it was, about black activities, was ignored entirely. (This neglect would persist; incomplete runs of white Republican organs survive, but for many of their black counterparts, only the name survived in the historical record. Of the Montgomery *Watchman* and the Huntsville *Herald*, not a single issue exists; only one is extant from the Montgomery *Advance*.)[50]

How would the picture have changed had there been a strong, biracial press and had it been exploited to the full by the Associated Press? The answer is necessarily conjectural, but from those surviving issues of black journals like the Arkansas *Freeman* or the Washington *National New Era*, one can surmise a few things. First, the terrorism and violence that was used against Southern Republicans would have received greater coverage; the freedmen would have appeared as less comic figures, less the passive followers of white leaders, and the issues on which Southern politics turned might have shown a smaller emphasis on taxes, railroads, levees, and development, and more on the transformation of social custom, religion, and educational practice. The radical character of the South's transformation and the successes of that change would have been more visible; so would the abuses of the convict-lease system.[51] With all that publicity, Northern whites might not have been convinced that federal intervention to perpetuate the Reconstruction experiment was called for; but the argument on that side would have been stronger, the argument for the utter failure of the Republican experiment would have been more on the defensive.

Press or no press, the gains of Reconstruction might have been lost.

The odds against its long-term success were enormous, the temptation of Republicans to fight each other was intense, and the economic and military power of conservative whites was almost insurmountable. When members of the biracial coalition saw each other as "political *bastards*, and renegades, and newly converted traitors," or just plain cowards, and when they lacked the guns and land to protect themselves from threats, the power of an editor, even one "true as steel to the flint," was a puny one, indeed.[52] But if a strong press might not have made Reconstruction work, its lack ensured Reconstruction's failure. Until Southern citizens had newspapers that published all the news fit to print, they would have their views shaped by papers that broadcast only the news that fitted the printer.

CHAPTER 14

An Extraordinary State of Affairs at Vicksburg

On December 7, 1874, alarming reports reached the Northern press of "an extraordinary state of affairs" in Vicksburg, Mississippi. Some seven hundred blacks, heavily armed, were marching on the town. Businesses had closed down, as the citizens, badly outnumbered, mustered under arms to meet them.[1] Quickly, additional information presented itself. The two sides had met. The attackers had been turned back; one white was killed, and some twenty-five blacks. But the fight was not over. "The negroes in the country are reported as burning dwellings and gin-houses."[2]

What could have caused so bloody a contretemps? At first the messages were cryptic. "The object of the assault is said to have been to reinstate a sheriff," said the New York *Tribune*. It was, as the dispatches quickly made clear, a *Negro* sheriff, one Peter Crosby, "who was requested to resign because he had not given a bond." As other reports soon clarified, the request had been made in no uncertain terms. According to the wire services, there had been trouble for some time between the taxpayers' association and county officials, many of whom were under indictment for forgery and embezzlement; citizens had tried to induce the county board of supervisors to make Crosby give a new bond and were rebuffed. Exasperated, "citizens" met to demand a general resignation by all the malefactors. Their guilt beyond question, the others fled, but Crosby refused to do so. Instead, he resigned. Then, on Saturday, December 5, a publication appeared on the streets of Vicksburg using the most inflammatory language to summon an armed force for his restoration. At its behest, field hands came marching on the town. They were met and were ordered to turn back. When they refused to do so, the firing began on both sides and the blacks fled.[3]

Who was to blame for the fight? About that, too, the sources had no doubt at all. According to the AP report, carpetbagger Governor Adelbert Ames had incited "the invasion of this city by negroes" and had the help of his attorney general, a misdeed for which "the ablest lawyers" now held unquestionable evidence and would arraign both men. More generally, the fight must be blamed on the belligerence of the blacks, filled with race hatred by their demagogic leaders, like State Superintendent of Education Thomas W. Cardozo, "than whom no man has done more to create this trouble." Cardozo allegedly declared that "the race conflict is now on us, and the negro women are ready to commence with axe and knife to slaughter the white women and children."[4]

Other reports asserted that at the moment of actual contact, the black mob had provoked a fight. It fired the first shots. Sources in Washington informed reporters that the black chancery clerk of Warren County had boasted in a public speech that white women would yet be proud to marry colored gentlemen, and that he could get any white belle in the county he wanted. By refreshing contrast, the fight on the white side had had nothing to do with race at all. It was simply a struggle for the protection of taxpayers' rights, open to all men of property.[5]

Nothing less than deposition of the sheriff and public officers would have been possible for the frustrated taxpayers. Every other alternative had been thwarted. "Finally, the respectable tax-payers, who had the best interests of the State at heart, driven to desperation by their wrongs, demanded the expulsion from office of these unprincipled scoundrels."[6] The right of revolution, therefore, had been invoked by hitherto conservative men.

A tidy explanation! But journalists should have wondered about a few of the most obvious difficulties with their accounts. The first was with the original descriptions of the armed engagement: reports put it in terms of a formal battle, with each side massing in columns and maneuvering for position.[7] Had the two sides been as well matched as the descriptions implied either in discipline or numbers, this reporting would have made sense, but if so, why did one side flee so soon, and after having inflicted so little damage? Why were virtually all the casualties on one side?

"H. C." of the New York *Times* offered one possible explanation. The Negro had "a natural fear of white men." Understanding neither the principles of warfare nor basic tactics, blacks failed to station themselves behind the breastworks, left over since the war. Whites positioned on the cliffs above were therefore able to "kill them by the dozen."[8] But this explanation only made the event more perplexing. Why would men bent on sacking a city defended by well-armed and experienced whites, before whom they trembled, come so ill-organized and badly armed that they would be beaten in an encounter by forces so much smaller than themselves? Why would blacks filled with such a "natural fear" provoke a fight rather than withdraw?

Journalists did not explore another possibility, that the number of "attackers" had been exaggerated, the defenders' advantages minimized, and the conditions under which blacks were fired on misstated. But a House committee did. For all the reports of terrible, bloodthirsty hordes of freedmen menacing Vicksburg, it turned out that no more than a few hundred blacks had gathered in several tatterdemalion armies. They had no military training and no well-drilled leaders. In every contact with the enemy, they were badly outnumbered. Their weapons were whatever they had on hand. Some had shotguns, some pistols, and half had no weapons at all.[9] The origins of the clash in Vicksburg raised other puzzling questions. How could the helplessness of conservatives to redress grievances be squared with their success at the polls just four months before? How could it be reconciled with the indictments that a biracial grand jury had handed down against the leading county officials and with the effective work done by a Republican district attorney?

Nor did the dichotomy make sense, of city whites who thought only in terms of taxes and country blacks who saw the crisis only in terms of race. How could the two groups' thinking be so opposed? Why did the taxpayers call their associations White Leagues? Why did no black property holders belong? Why did the citizens' army that marched out to meet the invaders have no blacks in it? On close examination, the story sent north fell apart.

What, then, had actually happened? The answer is not easy to come by. Some witnesses lied. Others declined to testify out of fear. Still, a basic picture emerges, and it was far from that sketched by the newspapers.

Race had been an issue all along on both sides. The forces that had overthrown the Republican city government that summer deplored corruption and high taxes, but their campaign drew the color line sharply as well. Voters were warned that blacks were mustering secret armies, that they were colonizing Negroes from beyond city limits, that the real issue was race mixing in the schools, that local blacks had threatened to burn the town if whites won a majority. As Election Day neared, armed white bands rode the streets and paid visits on black voters. Many Republicans found reason to shun the polls. "The day is ours," a resident exulted as the returns came in; but to ensure lasting victory, he added, white men must wipe out Negro economic power. Let the people discountenance "all negro hackmen, barbers, waiters, servants (male and female), and compel them to go back to their proper sphere, the corn and cotton fields. The war has commenced, and before it ends our city . . . will have lost a large number of idle, vagabond negroes—the men infamous vagrants all, the women unworthy of any name but strumpet." [10]

At once the campaign began to overturn county officials a year before their terms expired. Whites pressured Sheriff Crosby's bondsmen; it was not just his own insolvency that kept him from raising legal bond. Sponsors withdrew their names or challenged Crosby's right to serve. At the moment that the whites met in a hall to consider means of removing the sheriff on December 2, legal methods of driving him from office remained untried. [11] Indeed, a resolution proposing legal remedies was voted down and another put through demanding the resignation of *all* county officials, including the county treasurer, against whom no accusation had been made but whose color was self-evident. [12] A committee was chosen to call on Crosby and force an immediate answer from him. When, after a half hour of grace, he had failed to submit, the committee reported back to the meeting, which adjourned, its members five hundred strong marching on the courthouse to compel a different response. With guns being brandished in his face and a few members of the crowd calling for his lynching, Crosby signed the resignation written out for him. But the sheriff was not so easily defeated. Sending a written protest to Judge George F. Brown of the circuit court, he made clear that only duress had made him yield, and that he would do what he could to get his office back. The next day Crosby was seated in the Governor's Mansion, telling his tale to Adelbert Ames.

Ames knew little about the frustrations of taxpayers but more than he liked about the aims of the White League, and he was determined to uphold the due process of law. The sheriff wanted help. He was promised a semblance of it, but not federal troops, which Ames had failed to obtain to keep order in the recent city election, nor state militiamen, most of whom were white and unreliable guardians for black officials. Rather, the governor advised Crosby to appeal to the courts, promised to back any favorable decision, and encouraged him to raise a *posse comitatus* to uphold his authority.[13]

That was where things went disastrously wrong. The governor assumed that Crosby would go to court first and call for force afterward. Instead, Crosby returned to town, bent on regaining his office. At first, he considered making a posse "of the best lawyers and business men" of Warren County, the very group that had thrown him out. He was quickly advised of how useless the attempt would be. In the end, he deputized two of his friends to bring him a body of men to town the following Monday evening to serve as deputies.[14]

Then on Saturday, December 5, a flier appeared, distributed throughout the county over his signature. Crosby denied having written or issued it, which was technically correct, though he authorized its publication in the *Plaindealer*, a black weekly, and signed the statement without reading it. He was astonished to find it passed out as a handbill that spread far beyond city limits and employed a perilously ambiguous choice of words. It was not quite the call to arms that newspapers later pronounced it, but it did appeal for support and left the kind unsaid. Conceivably it could have been read as a summons to Crosby's friends to back him with all the force at their command.[15]

That was how it was read in the countryside. Some blacks mistook it for an official document giving them authority to gather together at Vicksburg as a posse to enforce the law. However both sides may have read it, it was issued without the governor's support or even his knowledge. When it became public, nearly every prominent Republican in town denounced it, including the governor's emissaries. By the evening of Sunday, December 6, Crosby and Republican leaders were sending out all the runners they could to retract the proclamation, but it was too late. Already blacks had begun to amass what weapons they had and march on the town.[16]

Many of them were not even sure what they were marching to *do*. The sheriff needed their help, but how? doing what? Some of them had heard that the board of supervisors wanted them to rally in town for a protest meeting to show the people's will. Others believed that they would "see Peter Crosby take his seat, and serenade him for it." "It looks right for we colored people to stick to one another as much as the white people," one of the volunteers explained later, "to try to be a nation of people if we could." [17]

Long before the crowds took to the road, the news of their coming had reached the white men in charge at Vicksburg. At first, there was incredulity; then, as the reports were confirmed, alarm, even panic. At three in the morning, city bells rang a tocsin. With Crosby lodged in the city jail, whites mustered to arms. The mayor put Horace H. Miller, a one-time Confederate officer in charge of the soldiery, and just after dawn they set out.

The first skirmish took place on Grove Street. There some 125 blacks under Andrew Owen had marched toward the town. But they halted on the outskirts, and Owen rode to parley with Miller. They had come, he explained, in obedience to the sheriff's order. Miller offered to bring Owen and the sheriff face-to-face to clear up matters; on reaching the jail, Owen found that he was not wanted after all. His men should be sent home at once. Owen cursed, and with good reason, for as he later remarked, Crosby "had got us into a little trouble." It cannot have escaped his thoughts that his men were badly outgunned and he, with them, stood an excellent chance of being killed. So he was nothing loath to return to his followers and order them home. [18]

It was as they were withdrawing—indeed, had withdrawn half a mile—that the firing began. Who fired first? Colonel Miller came the closest of any witness to accusing the blacks, and he declared the shooting "simultaneous" on either side. Other witnesses agreed that a mounted group of whites had begun the shooting. [19] "There wasn't any danger," one white explained later, "for we were firing with long-range guns at long range, and they with shot-guns or short-range guns." Many of them were not firing at all: Owen saw to that. As they heard the shots, some blacks wanted to stand and make a fighting line. Owen forbade it. At first, he tried to convince his men that the gunfire was merely for effect, but as the firing persisted and bullets struck closer, he had to draw his own revolver to keep the stragglers from forming into a line. "If you return the fire, I will give you the next volley," he told them, remembering afterward that this threat "squashed them. They marched on after the balance, and I saw one of them in a few minutes fall upon the hill." At that point the lines broke. Men ran for their lives. Owen leaped into a ditch, and it was there that he was captured.[20]

That and the other skirmishes did not complete the killing. Spurred by the false and exaggerated statements spread through the Associated Press, whites rushed from outlying areas to aid their race. "Can raise good crowd within twenty-four hours to kill out your negroes," one Texan wired the authorities. That evening, 160 armed men crossed over from Louisiana to tender their services. Whites broke into private dwellings and seized the personal firearms of blacks and anything else they fancied. An old black huntsman sitting in his neighbor's house was shot and killed. In an outlying house, a black father and son were murdered in their family's presence. An aged and decrepit man was met up with by one of the "patrols" sent to scour black districts and the top of his head was smashed in. Other blacks were shot, their throats cut and ears cut off, their bodies left unburied. Many more fled into the canebrake. When the House committee sought information, many refused to testify. Others called to the stand cut testimony short when they learned that their words would be published. Of casualties, no good estimate is possible. Early reports spoke of 50 blacks buried in one spot, and on hearsay historians have put the death toll at 300.[21] Pressed by Ames's adjutant general, Crosby again resigned his office. Even then his life was in such danger that his captors had to keep him safe in jail until they could arrange a clandestine passage out of town.[22]

Obviously the earliest press accounts made a hash of the truth. Nothing else would have been possible when the first reports, carried along the wire services, relied exclusively on Southern conservative newspapers in Vicksburg, New Orleans, and Memphis. A bit after that came letters north from "occasional correspondents," invariably white natives issuing editorial comment and protected by anonymity from challenge. If journalists' professional standards were low, that of the "occasionals" was nonexistent. They neither interviewed nor sought a range of sources beyond their neighbors and their own consciences. If "C. W. B.," writing in to the Louisville *Courier-Journal* was right, the blacks had wanted to burn the town in August and had been frustrated in their plans. Since that time, he declared, country Negroes had boasted "that *as soon as they got the money for their cotton and could buy arms, they intended to come in and 'whip out the Vicksburg white people.'*" Not one witness before the House committee backed up the statement, and as "C. W. B." admitted, all his knowledge of Vicksburg came from letters that friends sent him from there.[23]

Within a week, a few Northern reporters had reached the scene and sent back better reports. Even so, not having been there for the events and unfamiliar with the area, they put their faith in a very limited group of informants.

This was not all their own fault, as a correspondent sent south by the New York *Times* made clear. The blacks proved too guarded to advance his understanding at all. They preferred not to talk to strangers, especially on political matters. "Ask them the simplest question and they profess to be unable to give an answer. Touching the recent massacre they positively refuse to give any definite information. I have spent hours by day and by night seeking for one black man who could and would express an opinion upon the subject. I have been unsuccessful, and I do not think that in the whole State there is a colored man who can be induced to make any detailed statement regarding the trouble here." White sources talked freely, the journalist added, but only to justify their side's conduct.[24]

Having thrown up so strong a challenge to his sources, the *Times* reporter would have had every right to abandon hope of learning the truth. He might even have pondered the reasons that blacks were so reluctant to speak up. The reason should have been obvious: they were afraid, and their fear should have been an unmistakable clue that something was wrong in the interpretation of the crisis as essentially one over corruption, rather than color. Instead, the journalist took up the conservatives' line and accepted the same sources he had questioned before. The version of Republican officeholders he dismissed at once. Even white ones owed their place to "negro votes." That made them unworthy of trust. The reverse applied to "white men of education and apparent honor," all of them hostile to Ames's government, and to "fair-minded Republicans," which meant those taking the white side in the conflict.[25]

Indeed, the language of the accounts themselves sent signals to readers. Labeling the blacks marching on the city an "army" implied more organization than they had and a military intention, while "assailants" and "attackers" assumed in advance that they came with an aggressive purpose. The term "citizen" was equally loaded. It meant "white" exclusively. To refer to a "black citizen" would have sounded positively oxymoronic. He was a "negro," nothing more. Often the assumption was more heavily cloaked in language. When a special dispatch pronounced the governor's proclamation convening the legislature as "almost unanimously condemned," for example, it said what could not have been true unless the journalist considered white public opinion the only one that counted. After all, half the state's population was black, and blacks could hardly have deplored an action taken to protect their rights.[26]

What makes this misjudgment of events at Vicksburg more disturbing is how regularly Northern reporting made the same mistakes. All through that autumn, conservative Democrats had been raising white fears over proposed civil rights legislation and bitterness against Republican tax rates in order to divide voters along race lines. Building a panic from loose talk about secret black military companies, they had assembled paramilitary White Leagues to intimidate and kill active Republican politicians. Louisiana's government, however briefly, had been overthrown. Up the Red River in Coushatta, parish officers had been forced to resign and were then butchered. Minor slaughters of blacks took place in Tennessee, North Carolina, and Alabama.[27]

In each case, as the Chicago *Tribune* noted tartly, the process was the same:

One day we are told that the negroes who are marching on Vicksburg or some other Southern city are of the most ferocious character and prodigious numbers; that they are impaling children upon pitchforks, ravishing women, and are within an hour's march of the devoted city which is doomed to the fire and sword. The next day's telegraph brings the intelligence that seventy more negroes are slaughtered, and not a white man is hurt. In yesterday's dispatches we were informed that the black women were arming themselves with the view of butchering the white women. This, of course, is very dreadful intelligence, but isn't this intelligence getting a little too dreadful? If the black men are going to murder all the white men, and the black women all the white women, who knows but that the black pickaninnies may break loose some day, and, arming themselves with carving-knives, sirup bottles, safety-pins, and feather-bolsters, deliberately proceed to cut, maul, stick, slash, and suffocate all the white babies in their neighborhoods?

Yet Northern newspapers never seemed to learn. Each scare was accepted as credulously as if it were the first to appear. As the *Tribune* pointed out, every time the cry arose about blacks massing to butcher the whites, the casualty lists turned out the same way. "If any one is punished, it is a negro. If any one is driven from home, it is a negro. If any one is killed, it is a negro; and if any one is to blame, of course it is a negro." [28]

In every case, Northern reporters took "respectable" whites' version of events and balanced off the victims' death with allegations of their guilt. Witness the Election Day violence at Eufaula, Alabama, a month before Vicksburg's troubles. Zebulon White of the New York *Tribune* touched on it only briefly. Everyone deplored the outbreak, he insisted, adding that black aggression had started the fuss. The lesson Eufaula taught was how foolish a custom it was for the average citizen to carry a pistol. Both sides had blazed away, though the Negroes, being more poorly armed and less skilled, ended up worsted. [29]

In only one sense was White's account balanced: it blamed both sides, although whites took a slightly smaller share. At worst, a *Tribune* reader would assume, the clash was one about which they had no right to learn a partisan moral, and certainly it delivered no message about white Democrats' intentions toward the black voter.

What were the facts? The blacks had not been poorly armed. They had been wholly disarmed. To prevent any excuse for violence, the local Republican judge had ordered them to leave their guns at home. Those who brought weapons to the edge of town were induced to leave them stacked at camp sites that Republicans had set up. On entering town, a federal deputy marshal searched all blacks for what stray arms had eluded precautions. No one did the same for the Democrats, who came well supplied and could get more from the armory one floor above the polling place. Fighting had erupted over a Negro casting a Democratic vote. Underage and turned away by election officials when he showed up with a Republican ballot, he had been bullied into handing in one from the opposition. When another black tried to interfere, a white stuck a bowie knife in his shoulder and shouted, "Shoot the damned son of a bitch!" At that, firing broke out, all on one side. Blacks fled. They were shot down as they ran. Some dozen white Democrats were hit, too, and one was killed; their side had imperfect aim. A few miles away, a white mob descended on the judge's house and riddled his son with bullets. Those blacks who testified against their attackers before the grand jury were driven from the county. So was the judge. By such means a county largely black and Republican cast an overwhelming Democratic vote, in an election that White insisted was among the fairest and most temperate Alabama had ever known.[30]

The Eufaula riot was of a piece with other violence in Alabama that autumn. At issue was the most critical point on which the use of federal marshals and soldiers to guard the polls rested: that black Southerners really did risk their livelihood, and often their lives, in order to vote or hold office, and that local government could not protect them. Were Republicans really being threatened because of their race and party loyalty, or was this simply a political sham to whip up Northern voters against their own Democratic candidates? How much real blood was there on the "bloody shirt"?

The answer that White and others like him sent back again and again was clear: little or none. When Congressman Charles Hays of Alabama listed political murders in his state, his letter was broadcast nationwide. So was the rebuttal, led by White. In vain Hays pointed out that, if he had muddled some facts and invented some details, the general picture he had given was true. Republicans were shot and killed, bullied and beaten. But the *Tribune* and other papers were far more interested in proving Hays a liar on specifics than an honest man on the basics.[31]

This indictment of the press may seem unduly harsh. Careful readers could have spotted many of the contradictions for themselves; if they read the accounts of "H. C." and those of Sheriff Crosby and Governor Ames, which New York newspapers published, they might have come close to the truth about Vicksburg; but even there, they would have had to discard the biases and direct their attention resolutely away from the misinformation produced and credited in the same newspapers; they would have had to ignore the editorials founded on the earlier depiction of events and determined to award most of the blame to the Republican mob rather than to the civic lawlessness that led Crosby to issue his address to the people. To the end, the editors of the New York *Times* would insist that the issue had never been a white man's government, but taxpayer relief;

to the end, the *Tribune* would blame the conflict on "the system of governing a Southern State from Washington," on "partisan mismanagement and official corruption."[32]

There were two stories in Southern politics. The first was the effort of white conservatives, using violence and extralegal tactics, intimidation, and legitimate political organization, to overthrow Republican governments at the polls or in the streets. The other was an incompetence and corruption in which Republican officials often participated and against which white taxpayers objected with good reason. Vicksburg illustrated both stories. But the most extensive press reports only connected it to the second. In doing so, they added legitimacy to the means used to destroy duly elected governments and stilled Northern uneasiness at the rise of white supremacist violence. Such misreporting would cause many more blacks to lose their lives than those who marched unawares to their deaths on the outskirts of Vicksburg.

PART FIVE

THE BREAKUP OF THE PRESS GANG, 1872–1877

"Another Outrage"
(Thomas Nast, *Harper's Weekly*,
February 6, 1875).

CHAPTER 15

The Worst Thing Yet! 1872

In his portly old age, the bald head and spectacles made him the very image of Charles Dickens's Mr. Pickwick, and to generations yet unborn he would be remembered most for words he never uttered: "Go west, young man." But Horace Greeley of the New York *Tribune* had greatness in more than a Pickwickian sense. He was the foremost editor of his age and one of its most widely recognized men, truly a symbol of the political ambitions of the independent press. Who was more worthy to test that press's actual power? And yet the story of that challenge was as complex as Greeley's character; for the election of 1872, in which he starred so pathetically, was as much a political farce as it was a personal tragedy.

His reputation for oddity and ambition was well earned. Slouching, hot-tempered, benevolent, passionate, rude, the white-coated figure of the *Tribune*'s founder was a caricature easily drawn. Those who believed, as a Cincinnati journalist did, that Greeley did "more wrong through his perverse notions than any man alive," found it easy to like him.[1]

Those who admired his abilities found it easy to laugh at him. His book, *What I Know About Farming*, was automatically dismissed as a packet of conceit and ignorance. In fact, as one reviewer noted, there was plenty of good advice in it about planting forests and irrigating wasteland, and, indeed, "scarcely a page . . . from which even a well-informed farmer may not take a useful hint." But an anecdote about the work fitted the image of the "sage of Chappaqua" more. An admirer baffled Greeley by asking whether he should put manure on his strawberries. Perhaps that would do for a man whose taste was destroyed by tobacco and drink, the editor told him; as for himself, he preferred cream and sugar. His illegible scrawl was another comic legend. There was the story of how he had scribbled a note firing a compositor; it had been so unreadable that the recipient carried it across the street to the *Times*, brandishing it as a letter of recommendation and getting a job instantly.[2]

This fond, comic image led Greeley's critics to belittle the man, but his readers and the politicians knew better. They knew him as a man of principle and conscience, an early critic of slavery, and a founder of the Republican party, a businessman who combined strong views about public affairs with sound judgment about making a great newspaper. "Gath's" description is an apt one:

> He was a gigantic bull in the intellectual and commercial stock market—the editorial Vanderbilt,—ready to bet that a thing would succeed; that it must pan out well; that it had merit in it and must go. . . . The whole country is covered over with monuments of his faith. McCormick's reapers buzz his praises as they shear the harvest-fields. He told Mayor Joseph Medill to go to Chicago and wait there, and this vindicates the wise advice to "Go West." I met Adolph Sutro the tunnel-maker of Nevada the other day,—a man who is paying out from $30,000 to $50,000 a month in wages, and who, if he succeeds will have revolutionized silver-mining in this country, and he said: ". . . Everybody was laughing at me, and it looked dark ahead, when Horace Greeley spent a whole day reading my book. He asked no questions what public opinion had to say about it. He said: 'That is a great project, and I believe in you!' "[3]

To have Greeley's backing was worth a fortune, for "New York's most honest newspaper" had become a national institution. Its columns gave reform a fair hearing and full coverage. The editorials were derided by some but read with trust by many more, and while Greeley did not write all or even most of them, their utterances generally echoed his own. Those had a bluntness that was legend. New Yorkers remembered how Greeley had refuted an editorial in the *Evening Post* with "You lie, villain! wilfully, wickedly, basely lie!"—perhaps the shortest leading article on record. A story (characteristic, but certainly false) made the rounds of one crack journalist who committed the one unpardonable sin: he began an editorial with, "We fear." He was fired on the spot. "The Tribune fears nothing," Greeley told him.[4]

Others feared the *Tribune*, as well they should have. "Having him firmly behind me will be as helpful as an army of one hundred thousand men," Abraham Lincoln was reported to have said. After giving offense to Greeley, the Grant administration scrambled to make amends. It was quite true, as later critics would allege, that Greeley's resentment against the Grant presidency began when he was denied the mission to England that he had so hoped would come to him. (So did Benjamin F. Butler, one of Greeley's main targets: he wanted the editor out of the country.) It was not a deliberate snub; after all, the *Tribune* alone had been let into Grant's confidence as he was picking his cabinet. Without publicizing it, the president hastened to make the editor commissioner of the newly completed Pacific Railroad, a post immediately refused.[5] A year later, the president proposed giving Greeley the British mission after all and was only dissuaded by his alarmed secretary of state. By the end of 1870, the wooing was going on in earnest. Word was passed through John Russell Young that the administration was eager to know what Greeley wanted. As soon as official business began again after the Christmas holidays, the New York City postmaster wrote his superior, would it not be wise to invite Greeley to Washington and have the president spoil him with attention? The editor had ideas enough and was "easily satisfied."[6]

Wishful thinking! The scheme got Grant's backing, if not his open invitation, and the editor was assured of almost anything he wanted except the one demand that most mattered, administration abandonment of Roscoe Conkling's faction in New York. Greeley left Washington unreconciled to low-tariff Republicans like Garfield and as angry with Grant as ever.[7] By 1872 the *Tribune*'s master had come out for restricting presidents to a single term and embraced the cause of civil service reform. Touring the South and Midwest, Greeley had given cheering crowds the message that a sheaf of *Tribune* editorials should have made clear already: the nation could have harmony again only on a platform of equal rights and full amnesty to all former Confederates.[8]

Nor did Greeley go to perdition alone. That spring, Republican journals previously loyal to the party echoed his appeal and much of his platform of reconciliation and reform: Samuel Bowles's *Republican*, Murat Halstead's *Commercial*, Charles A. Dana's *Sun*, Horace White's Chicago *Tribune*, and Colonel William Grosvenor's St. Louis *Missouri Democrat*. Seconding their cry for a united front on reform's behalf were Democrats, notably Henry Watterson's Louisville *Courier-Journal*, Wilbur F. Storey's Chicago *Times*, and the McLeans's Cincinnati *Enquirer*, all of which, naturally, had every reason to cheer any movement that arrayed Republicans against each other.

By 1872, the independent Republican press had reason for disaffection. Many of Dana's allegations in the *Sun* of bribery and nepotism, like his evidence that Grant awarded rich men with cabinet seats in payment for their having endowed him with a mansion in earlier years, were more fabulous than true.[9] "The Worst Thing Yet!" a typical headline read (aptly, since it was the most baseless allegation of all). But Dana was readily believed when he was wrong because so often he was right, or nearly so. "I send you a letter written by a friend of the office to one of our men," Amos J. Cummings, editor of the *Sun*, wrote to Uriah Painter, who still provided news from Washington. "I want you to investigate it. . . . Don't show the enclosed letter to a living soul, for it is written by a navy officer who would get into a hell of a scrape if it were known that he wrote us." That letter led Painter to corruption, favoritism, and mismanagement in Secretary George Robeson's Navy Department. Midwinter, the headlines broke loose on "Robeson, Roach, Robbery."[10]

Not even party loyalists could dismiss the evidence assembled by the winter of 1872. Slow though it might be to abandon Republicanism, the New York *Evening Post* had to admit the Grant administration's involvement in what it called "The Criminal Epidemic." Seen from Newspaper Row, the administration seemed to be lurching from blunder to blunder. Among the growing band of disaffected Republicans, soon known as the "Liberals," there was grumbling that the president's support for Southern governments grew stronger as those he protected grew ever more unworthy: a Georgia executive whose well-financed lobby tried to make Congress put off elections another two years, a North Carolina governor whose use of state militia against the Ku Klux Klan led to his impeachment and conviction, a gang of rascals led by the president's brother-in-law that used bayonets and gunboats to wrest control of the party from rogues as avaricious as themselves. As reformers were tossed out of the cabinet and fresh mediocrities tossed in, as the administration pushed for fresh territory in the Caribbean and fresh powers over the Southern courts, the journalistic outcry grew.[11]

Newsmen found plenty of friends among the disaffected Republicans. From Senator Lyman Trumbull, challenged for control of Illinois politics by the veterans' organizations and the disciplined machine of Black Jack Logan, the Chicago *Tribune* received a clear sense of Washington on the inside, and Trumbull readily leaked damaging information about Logan's cousin in federal office to the New York *Sun* for further investigation. Losing his war with Senator Roscoe Conkling for control of the New York party organization, Senator Reuben Fenton was always ready to feed Greeley's reporters information, and Senator Carl Schurz of Missouri could rely not only on the loud and influential voice of Grosvenor of the *Missouri Democrat*, but also on his contacts among the independent press. Donn Piatt smoked cigars in the senator's library, and George Alfred Townsend attended his parties, even joining the choruses around the piano.[12]

Could Greeley be converted into an active bolter, too? For all his fondness for utopian and humanitarian reforms that many a liberal considered sentimental rubbish, his alliance with Fenton was one bridge to the liberals. Southern issues were another. Reconciliation was an ideal he had long embraced, with sincerity. When the government lagged in bringing Jefferson Davis to trial for treason, it had been Greeley who led the campaign to set the Confederate president free and raised the money to post bail. Subscribers fled, Republicans cried treason, but Davis was released, and the *Tribune* never recanted.[13]

By early 1872, hopes had risen that dissidents inside the party might unhorse Grant before the Republican convention with a gathering at Cincinnati. That failing, the reformers' conclave might run a Liberal nominee who would win enough Democratic support to wage a winning campaign in November. The Chicago *Tribune* wanted Lyman Trumbull, the Springfield *Republican* preferred former minister to Great Britain Charles Francis Adams, and William Grosvenor gave uneasy support to Missouri's favorite son, B. Gratz Brown. From the New York *Tribune* came not only a growing willingness to endorse the Cincinnati movement, but also coy suggestions that its guiding spirit would answer the call of the people, much to the alarm of liberal dissidents who wanted Greeley to support them rather than face having to support him.[14]

That Greeley was a candidate, and not just a commentator, however, brought up one of the two serious problems that the alliance of independent press and dissident politics faced that year. "We shall yet achieve a Civil Service Reform, nay; we *must*," Greeley had told his readers the summer before. "Office-seeking is our national vice."[15] As such a longtime seeker and so regularly a disappointed one, the editor was certainly in a position to know. Rarely had he enjoyed the success that the *Tribune*'s endorsement had brought less worthy candidates. Now might be his chance. As he traveled south and midwest, he caught tantalizing hints. "Iowa loves Mr. Greeley—nay, reveres him," a reporter noted; "and the people here will go through fire and water to see and hear him." "There is no man in the North . . . who can command the vote Mr. Greeley can," the St. Paul *Dispatch* assured readers. From both the Cincinnati *Commercial* and the New York *Sun* editorials advanced their colleague as the ideal nominee. No message could have struck a more pleasing note on Greeley's ear.[16]

No message could have struck a more alarming note for some of the most articulate liberals. Greeley's position as reformer was all the more complicated by the company he kept. Where ethics or issues were concerned, purists would have found little to choose from between the state's two senators. Fenton and Conkling both knew how to use federal officeholders and club-wielding mobs of New York toughs to carry party conventions. Greeley's cries against Conkling's collector of the port as a rogue, cheek by jowl with Tammany Hall corruptionists, may have irritated Conkling more when he looked at the New York City Republican committee that Greeley headed: as despicable a gang of Tammany Republicans and artists of the party sell-out as could be found anywhere outside of jail. Fenton had had his chance to run the customhouse in New York City already, and, as Conkling would sneer in quite another context, when Dr. Johnson pronounced patriotism the last refuge of a scoundrel, he had underestimated the possibilities in the word *reform*.[17]

Standing in so compromised a position was inevitable for news gatherers like Greeley as long as they wanted to be the news themselves. Political ambitions generally recognized gave a different look to every stand on principle an editor assumed. This opportunism and apparent insincerity would taint the whole liberal revolt, and the fault would be as much Greeley's as anyone's.

Direct political involvement was only one side of the problem for the "independent press." By early 1872, its managers saw themselves, if not as aspirants, at least as power brokers, the one true voice of the people. From them came rhetoric radiating confidence of victory, and back came the echo of politicians, convinced that triumph would befall those who had such backers as the independent press. Might not even a president be unhorsed? "Privately we don't believe here that Grant is to be the next candidate," Whitelaw Reid wrote from New York in late 1870. Nine months only made Reid more sanguine that the incumbent would "have his throat cut" when the convention met.[18] Greeley's very candidacy rested on the assumption that his leading articles would lead Republicans into any party he headed.[19]

Was this an arrogance misplaced? The "independents" had shown their power, to some extent, in the past four years. They could embarrass the administration and define the issues. Their fire could force Grant to drop his collector of the port in New York or save face on Santo Domingo by proposing a fact-finding commission in place of an annexation treaty. That the president moved to endorse civil service reform, amnesty, and tariff reform owed much to the clamor that the press had raised; that congressmen shied away from land grant bills and hesitated before defending the spoils system outright showed how well the independents had shaped the debate. But when it came to breaking party ties or discrediting candidates, the record was nowhere near so plain. The Chicago *Tribune* battled hard against "Black Jack" Logan's bid for a Senate seat in late 1870 and lost ignominiously.[20] Greeley's own endorsement of Fenton's faction had gained the senator precisely nothing. Wisely, Senator Justin Morrill of Vermont pleaded with Greeley not to leave the party ranks, if not for the party's sake, then for his own. Work from within would do some good; work from without might mean his ruin. "Greeley, like others before him, has been strong when leading his friends," an astute observer commented. "He will be *impotent* when he attempts to lead his *enemies*."[21]

The "independent press," therefore, may have missed two crucial points. First, involvement as players in party brawls injured editors' standing as opinion makers. Second, personal and party loyalties were more deeply rooted than concern with immediate issues, especially when those under fire shifted ground on those issues just far enough to make themselves credible reformers. A third point is also worth considering and follows from the second. Powerful as the independents thought themselves, they underestimated the lingering force of the partisan press in shaping campaign opinion, however it had declined relatively as a source of news or even as a power in defining the basic issues.

With the newspaper cadre issuing its benison, dissident Republicans converged on the convention hall in Cincinnati at the end of April 1872 to write a platform full of reform sentiments and choose a winning candidate. Those candidates were ones tested and touted by newspapers alone. Among them were Judge David Davis and the increasingly apolitical Charles Francis Adams, neither of whom had endured the rigors of a popular campaign to reach the position that he had attained. But Davis had the Chicago *Times* behind him, and the *World*, the Springfield *Republican*, and other liberal papers argued for Adams, whom "Gath," then his earnest backer, would later describe with cruel aptness as "that lonely political Selkirk whose cold family lies around him like seals on the Island of Juan Fernandez."[22]

When the convention began, it must have looked at times like an impromptu press club. Not all the journalists present came to further reform. A hearty Grant man, "Mack" sat at the reporter's tables, enjoying the fun, while "Gath" and Piatt showed up to sing the convention's praises and abuse its foes—"a beautiful twain of literary prize-fighters," sneered a contemporary. But the editors converged with higher ambitions. It was clear, at least to their minds, that they could run the body not just through parliamentary maneuver and the rallying of delegates, but through manipulating opinion. Horace White, "short and dark like a cowld winter's day," had come to stack the credentials committee on Trumbull's behalf. Bowles threaded his way through the crowds to round up four of the six New England states for Adams. Watterson, when he was not trying to bluff old friends at poker with two deuces in his hand and fourteen drinks under his belt, was there to represent the Democrats' will (his more orthodox ally Manton Marble of the *World* attended, too, but was shut out of the inner councils). Now the quill drivers came together over dinner— and the editors of the *Commercial*, *Nation*, and St. Louis *Democrat* with them. Dubbing themselves the "Quadrilateral," a name reminiscent of the Austrian fortresses that held Italy in thrall until 1859 rather than a precise numerical description, the editors resolved to narrow the field of candidates down to ones mutually acceptable. They enlisted ready allies in Washington McLean's Cincinnati *Enquirer* and in Whitelaw Reid, whose influence with the New York *Tribune* far outweighed the risks that his management of Greeley's candidacy seemed to pose; for Greeley, the editors reassured each other, had no chance. Once committed to the nominee, he could do a world of good. As one, the editors opened fire on Davis's candidacy, smashing it to flinders.[23]

But the life of the movement was not on the editorial page; it was on the floor of the convention hall and in the hotel rooms where delegates pondered over their alternatives. When the hullabaloo died away after the sixth ballot, the Quadrilateral found itself outflanked and undone. They had broken Davis only to find themselves saddled with Greeley.[24]

To New York lawyer George Templeton Strong, the news was "scarcely credible," "the most preposterous and ludicrous nomination to the Presidency ever made on this continent." Plenty of good wine at a funereal banquet that evening reconciled the editors. Not even a flood of tears and a volley of curses could make them like it. A convention inclined to lower the tariff had chosen protection's most outspoken champion, a man who explained free traders as bought with British gold; a gathering hoping for Democratic endorsement at the party's convention that summer had nominated the man who once declared that, while not every Democrat was a horse thief, every horse thief was a Democrat.[25]

For chagrined editors, including a few erstwhile members of the Quadrilateral, the explanation was obvious and fully in keeping with the conspiratorial view of politics they had done so much to promote: intriguers had played the idealistic delegates for suckers. Naive reformers had been ill-prepared to discover *politics*, of all things, going on in a political convention! The interpretation bore some watery resemblance to the truth. Those who attended the convention on behalf of Davis felt betrayed; they had a score to repay the backers of Adams and Trumbull. There were wire pullers and jealous intriguers, and among them Governor B. Gratz Brown, who had arrived past midnight, convinced that his delegation meant to sell him out and ready to avenge the wrong by dictating the nomination for another, if not for himself. But the conspirators did not affect the outcome much.[26]

Greeley won because the delegates wanted him, and they wanted him in part because Greeley was the *Tribune*. One might be unsure of where Adams or even Trumbull stood on some issues. But the sage of Chappaqua's views, his personality, were widely known, and the personality excited very real affection; in a campaign where politics would be based largely on character, and where the personality of the Republican nominee was sure to be an issue, that character was important. Southern whites remembered how important the *Tribune* editorials had been on Jefferson Davis's behalf; as Southern blacks must also be aware, his hectoring in wartime helped hasten the day that slavery ended. If sectional reconciliation was the great issue, here stood the perfect spokesman for it. In view of the *Tribune*'s tart words for the Slave Power before the war, former Confederates could adopt no candidate more plausible as proof that they, too, had forgotten the hatreds of the past. Whatever the party of saloon keepers and blacklegs might think of his slurs, they had to admit his candor.[27]

Greeley's appeal went beyond himself. His newspaper meant votes. It was perfectly reasonable to imagine, as many delegates must have, that when the *Tribune* spoke, its readers would heed. "The farmers of the West have read, studied and profited by Mr. Greeley too long and too much not to . . . rally around him," the Springfield *Republican* assured readers. What could be more logical than that a party largely built up by newspapers should choose the strongest newspaperman of them all to lead it to victory?[28]

Of course, Greeley's openness worked both ways. Frank opinions made open enemies, and the rivalry of newspapers meant that among the least easily conciliated liberals were editors he had offended. The cheers of Samuel Bowles, Horace White, and Henry Watterson rang hollow and halfheartedly. If back him they must, Bowles told the staff of the Springfield *Republican*, they were "not to gush!" Murat Halstead finally accepted Greeley but vowed to print all the news, whether it hurt the nominee or not. White even convinced himself that a Greeley victory would ruin both parties, shatter old allegiances, and leave reformers to assemble a new system as they pleased.[29]

Others proved less forgiving. The New York *Evening Post* chose to stand by President Grant rather than with "a thorough-going, bigoted protectionist," and E. L. Godkin's *Nation* uttered a plague o' both political houses. Both journals took the cause of low tariffs too seriously to accept a protectionist nominee, but there was also an element of that spleen that editors' quarrelsomeness had fostered. William Cullen Bryant's animosity had been twenty years maturing. "Don't you know Mr. Greeley?" he was asked years before by a friend hoping to introduce the two men. "No, I don't," the old poet snapped, "he's a blackguard—he's a blackguard!" Now he insisted that "the grossness of [Greeley's] manners" made his candidacy unthinkable. If there had been any doubt of the Chicago *Times*'s having thrown off all party ties, there would be none now. To the end of the campaign, it resisted the reformers' ticket as a corrupt swindle in terms that its liberal counterpart aptly described as "pure cussedness."[30]

The *Times* lost nothing by doing so. On the contrary, independence of the "independents" acted on it like a tonic. That and one other factor should have given the liberals pause. In the two months between party conventions, scores of Democratic organs protested the nominations. "Of course no Democrat can or will endorse Greeley," Marble's *World* asserted. Vainly, Democratic congressmen urged their foremost journal to moderate its tone. "Let the trumpet blow no uncertain sound, though all the archangels beseech," the editor shot back. Untrammeled by alliance, Democrats must fight for good government with a ticket all their own. "God give us victory." The prayer went unanswered. Party leaders preferred to risk a coalition, and they, not Marble, ran the national convention that July. Greeley was nominated by his lifelong enemies. Instantly, the chorus of editors changed its tune, from dirge to anthem.[31]

The failure of Democratic editors only underscored the failure of the Quadrilateral. How much power had the press to drive the politicians where it would? And if that influence had been overrated, what chance had the papers to herd the rank and file to the polls? Equally troubling: how independent, in the end, was the mass of the press when so many newspapers could take one side and then the other, just as the party line dictated? Halstead and Bowles aside, how independent would the independent press itself be, in telling all the news, however its candidate was affected?

The last question was answered instantly. Long before the dog days, journals on both sides ran mad for one candidate or the other, and their editors plunged into the back rooms to plan strategy. Though Greeley relinquished editorial control of the *Tribune*, the change in leadership made no change in leading articles, all of which put the worst possible face on national affairs under Grant's presidency. With the Illinois liberal committee too disorganized to arrange local campaign needs, the Chicago *Tribune* printed documents instead. Democrats in northern Ohio clamored for a daily morning paper, and the Cleveland *Plain Dealer* prepared an edition especially for the canvass.[32]

The campaign that followed turned into a mud-wrestling match. Perpetrators of the Pacific Mail steamship subsidy, liberal Donn Piatt insisted, had kicked back half their loot to the Grant campaign. Compared to the abuse that the *Sun* was leveling at the "Office-Holders' Candidate," that was mild reproof. "Were I important enough to be worth assailing as an upholder of the Administration," George Templeton Strong wrote, the leading liberal papers would agree in declaring:

> "This corrupt scoundrel, Strong, was treasurer of the Sanitary Commission. We have no doubt he stole a large amount of its money. If he didn't, why doesn't he *prove* that he didn't? He got up a swindling concern called the Church Music Association, and we have reason to believe that he pocketed all its funds. Somebody said so. Let him disprove it if he can!" The next day we should read: "The atrocious corruptionist, Strong, has not ventured to attempt clearing himself by any kind of positive proof from a single one of the grave accusations with which we thought it our duty to charge him. We hope the People will at last hold these proven beyond all question. We are credibly informed that this infamous minion of a perjured and profligate Administration is affiliated with the Erie Railroad, the Credit Mobilier, and Bill Tweed; and further (*this on affidavit*) that he designs to go to Long Branch week after next and secure as the reward of his baseness from the Speechless Nullity who is reveling there with his cigars and his horses and his whiskey, the appointment of consul-general at the Galapagos Islands. *This we know.* The Hon. Snooks of Oregon has written a letter positively affirming the disgraceful fact! People of America!!! The Farmer of Chappaqua! the great and good Horace Greeley!!! Single-minded, pure, and patriotic! *Honest* Horace Greeley!" and the like.

The Republicans were just as bad, or worse. Liberal vice-presidential nominee B. Gratz Brown appeared as the man "who butters his watermelon and takes eight drinks in the forenoon." Behind his editorial desk at the *Tribune*, Whitelaw Reid quivered at the thought of opposing newspapers getting hold of private letters about his intrigues to become Greeley's second-in-command three years before—and with good reason.[33]

As Reid's anxiety showed, Greeley's candidacy had made sure that not just the politicians, but the press, would face a brutal scrutiny, one that went to the heart of the independents' right to dictate public morality. The Cleveland *Leader* alleged that the New York *Tribune* had taken bribes from Tammany thieves to keep silent on city government scandals, that the *World* had fattened on the Tweed Ring's payroll. Other papers mistakenly insisted that Greeley himself, a stern enemy of tobacco, had entered a firm for its manufacture along with Boss William M. Tweed.[34]

As the canvass closed, the *Nation* mockingly reminded the press that time was running out. Had they perhaps overlooked something? "Has no Greeleyite or Grantite minister been selling bad liquor on the sly in the basement of his church? Has no brother editor been carrying off the silver spoon out of the medicine glass of his dying friend? Has no senator been defrauding and brutally beating his sick washerwoman?" Was there, in short, nothing more they could find to smear a good name or make America look like "a den of drunken thieves, and thus exalt 'journalism' in the eyes of the community?"[35]

Personalities alone did not shape the campaign, of course. There were real issues: how far should the federal government involve itself to protect black voters and Republican authorities in the South? how safely could Northerners trust to former Confederates' professions of loyalty? How could government be reformed to work more efficiently, much less honestly? Government corruption did indeed exist, and the New York *Sun* did its part to expose the wrongdoing of congressmen in the Credit Mobilier scandal.

That scandal had real basis in fact. Though some insiders had known of wrongdoing for some time, it was only that summer that "a lawyer in Pennsylvania, of much ability, but of leaky speech," as George Alfred Townsend called him (very possibly former attorney general Jeremiah Black, who had known the facts for four years), unloaded the story in private conversation. The talk passed to A. M. Gibson of the *Sun*. He wanted to learn more. Learning that hard evidence lay on the record of the case of *McComb v. Credit Mobilier*, Gibson managed to glimpse the document as it was being transcribed. Taking no notes, he wrote a report largely based on his memory of what he had seen, and Dana published it early in September.[36]

Even here the issues were obscured by extravagance and absurdity (which, however, partisans privately seemed to believe). "The people must choose between Grantism and patriotism," thundered Henry Watterson's Louisville *Courier-Journal*. Let Americans remember how corruption killed the Roman republic, other editors warned. "If the people want liberty, they must vote to save it."[37] The *Sun*'s startling charges would have been more meritorious, too, if they had stuck to exposing the guilty. But that would have been too short a list by far; and so Dana's rogue's gallery of Credit Mobilier bribe takers included a host of statesmen who could offer convincing denials of all involvement. Faced with effective rebuttals, how were Americans to know the truth or to trust to a single one of the *Sun*'s allegations?[38] The press, in short, did not make the issues clear. It obscured them doubly: with personal charges and with distortions of the consequences.

Did it, in fact, wield any substantial effect over people's minds? That seems far less likely. If the independent press had any real force, it was in Chicago, in Cincinnati, in New York. But the bolt of liberals was a modest one in all three places, offset by the loss of Democrats. A loyal Democratic press could not hold its own troops. Not all the apocalyptic warnings could overcome rank-and-file apathy, to call it nothing worse.[39]

Indeed, the independents could not even rouse the forces of reform. Henry Boynton, Richard Smith, and George William Curtis remained committed to a purified government and President Grant both. "We *must* come together, and act together, for we think together," Charles Francis Adams, Jr., told Murat Halstead. But not yet: not until Greeley was beaten. Detest the administration though he did, author Richard Henry Dana would not sail four years before the mast on Greeley's ship, not even when his friend Samuel Bowles was a member of the crew. Even James Shepherd Pike hesitated long before casting his lot with his employer on the *Tribune*.[40]

Instead of rallying readers to the cause, editors found the readers rallying to rival presses. Postmasters actively encouraged the conversions. Owing their jobs to the administration, they repaid it by refusing to deliver liberal journals to subscribers, or by furnishing lists of subscribers to Republican organizers for conversion. With every local subscription agent for the Springfield *Republican* a postmaster, Bowles found himself forced to recruit an entirely new organization across New England; but no one would take the job except Democrats. New York Republicans switched their subscriptions from the *Tribune* to the *Evening Post* or the *Times*; Chicago partisans took up the newly established *Inter-Ocean* rather than follow Horace White further. By resigning command of the *Tribune*, the candidate only weakened its voice; he did not cut off the hatred that descended on it. Daily circulation tumbled, and weekly circulation was cut in half.[41]

By contrast, Grant Republicans were well equipped for battle. During the campaign, they made a concerted effort to coordinate the faithful. Where the *Weekly Tribune* circulated, the campaign committees sent out the New York *Times* for free distribution and, indeed, may well have used postmasters to open up packages of the *Tribune* and replace them with the Republican alternative. Washington organizers wrote editorial boilerplate and sent it on the congressional frank to the postmasters running small-town administration organs. As many as three hundred campaign workers ferreted out and quoted the candidate's most embarrassing editorial utterances to publish as, "What Horace Greeley Knows About Everything," and the New York *Times* issued a special supplement, in bold letters, made of nothing more than Greeley's own words—especially about Democrats. They also did what they could to swing the Irish and German presses behind Grant. The New York *Oestliche Post* declined to sell out without a subsidy; it got one. So did ethnic newspapers in other cities, as well as government advertising to sweeten the deal. Even when the negotiations to placate a paper broke down, the effect on a hostile newspaper could have advantages. In Cincinnati, the administration listened to a proposition to support Friedrich Hassaurek's *Volksblatt*; what they balked at was his price of $15,000:

> Would you buy a speculator?
> He is up "For Sale."
> Have you fifteen thousand dollars?
> Go to Avondale.
> There the Hassaurek will greet you,
> If you wish to buy,
> Fifteen thousand is his figure—
> "How is that for high?"
>
> .   .   .   .   .
>
> Fritz, since you have made a bargain,
> Should you now get mad?
> Don't tell lies and say you didn't—
> That would be *too* bad.

> Now, dear Fritz, your auction's over,
> And your sale is done;
> Long you'll hear the echo ringing—
> "Going, going, gone!"

Hassaurek's best defense when the story came out was that the fund was "not to bribe . . . but to remunerate him," "not corruption, but compensation." "Hassaurek is *dead as a smelt* in consequence of the exposure," a Republican gloated.[42]

Patronage and the persistence of the party press in small towns helped Grant win, but it did not explain why the independents did so poorly. Voters were not just missing the independents' message. They were dismissing it. Could that illuminate the limits of the independents' influence? Was it not possible that the news that most convinced appeared in newspapers whose editors kept a certain distance from politics—that taking one party's side destroyed the real effect of an "independent" press? Or could it be that readers took from the journals what they wanted to take and believed what they chose to believe?

Witness the case of George Templeton Strong of New York. The conservative businessman and social leader had many reservations about the Grant administration. His nose wrinkled at the "most nasty mess of corruption in the custom house," and Grant's diplomatic appointments embarrassed him. "One might as well try to spoil a rotten egg as to damage Dan's character," he wrote of Daniel Sickles, minister to Spain.[43] Yet there had never been any doubt of where Strong would stand. Foul as the customhouse revelations were, he had no truck with the *Tribune*'s attacks. They were "mephitic, fetid, ammoniacal, hippuric, cacodylic, and abominable." As the criticisms went on, Strong credited the *Tribune* and *World* abuse with making him a Grant partisan. "Everything is Grant's fault," he commented disgustedly. ". . . The prevalence of smallpox in New York is due to 'nepotism' and the recent baleful activity of Vesuvius is due to the 'Military Ring.'" By the time the campaign had begun in earnest, Strong could convince himself that the *Tribune*'s editorials were "vapid," secreting poison as impotent as dishwater.[44]

Strong's view of Greeley himself changed as well. "Greeley means right, I think," he wrote in April, "but he is ruined by overweening vanity and a most plentiful lack of practical common sense." The moment the editor ac-

"We Are on the Home Stretch!"—New York *Tribune* (Thomas Nast, *Harper's Weekly*, November 2, 1872). Senator Reuben Fenton and editor Whitelaw Reid carry Horace Greeley home to Chappaqua, while Theodore Tilton and Senator Carl Schurz mourn; an urchin is trying to return the tag, Greeley's running mate, who was made notorious for his obscurity by Nast's featuring him this way throughout the campaign. The cartoon was much crueler than Nast intended. He was unaware that Greeley's wife was dying and that the candidate himself was in failing health.

cepted the liberal nomination, that opinion changed for the worse. "Diogenes Slyboots" had "at last taken his place among mere trading politicians." Greeley's reputation only sank thereafter. "Miserable old charlatan and traitor!" stormed George Templeton Strong. "God grant that he may be squelched indeed!"[45]

Strong got his wish. By fall, it became clear that nothing could carry the North for Greeley, nor, indeed, carry the blacks of the South. As the state returns in North Carolina went against the liberal coalition, its press defenders soothed themselves with the explanation that victory had been bought. By the time Vermont, Maine, Ohio, and Pennsylvania had cast their lot with the administration party, that excuse had grown too threadbare to convince anybody except, perhaps, Horace White. With a landslide sweeping Grant back into power, the *Tribune* optimistically headed the returns "The Liberal Triumph Postponed."[46]

It was no such thing. The liberal bolt was dead, so clearly so that even Democrats declined to carry on the farce by changing their name the following year. "May we have better luck next time," one of the few surviving Democratic congressmen wrote; "d–d few of us reached dry land this time." Liberals were just as chapfallen with their allies. The movement died, Halstead wrote two years later, from "devouring hard-boiled Democrats— . . . and an insufficiency of gastric juice led to fatal consequences."[47]

The consequences were quite literally fatal for Greeley. Already a tired man before he took to the stump that fall, he found himself worn down still more by the vigil at his dying wife's bedside. Sleepless, heartbroken, it would not have taken much to shatter him completely, and the campaign was more than sufficient. Attacked until, as he put it, he could hardly tell whether he ran for the presidency or the penitentiary, he read the returns not as a rebuke to reform, but as a personal judgment on himself, which in some ways it was. The constant quotation of his editorial attacks on Democrats, on Southerners, on fellow editors and free traders had taken the fight out of so many who would have been his partisans; his advocacy of so many odd and radical reforms over time had made the solid business community rally to the comparatively safe Ulysses S. Grant. "O, that mine enemy had written a book," John Adams had once lamented; Greeley had written enough for a library.[48]

It was a shattered man, his reputation squandered, who returned to the *Tribune* offices, and there he found himself no longer wanted, indeed, scarcely welcome. That was the finish. Within a few days, mind and body gave way. Within a month, members of the administration were attending his funeral—a pitiful end to the "second Franklin."[49]

In the end, what precisely had the "independent press" lost? The New York *Tribune* survived and, for the moment, remained as aggressive in exposing administration misdeeds as ever. From a year's distance, other liberal organs did not look on the campaign quite so dispiritedly. The issues had not been entirely of their choosing. They could not turn Republicans away from memories of the war, nor from appeals to party loyalty. But neither had Republican orators been able to dismiss the issues of corruption and sectional reconciliation. They had to address both, and on terms of the liberals' choosing: that sectional reconciliation mattered too much to be risked by aggressive federal action on blacks' behalf, that corruption's cure was less government at less cost and a reformed civil service. When the Forty-second Congress returned to session in December, those issues would move to the fore again. Stirred up by the independent press, public clamor would force a rash of embarrassing and fruitful investigations into seat-buying senators and influence-peddling lobbyists. By Inauguration Day, the victors were in disarray, their mandate discredited.

Yet the independent press had lost much of its moral power by hazarding all on Greeley and losing so badly. It had been given a stinging lesson in effective politics. "You fought the senatorial contest with Trumbull and you 'unhorsed him': 'wiped him out,'" a supporter of Illinois's senator-elect exulted. "You rolled him up in the sheets of his pet paper the Tribune and buried him out of sight." A few newspapers died outright. The Washington *Patriot*, a Democratic organ, gave up the ghost the moment Grant was elected. Others felt a marked break in their influence. There was all too much truth in the remark of one Boston correspondent that the moment a Republican candidate won Bowles's endorsement, he knew the game was up with him. Something animating had passed into the grave with Greeley; the press gang would not see it restored.[50]

CHAPTER 16

The Wild Animals Loose

The Panic of 1874

Early in January 1874, the proprietor of the Washington *Sunday Capital* had some unexpected callers at home. Two men armed with heavy sticks were standing on the threshold, with great interest in seeing Donn Piatt. And what were their names? Neither man would say. The servant answering the door could not fetch Piatt, who was at the office, but he went to summon the editor's kinsman General Banning from the library. One glance at Banning's face and the callers fled, but not quickly enough to escape recognition. One was President Ulysses S. Grant's son, Second Lieutenant Colonel Frederick Grant, and the other the president's notorious brother-in-law, New Orleans collector of the port James Casey. If the chief executive was entitled to two assassins, Banning joked, how many was a congressman allowed?[1]

When it was over, no one ended up hurt, though Piatt's invalid wife was given a fright. Piatt published a card inviting the bullies to call on him at his office "during business hours" for satisfaction. Privately, he joked that the stir did wonders for the paper's circulation and told a friend of the Grants that if the president's son would drop by the office to finish his business, "I would pay the family a premium on my increased circulation." He was doomed to disappointment. At his mother's appeal, Fred agreed to let the quarrel drop. "He says he did not intend to shoot Piatt, but to give him a good thrashing," a reporter explained (and Casey hastily assured another journalist that he had gone along only to reason with the headstrong young man, and that neither of them intended even so much as a drubbing).[2]

Young Fred had his reasons. Reporting the New Year's reception at the White House, a woman correspondent of the *Sunday Capital* had made unflattering personal remarks about his mother and sister. Among them was the brutal and unfair suggestion that holding the social function showed the First Lady's lack of family feeling, her late father just having been buried. Piatt himself admitted that he was in the wrong and added that his only contribution to the offending article was to "soften it down." Apparently, he did not soften it enough.[3]

The incident touched the relationship between the press and the president with special drama, but it fit the general mood in Washington by 1874. As the Forty-third Congress opened session, the uneasy relationship between government and press gang took on a new acrimony. Worse was to follow: a year of panics, imaginary perils, and persecutions. To hear the independents tell it, the elections that fall marked a crisis for the republic. In fact, they marked a crisis in the interaction of the press and politicians.

The ill will had been building for some time, and in the months just after Horace Greeley's defeat, a series of scandals publicized by the press made the mutual distaste even sharper. Senator Samuel ("Subsidy") Pomeroy's attempt to buy his own reelection, the storm of abuse that lame-duck congressmen met for raising their own salaries retroactively, and, most of all, the Credit Mobilier hearings left public figures cautious to the point of discretion. "All we have to do is to wave the black flag at them and they take to their heels," a Democratic congressman boasted of his Republican colleagues.[4]

Perhaps so, but they also took to verbal cudgels against the muckrakers for stirring up the public. Most outspoken were public officials closest to the administration, notably Congressman Benjamin F. Butler, Senators Matthew Carpenter of Wisconsin and Zachariah Chandler of Michigan, and the leaders of the so-called District Ring. Butler's hatred for "that damnable engine of libel and slander" was only strengthened by the press's pursuit of his friend, Congressman Oakes Ames, the master spirit of Credit Mobilier, and of his own success in shoving through the "back pay grab."[5] Carpenter's forays against the press dated back to the treaty investigation of 1871. Two summers later, he upbraided the newspapers for fostering the sickly morality that a congressman had no right to invest in any business on which he might legislate. His feelings sharpened that August when his erstwhile victim, Hiram Ramsdell of the *Tribune*, spied him and a female companion being turned away from a Long Branch hotel. Within days readers across the country knew how the drunken satyr from Wisconsin had taken a notorious whore on his visit to America's most fashionable summer resort. Most of them, and Ramsdell himself, may actually have believed it to be true.[6]

The bibulous Zachariah Chandler enjoyed a less steamy, but more stormy relationship with the press. A self-made party boss whose scholarly ignorance was always good for a joke, and whose reputation as a blowhard and a drunk became a staple of Washington journalism, the Michigan senator paid his attackers as best he could, in one case, invading Newspaper Row, revolver in hand, to track down "Gath."[7]

Finally, there was the president's good friend and newly chosen governor of the District of Columbia, Alexander R. Shepherd. For three years, he had run the Board of Public Works with spectacular results. Under his guidance, Washington had been remade. Its swamps became spacious vistas, its muddy lanes turned into grand thoroughfares. "Why, this city is one vast park!" a journalist wrote. "It is Central Park filled with cottages and castles." Civic defenders would argue that the improvements were worth the cost.[8] That cost, however, included graft and fraud. As early as the fall of 1871, a few newspapermen were on Shepherd's trail, and loudest were Democrats looking for some Republican scandal to balance off the Tweed Ring's stealings in New York City. By early 1873, the story had become common property; by the following winter, it was too widespread for Congress to ignore. So was the District debt, which would turn out to be three times the limit set by law.[9]

By no coincidence, the District newspapers gorged on contracts and Board of Public Works advertising heaped personal abuse on Shepherd's critics, accusing them of wartime treason, extortion, and running houses of prostitution. Crosby Noyes of the *Evening Star* made sure that local AP dispatches summarized the testimony as clearing the boss of wrongdoing, until the Western Associated Press refused to receive his accounts any longer, and his superiors dispensed with his services. As long as Washington correspondents were sending back their own accounts, however, it scarcely mattered what AP said. Muzzling the journalists when the House investigation was front-page news was difficult, but not impossible. A few of them were put on the payroll in some cases, and one "of former brilliancy and promise," it was later charged, had been bought up to set down columns of abuse "over unknown signatures" against Shepherd's accusers (very likely this referred to George Alfred Townsend). By the time the House committee concluded its labors, as Henry Boynton reported, nearly every apologist for the District Ring relying on defamation had been shown up as a purchased penman.[10]

Where money would not work, other pressures were applied. The Washington *Patriot* reprinted other papers' allegations, until it was threatened with a libel suit. The terrified managers published not just one retraction, but two; bullied beyond what his dignity could bear, the managing editor resigned. Creatively interpreting an ambiguous sentence in a Washington dispatch, Shepherd lodged two suits for libel against the New York *Tribune*, though possibly more for effect than for damages. Troublesome reporters were told that they "enjoyed too much swing in this town." Not all of them took the hint in the proper spirit. When A. M. Gibson of the New York *Sun* was sworn in to back up his charges against the District Ring, he found himself face-to-face with District Attorney Harrington, a Shepherd ally. Harrington vowed to use the cross-examination to "inquire into your character." "All right, Mr. Harrington," snapped Gibson; "and now, sir, I give notice that I, too, shall enter upon an investigation, the subject whereof shall be you, Mr. Harrington. I promise, moreover, to make it both searching and thorough."[11]

Gibson kept that promise, but by that time, Shepherd's government was tottering. For three months, a joint committee took testimony, all of it broadcast nationwide. The facts backed up every charge but the open corruption of the boss himself. Money had been passed along to incompetent contractors, without check or safeguard by the city's financial officers. Board meetings to award contracts took place on the secretary's books and in Shepherd's mind, but nowhere else. Shoddy work, exorbitant expense, inside influence, and outright corruption marred policy so badly that the entire District government was beyond saving. It would be abolished, and with it the home rule that residents had enjoyed.[12]

Thorough investigation, indeed, was the order of the day in the Forty-second Congress—that and the mutual recrimination of press and politicians. The year began with a chorus of abuse against the president's choice for chief justice, a chorus so ferocious that first one nominee and then a second were forced to withdraw their names. Lurid revelations about shakedowns in the New York customhouse and profiteering tax collectors in the Treasury who worked for Ben Butler made good copy and proved beyond all doubt the imbecility or worse of Secretary of the Treasury William A. Richardson. Even Mary Clemmer Ames, generally one of the more sympathetic correspondents, lashed out at the administration and at the depravity she saw around her. Angrily she listened to the Senate chaplain invoke the Lord against slanderers; plainly, his prayer was directed against the press gallery. The truth, Ames asserted, was that nine out of every ten stories of misdeeds were true. Everywhere she saw evidences of "official corruption" and "a preposterous official caste, . . . based on money, 'jobs,' and power, howsoever gotten." It showed itself in cabinet members' families rolling in monogrammed "satin and mirror-lined 'establishments'" complete with footmen, when single-horse carriages would have been good enough, and in the Justice Department pretending that its official tasks required $3,000 of ice a year, when ice went for a penny a pound. But a trivial incident caught the viciousness of Washington best. When Charles Sumner died, thousands arrived to do honor to the last great champion of equal rights in public life. Among the most moving tributes came from Kate Brown. Years before, she had been thrown off of a city streetcar because of her race. So badly injured that she could no longer hold her job, she went to Sumner, and he found her employment as attendant in the ladies' retiring parlor off of the Senate gallery. Now she scraped together her savings to buy a pillar of flowers to rest against his bier, as he lay in state in the capitol rotunda. By nightfall, the memorial had vanished. Senator Simon Cameron, of Pennsylvania, the man who replaced Sumner as head of the Foreign Relations Committee, had filched it, put his card on it, and sent it as a love token to the hotel room of his paramour![13]

Not that the quarrel between press and politician was one-sided. Grant remained as outwardly imperturbable as ever, but his contempt for press clamor showed itself twice that spring. When congressional investigators found incapacity, influence-peddling, and financial irregularity in Shepherd's handling of the Board of Public Works, no one doubted that the "boss" had outlasted what small usefulness he had ever held. But when

Congress set up a special commission to run the District, the president declined to submit nominations for it. With the session about to end, he meant to delay until Congress had gone home and could not prevent the ad interim selection for six months. It took personal intervention and even bullying by prominent administration senators to change his mind. When the names were produced, Grant's reason for foot-dragging became clear. He wanted Shepherd to head the commission; most likely, he had made the nomination to show that press clamor could not drive him from his associates. An embarrassed Senate defeated the nomination and Shepherd's public career ended on the spot.[14]

The same proved true of Secretary Richardson. For months the leading newspapers demanded his dismissal and forecast its imminence. Yet no resignation followed. Grant was holding fast until a House committee had Richardson "vindicated" by dropping all charges. Very possibly Grant also imposed a second condition, that Richardson be confirmed as judge on the court of claims, a position he had wanted in the first place.[15]

The press's reception on Capitol Hill was more hostile still. Labeled a "legislative pumpkinhead," a Mississippi congressman proved it by searching out the columnist for a beating and, when he failed to find him, administering it to the offender's cousin. There were minor insults aplenty. Goaded by newspaper criticisms of official extravagance, Congress found a way to cut costs: it denied correspondents the use of government ink, pens, pencils, and paper, at a saving to taxpayers of some $250. Matthew Carpenter led the economy move in the Senate, but his newfound concern about government's spendthrift habits was shared by his old ally in the treaty fight, Senator Roscoe Conkling of New York. The independent journals suggested that what the reporters wrote about and not what they wrote with was what concerned the two senators. Perhaps they should put forth an edict regulating the daily press, modeled on one recently passed in Japan. There, journals were allowed to announce prices, births, deaths, marriages, and wars but were forbidden to discuss the laws or advocate "foreign ideas" and "uncalled for remarks."[16]

Could that be what the administration spokesmen had in mind? Early in the session, Conkling told a friend that he had a bill prepared to "fix those fellows" in the press gallery; in a conversation with a reporter, Carpenter raged against the licentiousness of the press, as well as against the weakness in state courts and libel laws that let rogues like Hiram Ramsdell run at large. It was a deficiency, he added, that would need attending to.[17]

Carpenter's threat was uttered to Augustus C. Buell, correspondent for the Detroit *Free Press* and St. Louis *Democrat*, who was particularly sensitive to veiled threats. A month before, he had published the report that Zachariah Chandler had arrived in the Senate so drunk that his colleagues had to carry him out and lay him on the cloakroom sofa. Buell's source took back the story at once, and Buell himself admitted he may have been mistaken, but the account was repeated. When it appeared in Donn Piatt's *Sunday Capital*, Chandler had the reporter arrested for libel and started a civil suit against the *Free Press* for $100,000.[18]

That the story itself, as another reporter acknowledged, was "as pure an invention as ever obtained a copyright" was not what made Buell's case so disturbing. Nor was it the murkiness of the law itself. The district statute book, in fact, said nothing about libel; but the territory had once belonged to Maryland, and there libel could be punished under the common law. But how could it be punished? The most specific statute anyone could find dated back more than a century and meted out the pillory, branding, and whipping through the streets as punishment—none of them seriously considered any longer. Still, all of these were trivial points compared to the main ground for concern, the place where Chandler chose to make the arrest: the police court of the district. Under the law of 1870 establishing the tribunal, the presiding officer could sentence offenders without jury trial and was empowered to decide the facts of the case as well as the law. Worse still, if an article published in Detroit could be punished in Washington, where influential lawmakers could control the judges, who on Newspaper Row would feel safe criticizing government's doings? So it came as no surprise that when Buell got out on bail he fled the District for St. Louis, nor that his two lawyers, both former attorney generals, would pronounce him "the Hampden of our journalism" and appeal his case to the District Supreme Court. Nor should it have surprised anyone that the higher tribunal's decision that jurisdiction ought to be given to the local criminal court, jury and all, did nothing to allay reporters' uneasiness. They knew how easily a jury could be packed, and what weight a judge might have there. "These juries here in my court watch me like children," Judge David Cartter boasted, "& they generally follow the least intimation from me."[19] (Cartter actually meant to reassure one editor, who feared conviction.)

This was not, indeed, the first time injured parties had tried to use the police court against offending newsmen. A year before, Boss Shepherd had gone after Charles A. Dana of the *Sun* with a libel suit. District Attorney Harrington had appealed to Judge Samuel Blatchford of the Second Circuit in New York for a warrant on which to transport Dana down to the capital for trial. Even if Dana had committed libel, his attorney argued, action by the police court was unconstitutional, depriving the defendant of his right to a jury trial. Blatchford agreed fully.[20]

Only in the context of those two cases and the heightened tensions surrounding press relations that spring does the outcry over two pieces of legislation in June 1874 make sense, for neither bill on its own seemed all that alarming. In a calmer time, no one would have imagined anything wrong with Carpenter sponsoring the Senate measure. Its aim was to repair oversights in the 1789 Judiciary Act, and the "Webster of the West" was one of the shrewdest lawyers in the chamber. The problem Carpenter hoped to solve had nothing to do with journalists, or so he said. Northern firms doing business found sectional prejudices too strong to permit them a fair hearing in state courts. Procedures must be streamlined to make it easier to transfer a case into the federal courts. That was what the Senate bill did, by allowing any circuit or territorial court of the United States and any court of the District of Columbia to take up a suit against any corporation that had an agent residing in the place where the suit was brought.[21]

Partway through the debate, Senator Thomas F. Bayard of Delaware rose to point out an unsettling ambiguity in the term *agent*. It might indeed mean the branch office of any larger firm. It might also mean the Washington correspondent of a paper published elsewhere—the *Sun*, for example—and allow the editor's trial in a District court. A proviso exempting slander and libel from the terms of the bill would prevent any such misunderstanding. Other senators were not so sure it was a misunderstanding after all. "Mr. President, this strikes at public liberty itself," one of them warned. The warning went unheeded or, worse, unappreciated. Led by Carpenter and Conkling, the Republican majority drove the section through unchanged.[22]

Later, as the storm rose, Carpenter insisted that journalists' fears were groundless, but in terms that could hardly have made publishers feel that much safer. "They seem to think that they may be sued in Washington for libel. Well, why should they not be, if they commit that injury by an agent in this District?" Honest men need never fear the law; what did that say about the editors trembling behind their desks? And though he declared that Washington correspondents did not fit the definition of agents, his claim held less conviction than the vote against Bayard's amendment and his own proposal of a resolution a month before to look into the validity of cases brought in the District police court. More persuasive was the Cincinnati *Commercial*'s charge that Carpenter's bill would have placed "censorship of the press in the hands of some played out and vicious politician, furnished an asylum as a Judge of the District of Columbia—some abject appointee of the President and beggarly sycophant of the Ring."[23]

Carpenter's bill did not get through the House, though the Judiciary Committee chairman, Ben Butler, energetically urged its passage, itself a sinister portent. Already "fuming accounts" flew across the telegraph wires, and reporters raised a lobby of their own. Not even Carpenter "when he is chasing a new drab" was as persistent as the journalists, one of them boasted. Theirs proved a hollow victory. Instead, Carpenter's apparent purposes were met with a bill offered by Luke Poland of Vermont. It conferred concurrent jurisdiction for all charges brought before the police court on the criminal court of the District of Columbia.[24]

Poland seemed hardly fitted for a conspirator's role. Fond of ruffle shirts, swallowtails, and brass buttons, he looked like a statesman out of some other time. "Respectability" was a word that came naturally to those describing him. Unlike other members, he never acted hastily or angrily in Congress, the *Nation* admitted, never called his colleagues liars nor shook his fists at them. When the House considered punishing the malefactors in Credit Mobilier, Poland's gravity as chairman made up for his lack of oratorical flash and drove the arguments for censure home.[25]

Nor, on the face of it, did Poland's bill seem unreasonable in view of Blatchford's decision. If the police court lacked the authority to try certain crimes given to its exclusive jurisdiction, the law must be corrected to lodge the jurisdiction for them elsewhere. How this might affect newspapers had been the last thing in the Vermonter's mind. But it was the first thing in editors'. This was Shepherd's bill, they warned, drawn up to enable some District court under the "boss's" thumb to grasp Dana.[26]

They were right. Months later, Poland admitted that District Attorney Harrington had written the bill and Butler, knowing perfectly well how anything he proposed would be interpreted (and possibly with a sense

of the political uproar that such a measure would raise and eager to re-
pay Poland for having brought about the censure of Butler's friend Oakes
Ames in the Credit Mobilier scandal), had induced the gentleman from
Vermont to condense and report it. It had been a put-up job.[27]

Within a month, dark suspicions had turned to open alarm. The two
libel suits were revived under the gag law's provisions almost at once.
Before the end of June, the grand jury for the District court had found
an indictment against Buell. A fortnight later, it laid two indictments on
Dana on the basis of a sheaf of editorials brandished by Shepherd. Lest
anyone doubt that political influence would be used to sway Washington
jurors, Senator Chandler laid them to rest by making an offer to hand
the $100,000 damages to the District if he succeeded. This, as *Harper's
Weekly* put it, was "an immense and tempting premium upon injustice."[28]

With reason, then, newspapers saw the two bills as "a conspiracy of
politicians against the press." Apparently, they had exactly the same objects that New York's notorious boss, William Tweed, had had in mind
a few years before, when he pushed along a bill letting judges mete out
contempt-of-court citations and jail terms to any editorial comment on
juridical doings. Even rational Republican journalists gave their analyses
a paranoid edge. "It is only another means tried by the District ring to
bring editors here from all parts of the country for trial," Boynton wrote:

> First came the Dana case, which failed because the Police Court had
> no jurisdiction. Then the Poland law was prepared by Harrington and
> Shepherd, not naming libel it is true, but giving the Police Court con-
> current jurisdiction with the District Court, and thus removing the
> obstacle found to exist in the Dana case. Then the attempt was made
> to indict Dana, but the Grand Jury refused. Now the purpose is to use
> the power of Congress to bring editors here, and file suit against them,
> without the necessity of asking a Grand Jury whether they see fit to
> indict.[29]

Or was that too narrow an explanation? The more alarmist editors saw
a larger aim: the silencing of the muckrakers in general. Had there been
no free press, the public would never have heard of swindles in the Treasury, senators who bought their Senate seats, or Boss Shepherd. Vice-
President Schuyler Colfax would have returned to politics with reason
to smile, and Secretary of the Treasury Richardson would have escaped

his present reputation as "a drivelling idiot." With the silencing of a free press, good government would be stifled and free institutions put in the gravest danger.[30]

But were those institutions not in grave danger already? The Poland gag law was only one threat among many. By that summer, the independent press was warning of another far more pervasive: "Butlerism." Editors meant more than the grafting and special influence associated with Benjamin Butler himself, or the alacrity with which his demands were met by the administration. There were Butlers everywhere, politicians who used public office for private gain and cloaked their robbers' garb in partisan appeals. Such selfishness threatened the trust on which institutions rested and, in the long run, the republic itself.[31]

A third terror was the worst and the most farfetched of the lot: "Grantism." By 1874, the term covered more than corruption. As some of the most prominent journals used it, it meant the use of political muscle and favors to perpetuate the president in power for six more years.

The third-term panic actually started before Grant began his first year. Even as he ran for president in 1868, Democrats uttered dire warnings that the general was not simply ignorant of civilian institutions, but downright contemptuous of them. Given the chance to reign, he would seek the chance to rule as well. With thousands of offices to fill with his servitors, and a Congress led by men of pliant principles, it would be easy to make himself dictator, with every election a rigged plebiscite.[32]

So wild a notion was less inconceivable just after the Civil War. Scarcely twenty years since, Louis Napoleon, president of France, had made himself emperor. Free governments had fallen in Mexico before and would again. History was littered with the ruins of republics overthrown by overweening generals. Begun as a campaign sensation, perhaps, the idea took on a life of its own. "May God the Almighty . . . save the Republic whom men would destroy," former senator James R. Doolittle of Wisconsin wrote his wife gloomily. "I fear the time is coming when like the Jews our degenerate people want a king to rule over them and when God in his wrath will give us one." Even conservative men would acquiesce in a coup, a Missourian confided to his diary. "We shall have a consolidated imperialism—in fact we have one now."[33]

Four years of Grant's rather desultory governing style did not dispel Democrats' anxieties. Clearly the continued use of federal marshals and

"There It Is Again!"
(Thomas Nast, *Harper's Weekly*, July 25, 1874).

soldiers to keep the bare semblance of law and order across the Republican South kept fears of tyranny alive; probably the conservatives' view that every step to protect black voters' rights violated the Constitution strengthened the delusion that the president would stick at nothing where his aims were concerned. So the Democratic press made the 1872 campaign ring with warnings of tyranny to come. "The great issue before the people of the United States in 1872 is reduced to this simple but pregnant question," the Harrisburg *Patriot* summed up: "CINCINNATUS or CAESAR, which shall it be?"[34]

When the voters favored Caesar, the alarmist cries silenced, but only for six months. Then, the following summer, with Congress adjourned and no important news to rouse the drowsing readers, the New York *Herald* took up the cry.

The younger James Gordon Bennett's *Herald* remained what his father had made it: one of the most popular and profitable newspapers in the land, so independent among the "independent press" that it kept out of Greeley's bolt and sniped at both sides. It was from no long-held fears, then, that Bennett now made an issue of "Caesarism." His real aim was to boost circulation through the dog days, when a lack of news usually cut into sales. Two other reasons may explain why the *Herald* came out with that particular issue, and just then. Perhaps the topic occurred more naturally to editors' minds because of the struggle for free government that seemed to be breaking out across Western Europe. In Spain, republicans had managed to overthrow the Bourbons and put themselves in power, precariously. Germany's Iron Chancellor had begun to show an iron fist against the Catholic church and political opposition; and in France, a constitutional crisis had driven one of the founders of the Third Republic into the last of a series of retirements.[35]

Most of all, the choice showed the way caprice and competitiveness mingled. A peevish tyrant, Bennett treated the *Herald* as if it were a toy to be played with or used to smash things to which he had taken a dislike. "I want you fellows to remember that I am the only reader of this paper," he told his underlings once. ". . . If I want it to be turned upside down, it must be turned upside down." But there is also no doubt that he loved to show off what was commonly referred to as "the mysterious power of the Herald," and the best way of doing so was to create a sensation from nothing, or make a news topic that every rival paper in New York would have to pick up for its own sake.[36] That summer the New York *World* gave him a special incentive. With the election of 1872 having apparently settled the issues of the Civil War and Reconstruction beyond revival, Manton Marble had faced the double problem of finding a new rallying cry for the Democrats and reasserting the *World*'s role as the party's opinion maker, for debt and dissidence alike had made the paper, as one journalist put it, "gummy about the eyes—slobbery, decrepit—blank." The issue he hit upon was the tariff. Editorials calling for the Democratic party to endorse free trade sparked plenty of debate.[37] Conceivably, in firing a round at "Caesar," Bennett took aim at Grant to hit Marble. What better weapon could he have chosen than an issue by now almost second nature to the Democrats that Marble was appealing to?

Whatever his intentions, on July 7, 1873, Bennett launched a campaign to alert the republic to its peril. Americans should put aside such "sentimental issues" as free trade or protection, the editorial warned. They should focus on the only question that mattered: "Shall we have Caesarism or republicanism?" Grant's henchmen meant to win him the nomination, the *Herald* insisted; he had the power to make it certain. The sword of impeachment had proven a poor lath; no political institution could block a president's will. All the ominous parallels were drawn: Caesar offered the crown on the Lupercal, Napoleon encouraged to overthrow the French Directory, Lord Protector Oliver Cromwell dismissing England's Parliament in God's name and for his own sake.

The only thing lacking was proof that anyone had so much as considered Grant for a third term. From so much nothing, Bennett proved that there must be a conspiracy. No Republican was talking about the issue at all: "a grave indication." Obviously, partisans were "negatively committing themselves to the principle of Caesarism." If Grant actually declared that he would not accept a renomination under any circumstances, the *Herald* added, America would be in just as much danger as ever: no country "should have its liberties at the mercy of any man's magnanimity." The only way the issue could be quelled, Bennett argued, was by the president fulfilling certain conditions. He must renounce all ambitions, publicly denounce the Constitution as fatally flawed in coping with potential tyrants, and show his love for peace by sending armies to liberate Mexico and Cuba.[38]

Such logic chopping should have raised a roar of laughter across the nation. It did in some places (Thomas Nast found two years of cartoon material), but among those inclined to believe, it also raised a clamor of alarmed prognostications. Democratic journals took up the *Herald*'s cry. Some rebuked the *World* for fiddling with tariffs while Rome fell. Others chided the *Herald* for taking so long to discover what they had known all along. Though more skeptical of any threat to the republic, liberal Republican papers like the Chicago *Tribune* took Grant's ambition as plain fact.[39]

Just then, at the very start of the scare campaign, Republicans blundered badly. While their editors were right to dismiss third-termism as a groundless fear, they let it go. The president could have issued a statement denying all desire for a third term. Instead, contemptuous of his critics, still more contemptuous of the *Herald*, and unwilling to offend his wife, who liked the idea of staying on as first lady, Grant said nothing and authorized no one in his administration to speak for him.[40] The response seemed to make sense at first. After all, Bennett's campaign was palpably a newspaper stunt. Fustian like that deserved no official reply. Even a few journalists hostile to the president passed the topic off lightly. "I have read nothing great on Caesarism—only pleasant," a onetime employee of the *Herald* wrote. "For there is no danger & you can't hatch a bear out of a wren's egg." As late as July 1874, the Cincinnati *Commercial* could see the talk petering out. Third-term "fiddle-faddle" arose only to give journals some week's theme, it explained, declining only to rise whenever "dull times" made it necessary. But dull times were over: the scandal over the Reverend Henry Ward Beecher's adultery with the wife of his friend Theodore Tilton gave newspapers something to talk about.[41]

The *Commercial* was right in essential principles of news manufacturing, but it was wrong about the *Herald*'s hobbyhorse. By July 1874, the cry was spreading fast. Of course Grant was aiming at a third term, the Wilmington *Morning Star* insisted; that he could compel Republicans to give him another nomination was beyond doubt.[42] In the Cincinnati *Commercial*, "X. Y. Z." described how it would be done. Under Collector of the Port Chester Arthur, New York's spoilsmen would assemble and force the state convention to endorse the war hero. South of Pennsylvania, executive patronage could control at least half the delegations, especially those in which hungry Republicans were shut out of the state offices. A little pressure from the customhouse employees would make loyalists of every merchant. The moneyed classes, fearful of radical farmers' movements and restive workers in the cities, would embrace any nominee who could protect their corporate privileges. Grant filled the requirements better than any other possible nominee, critics pointed out. His adulation of magnates was well known. So was his use of judicial appointments to shift the Supreme Court's opinion on whether paper money could be considered a legal tender. Financiers owed him a still greater debt for his veto of the "Inflation bill," which would have reversed the Treasury's contraction of the money supply. Allegedly, three Wall Street operators in four pronounced the president a "safe" man, and as the economy worsened, safety looked all the more enticing. The open endorsement of the well-to-do meant open coffers, and that would carry many a state as well.[43]

Looking southward, the alarmist press invented two scenarios. Some editors focused on the unlettered black voters, who would vote for any nominee as long as he had a Republican endorsement, and on the politicians more than usually dependent on federal largess for their own livelihood. Corrupt carpetbaggers and stealing scalawags were prime recruits for the third-term campaign. Rather than see Democrats in command, Senator William G. Brownlow told the *Herald*, he would favor having Grant as "Emperor for life and the country an absolute despotism."[44] Alternatively, there were the Southern whites, desperate for some means of ending Republican rule in the cotton states. If Grant would help them restore conservatism to power, they would repay the favor; and as observers on Printing-House Square pondered his Southern policy in the winter and spring of 1874, they wondered whether a deal had been struck already. Republican contenders, hoping to cling to power after a defeat at the polls, appealed to the president in vain for federal intervention. In Arkansas, two self-proclaimed governors, each of them with a tainted title, assembled armies and battled it out in the streets. Grant threw his influence to the one backed by most white Democrats. Sickened by the political debauch in South Carolina, he berated visiting Republicans for letting it go on and dropped hints that the administration might sustain a bolters' ticket.[45]

All of these signs could be read different ways, but the *Herald* and other newspapers did their best to connect the moves with the third term and found just enough conservative Southerners willing to utter corroborative gaffes. One of the most vocal and dangerous was Colonel John M. Mosby, who wanted to run for Congress as an independent on a platform backing Grant for a third term. "I have but one object," he told a reporter, "and that is to have the white men of the South and the white men of the North cooperate for the general good of the country." That might just mean endorsing Grant. In Atlanta, H. V. Redfield watched as the postmaster formed a Grant Club and boasted the support of some of Georgia's most solid men. "If Grant will do the fair thing by the South, if he will give us simple justice, we are for him for a third term or a fourth term," the governor told the Cincinnati *Commercial*'s correspondent. It was from such remarks as these that reporters were able to build a case for a new, conservative presidential party.[46]

Special significance was seen when the San Francisco *Alta California* suggested the possibility of running Grant on a hard-money ticket, for it was owned by Senator John P. Jones of Nevada, one of Grant's close confidants. But even more significant was the republication of the *Alta California*'s editorial by W. J. Murtagh's Washington *National Republican*, widely seen as the president's official mouthpiece.[47] Indeed, for lack of word from Grant himself, the alarmists took a cue from everything the *Republican* cared to say. When the paper published a letter by former governor Paul O. Hebert of Louisiana endorsing the third-term project and added an approving editorial, it was easy for critics to infer that the White House was actively flirting with conservative Southerners for the 1876 race. Coming upon Colonel Erastus Brooks, editor of the paper, a reporter asked him whether he was in favor of a third term. "Of course I am," Brooks exclaimed. ". . . I think Grant the best President the country has ever had."[48]

Level-headed observers treated these frail leads paraded through the press as the meaningless tokens that they were. It was ridiculous on the very face of it to assume that Grant would be the candidate of the regular Republicans who still feared ex-Confederate control in the South *and* of rebels like Mosby, of those who wanted the "carpetbagger" governments sustained with more military vigor *and* those who wanted those governments wiped out and had promises from Grant to do it. Whatever the *Alta California* said, its putative voice, Senator Jones, made clear that Grant's renomination was out of the question. Close associates of the president pointed out that he had never expressed any desire to run again, and that he had too much sense to want the job for another four years. Not a single Republican speaker of importance, not one important party newspaper outside the capital, and no state convention except South Carolina's gave the third-term project its endorsement. As the *Nation* said wryly, Grant seemed to be trying the unusual strategy of winning a nomination without votes. Southern conservatives quickly disassociated themselves from Mosby and the third-termites, or insisted that their support for a third term was strictly in the abstract. When two anonymous "Southern gentlemen" endorsed Grant for a third term on the Democratic ticket, the Rome *Courier* hoped that anyone of their way of thinking would meet with "a fatal railroad accident or a successful marine disaster before they return home."[49]

Yet the panic went on. Of course Grant wanted a third term, the Washington *Sunday Capital* argued. "Power with this man is an instinct." Eventually, otherwise staid newspapers began to accept, if not the president's plan to usurp power, at least his readiness to succeed himself. Even the Springfield *Republican*, coolheaded though it was, became half convinced, and Henry Watterson of the Louisville *Courier-Journal* thought the president's reelection a near certainty. When white Democrats massed a private army and overthrew Louisiana's Republican government that September and the president intervened, the alarm over a Caesar using force to keep himself in power grew stronger, though as one paper pointed out, the men behind the revolt themselves may have acted because they believed the third-term talk: they really imagined that Grant would let them get away with it in return for their political support.[50]

In vain *Harper's Weekly* joined a chorus of Republican newspapers in begging the president to make a formal renunciation. Congressman Joseph Hawley's Hartford *Courant*, one of the most respected Republican organs in the country, denounced the third term as "revolutionary." "Everybody here is against the third term—and against Grant," a visitor to Milwaukee wrote home. The party convention in Kansas pronounced the two-term limitation a vital part of America's unwritten law. Republicans in Nebraska, West Virginia, and Nevada spoke nearly as emphatically. Delegates in Pennsylvania made an indirect repudiation by endorsing their governor for president instead.[51]

Grant's silence made it all the more imperative for his party's candidates to speak out. Any shilly-shallying would cost them as dearly as it did New York Republican governor John A. Dix. True, his reelection campaign was crowded with obstacles enough without bringing in national issues. Temperance advocates seethed at his veto of a local prohibition bill; liquor dealers and German voters shunned him for having signed a measure nearly as objectionable. With a reform record to his credit, machine Republicans had to accept Dix at the convention but made no secret of their disgust, and on the Democratic side, reformers and Tammany Hall plug-uglies alike hurrahed for Samuel J. Tilden. Dix might have lost anyway, but the third-term panic made it certain.[52] From the *Herald*, *Tribune*, and *Sun* the cry came that the Republican platform's silence meant consent and demanded an unmistakable rebuke.[53]

Try as the governor might, he could not escape the third-term trap. In private conversations for public consumption, Dix insisted that he disapproved of any president serving more than eight years. If press reports were correct, the statement was strong enough to offend Grant himself. Having helped Dix win in 1872, the president thought such a statement as ungrateful as it was cowardly, and his friends passed the word that no Republican scratching Dix's name off the ticket would suffer for it. But so wan a statement as the governor's did not satisfy the *Herald*, the *Tribune*, the *Sun*, or the Democrats. "The question . . . was not what he thinks, but, What will he do?" former governor Horatio Seymour told a crowd. Would he actually resist Grant if an attempt was made?[54]

Across the North that fall, the voters spoke, and in no uncertain tones against the Republican incumbents in House and Senate. Hard times were to blame, as were the scandals in Washington and across the South. But there were plenty of signs, as well, that the newspaper panics had played a significant role. In Vermont, Luke Poland failed even to gain renomination—a result widely credited to his sponsorship of the gag law.[55] Butlerism suffered a mortal blow in Massachusetts when Butler was beaten, and Chandler and Carpenter found themselves fighting for their political lives, with legislatures usually safely Republican now leaning to the enemy. As for Caesarism, the election of a Democratic House ensured a rash of investigations into every administration department and reports sure to discredit Grant, if not bring his impeachment. Dix lost badly, too, and the independents thought that they knew where the credit lay. "The King is dead! Long live the King!" former *Times* editor John Bigelow wrote Whitelaw Reid. "The grave has been dug large but not too large to hold Dix, Grant, and the Third Term abomination." With justice, Tilden credited his victory to the two-term tradition. He might as well have credited it to the *Tribune* and the *Herald*.[56]

The election marked the high point of the panic of 1874, though that did not become clear immediately. The prosecution of Buell and Dana persisted; momentarily, indeed, the District Ring seemed about to claim another victim. Unable to arrest the editor and bring him into the District, Shepherd's friends arranged to have him called as witness in a case in the federal courts. The ploy was a little too transparent; the subpoena went out the night after a grand jury had dismissed the case, much to the bewilderment of the jurors, judge, and prosecutor in the case, none of whom imagined that Dana could be of the slightest service to them. Once the editor set foot in Washington, it was alleged, any number of suits could be cooked up against him. A packed jury could pick the *Sun* clean with a large settlement for damages. Dana was not so easily taken in: the trick already had been tried with Reid of the *Tribune* in January 1875 by arresting him after the House summoned him to the capital to testify in the Pacific Mail Steamship subsidy investigation.[57]

Caesarism proved virtually indestructible, perhaps because something that never existed was difficult to extinguish. Early in the new year, even Speaker James G. Blaine fretted that the dream of a new lease on power had "taken firm hold" with the president and expressed alarm at the means likely to be used for its fulfillment. A bill to strengthen the government's power to protect blacks' right to vote became clear proof that Grant was grasping for power, and for what end but a third term? "Dead at Last!" the *Herald* exulted of Caesarism, as spring elections in 1875 gave Connecticut to the Democrats. Few deaths proved so short-lived: two weeks later, another editorial proclaimed Grant the most likely nominee in 1876.[58]

Yet in other ways, the changing political climate had been clear from Election Day. After all, the independent press could hardly keep up the same level of alarmism when it had won. Without Butler, Poland, or Carpenter, the perils that they symbolized looked nowhere as serious. As for Chandler, in Brick Pomeroy's gibing verse:

> No more, no more,
> Upon the Senate floor,
> We hear the fearful din,
> A half-and-half of eloquence and gin.[59]

The politicians had no stomach for renewed fights with the press gang. "Gideon" of the Chicago *Times* noticed it clearly when the lame-duck session of the House opened. No longer did lawmakers bellow at the press or threaten vengeance. Congressmen did rise as quickly as ever to correct press canards but no longer termed them "falsehoods." They were merely errors. On the very first day, even before receiving the president's message, a member rose to repeal the "press-gag law." By the day's end, Sunset Cox had moved to free newspapers from postage costs. Soon after that, Poland himself proposed changes exempting libel from the provisions of his ill-fated bill. Before the session closed the following March, the Vermont congressman had not only redeemed his good reputation but also enhanced it by leading the fight against the president and his carpetbagger friends in Arkansas who wanted the new Democratic state government set aside. Unanimously, the Senate Judiciary Committee reported that Poland's original law had not allowed the District's criminal court to

"How Many Times Shall Caesar Bleed in Sport" (Thomas Nast, *Harper's Weekly*,
November 21, 1874). With the elections over, Whitelaw Reid, Manton Marble,
and James Gordon Bennett, Jr., as assassins, finish off their antagonist.

handle libel cases in the first place: libel was a common-law offense, and
federal tribunals were limited to federal statutes.[60]

With that, the effort to indict Augustus Buell fell to pieces. A writ
of habeas corpus was obtained and the case appealed. Finding semantic
errors in the original indictment, which had somehow failed to mention
the publication of the libel in any newspaper printed in the District, the

court discharged Buell. When a new bill of indictment was worked up, a judge threw it out again, this time declaring that Buell's offense took place before Poland's law gave the District court jurisdiction over it. When Washington authorities sent a federal marshal to drag Dana to the capital in answer to a subpoena, Judge Blatchford dismissed the case (the delighted editor proposed that the jurist's portrait be hung in every newspaper office in the land). Proceedings would linger until 1882, but Dana's days of peril were effectively over. So were Reid's. District judge David Cartter had no intention of handling so controversial a case unless forced to do so and, as he assured Boynton, would see to it that no jury blundered into an unfair verdict.[61]

As for Caesarism, the question had been so nearly settled by the election returns that whatever Grant intended had become irrelevant, a point that by midspring was clear to most level-headed people. Even so, in late May 1875, the president wrote a public letter renouncing all desire for a third term. His letter was written in plain language, but not plain enough for the *Herald*. Reporters interviewed prominent politicians who found loopholes large enough to let a candidacy through. A few actually read the letter as a demand for a third term. One senator tried to dismiss the pronouncement as a forgery. Not even the presidential nominations a year later allayed the fears of the most suggestible readers, and when the election returns led to a dispute and legislative deadlock, a few easily frightened Democrats assumed that Caesar had crossed the Rubicon at last. With the army behind him, he could impose order, annul the returns, and put off the choice of a successor until 1880. The third term was his, after all! A real political crisis made such fears more plausible, yet they were not much believed, not even by the New York *Herald*.[62]

Other changes by 1875 had less to do with the politicians than with the press itself. The election proved to be the last hurrah of the independent press as a united, aggressive force in politics. Freed from the burden of supporting Grant, Murat Halstead and Whitelaw Reid would find their way back to the Republican party in short order. "Gath" had quit the Chicago *Tribune* and swung over to the New York *Graphic*, a newspaper far less hostile to the administration, for all its vaunted independence. Like Piatt, "Gath" had destroyed much of his credibility as a muckraker by his defense of Boss Shepherd, in any case. Manton Marble had long since sworn party fealty again; that, indeed, was the real meaning of his campaign for free trade, to set an agenda separate from that of the liberal Republicans with whom he had associated. The Chicago *Tribune*, too, fell back into stolid Republican hands; the New York *Times* rekindled its orthodoxy. Other independents were left, certainly, but there were not nearly enough to do the same sort of damage as in 1874.

And what of James Gordon Bennett? He continued his idiosyncratic ways, but with less and less force in politics. The reason why should have been clear within a week of the election, when Monday's front page produced one last panic: AWFUL CALAMITY! THE WILD ANIMALS BROKEN LOOSE FROM CENTRAL PARK! TERRIBLE SCENES OF MUTILATION! A SHOCKING SABBATH CARNIVAL OF DEATH! AWFUL COMBATS BETWEEN THE BEASTS AND THE CITIZENS! The story had every detail, but the only one that counted came at the end of the page-long article, where the author admitted that the whole account was a simple exercise in imagination.[63] Such practical jokes did much to undermine the *Herald*'s influence in defining public opinion: Caesarism itself might have been just one more of Bennett's jokes.

There was, however, another hoax that the press exploited that fall, and it was far from being a joke. Instead, it furthered the disintegration of the already loose alliance between the independent press establishments leagued, however loosely, to either party. Quite another kind of scare had won Democrats their victories in the South, the Border states, and even much of the Ohio valley: the politics of race-baiting. Seizing on the proposed civil rights bill still pending in the House, partisan newspapers had raised a panic about Negro rule and black uprisings. It was on this issue, one that Horace Greeley would have deplored and the old *Tribune* scorned, that the Democrats came to power. Not reformers but onetime Confederates would sit in the House from below the Mason-Dixon line.

The year 1874, then, was not such a contrast with 1872 after all, however much the election returns differed. In each case the independent press had helped shape the issues; in neither had it won anything for itself. The politicians had won. By 1877, their victory would be complete.

CHAPTER 17

James G. Blaine
Beats the Rap

House Democrats had no excuse for the blunder they made in early 1876. Eighteen years in the minority may have left them inexperienced at forging a policy. But they might have wondered why Northern voters kept electing a Republican House. Was it not possible, just remotely possible, that people still associated the party with treason? If so, was there not some danger in giving aid and comfort to former Confederates? Yet the Democrats did just that, the moment they came back to power. They offered a bill restoring the right to hold federal office to the last white Southerners still shut out by the Fourteenth Amendment.[1]

They had reckoned without the former Speaker. James G. Blaine of Maine was among the most remarkable politicians of his day and one of the craftiest. "Now there's Blaine, damn him!" one congressman exclaimed, "but I do love him." It was a love widely shared. Grizzled and amber-eyed, energetic and impetuous, attractive to men as well as women, Blaine had the kind of magnetism that would make crowds of Republicans support him to the end—or fight him to the death. In vain critics looked behind the accom-

plished performer for deep moral intuitions or the idealist's vision of what
should be, as well as the realist's of what was. One perceptive observer
described him as Disraeli without a classical mind. "Blaine's mental qualities are the subtle, instantaneous power you see in a baseball player who
can catch the ball over his shoulder, no matter who bats it," George Alfred
Townsend marveled. "In the power of catching out the other side he is
unrivaled."[2]

Divided, turbulent, fecklessly led, the other side was just asking to be
caught out. With a Republican party hungry for good leadership, with his
own ambition and shrewdness to drive him on, James G. Blaine might no
longer preside over the House, but he could still run it. Within days of
the opening of the Forty-fourth Congress, Blaine had turned the Southern
issue in Republicans' favor and broken the Democratic ranks so badly that
not even their Speaker could undo the damage.[3]

Then came the amnesty bill. Blaine's weapon was simple: an amendment
excluding Jefferson Davis, former president of the Confederacy, from its
provisions. Pardon for rebels there might be, the former Speaker agreed.
Republicans themselves had given it generously, and every year they extended their generosity further, until no more than a paltry few hundred
remained unabsolved. Let them be relieved of their burdens now! Only
for one should there be no forgiveness. Thousands of Union soldiers had
died of hunger, neglect, and cruelty within the prison gates of Andersonville. Now these dead Blaine laid at Davis's own door and his alone. He
could keep his freedom; no one would deprive him of the right to vote or
travel, to buy or sell as he pleased, or to hold state and local office. But
in the name of those who died at Andersonville, the House must not call
back and crown "with the honors of full American citizenship the man who
organized that murder."[4]

A year before, Blaine himself had been ready to pass an amnesty bill
with no exceptions. This is one reason that critics then and historians since
have dismissed the speech as crude demagoguery. There was really nothing crude about it. Absolving white Southerners of guilt in war crimes,
extending amnesty to every man but one, the appeal was perfectly framed
to unite Republicans and to make former Confederates angry enough to
make fools of themselves. They did. Northern Democrats helped them.
Shouting at "the hyena from Maine," Samuel Cox of New York exposed
his party's biases by hurling more abuse at black Union soldiers than at
white Confederate ones. Later honored for eloquence and valor on this

occasion, Benjamin Hill of Georgia would have served his party better by displaying neither. The last thing Democrats needed was a onetime rebel officeholder declaring the Northern prison camps more inhumane than the Southern ones and Jefferson Davis a better man than President Grant.[5] The party hoped to carry the presidency that year by exposing the corruption that sixteen years of Republican rule had brought; but the mantle of reform looked less attractive when it was dyed a Confederate gray and very possibly made of the whole cloth, as well.[6]

Undoubtedly Blaine was a clever man, clever enough to be nominated for president, and after the amnesty debate, there was every chance that the honor would be his for the taking. Other candidates vied for the office. For those who liked to see the bloody shirt waved in a more violent manner, or felt that the Southern blacks' rights were still worth protecting, the fierce senator from Indiana, Oliver P. Morton, seemed a better prospect. Reformers looked to Secretary of the Treasury Benjamin H. Bristow, whose vigor in exposing frauds in the collection of the whiskey tax had revealed a trail of graft running all the way to the desk of President Grant's personal secretary. Party machines in New York and Pennsylvania had favorite sons, and Ohio Republicans advanced the claims of their newly elected governor, Rutherford B. Hayes. But every state convention showed that the nomination was Blaine's to lose.[7]

Blaine did lose it in the end, but by so little that for the next sixteen years, no Republican convention would pass on presidential nominees without first taking a good look at "the plumed knight," "the magnetic man."[8] Why that was so had a lot to do with the newspapers. It tells a great deal not just about how they could wreck a politician's career but how they could save it—and how even the muckrakers raked the muck with party advantage in mind.

With the amnesty debate, two forces converged: the Democrats clamoring for revenge, and the backers of other Republican candidates, determined to stop a rising man. Something must be found on Blaine. Finding it would not be all that difficult; for quite some time, reporters had been aware of leads. All that was needed, it would seem, was to follow some of them up. The summer before, rumors had circulated about personal matters touching the former Speaker. Congressman William W. Phelps, of New Jersey, a close friend of both Blaine and editor Whitelaw Reid, had heard them—or, rather, refused to hear them—when a Kentuckian had offered to tell.[9]

No doubt it was the story that would surface just before the convention in several obscure Tennessee and Kentucky newspapers. Years before the Civil War, when Blaine had taught school in Kentucky, he had married and within a surprisingly brief time become a father. Common rumor suggested that the pregnancy had preceded, even explained the marriage. An even wilder variant told how the young teacher had seduced an instructress, got her pregnant, and been confronted by members of the family. They threatened to kill him unless he made an honest woman of her. As the tale went, Blaine fled and when captured, fell on his knees to beg for mercy; the marriage took place, though it was cut short by the wife's death soon after.[10]

The story would surface over and over during Blaine's career, a fantasy built around a particle of truth. Blaine had indeed been married twice, but both times to the same woman, once privately in Kentucky and then six months later in the presence of her family in Pennsylvania. It was the second wedding that preceded the child's birth by so suspiciously short a time.[11] An unprovable story based on winks and nudges, however, could only discredit the tellers, and most newspapers let the allegation strictly alone.

Other reports were much more discreditable because they were much more usable. Rumors of corruption had been afloat for some time. Democratic newspapers in Maine had traced a connection between Blaine's legendary wealth—which was, in fact, mythical—and the vast land grant that the Northern Pacific Railroad had been assured during his first Speakership. Had there been a payoff from Jay Cooke & Company, the banking firm promoting the venture?[12]

The evidence was there. In early 1874, when a member of the Cooke firm died, he left behind private papers relating to the mismanagement of the District of Columbia, over which Henry Cooke, as governor, had presided. As congressmen called for an investigation, Speaker Blaine blocked the way. Gradually it dawned on Zebulon L. White, bureau chief for the New York *Tribune*, that there was a connection between Blaine's conduct and those letters. When the Speaker arranged for a bank examiner to look over the papers of the deceased, there were suspicions that the man he chose was selected "in order to have those letters suppressed."[13] Years after Blaine's death, indeed, letters surfaced showing that the Speaker's friendship for the Northern Pacific had been well watered with loans on easy terms. Blaine had practically demanded favors, reminding the Cookes of how his official powers could be used for their benefit. "You must see and satisfy Blaine," Henry wrote Jay Cooke anxiously. "I have been working up the idea of a gov't subsidy with him and others, and think it can be carried through, with good management."[14]

Now Blaine's "good management" in railroad matters was coming back to haunt him, but not, as it happened, his relationship with the Cookes. Soon Democrats were boasting that they had found something. Word reached the Republicans through that sharp-eared correspondent, Henry Van Ness Boynton. On February 6, 1876, he wrote to his editor, Richard ("Deacon") Smith of the Cincinnati *Gazette* of unsettling reports. The charge was that in 1864, when Blaine was a freshman in Congress, he had received a $15,000 bribe through the lawyer and lobbyist Joseph Stewart of the Kansas Pacific Railroad just when legislation was pending to change the government's lien on the road to a second mortgage. Worse still, the evidence could be found on the company books, fit for any partisan accuser to reveal.[15]

Boynton's story had drifted up and down Newspaper Row for three years and could be traced back to two reporters, James W. Knowlton of the Chicago *Tribune* and A. M. Gibson of the New York *Sun*. One reporter described Knowlton as boyish, easily mistaken for "a medical student off on a lark." A law student would have been a more appropriate description. It was while studying with the law firm of Joseph Stewart & A. G. Riddle that he had witnessed the signing of the bonds in Blaine's presence, though he never saw them handed over.[16]

Knowlton's story was conjectural at best and when he passed it on to Gibson in 1873, he was appalled to see it published as an actual accusation of bribery. Hastening to Gibson, he assured him that idle remarks had been misunderstood. Accompanied by J. M. Macfarland of the New York *Herald* and later of the Philadelphia *Press*, he rushed to Blaine's home to tender apologies and repudiate any suspicions. (That, at least, was how Gibson and Macfarland remembered it; Knowlton's version had Blaine summoning them and persuading them that the story was untrue). Within a day of making the charge, Gibson published a retraction.

Gibson and Macfarland were still alive to correct the specific allegation if it came up again, but Boynton rested his case on stronger grounds than them. There was something in the charge of involvement in the Kansas Pacific, more than the retraction implied. Knowlton's apprehensions arose only from his own peculiar situation: he was about to marry A. G. Riddle's daughter. The reporter's prospective father-in-law would find his own position in the law firm badly compromised by the allegations. But Knowlton continued to suspect Blaine. Before dying late in 1873, he passed his thoughts on to his mother and sister, and, more important, to Boynton himself. At first believing the Maine congressman innocent, Riddle, too, grew convinced that corruption lay behind the bonds. In addition, another student in the law office recalled seeing Blaine visit there frequently, in flat contradiction of what the former Speaker claimed. There was a story there, and Boynton suspected that with a little more digging he could find the documents to prove it.[17]

What is most interesting is not Boynton's determination, but his timing and discretion. The same charge might be made of other reporters. Zebulon White could have followed up his suspicions about incriminating letters two years before—but he did not; William W. Phelps was concerned enough about the sex scandal to get in touch with Charles Nordhoff of the New York *Herald* and let him know that there was something worth pursuing.[18] But Nordhoff never followed up on it. As for Boynton, in more than two years since Knowlton's death, he had shown a complete lack of interest in delving into Blaine's money-making.

Boynton's indignation was undoubtedly sincere. In the past year he had exposed the sinuous intrigues of Grant's secretary of the interior, unearthed evidence of corrupt lobbying by the Pacific Mail Steamship company and the attempt by District Ring cohorts to frame one of their accusers, and torn apart General William Tecumseh Sherman's use of facts in his memoirs. But was there not another reason for Boynton's sudden appreciation of the Blaine matter? In his letter to Smith, he added a revealing argument for bringing the scandal out: "prominent democrats know enough of this record to make it certain that it will become widely known, the moment [Blaine's] name is placed on the ticket."[19] There it was: as a Republican, Boynton wanted to handle the scandal before it harmed his party's chances.

The point needs emphasis. Democrats stood a good chance of winning the presidency, an excellent one if they could taint the Republican nominee. Not until the amnesty debate did the peril of Blaine's nomination become serious enough to warrant action. "You may be sure it's a true bill," Boynton would write on the eighteenth, "—whatever Blaine may say—at any rate he will have to meet it before long—though not from me. If he can give an entirely satisfactory answer, well, but if he can not, no party could elect him."[20] For the party's sake, Blaine must be cleared, persuaded to withdraw, or broken within before the nomination.

Yet even in making this argument, Boynton was not being wholly frank. He and Deacon Smith had another reason for wanting the scandal broached early and for hoping the charges were unanswerable ones. They wanted Secretary of the Treasury Bristow nominated, and Boynton was not just an advocate but an associate in the fight against Treasury corruption. When the Whiskey Ring was broken in St. Louis, the secretary of the Treasury had made his preparations outside of official channels. He could trust neither members of the Internal Revenue nor the telegraph operators not to reveal the government raid in advance. It was Boynton who helped him out, by arranging that all messages be sent in a special code that he and another journalist, George Fishback of the St. Louis *Democrat*, shared. Through them the traps were laid and the communications would pass. Now he meant to give Bristow the highest office in the land, to roust out the thieves from every branch of government.[21]

Boynton's mixing up of his role as journalist and political kingmaker was nothing unusual. The whole press gang had chosen sides. Among the reformers, Bristow had become the candidate of choice. Murat Halstead, editor of the Cincinnati *Commercial*, favored him. So did Horace White, formerly of the Chicago *Tribune*. Samuel Bowles of the Springfield *Republican* was ready to support Bristow as well, when it was clear that the glacial Charles Francis Adams would have no more to do with the Republicans than they would with him. Governor Hayes had friends, as well, most notably William Henry Smith, agent for the Western Associated Press, and Oliver Morton could rely on Will Holloway, his brother-in-law, postmaster of Indianapolis and master spirit of the Indianapolis *Journal*.[22]

Boynton's allegation spread from the Bristow camp almost at once. Sharing stories with each other, as we have seen, was standard practice, and Boynton was never one to keep a good tale to himself. By February 11, the Washington press corps was seething. Zebulon White sent word back to Whitelaw Reid in New York. Thanks to their connections with the Chicago *Tribune*, E. B. Wight and Horace White were able to inform the managers of the Boston *Morning Journal* and the Springfield *Republican*.[23]

As for the Chicago *Tribune*, it got the news when Deacon Smith thought the revelations too important to handle alone. He turned for advice to William Henry Smith, and Smith told Joseph Medill of the *Tribune*. What

The Present Portentous Aspect of the Political Heavens (New York *Daily Graphic*, April 18, 1876). Editors carry their favorite candidates. Highest is Secretary of the Treasury Benjamin H. Bristow, riding Murat Halstead; below him, Henry Watterson's *Courier-Journal* bears Samuel J. Tilden, with James G. Blaine astride Whitelaw Reid. Charles Francis Adams, Sr., dourly rides Samuel Bowles, while above him "the Great Unknown" takes a flier on Horace White and former senator Carl Schurz (both men went for Bristow; so did Bowles). But "upon the horizon's verge / Through Hayes the rising sunbeams surge."

this meant was that within a fortnight of having made the original charge, Boynton and the Deacon had alerted the newspaper representatives of every important candidate except Morton's.[24]

One historian since and more than one Blaine loyalist at the time, describing the dark maneuvers that followed, would interpret the intrigues as a plot to destroy Blaine, restrained only by a common desire to fob the responsibility for exposure on someone else's candidate.[25] If it had only been that simple! Most of the insiders would have breathed easier if Blaine's fall had raised their own candidates' fortunes. But that was a small matter compared to the big one: how to keep the Democrats from "keeping a rod in pickle" to use on Blaine when it was too late for the Republicans to choose another nominee.

Boynton was the least cautious. Still, the warning recurred even in his letters: unless great care were taken, the story would get out. Did Medill propose a trip to Washington to quiz Boynton's authority? Boynton reminded him of the risk that a flying trip to Washington by so important a party editor as Medill would run. Questions would be asked, and the answer would not be long in coming, he warned. To connect that exposure with Medill or William Henry Smith would make them a party "to a very annoying business." Instead, he offered to meet with Medill and the two Smiths at Cincinnati some weekend, bringing with him the documents to prove his charges about the Kansas Pacific matter.[26]

Those documents he had little trouble in finding. From the clerk of the federal district court of Kansas came a transcript of its records on the settlement of Stewart's affairs. From the information, it seemed that Stewart, as a lobbyist for the Pacific Railroads, had received $240,000 in construction bonds from the president of the Kansas Pacific. Blaine's cousin, the railroad promoter and Democratic politician General Thomas Ewing, Jr., got $10,000, a prominent lobbyist received $24,000, and $15,000 more went to "—Blaine." All parties later insisted that it was the congressman's brother John who was meant; and John had been a court clerk at the time in either Kansas or Nebraska. But Boynton had heard tales that in Stewart's own copy of the written arrangement, the name was set down James, not John.[27]

Even as Boynton assembled his evidence, however, the "very annoying business" was being passed on to Blaine—as everyone knew and most of them hoped. As soon as Zebulon L. White and Medill were informed, Blaine had to know what was coming, for both the Chicago and the New

York *Tribune* leaned toward his candidacy. Confiding in Blaine would make no sense if the two Smiths, Boynton, and Medill had been planning his public destruction. What they wanted was an explanation that could overcome the accusations. As early as mid-February, Blaine had given a plausible refutation and his reply had been passed on to Boynton. That was why more evidence needed to be collected in the first place.[28]

By the time the cabal met on March 18, Boynton had compelling proof, including the court transcripts. His evidence was good enough to persuade Medill and Richard Smith to write Blaine again. The Deacon went into specifics about the $15,000 in bonds, but he added a second alarming note. While he would leave it to Medill to discuss the $75,000 in Little Rock & Fort Smith Railroad bonds, he cautioned the candidate, that piece of information looked very damaging.[29]

Seventy-five thousand dollars in Little Rock & Fort Smith securities? Here was a new item! The fact that it came up at all showed how wide the newspaper conspiracy had spread. Before the Cincinnati meeting could take place, before, indeed, it was so much as proposed, the cabal had suddenly taken on a new recruit and with him a fresh charge against Blaine. Somehow, in his editorial office at Indianapolis, Will Holloway had caught word that something was up. Perhaps the news reached him through his old acquaintances on the Chicago *Tribune*, where he had worked as a wartime correspondent.[30]

Holloway knew nothing about the Kansas Pacific, but he could tell a story all his own. It related to Blaine's dealings with the Union Pacific Railroad and with Tom Scott, whose Texas & Pacific Railroad had won the last great land grant Congress gave, while Blaine was Speaker. As William Henry Smith headed back to Chicago from press business in Cincinnati in late February, Holloway found time to wait at the Indianapolis depot to talk with him. Apparently, the Union Pacific owned bonds in the Little Rock & Fort Smith, with a face value of $75,000. Their actual value was next to nothing and had been so in 1872, but the Union Pacific took them as collateral in exchange for a $64,000 loan that was never meant to be repaid. The man who forced the company into such a curious business transaction was Tom Scott, then president of the Union Pacific. The loan's beneficiary was Blaine.[31]

The story was dynamite if true, and Holloway had the best of reasons for thinking it true. He had heard it from J. C. S. Harrison, a director on the Union Pacific, who had been informed of the bonds' origins four years before, during the 1872 campaign, by E. H. Rollins, secretary of the line. What made Harrison so voluble now was the same inspiration that loosened Holloway's tongue. Both were Morton henchmen, determined to wreck their candidate's most dangerous rival. Neither of them had any scruples about Blaine's being exposed in the press, and at once; the editor was particularly uneasy lest Blaine be informed of what the charges were against him. Let Boynton be put on the trail before the man from Maine could cover his tracks or induce Rollins to doctor the records for the Union Pacific, he urged. Far more than Boynton, Medill, or the Smiths, Holloway had only one fear: that the revelations would be traced back to the Morton camp, particularly since, as he insisted, the senator knew nothing about the evidence.[32]

Now William Henry Smith, Medill, and Holloway knew that they had a hot new story on their hands. So did Blaine. Primed by both Smith and Holloway, Medill had written the candidate an early warning and after the Cincinnati meeting, a second one. Blaine's answers were no longer as quick in coming. Perhaps he no longer saw the point. The secret scandal was bursting the confines of the cabal. Any reply he made to its members would only need repetition to a larger audience soon enough; time was running out. As confidences spread from person to person, the information was getting beyond any one group's control. By early March Reid knew that there was a story out there, and most likely it was larger than the one Zebulon White had passed along three weeks before. He turned to Charles Nordhoff of the *Herald*. "I guess you'll think I'm very stupid," Nordhoff wrote back apologetically, "but I really & truly don't know what scandals are going, abt. Blaine. Do you mean the Catholic business?[33] That's only one, & I don't attach much importance to it, though it annoys him I notice. I wish you would—if there is anything going likely to hurt him, & which could be explained, let me hear. I'll keep you out of it, with the most faithful secrecy."[34] Murat Halstead, of the Cincinnati *Commercial*, also had been let into the secret by the conferees. Horace White now not only knew the basics, but also had found more corroboration for the $64,000 question on his own: former congressman James F. Wilson, government director on the Union Pacific, backed up Harrison's original recollection. From Massachusetts to Missouri, reports filtered back to leading reform Republican politicians that Blaine's exposure was only a matter of time.[35]

The only question, then, was when and where the news would break. On April 11, that, too, was answered when the Indianapolis *Sentinel*, a Democratic newspaper, revealed the tale of the Union Pacific bonds.

How did it get there? To Medill and the Chicago *Tribune*, the place of publication explained everything. Morton's men had broken the story. Perhaps they did, but not Holloway. Understandably horrified, lest Blaine's supporters pin the blame on the Indiana senator (which they did), he swore that someone else must have primed the *Sentinel* for that very purpose. William Henry Smith protested that the story's appearance took him by surprise and that he had even tried to prevent the wire service from carrying it.[36]

Blaine's friends would blame Boynton and Bristow's Cincinnati friends. Were they right? Was there significance, perhaps, in the fact that George Fishback, Boynton's friend and contact in the Whiskey Ring investigation, had two brothers in Indianapolis journalism, one of them in charge of the Indianapolis *Sentinel*? Two weeks later, the New York *Herald* brought up the Kansas Pacific matter. Boynton had used the *Herald* before to plant allegations and escape paternity for them. Might he have been the source again?[37] Possibly, or the final responsibility may fall elsewhere. For three months Democrats had been boasting of what they held on Blaine. Too much talk could well have ended with one of their newspapers unable to hold its peace any longer.[38]

Who published first scarcely mattered. By the time the *Sentinel* broke the news, Blaine had stirred himself. The Republican journalists had seen to that. Time was precious. It could be put to use preparing a reply to the allegations thrown at him, and that was how Blaine used it.[39]

On April 24, with House and galleries in breathless attention, reading his speech from printed slips, Blaine made a full, emphatic denial of the charges leveled against him. He owned a few securities in Little Rock & Fort Smith, paid the market price for them, and lost heavily. "I never had any transaction of any kind with Thomas A. Scott concerning bonds of the Little Rock & Fort Smith road," he told his colleagues, "or the bonds of any other railroad, or any business in any way connected with railroads, directly or indirectly, immediately or remotely. I never had any business transaction whatever with the Union Pacific Railroad Company, or any of its officers or agents or representatives, and never in any manner received a single dollar in money or stocks or bonds, or any other form of value from them." Leading lawyers on both sides of the aisle agreed that the ex-

Speaker's case was so well made that "his enemies must put up or shut up." They could hardly have helped thinking so when Blaine read Rollins's letter as treasurer and two wires from Morton, Bliss & Company, which was alleged to have cashed a draft on Blaine's behalf in the sale of the seventy-five Little Rock & Fort Smith bonds, as well as a note from Tom Scott himself.[40] Five days later, he waved letters from Gibson, Macfarland, and Stewart to disprove the Kansas Pacific story, which had just appeared in the New York *Herald*.[41]

What made the two speeches persuasive was not Blaine's eloquence, but his documents, and those he had begun gathering more than a month before, as the editors' warnings intensified. By the end of March, Rollins, Macfarland, and Gibson had put their assurances on paper, and Stewart and Morton, Bliss & Company had their answers ready before the *Sentinel* had thrown out its charges. Indeed, the refutation of Rollins and Morton, Bliss & Company hit the press on the same day as the *Sentinel*'s allegations.[42] There had been time enough for all the responsible parties to prod their memories or their imaginations, and for some of them to prepare statements as misleading, even dishonest, as Blaine's own. For the fact was that the transaction with the Union Pacific had taken place, just as Harrison had said.

That fact was not so easily arrived at. When House Democrats launched an investigation, the Union Pacific officers stuck to their story. No bonds had been unloaded on them, certainly not in return for favors. A few journalists, Boynton among them, were able to spot discrepancies in Blaine's account. They could not shake it further. Late in May with the convention barely three weeks away, it seemed that the former Speaker had bested his challengers.[43]

All but one. Just at the end of the month, the subcommittee called James Mulligan to testify. Once the clerk for Blaine's brother-in-law and still nursing a grudge over the quarrel that marked his departure, Mulligan had a score to settle. He also had the weapons to do it with. The first was his own knowledge that Blaine had lied about dealings with Tom Scott. The bonds that Scott had claimed were his to sell to the Union Pacific had come through Blaine, to oblige his friends who had invested in them and lost badly on the deal; the reason Blaine was doing his friends the favor was that he had been the one who fobbed the bonds on them and took a big commission for doing so.[44]

The Speaker as stockbroker: the scandal was all the messier because it fit another letter that had leaked out just days before. In that note, Blaine had apparently arranged the sale of a share in the Northern Pacific Railroad within months of smoothing House passage of a bill on the road's behalf.[45] The way in which Blaine's involvement with securities and the fortunes of railroads needing the Speaker's aid kept coming together was more than a little suspicious.

Mulligan's word alone would hardly earn him a day's headlines. Blaine could call witnesses to refute everything and journalists ready to dig up enough to prove the bookkeeper a warped, frustrated little man. Mulligan knew it. Other witnesses in that spring of investigations had testified and later had had the press unleashed against them. He would not let it happen to him. Partly to fix his own memory on the details, but also for public release the moment smears began, Mulligan carried a cache of letters between his employer Warren Fisher, contractor of the Little Rock & Fort Smith Railroad, and Blaine. They were among many that Blaine had written years before and, when his dealings with Fisher ended, had asked to be returned. Most had been returned, but these sat in Fisher's safe until he and Mulligan went down to Washington for the hearings.[46]

Understandably, Blaine paled when Mulligan let slip that these letters now were ready to be produced (friendly AP services carefully cut the revelation out of their account).[47] It was a stroke for which he was completely unprepared, because the muckraking newspapermen had not done their job well enough. They may have suspected Blaine of many things, but never of stockbroking for Little Rock & Fort Smith. They could hardly give him advance warning of something that none of them knew anything about.

This time, therefore, Blaine had to move quickly—all too quickly, indeed, for the urgency gave his manipulation of public opinion a transparency that would cost him dearly in the long run. Before Mulligan could place the letters in the public record, Republicans got the investigating subcommittee to adjourn for the weekend. That gave Blaine time to call on Mulligan at his hotel and beg for the letters. As Mulligan told the story, the former Speaker practically fell on his knees, wept and pleaded for the sake of his wife and six children, threatened suicide, and offered a consulship. Any of those acts was more believable than what actually followed. Blaine asked to see the letters, and, having resisted every appeal to greed or pity, Mulligan handed them over. He never got them back.[48]

That was not how public opinion was won, not as long as the press held sway over reputations. No matter how badly his letters would have looked on the front page of the dailies, their suppression would look worse, especially if the House held Blaine in contempt. Pettifogging lawyers and former attorney generals could call a man's private correspondence inviolable, but was this the plea of a man with nothing to hide? Whatever the House decided, Blaine's real trial would come before the court of public opinion, presided over by several dozen hanging judges in the press gallery and along every city's Printing-House Square. The reliable old party press establishment could no longer protect a favorite's reputation. Blaine got more advice on that score from Zebulon White of the *Tribune*. As bureau head for an acknowledged "Blaine organ," his admonition for a candid explanation may have had special weight.[49]

Only audacity could redeem audacity. On June 5, before the subcommittee could report against him, Blaine arose. The galleries overflowed, senators scrambled for places in the back of the hall, and correspondents were virtually piled upon each other.[50] They came for spectacle and got it. Blaine was at his most aggressive, but not against the press gang. It was the onetime Confederates, Jefferson Davis's apologists, whom he scored. Smarting from his blows, onetime traitors and their friends had unearthed this scandal to smear him! Now they would invade his private life by nosing through his correspondence. That intrusion anyone who cherished his manhood would defy to the end.

But not because he was guilty. "I am not ashamed to show the letters," he exclaimed. "Thank God Almighty! I am not ashamed to show them." Out of his coat he pulled a packet and flourished it over his head. Wave on wave of applause rolled across the House. "There they are. There is the very original package. And with some sense of humiliation, with a mortification which I do not pretend to conceal, with a sense of outrage which I trust any man in my position would feel, I invite the confidence of 44,000,000 of my fellow countrymen while I read those letters from my desk." So he did, or at least those excerpts he pleased, in no apparent order. It was impossible for any listener to put together a pattern or even to conclude that there was one.[51]

Nor was he supposed to. This was theater, pure and simple. As Blaine began to read, some Republicans wept with admiration. When he advanced on the head of the committee and put him on the spot for suppressing evidence on Blaine's behalf, a telegram of supposed vindication against the charges by one of the principal parties, the galleries went mad. Even some Democrats joined in the applause, and not all the hammering of the Speaker's gavel could still the uproar.[52] Playing for the crowd and for the press gallery, Blaine very nearly won both. The performance would go far to efface the correspondence itself. "The letters show absolutely no wrong," Charles Nordhoff wrote back to Reid exultantly. "A decided and unanimous revulsion of sentiment for him," Zebulon White agreed.[53]

Decided it may have been, but the revulsion was far from unanimous. Blaine withheld the originals from the subcommittee and press, but even as read aloud, the letters offered a damning case when reduced to print. They provided that connection between private financial transactions and the Speaker's official acts that the muckrakers had never been able to weld. Not even Mulligan had noted how Blaine got his Little Rock & Fort Smith bonds in the first place: by indelicately reminding the firm of how he had saved its land grant in the House and by promising future diligence on its behalf. It was perhaps no coincidence that the Washington bureau of the Associated Press, friendly as ever to Blaine, failed to send along the letters in question to its readers on the day that it reported Blaine's theatrical triumph. Indeed, it tried to suppress them all, until the special correspondents banded together to force their transmission along the wires.[54]

Acute observers, among them Richard Smith and George Alfred Townsend, spotted the damaging passages right away. No bribe and no act of official misconduct from the chair had been proven. But the suggestion was palpable and pervasive, and when it came out that the telegram "vindicating" the former Speaker not only did no such thing except by misleading implication, but also had been dictated by Blaine himself to be planted on the committee—that, indeed, the investigating committee had had good reasons to suppress a piece of bogus evidence as a trick— the suspicion hardened to a certainty. "He stands there conspicuous as a man who has parted with his shadow," Townsend wrote. "There is all of him that was, but something else is missing. He lacks the good defect, the wondrous scruple."[55]

Blaine's coup de theatre kept him in the race for the presidency, but newspaper sensation, like a magician's tricks, is one of the most perishable of wonders. As time went on, the speech itself looked more like what it was, a stunt contrived from the desperation that sudden challenge thrust upon a man justly brought to bay. It would be partly an uneasiness at the content of those letters when they were published, but partly, too,

Mr. Blaine Showing His Hand (Joseph Keppler, *Leslie's Weekly*, June 24, 1876). James G. Blaine turns the tables on Congressman Proctor Knott, head of the subcommittee investigating him.

a well-founded distrust of so tricky a character that would be enough to deprive him of the nomination that year and four years later. By 1884, some of his newspaper critics had made peace with him, "Gath" among them. Others had not. Indeed, the ranks of the Republican city press split wide open. Never had so many proclaimed independence of party rather than swallow his presidential candidacy. The very theatricality that gave Blaine such popular appeal worked against him among the sober reformers. "He is essentially a rockety, journalistic kind of man, fond of rows and sensations," the *Nation* had commented, and if its readers agreed, the spectacular vindication of June 5 was one reason why they did.[56]

Still another try at news management went awry that spring. Blaine was not nominated, but neither was Benjamin H. Bristow, and one reason lay with the journalists themselves. As friends of President Grant and backers of the other candidates watched the charges of corruption mount against themselves, they rightly suspected that newsmen on Bristow's side were digging up the dirt. They could play the same game. Allegation met allegation. Democratic committees were glad to look into charges that the secretary of the Treasury had covered up for friends who evaded whiskey taxes or had made sly deals with lawbreakers for political advantage. None of the charges stuck. Bristow exploded them one after the other, but the campaign against him added to the bitterness of the rivalry on the Republican side.

"I have never been enthusiastic for the nomination," Mrs. Blaine wrote. ". . . But now I want Mr. Blaine to have it, and to go to it, as it were, on men's shoulders. I hate to hate but I am in danger of that feeling now." Most of all she hated Bristow. When stories arose once more about Blaine's marriage, it was only natural to suspect Bristow's friends. For that suspicion, there is no basis whatsoever. Blaine himself assured the secretary that he never imagined any such connection. Perhaps not, but Mrs. Blaine did. On the eve of the convention, as the former Speaker was on his way to church, he collapsed. Carried home senseless, he lay desperately ill for days. Well-wishers hastened to call on him, and one of them was Bristow. But when he reached the front door, he was confronted by Blaine's wife. "Mr. Bristow," she cried, "you have had your will. Now leave us!" The mortified secretary fled. "Everybody will forgive her but him," Senator Henry Dawes wrote his wife.[57]

The incident was ominously significant. Bristow could not win without votes from Blaine's delegations, nor Blaine without Bristow's. But the scandalmongers had made an alliance impossible. When the convention met and deadlocked, it was Bristow men, determined at all costs not to have Blaine, and Blaine men, resolved not to let Bristow or Morton come close to the prize, who shifted the convention to the bland, easygoing candidacy of Rutherford B. Hayes of Ohio. Neither side would forget nor forgive the other. Two years later, Deacon Smith and Bristow's backers still felt the hatred from Blaine's friends. They would repay it cordially. When Blaine at last got his presidential nomination in 1884, there was no chance of winning Boynton over. Rather than win the White House with such a choice, the reporter growled, he wanted to see Republicans "go into a minority and start again on an honest basis."[58]

The story of Blaine's dealing with the press in the spring of 1876, therefore, is not just the easy story of a vigilant press tracking down wrongdoers or a public figure destroyed by scandalmongering journalists. Instead, it is also a complicated fable of the way in which postwar improvisations in news management had changed the way scandals broke or their force was broken, with Blaine using the press so cleverly that his smartness would become legendary. From his reputation he would never recover.

CHAPTER 18

The Hayesociated Press

For once, Donn Piatt had just cause for his fury. As President Grant's term dwindled down to a matter of weeks in 1877, it became increasingly clear that his successor would be the Republican governor of Ohio, Rutherford B. Hayes. The change could only be an improvement, but that did not sweeten Piatt's temper. His candidate, the reform governor of New York, Samuel J. Tilden, had carried the popular vote and the Electoral College, or would have if partisan officials in three Southern states had not used their influence over the count to certify just enough electors to give Hayes the presidential title. For a brief time, it looked as though this cheating would come to nothing. Congress had left the decision of who carried the disputed states to a special Electoral Commission. If the commissioners only went behind the official returns, if even one Republican member of the tribunal put his partisanship aside in counting just one electoral vote, it would have been Tilden, not Hayes, who took the oath a fortnight hence. But as the commission handed down its decisions, Democrats discovered that they had simply set up one more body to coat the stolen election with the gloss of legitimacy.[1]

And so Piatt lost his temper as Tilden lost his last chance. Once more the *Capital*'s editor thrust his pen at the thieves, from the bayonet-backed carpetbagger to the "coarse, brutal and ignorant" president surrounded by "sycophantic pimps." Against a subsidized press and a horde "of Treasury-eaters," with monopoly capital ranged on the oppressors' side, the people had won the government back, only to be cheated of it by penitentiary convicts. Would Americans submit? Let them be warned: *"If a man thus returned to power can ride in safety from the Executive Mansion to the Capitol to be inaugurated, we are fitted for the slavery that will follow the inauguration.* . . . Notice is now served on the citizens of Louisiana and South Carolina that they must care for themselves, how soon the lamp-posts will bear fruit is for them to say. If there is a law for fraud, there is a reason for violence, and to that we make our last appeal."[2] Was this another of Piatt's jokes? Or had he been misunderstood? Piatt's explanation soon afterward was not reassuring. He protested that he had never urged killing anyone. Instead, the people must "take up arms . . . and use them in the open field."[3]

In a capital already jittery with cries of "Tilden or Blood!" ten thousand copies of the *Capital* could do a great deal of damage. The administration quickly put him under arrest and the district attorney was instructed to indict him for sedition. Beyond that, nothing stopped Piatt's paper or Piatt's pen. For all the suggestions that some public-spirited citizen stave in the editor's head, he met no further inconvenience than piles of threatening mail and the knowledge that the police would shadow him on Inauguration Day.[4]

If the savage feelings of that editorial were any guide, however, the relationship between politicians and the press would not get any better under the new regime than under the old. As it turned out, they were no guide at all. Much of the old rancor would persist. It would mark the editorials of party organs for the rest of the century. But the conditions that had embittered press and politician alike were vanishing. Both sides were sick of their quarrel; some of the muckrakers had worn out their indignation, while their publishers had found excuses to make peace with the party organizations. As James G. Blaine's coup de theatre showed, public officials were reaching a new sophistication in the co-opting and control of reporters' dispatches. Reconstruction's end removed one of the most divisive issues and Grant's retirement one of the most controversial public figures. If the Caesarism scare marked the beginning of the end for the postwar order in journalism, Caesar's departure from Washington made the transition clear enough even for newspaper readers to see.

That would have been so, probably, no matter which candidate had won in 1876. Both of them took a special interest in fostering a friendly press. Tilden's interest was certainly more widely known. A cautious, calculating partisan, he had none of the magnetism of other prominent figures, and though reporters were welcomed into his home and courteously treated, they left with far less to say about his views than about his library or his looks. Absent from the public persona were the usual anecdotes about a candidate's simple tastes, peaceful home life, or the kindnesses that the "Great Forecloser" had done for widows and orphans. That lack of charisma was assiduously cultivated: the man for whom public responsibility and reform mattered more than worldly pleasure.[5]

More than any presidential candidate before him, Tilden knew the uses of managed publicity. To bend the legislature to his will, he pushed his program, one critic complained, like a businessman selling wares. His home on Gramercy Park became "a sort of political factory," where clerks attended not just to politics and business, but to currying the press. Through his private secretary, John Bigelow, an old newspaperman himself, the governor kept the residents on Printing-House Square friendly.[6]

Now the publicity machinery was stoked for a presidential bid. Like his rivals for the nomination, Tilden had workers everywhere; unlike them, he paid special attention to the press. Assured of support from Charles A. Dana's New York *Sun* and Manton Marble's *World,* the governor's friends sought out press spokesmen in Philadelphia, St. Paul, and Baltimore as well. In Des Moines, the *Iowa State Press* put not just its columns but its employees at his disposal, and its publisher wrote the state convention's resolutions. Under the scrutiny of William L. Pelton, the governor's nephew, the Tilden campaign looked over friendly articles and sent them out to 1,200 local papers for republication. Pelton even considered sending copies of the *World* to 2,600 journals for every day of the three months preceding the national convention. In the meantime, A. F. Boyle, Tilden's man in Washington, sent out helpful letters on boilerplate to publishers of weeklies across the land.[7]

The South had a special bureau to manage its press releases for Tilden. When Henry Watterson of the Louisville *Courier-Journal* went to New York, Tilden invited him to dine. Watterson was captivated and remained under the governor's spell lifelong. Years later, he would pronounce Tilden "the nearest approach to the ideal statesman I have known." When John Bigelow prepared a campaign biography especially suited for Southern readers, Watterson plastered it across a full page of his newspaper and led the Tilden forces to mastery of the Kentucky delegation soon after.[8]

By no means did the governor put the whole press in his pocket, nor even all the Democratic papers. The Cincinnati *Enquirer* inveighed against him, though it did his campaign good service by destroying Ohio's most promising favorite son, Senator Allen G. Thurman. But no one else managed the newspapers as efficiently. When Tilden was nominated and the platform prepared, it was only proper that the task of shaping it to suit Tilden went to Manton Marble.[9]

Throughout the campaign, the innovative use of the press release continued. Propaganda would no longer be every editor and orator for himself. It would be given system through a "bureau of correspondence," with weekly newsletters containing extracts from Democratic speeches, squibs from other newspapers, and appropriate editorials. It was the Republican strategy of 1872 on a massive scale. In return for the free filler, each subscribing newspaper had to send its own issues to the bureau so that its expressions could be monitored. Every week, two million readers could peruse the arguments that Manton Marble penned, and no two adjoining counties saw quite the same ones, thanks to "careful adjustments."[10]

Of course, the system depended on the quality of what Tilden sent out, and here the limitations in the governor's approach began to emerge. It was with facts that the Democratic case would be made, and these could be made better by mailing out documents than by relying on partisan newspapers. So the documents were sent, ten million of them by mid-September, five times as many as in the whole campaign of four years before. Piles of pamphlets met "Gath's" eye, "all of the form and size of a folded mortgage or a note-book," and with the most high-toned reading matter. The more statistics they had, the better the bureau liked them. *Sun* reporter A. M. Gibson prepared a campaign textbook, 750 pages long and detailed on Republican crimes. Perhaps, as one of Tilden's backers would boast, the book determined the result by priming party campaign workers with the evidence they needed. But more attention to documents meant less for the raucous sort of propaganda that the party press did best.[11]

When it came to day-to-day news, however, Tilden lost his grip entirely.

A ringing letter accepting the nomination might have stirred the independent press. Instead, he dallied for nearly two months and then submitted an address that tried to make up for its dullness with extreme length. When the New York *Times* leveled charges against him of income tax evasion, Tilden should have replied instantly. But a month passed as he put off action and worried over every small phrase until, as his secretary John Bigelow put it, "he is scarcely fit or able to do anything." Finally, after weeks of repeated allegations, Bigelow and his former law clerk put together a full refutation of the charges. When Republicans warned that Tilden would pay the Confederate war debt and other "rebel claims," the story lingered on the front pages day after day, until late October. Tilden's letter was forceful, irrefutable—and a month late.[12]

How could so canny an operator have stumbled so badly? There are two possible answers. Reporters noted the first, and more so as time went on: Tilden was an ailing man. Whether he suffered a series of strokes or felt the increasing debilitation of Parkinson's disease, the governor became more an invalid every day. Querulous, irritable, hands trembling, voice dwindling to a whisper, mind detached from daily events, he no longer could muster the energy or the will to conduct an aggressive campaign.[13] But there is a second possibility. As befitted one of the nation's foremost corporation lawyers, Tilden believed in argument, detail, and fact. Sending out matter for the editorial pages was a skill that came naturally. That talent remained to the end. But the effect that news stories had on public opinion, or the immediate power of the "scoop," he had never understood, even when in good health.

There was also one final ironic weakness to Tilden's management of the press. Manipulation works only when it is so unobtrusive that it remains unnoticed. In this sense, Tilden's cleverness was like Blaine's—the sort out of which ultimate defeats were made. By the time the campaign began in earnest, his manipulation of journalists was common knowledge. It became one more proof that beneath the image making lurked an unusually tricky character, "Shammy Tilden," "Slippery Sammy," the "Spider of Gramercy Park."[14]

No one thought of Rutherford B. Hayes as tricky. The quiet, plodding Ohio governor had none of Tilden's experience in pulling wires and raising party funds. But his understanding of the new power of the press and the way that the rules had changed since the Civil War may have been more shrewd, more complete. He had not maneuvered his way through the treacherous factionalism of Ohio politics by leaving the press alone. He had listened to the editors, cultivated and honored them. By 1876, as his campaign for the presidency got under way, he could rely on them to give him good advice and to tell him where his campaign was going right. He could also rely on plenty of Ohio newspapermen, men of national influence, to support his candidacy.[15]

Three stood ahead of the rest: William D. Bickham, Murat Halstead, and William Henry Smith. The contrast between them was significant. Bickham was as regular a partisan as Ohio could boast, while Halstead still kept one foot in the reformers' camp, and Smith, a strong Republican, controlled the Western Associated Press. All of them had received Hayes's attentions for years. To Smith, there were notes of correction and letters of thanks when personal opinions were offered; to Bickham, the flattering attention due to a major player in Ohio politics.[16] Now both were ready to champion him and publicize his candidacy. So zealously did AP distribute allegations against Tilden and bury news supporting his side just after the election that Democrats dubbed it the "Hayesociated Press." In all this work the governor kept aloof, but his attention never wavered. When Bickham's praise for his favorite-son candidacy was too fulsome, the governor sent him a gentle note urging him not to slight certain of his rivals. "You must also see that . . . some of my best friends are Bristow men," he reminded him. "If others lose temper we must not."[17]

Supporting Benjamin Bristow for the Republican nomination, Halstead took more delicate handling, but his support was worth more for his belated conversion. After Hayes's nomination, it was through Halstead that the backers of civil service registered their complaints; even beforehand, it was through Halstead that they got assurances of Hayes's good faith.[18]

Because he was a prominent public figure, Halstead's editorial services during the campaign took second place to his role as political strategist. Between him and the candidate, letters passed discussing which issues needed more emphasis and in which states to concentrate campaign funds. Halstead suggested sending supplements to the New York newspapers, "using large type and making it red hot," to ventilate Tilden's record on "Rebel claims." He spoke at Cooper Institute on Hayes's behalf, having submitted his remarks to Hayes beforehand. Tilden's letter refuting the Southern claims bugaboo appeared nationwide—but not in the Cincinnati *Commercial*.[19]

When the election returns brought chaos, with Democrats claiming victory and threatening deadlock in the capital, Halstead proved his usefulness once more. As delicate negotiations went on between Republican policymakers and Southern Democrats ready to sell out their Northern colleagues for the right price, the editor of the Cincinnati *Commercial* took a leading role. When the editor of the New Orleans *Times* went North for information about Hayes's intentions, the assurances were passed along through Halstead and the editor's hints of a possible settlement passed back to the president-elect. When Democrats in South Carolina wanted to contact Hayes with their own overtures for a deal, they sent an emissary to Halstead, as well. Advice on the cabinet, complaints from the publisher of the Chicago *Tribune*—all came through Halstead.[20]

Indeed, Hayes had a full brigade of journalists doing his work that winter. James M. Comly of the *Ohio State Journal* acted as his ambassador to restive Republican senators in Washington, as the crisis went on, and Southern Democrats scanned his editorials for signs of what Hayes's new policy would be. When plain talk from President Grant was needed, Comly went to the White House to find out where he stood; when Hayes's friends met at the attorney general's office, Comly was there.[21]

Equally important was Henry Boynton, whose support for Bristow's candidacy had turned into a passion to see his friend restored to cabinet office or even to the Supreme Court. If the reform Republicans were to control the new administration, they must put Hayes in their debt. This Boynton promised to do by stitching together an alliance of railroad lobbyists, led by Tom Scott of the Texas & Pacific, with Southern Democrats hungry for subsidies and patronage and eager for an administration that would bring a formal renunciation of the Southern Republican governments. The "King of the Bohemians" may have been promising more than he had the power to deliver. Southern Democrats could not be bought on the conditions that Boynton set. They could not even be rented for a few crucial days, and Northern Republicans would not have paid his price anyway. But that did not make Boynton any less energetic or any less convinced that it was he and his friends who were breaking the deadlock in the Democratic House and permitting the count of electoral votes to continue to the end. And, in a general way, they may have been right. Their specific promises may not have changed many votes, but the general message that Hayes would be receptive to white Southern requests made the real bargaining and sellout of Southern Republicans easier for other negotiators to arrange.[22]

Fire and Water Make Vapor: What a Cooling Off will be there, my countrymen!
(Thomas Nast, *Harper's Weekly*, February 3, 1877). Henry Watterson of the
Louisville *Courier-Journal* (for Samuel J. Tilden) blusters; Murat Halstead of the
Cincinnati *Commercial* (for Rutherford B. Hayes) eases matters.

That gift for bringing journalists to his side did not desert Hayes once he reached the White House. At times, he may have resented the editors' clamor for patronage. There was a story, for example, about his audience with E. C. Cowles, of the Cleveland *Leader*, who, like so many others, wanted a government job. As Cowles had supported another man for the nomination, Hayes was astonished at the demand. He led the editor to a window and pointed to the statue of Andrew Jackson in the nearby park. Did Cowles know how many tons of brass it contained? "[T]here is more brass in . . . the cheek of other Ohio editors I might name, than there is in that piece of statuary." And, like Jackson's horse, the journalists back home "always seem to be rearing upon their hind legs for something." [23]

The incident sounds out of character, most of all in Hayes's refusal to endow an editor. William Henry Smith became collector of the port of Chicago, though he was unable to keep the place for long. Whitelaw Reid was offered the Berlin mission, James Comly the post in Hawaii. [24]

Reporters found the chief executive eager to give no offense. One incident was particularly revealing. A diplomatic reception was held at the White House, and journalists were shut out of it, just as had happened in Grant's term; but Hayes moved at once to assure them that he had known nothing of the slight, regretted it, and would see that it never happened in the future. Even the more prickly residents of Newspaper Row felt that the president had made amends. [25]

For others, presidential attentiveness was enough. When Joseph Medill of the Chicago *Tribune* voiced concerns that the administration would favor the wrong wing of the party in Illinois, Hayes invited him to Washington to confer about "a world of matters." [26] Samuel Bowles of the Springfield *Republican*, too, basked in attention. By autumn, Bowles was in the unusual position of supporting an administration. [27]

Even Donn Piatt fell under the president's spell, and not just because he approved of Hayes's policies, which he did. The charges against the publisher were dropped. When, the following winter, the president invited Piatt to his silver wedding anniversary, the editor was touched and grateful. In later years, he would ask patronage favors from Hayes and invite him home. [28]

Boynton took particularly delicate handling. Part of his anger came from the sense that his own advice had been slighted, still more because Bristow ended up with nothing. When the correspondent tried to find a job for the son of "Deacon" Richard Smith, of the Cincinnati *Gazette*, the request was turned down without an explanation. But the president meant no offense and did his best to make amends. Boynton was given reassurances through Hayes's friends and was even invited to the White House for a talk. "Personally he will be and is, friendly to me," the president wrote. "*I am sure of it.* He does not like some of my associates, and opposes some of my doings, but I look only for a friendly criticism hereafter."[29] That, indeed, was all he got, though Boynton's reasons were different from those the president understood. His own knowledge of the inside deals the winter before would have made a scoop devastating to the administration—and to himself, as an active accomplice in them. Like William Henry Smith and Richard Smith, the last thing Boynton wanted was to set the House investigating the ways in which Hayes's friends beat the Democratic filibuster.[30]

So Hayes had every reason for self-congratulation. Nothing, of course, could make the press one unanimous voice in the president's favor. Partisan organs on both sides lit into him, either for being too good a Republican or not a good enough one. But even in the doldrums of his administration, Hayes could count on the strongest and most independent Republican papers, including the New York *Evening Post*, the Boston *Daily Advertiser*, and of course Halstead's *Commercial*. As his term went on, the president found his support actually strengthening. By July 1879, he could boast that never before had "the stream of commendation run so full."[31]

Two incidents in 1878 showed just how valuable press support could be. Although the president never authorized interviews, "Gath" had one anyway while the two men were guests at a reception held at Gettysburg. It was not the fighting fifteen years past that concerned Hayes, but the fight to come in the House. That long-foreshadowed investigation into the election returns had begun. Assuming that convincing proof of Republican fraud could be assembled, would Democrats annul the election? Some Americans thought so, and the thought may well have crossed Hayes's own mind. So he spoke freely with an acquaintance as "Gath" stood by eavesdropping. When Democrats opened their newspapers the following day, they learned that any such revolutionary act would be matched, even if it took some timely executions. Hayes may not have said that, precisely; but his willingness to put the Democrats on the spot as incendiaries forced them to speak up instantly, denying any such intentions. But then, there was no chance of their trying to depose him by the time the hearings were over. For that, the president had Reid's *Tribune* to thank. Having come into possession of coded telegrams sent between prominent Democrats (Manton Marble among them) in the days just after the election, the paper turned their peculiar language into a puzzle on page one and then, having grabbed public attention, deciphered them. The dispatches referred to efforts to buy up members of the Florida Returning Board and deliver the state to Tilden, a conspiracy managed from the candidate's own house.[32]

The end of such divisive issues as Reconstruction certainly helped promote an era of good feelings. The only thing enlivening one debate in Congress was the level of boredom itself, which made a member of the press gallery yawn so widely that he dislocated his jaw and a surgeon had to be brought in.[33] "Gath's" goodwill and Reid's good services, however, point to a third reason why the battle of politicians and press was moving toward a lull. Not just the presidents and the politics, but the press gallery had changed, and with it the conditions under which newspapers operated.

Start, then, with the correspondents: George Alfred Townsend himself had lost his crusader's spirit when the press gang turned its muckraking on Boss Shepherd. He never regained it and by 1877 had come to deplore the very idea of investigative journalism. "Having honest hands," he wrote, "I would not soil them by taking in old archives to find insignificant trails of insignificant bugs." "Playing the Christian detective," combining the snooper's officiousness with the moralist's sanctimony, was not for him![34]

Poet Townsend had begun and poet he remained. Some of his energies now went to writing short stories and novels. Yet, it is hard on reading his columns not to sense two real reasons for his change of attitude, both of which applied to other Washington correspondents as well. First, eight years of looking for fresh material had worn him out. Increasingly, he let others do the talking, as his columns went from analysis and description to transcribed interviews. His departure from the capital for New York in 1880 only accelerated the change. His columns became longer but less substantial: compendiums of chitchat with whatever celebrity he had cultivated. By 1884, another reporter, with perhaps slight exaggeration, called the emissions of the most admired correspondent in America "an overflowing fountain of drool," short on news, bare of significance, replete with balderdash. "To Gath a cockroach demands as much of his erudition as a comet. He displays as much astuteness in discussing a snuff-box as he would a ballot-box." His career had yet a score of years to run, but his contribution to aggressive news making was passed. In the 1890s, if he was noted at all by editors, it was as one Texas detractor did when he sneered at "that journalistic archaism and irrepressible struldbrug . . . Touchstone."[35]

The reliance on interviewing only intensified "Gath's" need to cultivate important people. Later he would insist that his conversion to officials' defender took place just after the war and was based on the conviction that government was "better than any of the institutions which berate it." If so, he harbored that conviction in secret until the late 1870s. A more skeptical observer might point out that abused officeholders tend to be reticent with those abusing them.[36]

Exhaustion and intimate relationships alike eroded the crusading zeal of the entire Bohemian Brigade. By 1882, the Washington press corps had lost its most prominent muckrakers. The New York *Tribune*'s three star reporters, Hiram J. Ramsdell, Eugene V. Smalley, and Zebulon L. White all had retired to take up editorial duties; so did Wilson J. Vance, the Cincinnati *Commercial* reporter who had exposed James A. Garfield's involvement in fraudulent pavement contracts.[37] Among the great Southern correspondents, most of whom had done service in Washington, Sidney Andrews died in 1880 after years as an invalid; Horace V. Redfield served two years as the *Commercial*'s bureau chief in the capital before dying in late 1881, and a few months later, James Shepherd Pike, nearly forgotten even by the South Carolina conservatives he had done so much to put into power, died quietly in Maine.[38] Head injuries had forced Mary Clemmer Ames into semiretirement in 1878, and Emily "Olivia" Briggs would leave the society beat four years later, though not the Washington scene: she became one of the city's most celebrated hostesses. A. M. Gibson gave up his duties at the *Sun* to resume his legal career, with a little lobbying on the side, and Uriah Hunt Painter virtually abandoned his place in the press gallery for one in company boardrooms. He and William B. Shaw would die almost wealthy enough to earn their former colleagues' respect.[39] New journalists would replace the old, but a shift in generations brought, if nothing else, a shift in common memory. The old fights and resentments, the wartime experiences that so many reporters had shared, and the set-tos with Congress, from the Treaty of Washington fight to the Poland gag law, were increasingly events that reporters had heard about rather than experienced. Anyone returning to the press gallery after ten years' absence in 1886 would have spotted no more than fifteen familiar faces. When Henry Boynton retired in 1891 (or was forced out), one of the last bearers of the old tradition carried a large part of collective memory with him.[40]

The more memory faded, the easier it was for reporters to deal on an intimate basis with their official sources. The process was all the easier because, however much the Standing Committee of Correspondents frowned on reporters earning outside money as lobby agents, it still permitted them to hold government jobs doled out by the very House and Senate members on whom they were reporting. To the end of the century, reporters held clerkships, wrote eulogizing campaign biographies,[41] helped lawmakers with their speeches, and shared in the perquisites of sinecures. The price with them was the same as with "Gath." Those privy to officials' secrets began to see themselves less as adversaries than allies.[42]

Lapses did occur: Boynton's mustering of the correspondents to hold the press gallery against outside intruders in early 1883, for example, and the effort of a furious Speaker to smear him as a bribe giver (one last scandal that arose from poor William McGarrahan's efforts to win his claim to the Panoche Grande tract in California). In 1890, a correspondent from Kentucky killed a congressman; in 1903, a South Carolina lieutenant governor murdered N. G. Gonzales, who had risen from Washington reporter to crusading editor. There may even have been a touch of malice in the response of the press gallery as the "Billion Dollar Congress" adjourned in 1891: the correspondents burst into a chorus of "Praise God from Whom All Blessings Flow." But the general patterns were increasingly clear, of reporters increasingly discreet as they came to see themselves as members of the Washington establishment. At the close of his career, Boynton would defend his colleagues from the charge of having done their job of informing the public by insisting that they had done no such thing. "If any half-dozen of the older correspondents in Washington should agree to sit down and send to the country upon any given night their knowledge [of the most sensational misdeeds of government], their narratives, which should not vary from the truth in any particular, or be in any sense exaggerated, would come as near pulling down the very pillars of the temple as anything that could be put in print," he explained.[43]

If Grant's departure marked the end of the age of scandal, then, some reasons for the change may have had more to do with reporters than with the welling virtue of public men. But there was a final reason for the transformation. The adversarial relationship enjoyed by so many Washington reporters had rested on the combination of a heightened sense of their own importance as journalists and the lack of firm professional standards in reporting: a lack of objectivity, the failure to provide news rather than gossip, participation in events as well as the recording of them, and emphasis on a lively style of the kind that Piatt, "Gath," "Mack," "Olivia," and Ames had mastered. But by 1891, much that set the Washington correspondent apart had vanished. The initials that once served as a byline were disappearing, and with them the long commentaries sent by mail. The demand for news meant that whatever was printed must hit the stands immediately. It was no longer in the province of reporters to reflect; nor did they have the same control over the length of their letters. Gradually, the emphasis on objectivity and detachment, and on the separation of the lobby from the press gallery, reduced the discretion journalists had in doing their job.

The transformation in the press gallery reflected a change in editorial offices. By 1877, the old independent press establishment itself was on the wane. Some of the alteration was a mere matter of mortality. Samuel Bowles would die late in 1877 with no worthy successor, but other independent prophets had joined the Philistines outright. In their pride the editors had overestimated their own strength with the reading public and badly underestimated the power of party ties. Horace Greeley's defeat did lose them subscribers, while the depression that followed the panic of 1873 cut into their advertising revenues. Now a steady, regular clientele, partisan though it might be, looked more attractive. Marble's *World* turned into an organ, which may well have hastened its decline. Admittedly, that had gone pretty far already. Weekly profits by 1872 scarcely exceeded one hundred dollars. Within four years, Marble had opened negotiations for sale of the paper. Tom Scott's money helped William Henry Hurlbert take control; in 1879, Jay Gould's money finished its influence in politics, seemingly forever.[44] Long before then, Charles A. Dana's *Sun* spoke better for Democrats: however idiosyncratic its editor might be, he was no independent. His views were aligned as unshakably on the one side as William Cullen Bryant's *Evening Post* was on the other. By 1875, Murat Halstead and Whitelaw Reid were searching for some common ground with orthodox Republicanism. Both found it in the politics of the money supply and the Confederate constituency of the Democratic party. Protesting their right to differ with the administration to the end, both men accepted Hayes, dropped the reform issue, and donned the bloody shirt.[45]

Horace White made no such conversion, but his Chicago *Tribune* did. Just as the Caesarism cry reached its climax in late 1874, the paper was restored to Joseph Medill's hands. Well paid for his shares and eager for a honeymoon, White departed gladly. The stockholders were just as happy to see him go, and his independent notions with him. "Like [an] engine-house, turned into a hen-house," said a disgusted reformer, "that once compact citadel of influence [is] only feathers, cackle, and rotten eggs."[46]

Of all the original independent editorial crew, virtually no one but Donn Piatt was left, and his time, too, was near its close. His power already waning before his call to arms against Hayes, he would edit and write until 1880, but his wife's health forced him to sell the *Capital* and go into political exile at his mansion in Ohio. The paper outlived him, under the editorial control of Augustus C. Buell, Zachariah Chandler's old nemesis, but it never cut much of a swath again.[47]

The independent press itself did not pass away. But it changed, as a second generation replaced the first, and became further wedded to the impersonality and objectivity of the news. The first generation freed readers from their reliance on politicians' opinions; the second insisted that it wanted to free them from those of the editors, too. "The epoch in which the editor imagined that he must do all the thinking for the people is about past," the New Haven *Morning News* commented. "The people now think for themselves and what they ask of the editor is simply a text of fact."[48]

This was, admittedly, as much a pose as political independence had been for editors like Marble. More than overviews of journalism generally admit, the party press survived, and with it the intermingling of editors and publishers with politicians. Many journalists went to Congress or into the diplomatic service. Others remained the unofficial canvassers and pollsters and the authorized spokesmen for administration policy.[49] The change in what independence itself meant certainly can be overstated. Journals still defined what constituted news and, by what they printed, defined how their readers would react. Joseph Pulitzer's definition of what the people should know had plenty to do with his ambitions in Democratic politics.

Still, the independent label was more in vogue than ever before, and with it went increasingly rigid standards of how far reporters could go to inject themselves or their own opinions into new accounts. With the election of 1884, the ranks of the old-fashioned maverick Republicans, for whom liberal reform meant more than party labels, swelled. Not just the Springfield *Republican* and New York *Evening Post*, but the New York *Times* and Boston *Transcript* fled the party. Equally important, the declining importance of politics as a story meant that the space into which partisans could inject their point of view grew steadily smaller. That, perhaps, and not a growing professionalism, checked the political importance of the press gang. By 1892, as one commentator noted, not one reader in a million could give the name of the editors of the five leading journals in New York. "The model newspaper of the future will have no editorials," he predicted, somewhat prematurely.[50]

Was this, then, the ultimate legacy of the antipolitics that Reid and Halstead had embraced: the abdication of the press lords' authority? What, beyond the destruction of President Grant, had the Civil War journalists accomplished?

Final Edition

For the postwar generation of journalists, no lachrymose obituary need be written, and encomiums on their own behalf they had written quite enough of already. Too long have studies of newspaper history centered their attention on the publishers and editors-in-chief rather than on the men and women who worked for them, on the importance of gathering news rather than the quality of that news once gathered, and on the energy of the press rather than its malice; with honorable exceptions, scholars have overlooked the relationship between nineteenth-century reporters and the politicians with whom they dealt.

To describe that relationship, bias is too gentle and general a term. When "Mack" published interviews with President Andrew Johnson, he served as the knowing propaganda outlet for a beleaguered official; but when he worked behind the scenes to keep one of the president's Senate supporters sober for the impeachment vote, he became an active agent in making the news he was employed to report.[1] It was behavior no different from that of Horace Greeley and Charles A. Dana soliciting patronage posts for themselves, or Manton Marble writing Democratic platforms. But in each case, it affected the way the news would be reported and the slant put on it. It can also be argued that while the involvement of editors in public events was established practice, it was a practice with greater perils for the reading public in an age when newspapers professed their primary purpose to be the retailing of the news. Reporters, too, had been political players before the war; the same James Shepherd Pike who deplored corruption in South Carolina had seen nothing wrong with handling the money for Republican vote buying in Maine before the war, or with acting as an official investigator of Democrats who outdid him at the game.[2] But as the reporters' craft divorced itself, at least officially, from the politician's, and as the Washington correspondents' columns expanded in their coverage, the confusion of roles became increasingly problematic.

Political engagement and a white-hot indignation had advantages, to be sure. Outcry over the very real corruption of the Grant administration and the carpetbagger governments might have taken a more muted tone, or have been stifled entirely, had it not been for the vigilance, the anger, and the political ambitions of the so-called independent press. Railroad land grants, spoilsmanship, and election fraud deserved their notoriety. If a deal between Southern Democrats and Northern Republicans to count Hayes in and push through aid for the Texas & Pacific Railroad came to nothing in 1877, the credit belongs to revelations in Dana's *Sun* and the invective of every other powerful newspaper in the North at rumors of a bargain. The clash of politicians and press, the professional and personal relationships between journalists, made Americans among the best-informed readers in the world. Certainly the country was better off for the work of Horace Redfield, Henry Boynton, and Charles Nordhoff; it could even glean substance from the malevolent aspersions of Donn Piatt and James Shepherd Pike. Year by year, too, the press was growing more professional in the best sense of the word: more responsible, more thorough, less openly corruptible by party councils and lobbyists' coffers.

This defense palliates for the press gang's abuses of power. It cannot efface them entirely. Against Pike, Redfield, and Zebulon White, the freedmen of the South had a real grievance. The reputation that Grant endured, the disgrace that Greeley brought upon himself, and the financial ruin that small investors in Jay Cooke's railroad schemes suffered all owed much to the venality and venom of the journalistic fraternity.

Rightly, then, party managers and public officials came to fear the power of the press just after the war. Newspapers helped define the issues

Fun for the Press, but Death to Public Men (Thomas Nast, *Harper's Weekly*,
March 13, 1875). As it turned out, Luke Poland's death was greatly exaggerated.
Eight years later, brass buttons, blue swallowtail, and all, he would
be back in Congress.

and in many cases distorted them beyond recognition. By determining
just what reform was, they did a great deal to limit what government
could do, for good as well as for evil. Ben Butler, Zachariah Chandler,
former secretary William A. Richardson, and Luke Poland all could attest
to the damage that a hostile press could do. Gradually, politicians adapted
new means of tempering the judgment of members of the press. Where
party ties no longer held, the assiduous personal attention that a James G.
Blaine or a James A. Garfield practiced could restore to men in public life
an influence, if not a mastery, over the news. Thanks both to the shift-

"L'Homme Qui Rit." J. G. B., Jun. "If Grant isn't careful, I'll let the Wild Animals loose again" (Thomas Nast, *Harper's Weekly*, June 19, 1875).

ing standards within the journalistic community and the new energy with which politicians cultivated the media, there would be fewer Donn Piatts in the generations to come, and they would be handled more effectively.

A cynic like Piatt could have pointed out the moral of the independent newspaper revolt of the 1870s. As long as independence, behind an editorial desk or from the press gallery, was based on a desire to wield political power, it could be bought off by those who had political power already. A Murat Halstead did not need to be nominated for a diplomatic post or a Whitelaw Reid to the vice-presidency; to be allowed into the inner councils of the politicians might be reward enough. That did not mean that the conflict of officeholders and journalists left no lasting legacy, of course.

It did. But true independence could not last, not until newspapers took themselves further from the political arena and acted as spectators rather than gladiators, and even then it was an independence biased strongly toward the respectability and ideology of its commercial sponsors.

As for Piatt himself, he retreated as far from the political arena as his wife's fortune would let him. His remaining years were devoted almost exclusively to writing, little of it on politics. Since he would not leave home and Democrats wanted to reward him on coming to power in 1885, the administration declared his house a fourth-class post office and put him in charge. The honor was a dubious one; Piatt's watchdogs drove away anyone coming to pick up mail. He had ideas for how to reform the postal service that he sent in letters of such miserable penmanship that the postmaster general could not make them out. He left no successor and an increasingly sweet memory, and when he died in 1891, a reporter noted the extraordinary length of the funeral procession. But then, Piatt carried so much of what was exciting, so much of what was pernicious, about newspaper work in the postwar years to the grave with him.[3]

Notes

CHS   Cincinnati Historical Society
HML   Rutherford B. Hayes Memorial Library, Fremont, Ohio
HSP   Historical Society of Pennsylvania, Philadelphia
ISDAH   Iowa State Department of Archives and History, Des Moines
ISHS   Illinois State Historical Society, Springfield
ISL   Indiana State Library, Indianapolis
LC   Library of Congress, Washington, D.C.
LL/IU   Lilly Library, Indiana University, Bloomington
LSU   Louisiana State University, Baton Rouge
MHS   Massachusetts Historical Society, Boston
NHHS   New Hampshire Historical Society, Concord
NYPL   New York Public Library
OHS   Ohio Historical Society, Columbus
SC   Smith College, Northampton, Massachusetts
SHC   Southern Historical Collection, University of North Carolina at Chapel Hill
SML/YU   Sterling Memorial Library, Yale University, New Haven
UP   University of Pennsylvania, Philadelphia
UV   University of Virginia, Charlottesville

INTRODUCTION

1. *Harper's Weekly*, November 7, 1874; see also November 21, 1874. The epigraph is quoted, and titled "Washington Correspondents," in Washington *Sunday Capital*, April 23, 1871.

2. Albert Bigelow Paine, *Thomas Nast: His Period and His Pictures* (New York: Pearson, 1904), 278–81, 295–97.

3. For just such mathematics, see New York *Times*, October 17, 1874.

4. *Harper's Weekly*, November 3, 1866, February 3, 1877. See also July 27, October 26, November 23, 1872, February 28, 1874, April 15, 1876, and, in the backgrounds of "Amphitheatrum Johnsonianum," March 30, 1867. While seeking to avoid the use of gender-specific language in this book, I have retained the term *newspapermen* when it applies historically. The plain truth is that women report-

ers were few, editors even fewer; as will be noted later, women correspondents went not to cover events or news, but to add touches of color to the journals' account of Washington affairs. There were a few conspicuous exceptions—but, as far as the daily workings of "the press gang" were concerned, it was a man's world.

5. The same was true in England. See Stephen Koss, *The Rise and Fall of the Political Press in Britain: The Nineteenth Century* (Chapel Hill: University of North Carolina Press, 1981), 135, 154, as well as *Punch*, February 15, 1856, May 3, 1862, April 17, 1880, August 28, 1886, March 9, 1889, all illustrations in Koss, ibid.

6. See, for example, Frank Luther Mott, *American Journalism: A History of Newspapers in the United States through 260 Years*, rev. ed. (New York: Macmillan, 1950); Alfred McClung Lee, *The Daily Newspaper in America: The Evolution of a Social Instrument* (New York: Macmillan, 1937); Thomas C. Leonard, *The Power of the Press: The Birth of American Political Reporting* (New York: Oxford University Press, 1987); Donald A. Ritchie, *Press Gallery: Congress and the Washington Correspondents* (Cambridge: Harvard University Press, 1991).

Institutional histories, better than most but frustratingly mute on newspaper ideology or news-gathering methods in the nineteenth century, include Thomas H. Baker, *The Memphis Commercial Appeal: The History of a Southern Newspaper* (Baton Rouge: Louisiana State University Press, 1971), John B. McNulty, *Older Than the Nation: The Story of the Hartford Courant* (Stonington, Conn.: Pequot Press, 1964), Raymond A. Schroth, *The Eagle and Brooklyn: A Community Newspaper, 1841–1955* (Westport, Conn.: Greenwood Press, 1974), and Harold A. Williams, *The Baltimore Sun, 1837–1987* (Baltimore: Johns Hopkins, 1987). There are honorable exceptions, including the works of James L. Crouthamel and a number of studies of the New York *Tribune* and of Pulitzer's newspapers, which will be cited later.

7. Characteristic biographies of the younger Bennett include Richard O'Connor, *The Scandalous Mr. Bennett* (Garden City, N.Y.: Doubleday, 1962), and Albert Stevens Crockett, *When James Gordon Bennett Was Caliph of Bagdad* (New York: Funk & Wagnalls, 1926).

8. Appropriate models might be found in two works in English journalism history: Koss, *Rise and Fall of the Political Press*, and Lucy Brown, *Victorian News and Newspapers* (Oxford: Clarendon Press, 1985).

CHAPTER ONE

1. "H. V. R.," Cincinnati *Commercial*, February 23, 1871; George Augustus Sala, *America Revisited: From the Bay of New York to the Gulf of Mexico, and from Lake Michigan to the Pacific* (London: Vizetelly & Co., 1886), 373–74; David Macrae, *The Americans at Home: Pen and Ink Sketches of American Men, Manners, and Institutions* (Edinburgh: Edmonston & Douglas, 1870), 1:582. Where possible, newspaper articles cited will include their bylines, as has been done above with Horace V. Redfield ("H. V. R.").

2. *Nation*, January 28, 1869; Indianapolis *News*, October 26, 1874; "Rocoligny," Chicago *Times*, December 20, 1874; "Horns," Springfield *Republican*, February 25 (both quotations), March 15, June 2, 1871. The national distinctions in newspapers were widely noticed on both sides of the Atlantic, and in England the interview continued to be considered a "distinctly shocking American practice" well into the 1880s (though it was not universally backed here, either: see Philadelphia *North American*, August 12, 1874). See *Punch*, October 4, 1890; Stephen Koss, *The Rise and Fall of the Political Press in Britain: The Nineteenth Century* (Chapel Hill: University of North Carolina Press, 1981), 70, 125, 342. On the character of the French press, see Theodore Zeldin, *France, 1848–1945: Taste & Corruption* (New York: Oxford University Press, 1980), 144–225.

3. By 1871, London alone had 261 newspapers, and there were 120 dailies in the United Kingdom. For more accurate figures, see John Vincent, *The Formation of the British Liberal Party, 1857–68* (London: Constable, 1966), 100–101.

4. Peter R. Knights, "'Competition' in the U.S. Daily Newspaper Industry, 1865–68," *Journalism Quarterly* 45 (Autumn 1968): 473–76; George P. Rowell & Co., *American Newspaper Directory Containing Accurate Lists of All the Newspapers and Periodicals Published in the United States and Territories, and the Dominion of Canada and British Colonies of North America* (New York: Geo. P. Rowell & Co., 1872), 11–291. Circulation figures were given by the newspaper proprietors, whose modesty about their own success should not be overestimated— nor their honesty. See Ted Curtis Smythe, "The Advertisers' War to Verify Newspaper Circulation, 1870–1914," *American Journalism* 3 (1986): 167–80; Carolyn S. Dyer, "Census Manuscripts and Circulation Data for Mid-19th Century Newspapers," *Journalism History* 7 (Summer 1980): 47–48, 67.

5. *Ninth Census: Statistics of the Population of the United States* (Washington, D.C.: Government Printing Office, 1872), 482–97; Augustus Maverick, *Henry J. Raymond and the New York Press, for Thirty Years* (Hartford: A. S. Hale & Co., 1870), 330–32; New York *Times*, May 22, 1870; Vincent Howard, "The Two Congresses: A Study of the Changing Roles and Relationships of the National Legislature and Washington Reporters, Revealed Particularly in the Press Accounts of Legislative Activity, 1860–1913" (Ph.D. diss., University of Chicago, 1976), 59–60. For figures challenging Macrae's own, see James Macauley, *Across the Ferry: First Impressions of America and Its People* (London: Hodder & Stoughton, 1871), 117–19. All figures, however, were unreliable. New presses began printing and old ones closed down every day. For data on Dutch-language presses, see Rowell & Co., *American Newspaper Directory*, 83.

6. Little Rock *Arkansas Gazette*, February 24–March 16, 1870.

7. Chicago *Times*, April 1, 1876. A recent monograph has contended that by the 1870s, local news reports were practically universal, and perhaps "Viator" picked up his paper on a bad day; my own examination of country papers suggests that there would have been plenty of bad days to choose from. See David J. Russo, "The Origins of Local News in the U.S. Country Press, 1840s–1870s," *Journalism Monographs* 65 (February 1980):11.

8. Edwin Emery, *The Press in America: An Interpretative History of Mass Media* (Englewood Cliffs, N.J.: Prentice-Hall, 1972), 160–62, 201–2.

9. Rowell & Co., *American Newspaper Directory*, 361.

10. New York *World*, September 8, 1866; Crystal Springs *Monitor*, October 28, 1882 (quotation).

11. New York *Tribune*, January 19, 1867; Justin E. Walsh, *To Print the News and to Raise Hell! A Biography of Wilbur F. Storey* (Chapel Hill: University of North Carolina, 1968), 268; Baker, *Memphis Commercial Appeal*, 130; *Congressional Globe*, 41st Cong., 2d sess., 25 (December 7, 1869).

12. "Carlfried," Springfield *Republican*, February 24, March 27, 1871; New York *Tribune*, January 19, 1867; Victor Rosewater, *History of Cooperative News-Gathering in the United States* (New York: Appleton, 1930), 157; Harry W. Baehr, Jr., *The New York Tribune Since the Civil War* (New York: Dodd, Mead, 1936), 78–79.

13. New York *Tribune*, January 19, 1867. These were the figures for 1865 (the numbers do not total because the list is incomplete). Though 1866 had no Civil War to cover, expenses rose to $885,158. News by wire had more than doubled.

14. In Cleveland, for example, the *Leader* turned from a proprietor-owned paper into a corporation in 1867, with $300,000 capital. Ten years later, the *Plain Dealer* did the same, though it put its capital at $75,000. Archer H. Shaw, *The Plain Dealer: One Hundred Years in Cleveland* (New York: Knopf, 1942), 221–22.

15. W. G. F. Shanks, "How We Get Our News," *Harper's Magazine* 34 (March 1867): 520; Maverick, *Raymond and the New York Press*, 324–26; Emery, *The Press in America*, 201–2; New York *Times*, May 22, 1870; Therese Yelverton, *Teresina in America* (London: Richard Bentley & Son, 1875), 2:137; Rowell & Co., *American Newspaper Directory*, 352; Sam Acheson, *35,000 Days in Texas: A History of the Dallas News and Its Forbears* (New York: Macmillan, 1938), 86; "Carlfried," Springfield *Republican*, March 27, 1871.

16. "Carlfried," Springfield *Republican*, March 27, 1871. These were New York City salaries, among the highest in the country. Later in the decade, the Washington *Post* paid its local reporter $7 a week for news from Georgetown and the executive departments. Cincinnati editors paid their Chicago correspondent $5 a letter and their Indianapolis contributor $10 only during the legislative session. "A reporter with a $30 salary is as great a curiosity as a live June bug in January, while the editor who receives $40 a week must eclipse an electric light in brilliancy," a Boston correspondent wrote thirteen years later. Chalmers M. Roberts, *The Washington Post: The First Hundred Years* (Boston: Houghton Mifflin, 1977), 6; R. H. Stephenson to William Henry Smith, January 31, 1868, Smith MSS, OHS; *The Journalist*, April 12, 1884.

17. Richard Kluger, *The Paper: The Life and Death of the New York Herald Tribune* (New York: Knopf, 1986), 119–25; New York *Tribune*, September 17, 1866; Horace Greeley to James M. Comly, July 30, 1867, Comly MSS, OHS.

18. For the term's origins, see Louis M. Starr, *Bohemian Brigade: Civil War Newsmen in Action* (New York: Knopf, 1954), 4–7.

19. William E. Ames, *A History of the National Intelligencer* (Chapel Hill: University of North Carolina Press, 1972), 310. For the rise of the reporter and his comparative lack, see Richard B. Kielbowicz, "Newsgathering by Printers' Exchanges Before the Telegraph," *Journalism History* 9 (Summer 1982): 42–47, and Donald L. Shaw, "Change and Continuity in American Press News, 1820–1860," *Journalism History* 8 (Summer 1981): 38–50. For a similar reputation in France, including bohemianism, see Zeldin, *France,* 156–58.

20. How little most newspapers altered, except in providing local news, is ably pointed out in Shaw, "Change and Continuity," 38–50.

21. J. Cutler Andrews, *The North Reports the Civil War* (Pittsburgh: University of Pittsburgh Press, 1955); Philadelphia *Press,* February 22, 1870; Henry Villard, "Army Correspondence: Its History," *Nation,* July 20, 27, August 3, 1865; George Alfred Townsend, *Campaigns of a Non-Combatant, and His Romaunt Abroad During the War* (New York: Blelock & Co., 1866), 368.

22. Starr, *Bohemian Brigade,* 251, 353–59; Frank Luther Mott, *American Journalism: A History of Newspapers in the United States through 260 Years,* rev. ed. (New York: Macmillan, 1950), 385 (Parton quotation); Howard, "The Two Congresses," 63–64; Washington *Chronicle,* July 28, 1874.

23. New York *Citizen,* January 20, 1866; New York *Graphic,* February 1, 1875 (quotation).

24. Sala, *America Revisited,* 226, 404–7.

25. Ernest Duvergier de Hauranne, *A Frenchman in Lincoln's America* (Chicago: Lakeside Press, 1974–75), 1:398. For the best study of the *Herald* through 1866, see James L. Crouthamel, *Bennett's New York Herald and the Rise of the Popular Press* (Syracuse: Syracuse University Press, 1989).

26. New York *Herald,* March 16, 1873, September 25, 1874; James Parton, "Newspapers Gone to Seed," *Forum* 1 (1886): 15; Frederic Hudson, *Journalism in the United States, from 1690 to 1872* (New York: Harper & Brothers, 1873), 428–90. Of course, the *Herald* also held a special place for the freshest misinformation in town. See New York *World,* August 13, 16, 1866; "Bueno Buro," New York *Citizen,* January 19, 1867.

27. Walsh, *To Print the News and to Raise Hell!,* 203–20; Chicago *Times,* February 10, 1876 (quotation).

28. New York *Tribune,* September 20, 1868; Cincinnati *Commercial,* January 17, 1870.

29. William H. Hale, *Horace Greeley: Voice of the People* (New York: Harper, 1950), 310–11.

30. "Seymour," Mobile *Register,* February 12, 1875; Charleston *News and Courier,* December 16, 1881.

31. Memphis *Daily Appeal,* August 1, 1873, March 16, 1876. For early trains, see Cincinnati *Commercial,* March 31, 1873; Cincinnati *Enquirer,* January 13, 1877; Cincinnati *Gazette,* September 2, 1869; and Chicago *Times,* March 20, 1876. For *Times* figures, see "Supremacy," Chicago *Times,* April 29, 1876. For "Viator," see Chicago *Times,* April 1, 1876. For circulation figures, see Rowell & Co.,

American Newspaper Directory, 287–91.Examples of daily and weekly circulation include the following:

Newspaper	Daily	Semiweekly	Weekly
Cincinnati *Gazette*	22,000	4,000	56,000
Cincinnati *Enquirer*	18,000		80,000
Cincinnati *Times and Chronicle*	13,000		95,000
Detroit *Free Press*	8,328	1,704	16,440
Nashville *Republican Banner*	5,800	1,500	9,000
New York *Times*	50,000	15,000	60,000
New York *Tribune*	45,000	25,000	150,000
New York *World*	26,000	5,200	72,000
Philadelphia *Age*	16,000		25,000
Springfield *Republican*	10,000		15,000
St. Paul *Pioneer*	7,125	3,601	22,319

The weekly was not necessarily the one that made the biggest return, however. The *Tribune*, which in 1868 claimed that its total printing was over 300,000 (and of the weekly, over 240,000), proudly pronounced its weekly the largest, best, and cheapest in America; though, it stressed, the weekly lost money, the paper recouped its losses on the daily and the semiweekly. New York *Tribune*, September 20, 1868.

32. Oliver Gramling, *AP: The Story of News* (Port Washington, N.Y.: Kennikat Press, 1969), 19–31, 60–83; Rosewater, *History of Cooperative News-Gathering*; Shanks, "How We Get Our News," 515–17; Cincinnati *Commercial*, September 14, 1874; Chicago *Times*, March 20, 1875; Eugene Casserly to Samuel Jones Tilden, July 15, 1876, Tilden MSS, NYPL (first quotation); "D. P.," Cincinnati *Enquirer*, June 1, 1877 (second quotation); New York *Graphic*, August 16, September 11, 1875.

33. Macrae, *Americans at Home*, 584; Charles F. Wingate, *Views and Interviews on Journalism* (New York: F. B. Patterson, 1875), 105; Whitelaw Reid to H. G. Parker, April 13, 1873, Reid MSS, LC; Kielbowicz, "Newsgathering by Printers' Exchanges," 42–47. Kielbowicz argues that, by having the same story through a number of exchanges, editors could minimize distortion. So they could, if the truth was their aim. For some, it may have been so; the Indianapolis *News* regularly republished the Washington dispatches of all three of Cincinnati's big dailies, one after the other (see, for example, any issue in July 1874). But like the papers they exchanged with, the receiving editors were more likely to pick the account fitting their own partisan biases.

34. Rowell & Co., *American Newspaper Directory*, 289.

35. "D. P.," Cincinnati *Commercial*, December 16, 1869. For a telling commentary on newspaper self-puffery, see *Nation*, February 18, 1869.

36. Edward Dicey, *Spectator of America*, ed. by Herbert Mitgang (Athens: University of Georgia Press, 1971 reissue of 1863 vol.), 30–31.

37. Alan Bussel, "The Atlanta *Daily Intelligencer* Covers Sherman's March," *Journalism Quarterly* (Autumn 1974): 405–10; Peter H. Langley, "Pessimism-Optimism of Civil War Military News: June 1863–March 1865," *Journalism Quarterly* 49 (1972): 74–78; Thomas A. Hughes, "The Civil War Press: Promoter of Unity or Neutral Reporter?," *American Journalism* 6 (1989): 179–99; Starr, *Bohemian Brigade*, 9–10, 244–45 (first quotation); New York *Citizen*, July 22, 1865 (second quotation).

38. Storey had contracted paresis in the 1860s, a brain disease brought on by syphilis.

39. Walsh, *To Print the News and to Raise Hell!*, 207; Chicago *Times*, January 6, 1877; Washington *Chronicle*, August 31, 1874 (first atrocity); Topeka *State Record*, March 22, 1871 (second atrocity). For more horrible headlines, see Kansas City *Times*, March 1, 1876; for more idiotic rhetoric, see Raleigh *Sentinel*, March 2, 1876.

40. Walsh, *To Print the News and to Raise Hell!*, 212 (first quotation), 220; Boston *Commonwealth*, July 4 (second quotation), August 8, 1868.

41. Mott, *American Journalism*, 415.

42. Ibid., 264–65 (Greeley quotation, p. 265); Emery, *The Press in America*, 183–86.

43. George S. Merriam, *The Life and Times of Samuel Bowles* (New York: Appleton-Century-Crofts, 1885), 1:358–65, 380–90, 2:68–76. Indeed, "Warrington's" Boston letter in its entirety took up much of the Boston *Commonwealth*'s front page every week and was one of the features in which it took special pride. See issue for July 11, 1868.

44. Watterson in Wingate, *Views and Interviews*, 13; "H. J. R.," Cincinnati *Commercial*, January 9, 1871.

CHAPTER TWO

1. Charleston *Courier*, November 2, 1869; New York *Times*, January 7, 1881. For the gold ring conspiracy, see Kenneth D. Ackerman, *The Gold Ring: Jim Fisk, Jay Gould, and Black Friday, 1869* (New York: Harper Business, 1988).

2. Indianapolis *News*, October 8, 13, 1876. See also "Newspapers and Nominations," *Harper's Weekly*, October 10, 1874. For historical corroboration (and cautions about placing the change too early), see Michael E. McGerr, *The Decline of Popular Politics: The American North, 1865–1928* (New York: Oxford University Press, 1986), 3–106.

3. *Appeal* quoted in Raleigh *Sentinel*, January 4, 1874; Cincinnati *Commercial*, May 31, 1874.

4. C. E. Henry to James A. Garfield, September 3, 1871, Garfield MSS, LC.

5. Lyman Trumbull to Whitelaw Reid, July 9, 1872, George Pendleton to Reid, 1876, Reid MSS, LC; Charles Sumner to Samuel Bowles, March 3, 1874, Bowles MSS, Yale University, New Haven.

6. See, for example, Allan Nevins and Milton H. Thomas, eds., *The Diary of George Templeton Strong* (New York: Macmillan, 1952), 4:17 (July 8, 1865).

7. Eric Foner, *Reconstruction: America's Unfinished Revolution, 1865–1877* (New York: Harper & Row, 1988), 1–34.

8. Joel H. Silbey, *A Respectable Minority: The Democratic Party in the Civil War Era, 1860–68* (New York: Norton, 1977), 189–95.

9. Michael Les Benedict, *A Compromise of Principle: Congressional Republicans and Reconstruction, 1863–69* (New York: Norton, 1974), 21–69.

10. By far the best biography is Hans L. Trefousse, *Andrew Johnson: A Biography* (New York: Norton, 1989), but some shrewd insights into what made Johnson behave as he did appear in the generally indispensable Eric L. McKitrick, *Andrew Johnson and Reconstruction* (Chicago: University of Chicago Press, 1960), 85–92.

11. LaWanda and John Cox, *Politics, Principles, and Prejudice, 1865–66: Dilemmas of Reconstruction America* (New York: Macmillan, 1963), 88–106, 129–71; McKitrick, *Andrew Johnson and Reconstruction*, 134–213, 274–325, 355–58, 428–47; Jacob Dolson Cox to James Monroe, November 21, 1866, Cox MSS, Oberlin College (quotation).

12. Howard K. Beale, *The Critical Year: A Study of Andrew Johnson and Reconstruction* (New York: Harcourt, Brace, 1930), 315–29.

13. New York *World*, September 30, October 13, 1865.

14. "Republican," Cincinnati *Commercial*, March 5, 1866 (quotation); "Mack," ibid., November 22, 1865.

15. Washington *Chronicle*, February 10, 16, 1866; "Republican," Cincinnati *Commercial*, March 5, 1866 (quotation).

16. Where Democratic papers may actually have had influence was among Southern newspapers, almost all of which took the *World* and the *Daily News* as true oracles of Northern politics. Having assured the South that the North would vote for reunion on terms far more conservative than Congress was proposing, the *World* then had to explain away a Republican landslide in 1866. Sure enough, Democratic journals sensed a vast sea change in public opinion almost at once and conditions that left Democrats as masters of the situation. Let the South refuse the proposed amendment, the editors urged; Congress dared do nothing worse. A deadlock would force it to make more generous terms. From all available evidence, the argument was fantastic, though it fit Southern editors' hopes exactly, and they took it as gospel—all the way to the moment when their intransigence drove Congress to the very measures that the *World* had proven could not possibly happen. See *World*, November 30, December 1, 6, 1866; John Forsyth to Manton Marble, October 13, 1866, Marble MSS, LC.

17. Nevins and Thomas, *Diary of George Templeton Strong*, 4:9 (June 17, 1865—quotation), 17 (July 8, 1865), 76 (March 28, April 2, 1866); New York *Times*, July 11, 1866. See also New York *Tribune*, September 15, 1865.

18. An exceptional study of the divided opinion of Republican papers during 1865 is Anne Kusener Nelsen, "The North, the South, and the Republican Ideology" (Ph.D. diss., Vanderbilt University, 1977), 16–72.

19. "Agate," Cincinnati *Gazette*, December 2, 1865. For the identification of "Observer" and Truman's tours, see New York *Citizen*, August 5, 19, 26, 1865, January 6, 1866, and Richard Smith to James A. Garfield, January 14, 1866, Garfield MSS, LC.

20. For complaints at the lack of a presidential organ, see James Dixon to Andrew Johnson, September 17, 1866, Johnson MSS, LC.

21. Charles C. Clayton, *"Little Mack": Joseph B. McCullagh of the St. Louis Globe-Democrat* (Carbondale: Southern Illinois University Press, 1969), 1–50; "Bueno Buro," New York *Citizen*, February 2, 1867; J. B. McCullagh to Murat Halstead, February 20, 1867, Halstead MSS, CHS; Schuyler Colfax to John Russell Young, April 22, 1868, Young MSS, LC.

22. "Mack," in Washington *Chronicle*, August 15, 1875; Ritchie, *Press Gallery*, 81–82.

23. "D. W. B.," New York *Independent*, February 1, 8, 15, 1866; John T. Morse, ed., *Diary of Gideon Welles* (Boston: Houghton Mifflin, 1910), 2:448–49 (March 9, 1866), 495–97 (May 1, 1866).

24. McKitrick, *Andrew Johnson and Reconstruction*, 428–38.

25. See, for example, James R. Doolittle to Orville H. Browning, October 7, 1866, Browning MSS, ISHS.

26. Cincinnati *Commercial*, April 28, 1866.

27. New York *Tribune*, September 4–5, 1866.

28. James R. Doolittle to Orville H. Browning, October 7, 1866, Browning MSS, ISHS; R. "Del" Mussey to William Henry Smith, February 23, 1866 (quotation), Smith MSS, OHS. See also William D. Kelley to Carrie Kelley, February 23, 1866, Kelley MSS, HSP; M. S. Wilkinson to Henry S. Lane, March 14, 1866, Lane MSS, LL/IU; Henry L. Dawes to Mrs. Electa Dawes, February 23, 1866, Dawes MSS, LC.

29. Henry Cooke to Jay Cooke, September 12, 1866, Pitt Cooke to Jay Cooke, September 12, 1866, Cooke MSS, HSP; Orville H. Browning to James R. Doolittle, October 13, 1866, Doolittle MSS, Wisconsin State Historical Society; John W. Forney to William Pitt Fessenden, September 1, 1866, Forney MSS, LC; H. H. Van Dyck to Hugh McCulloch, September 5, 12, 1866, McCulloch Letter-Books, LL/IU; William H. Hulburt to Samuel J. Tilden, September 2, 1866, Manton Marble MSS, LC (quotation).

30. Charles Nordhoff to William Cullen Bryant, February 21, 1867, Nordhoff to Parke Godwin, October 24, 1866, February 16, 1869, Bryant-Godwin MSS, NYPL.

31. "Mack," Cincinnati *Commercial*, March 27, 1866.

32. On Forney's character, see "D. P.," Cincinnati *Commercial*, February 6, 1871, and New York *Citizen*, July 22, 1865. For patronage broking, see Forney to Frederick W. Seward, April 13, 1861, Forney to William H. Seward, March 12, 16, April 16, August 29, 1861, Seward MSS, University of Rochester; Milwaukee

Daily Wisconsin, July 3, 1866; and Paul H. Bergeron, ed., *The Papers of Andrew Johnson* (Knoxville: University of Tennessee Press, 1991), 8:354, 505, 9:268–69, 562–63.

33. "Mack," Cincinnati *Commercial,* June 7, 21, 1866.

34. Washington *Chronicle,* February 20, 23, 1866. What Johnson may actually have said—at least, this was how the *Chronicle* quoted him—was, "I do not waste my ammunition upon dead *cocks.*"

35. "Occasional," Washington *Daily Morning Chronicle,* February 10, 21, 1866.

36. Cincinnati *Commercial,* March 8, 1866 (quotation); John W. Forney to William Pitt Fessenden, February 8, 1867, Forney MSS, LC; New York *World,* September 26, 1866. Not all departments obliged the president, and Congress effectively restored Forney's right to government advertising the following May. See Morse, *Diary of Gideon Welles,* 2: 486–87 (April 17, 1866), 490 (April 20, 1866), 632 (December 4, 1866).

37. New York *World,* August 6, 16, September 19, October 2, 11, 1866; "Bueno Buro," New York *Citizen,* January 19, 1867.

38. "Mack," Cincinnati *Commercial,* January 30, February 4, 7, 1867. For his graceless retraction, see ibid., February 11, 1867, and *Congressional Globe,* 39th Cong., 2d sess., 1074–75 (February 7, 1867).

39. "Mack," Cincinnati *Commercial,* December 19–20, 24–25, 1865, February 12, April 30, 1866.

40. "V. H.," Cincinnati *Commercial,* August 23, September 15, 1865; "E. S.," New York *Tribune,* September 4, 1865 (quotation). See also "Observer" (November 18, 1865) and "Leo" and "Berwick" (November 25, 1865), New York *Tribune*; Sidney Andrews, *The South Since the War* (Boston: Ticknor & Fields, 1866); and Whitelaw Reid, *After the War: A Tour of the Southern States, 1865–1866* (Cincinnati: Moore, Wilstach & Baldwin, 1866). For the overt political uses of this correspondence, see Whitelaw Reid to William Henry Smith, August 8, 1865, Smith MSS, OHS; John A. Bingham to Moore, Wilstach & Baldwin, October 1, 1866, Bingham MSS, OHS.

41. New York *World,* August 17, October 23, 1866; "J. Q. T.," Cincinnati *Commercial,* October 25, 1865 (quotation); Cincinnati *Commercial,* May 28, October 19, 1866; Andrews, *The South Since the War,* 292–300; Hugh McCulloch to H. H. Van Dyck, August 20, 1866, McCulloch Letter-Books, LL/IU.

42. Reid, *After the War,* 580; "V. H.," Cincinnati *Commercial,* August 23, 1865. For a suggestive broader picture of press imagery of Southern blacks, see Nelsen, "The North, the South, and the Republican Ideology," 238–43.

43. "Observer," New York *Tribune,* November 18, 1865.

44. Dan T. Carter, *When the War Was Over: The Failure of Self-Reconstruction in the South, 1865–1867* (Baton Rouge: Louisiana State University Press, 1985), 57–58; "Q. P. F.," Cincinnati *Commercial,* October 11, 1865; Florida correspondent (September 5, 1865), R. A. Alston letter (September 1, 1865), "Rollo" (November 3, 1865), New York *Tribune.* The New York *Tribune* was, in fact, not all that radical. Greeley had no patience with confiscation schemes and deplored treason

trials; he also had doubts about the wisdom of letting ignorant former slaves vote. Supporting universal amnesty for Confederates, the *Tribune* was willing to make black would-be voters take property and literacy tests as long as whites had to take them too. See New York *Tribune*, September 12, 18, 1865.

45. Carter, *When the War Was Over*, 226–27; New York *Tribune*, September 20, 1865 (quotation).

46. Carter, *When the War Was Over*, 228–31; New York *Tribune*, November 3, 1865.

47. For the unanimity of Republican newspaper opposition in Wisconsin, see Milwaukee *Daily Wisconsin*, February 24, 27, 1866.

48. New York *Tribune*, September 29, 1866.

49. Francis Brown, *Raymond of the Times* (New York: Norton, 1951), 268–315; New York *Times*, July 14, 16, 1866; "Observer," Worcester *Spy*, June 21, 1866; "R. J. H.," Milwaukee *Sentinel*, January 16, 1866; Milwaukee *Wisconsin*, July 20, 1866 (quotation).

50. McKitrick, *Andrew Johnson and Reconstruction*, 439–47; New York *Times*, September 17, 24, 1866; Samuel J. Tilden to Hugh McCulloch, September 17, 1866, Tilden MSS, NYPL; S. S. Cox to Manton Marble, September 21, 1866, Marble MSS, LC.

51. R. P. Aller to Andrew Johnson, September 25, 1866, William Bigler to Johnson, October 1, 1866, James R. Doolittle to Johnson, October 14, 1866, Johnson MSS, LC; Bill Lyon to John D. Strong, September 24, 1866, Strong MSS, ISHS. For an argument basing public opinion on newspaper accessions, see New York *World*, September 5, 1866.

52. Douglas Fermer, *James Gordon Bennett and the New York Herald: A Study of Editorial Opinion in the Civil War Era, 1854–1867* (New York: St. Martin's Press, 1986), 299–309; John Cochrane to Andrew Johnson, January 23, 1866, William B. Phillips to Johnson, December 8, 1865, September 16 (quotation), October 14, 1866, Johnson MSS, LC.

53. Ritchie, *Press Gallery*, 84. For the popular assumption about Greeley's position, see "Pink," Charleston *Courier*, May 3, 1868. How effectively newspapers demanding conviction or acquittal helped their own cause is unclear. "Perley," of the Boston *Morning Journal*, himself hoping for Johnson's dismissal, reported that the president's enemies actually helped him by overdoing their pressure on doubtful senators. Boston *Morning Journal*, May 9, 1868.

54. "Warrington," Springfield *Republican*, May 9, 1868; Springfield *Republican*, May 7, 1868; Hugh McCulloch to H. H. Van Dyck, May 15, 1868, McCulloch Letter-Books, LL/IU.

55. W. S. Rosecrans to Horatio Seymour, September 6, 1868, Seymour MSS, NYSL; John Bigelow, ed., *Letters and Literary Memorials of Samuel J. Tilden* (New York: Harper & Brothers, 1908), 1:240, 246.

CHAPTER THREE

1. James R. Doolittle to Manton Marble, January 27, 1868, Marble MSS, LC; Sandusky *Register*, September 1, October 12, 1868; Bridgeport *Evening Standard*, November 3, 1868; Louisville *Courier*, July 15, 1868.

2. Charles Coleman, *The Election of 1868: The Democratic Effort to Regain Control* (New York: Columbia University Press, 1933), 257–59; "Gath," Chicago *Tribune*, July 20, 1868 (quotation); Marietta *Register*, October 15, 1868.

3. Louisville *Courier*, August 7, September 6, 1868; Springfield *Illinois State Register*, August 6, 13, 17, 1868; Chicago *Times*, September 5, November 2, 1868. For the anti-Semitism charge, see Joseph Medill to Elihu Washburne, June 16, 1868, Washburne MSS, LC.

4. Chicago *Times*, July 11, 1868. For a shrewd evaluation of the silly season, see Georges Clemenceau, *American Reconstruction, 1865–1870, and the Impeachment of President Johnson*, ed. Fernand Bladensperger (New York: L. McVeagh, 1928), 239–43.

5. Joel H. Silbey, *A Respectable Minority: The Democratic Party in the Civil War Era, 1860–68* (New York: Norton, 1977), 217–27.

6. Frederick B. Marbut, "Decline of the Official Press in Washington," *Journalism Quarterly* 33 (Summer 1956): 335–41.

7. For the background and expansion of the party press, see Gerald J. Baldasty, "The Press and Politics in the Age of Jackson," *Journalism Monographs* 89 (August 1984); William David Sloan, "'Purse and Pen': Party-Press Relationships, 1789–1816," *American Journalism* 6 (1989): 103–27; and Robert K. Stewart, "The Exchange System and the Development of American Politics in the 1820s," *American Journalism* 4 (1987): 30–42.

8. George P. Rowell & Co., *American Newspaper Directory Containing Accurate Lists of All the Newspapers and Periodicals Published in the United States and Territories, and the Dominion of Canada and British Colonies of North America* (New York: Geo. P. Rowell & Co., 1872), 342, 581, 584.

9. Ibid., 384, 572, 578, 602.

10. Ibid., 11, 16, 19–20, 25–26, 29–30, 32, 35, 38–40, 42–43, 46–47, 49, 52–54, 56–57, 59, 62, 65, 67–68, 70, 79, 81–82, 85–88, 92, 95–96, 103, 107, 110, 112, 117, 130–34, 148, 150, 187.

11. Rowell & Co., *American Newspaper Directory*, 56, 584.

12. A. S. Twichell to William E. Chandler, March 4, 1872, Chandler MSS, NHHS; Rowell & Co., *American Newspaper Directory*, 29, 356, 360. See also the directory, p. 55, Onawa *Monona Co. Gazette* and Osceola *Clarke Co. Sentinel*.

13. ———— to Alexander Long, January 28, 1874, Long MSS, CHS.

14. Michael E. McGerr, *The Decline of Popular Politics: The American North, 1865–1928* (New York: Oxford University Press, 1986), 14–22. For the impact of the political press elsewhere, see Theodore Zeldin, *France, 1848–1945: Taste & Corruption* (New York: Oxford University Press, 1980), 222–24.

15. John Forsyth to Manton Marble, February 27, 1874, J. D. Burns to Marble,

May 16, July 28, 1876, Marble MSS, LC; Montgomery Blair to Samuel J. Tilden, August 10, 1868, Tilden MSS, NYPL; William E. Chandler to Elihu Washburne, October 19, 1868, Washburne MSS, LC.

16. Detroit *Free Press*, August 16, 1868; George Washington to George F. Hatch, May 20, 1872, J. W. Grantham to Hatch, May 22, 1872, John G. Moore to William H. Hatch, July 23, 1872, Hatch MSS, Missouri Historical Society, St. Louis.

17. Moss and Boon to Manton Marble, December 31, 1873, John Kelly to Democrats, October 1, 1875, Marble MSS, LC.

18. Edwin D. Morgan to J. H. Straus, October 1, 1872, Morgan to William Claflin, September 23, 1872, Morgan MSS, NYSL.

19. Milo Blair to Burdett, December 4, 1872, John S. Mitchel to Edward McPherson, November 25, 1874, McPherson MSS, LC.

20. Washington *Chronicle*, May 27, 1874; Cincinnati *Commercial*, July 24, 1869.

21. Franklin H. Orvis to Charles W. Willard, October 19, 1872, Albert H. Tuttle to Willard, March 10, 17, 1874, Willard MSS, Vermont Historical Society; H. B. Hendershott and E. L. Burton to Charles Mason, February 28, 1866, Mason MSS, ISDAH.

22. Rowell & Co., *American Newspaper Directory*, 354, 549.

23. New York *Tribune*, May 24, 1867; R. H. McBride to William Boyd Allison, November 3, 1873, M. M. Ham to Allison, February 19, 1874, M. C. Woodruff to Allison, January 4, 1875, Allison MSS, ISDAH; Topeka *Kansas State Record*, December 11, 25, 1872. On the stamps fight, see "Seymour," Mobile *Register*, November 28, 1875.

24. John M. Carmack to Andrew Johnson, July 14, 1874, Johnson MSS, LC; A. H. Hamilton to William Boyd Allison, February 18, 1874, Allison MSS, ISDAH; B. F. Sloan to Samuel J. Randall, February 1, 1875, H. Frysinger to Randall, January 28, 1875, Randall MSS, UP; Joseph Medill to Elihu Washburne, May 1, June 16, July 10, 1868, Washburne MSS, LC.

25. "Pickaway," Cincinnati *Enquirer*, July 5, 1877; E. Bruce Thompson, *Matthew Hale Carpenter: Webster of the West* (Madison: Wisconsin Historical Society, 1954), 205–7; Milwaukee *News*, December 24, 1873, January 7, 13, 1874.

26. Archer H. Shaw, *The Plain Dealer: One Hundred Years in Cleveland* (New York: Knopf, 1942), 178; "Westerner," New York *Graphic*, October 3, 1874; New York *Graphic*, November 2, 1874; "Senator Conkling and Mr. Roberts," *Harper's Weekly*, December 12, 1874; Chicago *Times*, February 20, 1874; New York *Times*, July 6, 1876.

27. George T. McJimsey, *Genteel Partisan: Manton Marble, 1834–1917* (Ames: Iowa State University Press, 1971), 15–17, 83–105; "Gath," New York *Graphic*, May 26, 1876; Allan Nevins and Milton H. Thomas, eds., *The Diary of George Templeton Strong* (New York: Macmillan, 1952), 4 (September 22, 1871).

28. Sam Ward to Manton Marble, July 31, 1868, George Ticknor Curtis to Marble, September 10, 1868, Sam Ward to Marble, August 1, 1868, August Belmont to Marble, (July?) 1868, Marble MSS, LC.

29. New York *Pomeroy's Democrat,* October 6, November 27, December 11, 1875. For Pomeroy's wartime career, see Frank Klement, "'Brick' Pomeroy: Copperhead and Curmudgeon," *Wisconsin Magazine of History* 25 (Winter 1951): 106–13, 156; New York *Herald,* May 31, 1896; New York *Times,* May 31, 1896. For his national readership, see "Earnest," Boston *Commonwealth,* March 21, 1868, and "Sidney," Boston *Commonwealth,* August 22, 1868. A shrewd commentary on him can be found in Jean H. Baker, *Affairs of Party: The Political Culture of Northern Democrats in the Mid-Nineteenth Century* (Ithaca: Cornell University Press, 1983), 37–42.

30. Troy *Weekly Times,* September 5, 1868; Clemenceau, *American Reconstruction,* 232; New York *Pomeroy's Democrat,* January 2, July 20, 27, 1870.

31. New York *Graphic,* May 26, 1876; New York *World,* May 26, 1876; *Pomeroy's Democrat,* October 16, 1875.

32. Mary E. Tucker, *Life of Mark M. Pomeroy* (New York: G. W. Carleton, 1868), 136–49, 186–90; LaCrosse *Democrat,* July 11, 12, August 30, September 5, 1866.

33. Peter T. Luther to John B. Stoll, November 10, 1875, Stoll MSS, Indiana Historical Society; Chauncey F. Black to Samuel J. Randall, May 25, 1877, Randall MSS, UP.

34. Chicago *Times,* April 15, 1876.

35. Topeka *Kansas State Record,* October 23, 1872; Mark Howard to Zachariah Chandler, December 3, 1868, Z. Chandler MSS, LC; Louisville *Courier-Journal,* August 31, 1875.

36. Springfield *Republican,* April 19, 25, 1871; Chicago *Times,* March 2, 1876; Washington *Chronicle,* January 27, 1876.

37. Leon B. Richardson, *William E. Chandler: Republican* (New York: Dodd, Mead, 1940), 85–89; E. H. Rollins to William E. Chandler, February 28, 1869, Henry McFarland to John T. Perry, March 11, 1872, Chandler to A. H. Cragin, September 8, 1871, McFarland to Chandler, March 26, 1872, Oliver Pillsbury to Chandler, September 16, 1872, Chandler MSS, NHHS.

38. Chauncey F. Black to Samuel J. Randall, May 25, 1877, Randall MSS, UP.

39. Cincinnati *Commercial,* August 7, 1869, "Probo," ibid., December 25, 1869; Michael C. Kerr to Manton Marble, June 15, 1874, Marble MSS, LC; "Pickaway," Cincinnati *Enquirer,* July 5, 1877. For "confusion," see John L. Russ to William E. Chandler, January 25, 1876, Chandler MSS, NHHS.

40. McJimsey, *Genteel Partisan,* 130–31.

41. Alexander Long to Manton Marble, October 17, 1868, Wilbur F. Storey to Marble, October 16, 1868, S. L. M. Barlow to Marble, October 24, 1868, Charles H. Mantz to Marble, October 17, 1868, A. P. Hall, Sam Harrison, and others to Marble, October 20, 1868, "A Constant Reader" to Marble, October 19, 1868 (quotation), J. P. H. to Marble, October 18, 1868, Marble MSS, LC; Clemenceau, *American Reconstruction,* 254; New York *Herald,* October 17, 1868.

42. Springfield *Illinois State Register,* January 15, 1871, January 19, 1872.

43. St. Louis *Missouri Republican*, December 30, 1868, January 5, 12, 15, 1869.

44. New York *Graphic*, January 18, 1875.

45. Milwaukee *News*, December 24, 1874.

46. Cincinnati *Commercial*, September 10, 1866; Burlington *Times*, September 5, 1868. For the most detailed attack on Morton, see Chicago *Times*, April 15, 1876 (colloquy).

47. Rowell & Co., *American Newspaper Directory* (1874), 100.

48. New York *World*, February 14, 1870. See also George W. Tanner to Thomas Jenckes, October 31, 1870, Jenckes MSS, LC, and Providence *Journal*, November 15, 1870.

49. Providence *Journal*, November 5, 7, 1870; Newport *Mercury*, November 5, 12, 1870.

50. On the papers' affiliations, see Cincinnati *Gazette*, April 20, 1869; Henry R. Davis, *Half a Century with the Providence Journal* (Providence: Journal Co., 1904), 15–35. On the campaign dirt, see George Manchester to Thomas Jenckes, October 23, 1870, Thomas Coggeshall to Jenckes, October 29, 1870, Jenckes MSS, LC; Ari Hoogenboom, *Outlawing the Spoils: A History of the Civil Service Reform Movement, 1865–1883* (Urbana: University of Illinois Press, 1961), 81–82; and Providence *Journal*, November 2–5, 7, 9–11, 15, 1870.

51. Some did read several newspapers. More affluent city dwellers, like George Templeton Strong, were able to compare the disparate accounts and did so; in small towns, partisans seemed to be well aware of what the other side was saying. Cincinnati editors, for example, answered allegations printed in rival concerns as though their subscribers were too familiar with the charges to require their repetition. Whether information that was accessible was actually compared, however, is another matter. Strong himself seems to have read Democratic journals more to convince himself of the depravity of the opposition's scribes than to unearth the truth.

52. St. Louis *Missouri Republican*, December 28, 1868; James Redpath to Whitelaw Reid, November 9, 1876, Reid MSS, LC; Chicago *Tribune*, March 12, 1873; Springfield *Republican*, July 13, August 10, 1876; *Nation*, October 30, 1879; New York *Graphic*, September 7, 1875.

53. "Pickaway," Cincinnati *Enquirer*, February 23, 1875. See also Chicago *Times*, February 20, 1874, April 27, 1876.

54. Washington *Chronicle*, January 8 (quotation), October 31, 1874; Washington *Sunday Capital*, October 18, 1874.

55. Cleveland *Plain Dealer*, July 19, 1873; Springfield *Republican*, April 11, 1871; John Barr to Benjamin F. Butler, January 7, 1870, Butler MSS, LC; St. Louis *Republican* quoted in Washington *Chronicle*, November 3, 5, December 8, 1874; F. W. Dawson to Mrs. Dawson, September 3, 1874, Dawson MSS, Duke University, Durham.

56. Charles F. Wingate, *Views and Interviews on Journalism* (New York: F. B. Patterson, 1875), 135.

57. New York *Pomeroy's Democrat,* January 12, August 10, October 19, 1870; Cincinnati *Commercial,* May 17, 1869; Springfield *Republican,* May 15, June 23, 1871.

58. "Warrington," Springfield *Republican,* January 20, 1871.

59. Justin E. Walsh, *To Print the News and to Raise Hell! A Biography of Wilbur F. Storey* (Chapel Hill: University of North Carolina, 1968), 202.

CHAPTER FOUR

1. "Nym," Charleston *News and Courier,* April 6, 1875; New York *Times,* April 15, July 16, August 16–17, 24, 1875; New York *Sun,* September 16, October 12, 1875.

2. "Gath," New York *Graphic,* September 22, 1875; "Seymour," Mobile *Register,* April 13, 22, 1875; Charles Nordhoff to Whitelaw Reid, April 14, 1875, Reid MSS, LC.

3. Cincinnati *Gazette,* July 27, 1871; Justin E. Walsh, *To Print the News and to Raise Hell! A Biography of Wilbur F. Storey* (Chapel Hill: University of North Carolina, 1968), 258. For stupendous profits just after the war, see New York *Citizen,* January 13, 1866.

4. "Gath," Cincinnati *Enquirer,* April 2, 1877; Elmer Davis, *History of the New York Times, 1851–1921* (New York: New York Times, 1921), 129.

5. Julian S. Rammelkamp, *Pulitzer's Post-Dispatch, 1878–1883* (Princeton, N.J.: Princeton University Press, 1967), 1–3, 39–40.

6. Topeka *Kansas State Record,* December 31, 1868; Cincinnati *Commercial,* December 31, 1865; Chicago *Times,* April 24, 1876.

7. Charleston *Daily Courier,* October 2, 1869 (quotation); New York *Graphic,* September 7, 1875; Charles F. Wingate, *Views and Interviews on Journalism* (New York: F. B. Patterson, 1875), 135.

8. Chicago *Tribune,* June 19, 1868; New York *Graphic,* June 9, 1874 (quotation).

9. "Gath," Cincinnati *Enquirer,* April 2, 1877.

10. Detroit *Free Press,* August 16, 1868; Springfield *Republican,* March 29, 1871.

11. Springfield *Illinois State Register,* May 8, 1874; James F. Wilson to William B. Allison, January 8, 1873, Allison MSS, ISDAH; Louisville *Courier-Journal,* April 18, 1874; Warner Bateman to John Sherman, January 10, 1877, Sherman MSS, LC.

12. "H. B.," Springfield *Republican,* May 25, 1871; "Anchises," Cincinnati *Enquirer,* October 21, 1873; Chicago *Times,* April 4, 1870.

13. William D. Mallam, "General Benjamin Franklin Butler: A Critical Study" (Ph.D. diss., University of Minnesota, 1942), 243; Boston *Commonwealth,* July 27, 1872; Chicago *Times,* June 8, 1870; Benjamin F. Butler to John Russell Young, February 27, April 29, 1870, July 21, 1872, J. C. Goldsmith to Young, July 29,

1872, Young MSS, LC; O. J. Hollister, *Life of Schuyler Colfax* (New York: Funk & Wagnalls, 1886), 363.

14. On the *Union*, see Cincinnati *Commercial*, May 1, 1874; on Washington papers, see Mobile *Register*, March 15, 1875, Portland *Eastern Argus*, May 25, 1874, and "D. P.," Cincinnati *Enquirer*, August 25, 1877; on Cincinnati, see Richard Smith to William Henry Smith, January 26, 1873, Smith MSS, OHS. The contrast with the British experience of would-be independents is striking. See John Vincent, *The Formation of the British Liberal Party, 1857–68* (London: Constable, 1966), 97–100.

15. Frederic Hudson, *Journalism in the United States, from 1690 to 1872* (New York: Harper & Brothers, 1873), 677–79; Cincinnati *Gazette*, April 30, 1869; Washington *Chronicle*, February 26, 1875. The *Chronicle*, of course, meant the analogy in no such sense. Very likely it was referring to other qualities: the cancan was deemed vulgar to the verge of obscenity, a corruption of a genteel art, and fit for criminal prosecution.

16. Candace Stone, *Dana and the Sun* (New York: Dodd, Mead, 1938), 38–39, 53, 380–82; Charles A. Dana to Uriah H. Painter, June 28, 1868, J. W England to Painter, May 10, 1868, Painter Family MSS, HSP; Frank Luther Mott, *American Journalism: A History of Newspapers in the United States through 260 Years*, rev. ed. (New York: Macmillan, 1950), 374–76 (*Post* comparison, 376).

17. Washington *Chronicle*, May 25, 1875; Stone, *Dana and the Sun*, 92; Janet E. Steele, "From Paradise to Park Row: The Life, Opinions, and Newspapers of Charles A. Dana, 1819–1897" (Ph.D. diss., Johns Hopkins University, 1986), 100–101, 135–37.

18. Joseph Logsdon, *Horace White: Nineteenth-Century Liberal* (Westport, Conn.: Greenwood, 1971), 39, 98–100, 105–7, 117–18, 171–72.

19. Logsdon, *Horace White*, 78–94; Lloyd Wendt, *Chicago Tribune: The Rise of a Great American Newspaper* (Chicago: Rand McNally, 1979), 207–11, 221–22, 227; Cincinnati *Enquirer*, May 9, 1877; New York *Graphic*, January 4, 1876 (quotation).

20. Donald W. Curl, *Murat Halstead and the Cincinnati Commercial* (Boca Raton: A Florida Atlantic University Book: University Presses of Florida, 1980), 6–45; New York *Graphic*, May 11, 1875, October 27, 30, 1876.

21. Walsh, *To Print the News and to Raise Hell!*, 270; Harry W. Baehr, Jr., *The New York Tribune Since the Civil War* (New York: Dodd, Mead, 1936), 119.

22. Peter R. Knights, "'Competition' in the U.S. Daily Newspaper Industry, 1865–68," *Journalism Quarterly* 45 (Autumn 1968): 473–80; George P. Rowell & Co., *American Newspaper Directory Containing Accurate Lists of All the Newspapers and Periodicals Published in the United States and Territories, and the Dominion of Canada and British Colonies of North America* (New York: Geo. P. Rowell & Co., 1872), 350, 361, 383, 392, 410, 433, 438, 472, 527, 559; New York *World*, January 2, 1869. The *World*'s claim to independence was more than braggadocio; see Samuel Bowles to Manton Marble, January 20, 1870, Marble MSS, LC.

23. James L. Crouthamel, *Bennett's New York Herald and the Rise of the Popular Press* (Syracuse: Syracuse University Press, 1989), 57–91; New York *Graphic*, February 3, 1874; "Gath," New York *Graphic*, July 27, 1875; Springfield *Republican*, March 29, 1871; Elwyn B. Robinson, "The *Public Ledger*: An Independent Newspaper," *Pennsylvania Magazine of History and Biography* 64 (January 1940): 43–55.

24. New York *Graphic*, February 18, 1874 (quotation), September 29, 1875.

25. "Independent Journalism," *Harper's Weekly*, January 23, 1869.

26. Louisville *Courier-Journal*, September 6, 1875; Springfield *Republican*, August 22, 1876; New York *Graphic*, September 6, 1875. On the *Herald*, see Washington *Chronicle*, October 31, 1874; Horace Porter to Zachariah Chandler, July 25, 1872, Z. Chandler MSS, LC; and Manton Marble to Thomas F. Bayard, January 15, 1875, Bayard Family MSS, LC.

27. Rowell & Co., *American Newspaper Directory*, 347; Chicago *Times*, June 11, 1870.

28. *Nation*, January 28, 1869.

29. Newport *Mercury*, May 23, 1868; Bangor *Whig and Courier*, January 8, 1869; St. Louis *Missouri Republican*, January 4, 16, 1869; Springfield *Republican*, January 19, 1876; Henry V. Boynton to Whitelaw Reid, February 9, 1869, Reid MSS, LC. See also Michael Kerr to Manton Marble, March 17, 29, 1870, Marble MSS, LC.

30. Logsdon, *Horace White*, 97; Whitelaw Reid, "The Scholar in Politics," *Scribner's Monthly* 6 (September 1873): 607.

31. Harry J. Brown and Frederick D. Williams, eds., *Diary of James A. Garfield* (East Lansing: Michigan State University Press, 1973), 2:246 (November 17, 1873); L. J. Jennings to Hamilton Fish, March 16, 1875, Fish MSS. LC.

32. Philadelphia *North American*, September 22, 1874; Brown and Williams, *Diary of James A. Garfield*, 2:175 (May 2, 1873); Chauncey F. Black to Samuel J. Randall, September 17, 1876, Randall MSS, UP.

33. Cincinnati *Commercial*, August 20, 1869.

34. See, for example, *Nation*, January 4, 11, 1872, on the New York *Times*'s abuse of Senator Carl Schurz.

35. New York *Tribune*, May 21, 1874.

36. Chicago *Times*, April 15, 1876.

37. J. S. Moore to Manton Marble, January 31, April 25, 1870, David A. Wells to Marble, March 24, 1870, Marble MSS, LC; *Nation*, December 1, 1870.

38. Cleveland *Plain Dealer*, July 26, October 11, 1873.

39. Philadelphia *North American*, October 10, 1874.

40. "Carlfried," Springfield *Republican*, March 27, 1871. Italics added.

41. *Nation*, May 6, 1869; Richard Smith to Whitelaw Reid, May 7, 1869, Reid MSS, LC; J. C. Goldsmith to J. Russell Young, December 2, 9–10, 13, 1872, Benjamin F. Butler to Young, January 19, 1873, Young MSS, LC.

42. "Colstoun," Chicago *Tribune*, December 16, 1872, "Gath," ibid., December 31, 1872; Benjamin F. Butler to J. Russell Young, January 19, 1873, Young

MSS, LC; Schuyler Colfax to James M. Comly, December 21, 1872, Comly MSS, OHS. The issue of Credit Mobilier, according to Congressman Benjamin F. Butler, was the deciding one, which adds a special interest to the letter that Washington correspondent Zebulon L. White wrote to Whitelaw Reid, on December 22, 1872. At that point the House investigation continued behind closed doors, but there had been damaging leaks. All of them, White wrote, came from Butler himself. Reid MSS, LC.

43. Zebulon L. White to Whitelaw Reid, December 21, 1872 (first quotation), Hiram J. Ramsdell to Reid, May 15, 1874, Reid MSS, LC; Baehr, *Tribune Since the Civil War*, 119–23; Whitelaw Reid to James M. Comly, January 9, 1873, Comly MSS, OHS (second quotation); Reid to William Henry Smith, December 18, 1872, January 9, 1873, Smith MSS, OHS.

44. Richard Kluger, *The Paper: The Life and Death of the New York Herald Tribune* (New York: Knopf, 1986), 132–35; *New York Times*, July 16, August 8, 1875; "Seymour," Mobile *Register*, April 22, 1875; New York *Sun*, September 16, October 2, 1875.

45. New York *Herald*, June 11, 1874; New York *Graphic*, May 1, 4, 7, 30, June 11, 13, 1874, February 1, 26, 1875; New York *Tribune*, April 7, 1874.

46. "Are Trade Unions Conspiracies?," New York *Sun*, October 9, 1875; Stone, *Dana and the Sun*, 47, 359–62; Steele, "From Paradise to Park Row," 145–46, 169–78.

47. "Broadway," Cincinnati *Commercial*, April 20, 1874.

48. New York *Sun*, September 3, 1875; "Gath," New York *Graphic*, July 25, 1876; Allan Nevins, *The Evening Post: A Century of Journalism* (New York: Boni & Liveright, 1922), 400–405.

49. "Carlfried," Springfield *Republican*, March 27, 1871.

CHAPTER FIVE

1. Ben: Perley Poore, "Washington News," *Harper's Magazine* 48 (January 1874): 234; Poore to William Warland Clapp, November 30, 1868, Clapp MSS, LC.

2. Frankfort *Commonwealth*, August 18, 1865; Charles C. Clayton, *"Little Mack": Joseph B. McCullagh of the St. Louis Globe-Democrat* (Carbondale: Southern Illinois University Press, 1969), 32–33, 41; Royal Cortissoz, *The Life of Whitelaw Reid* (New York: Scribner, 1921), 1:99–115.

3. Poore, "Washington News," 227–28; Vincent Howard, "The Two Congresses: A Study of the Changing Roles and Relationships of the National Legislature and Washington Reporters, Revealed Particularly in the Press Accounts of Legislative Activity, 1860–1913" (Ph.D. diss., University of Chicago, 1976), 29.

4. Donald A. Ritchie, *Press Gallery: Congress and the Washington Correspondents* (Cambridge: Harvard University Press, 1991), 26.

5. New York *Tribune*, May 30, 1887; "Creighton," Washington *Chronicle*, April 25, 1875, and Raleigh *Sentinel*, January 4, 1874 (quotation).

6. Ritchie, *Press Gallery*, 7–56; Oliver Gramling, *AP: The Story of News* (Port Washington, N.Y.: Kennikat Press, 1969), 31; James L. Crouthamel, *Bennett's New York Herald and the Rise of the Popular Press* (Syracuse: Syracuse University Press, 1989), 48–50; F. B. Marbut, *News from the Capital: The Story of Washington Reporting* (Carbondale: Southern Illinois University Press, 1971), 71–73.

7. Joseph Medill to William Henry Smith, February 11, 1878, Smith MSS, OHS.

8. The free right to print had three other restrictions: the material must appear in the next day's paper, any other journal taking the "special's" dispatch must pay part of the telegraph tolls, and country newspapers were under no such requirement. What this meant was that, in practical terms, only major metropolitan newspapers could avail themselves regularly of the advantage that the New York Associated Press allowed them. Still, for most New York newspapers, that was hindrance enough. The Western Associated Press followed different rules.

9. W. G. F. Shanks, "How We Get Our News," *Harper's Magazine* 34 (March 1867): 518–19; George Alfred Townsend, "Recollections and Reflections," *Lippincott's Magazine* 38 (November 1886): 521.

10. Frederic Hudson, *Journalism in the United States, from 1690 to 1872* (New York: Harper & Brothers, 1873), 701–6; Howard, "The Two Congresses," 29–35; Edwin Emery, *The Press in America: An Interpretative History of Mass Media* (Englewood Cliffs, N.J.: Prentice-Hall, 1972), 193–94.

11. Howard, "The Two Congresses," 121–22; Ritchie, *Press Gallery*, 77; Charleston *News and Courier*, November 22, 1881 (quotation).

12. Springfield *Illinois State Register*, February 17, 1872; Louisville *Courier-Journal*, April 18, 1874; Washington *Chronicle*, May 11, 1875; N. G. Gonzales to Emmie, January 25, 1882, Elliott-Gonzales MSS, SHC; Cincinnati *Enquirer*, March 13, April 7, 1875.

13. Maurine Beasley, "Pens and Petticoats: Early Women Washington Correspondents," *Journalism History* 1 (Winter 1974–75): 112–15, 136, and "Mary Clemmer Ames: A Victorian Woman Journalist," *Hayes Historical Journal* (Spring 1978): 57–63; Poore, "Washington News," 235; "Creighton," Washington *Chronicle*, April 26, 1875; Ben: Perley Poore to William Warland Clapp, December 1, 1868, Clapp MSS, LC.

14. "Gath," Chicago *Tribune*, February 9, 1869 (quotation); Cincinnati *Enquirer*, March 10, 1877; Cincinnati *Commercial*, June 17, 1870; Chicago *Times*, March 4, 1875; *Nation*, January 9, 1869; "M. C. A.," *Independent*, January 18, 1872.

15. "Van," Springfield *Republican*, December 14, 1871; Washington *Chronicle*, January 25, 1875, January 31, 1876; Boston *Morning Journal*, February 12–13, 1872; "Gath," Chicago *Tribune*, March 15, 1874; Ben: Perley Poore to William Warland Clapp, January 21, 1877, Clapp MSS, LC. "Perley" tipped the scales at 250 pounds; see "Gideon," Chicago *Times*, March 6, 1874. For the description, see Washington *Evening Star*, November 19, 1870.

16. For the physical description, see Chicago *Tribune*, September 25, 1870. For the testimonials, see New York *Graphic*, October 30, 1876; Lloyd Wendt, *Chi-*

cago Tribune: The Rise of a Great American Newspaper (Chicago: Rand McNally, 1979), 220; Raleigh *Sentinel*, January 4, 1874; and Charles F. Wingate, *Views and Interviews on Journalism* (New York: F. B. Patterson, 1875), 20.

17. "An Interviewer Interviewed: A Talk with 'Gath,' " *Lippincott's* 48 (November 1891): 630–38; Wendt, *Chicago Tribune*, 220; George Alfred Townsend, *Campaigns of a Non-Combatant, and His Romaunt Abroad During the War* (New York: Blelock & Co., 1866), 277–78, 307–8; Louis M. Starr, *Bohemian Brigade: Civil War Newsmen in Action* (New York: Knopf, 1954), 267–68 (quotation).

18. New York *Graphic*, August 7, 1875; Raleigh *Sentinel*, January 4, 1874 (first quotation); "An Interviewer Interviewed," 630–38; *The Journalist*, May 21, 1891; Cincinnati *Enquirer*, July 27, 1876 (second quotation), February 28, March 15, 1877; Washington *Chronicle*, January 31, 1876.

19. "Bueno Buro," New York *Citizen*, February 2, 1867; *Who Was Who in America, 1897–1942*, 126; Harry J. Brown and Frederick D. Williams, eds., *Diary of James A. Garfield* (East Lansing: Michigan State University Press, 1973), 4:81–82 (June 16, 1878); *Nation*, August 26, 1869 (quotation).

20. Ritchie, *Press Gallery*, 113–20; "Bueno Buro," New York *Citizen*, February 2, 1867; Henry V. Boynton to Benjamin H. Bristow, October 21, 1877, February 27, 1879, Bristow MSS, LC.

21. Francis A. Richardson, "Recollections of a Washington Newspaper Correspondent," *Records of the Columbia Historical Society* 6 (Washington, 1903): 27; House Report 1112, "H. V. Boynton and Others," 48th Cong., 1st sess., 210–23. For the following of Boynton's leads, see especially Henry V. Boynton to Benjamin H. Bristow, February 27, 1877, March 15, 1878, Bristow MSS, LC.

22. "Creighton," Washington *Chronicle*, April 26, 1875.

23. Hartford *Courant*, February 7, 1866; Poore, "Washington News," 234–35; Zebulon L. White to Whitelaw Reid, November 21, 1874, Reid MSS, LC; "H. J. R.," Cincinnati *Commercial*, July 3, 1871.

24. To give some examples from among the most prominent Washington correspondents in 1866: George W. Adams of the *World* was 25; Sidney Andrews of the Boston *Daily Advertiser* was 31; George Alfred Townsend of the Chicago *Tribune* was 25; Hiram J. Ramsdell of the New York *Tribune* was 27, which made him senior to his colleague James R. Young by eight years, and to Zebulon White by three; and "Mack" of the Cincinnati *Enquirer* was 24.

25. Cincinnati *Commercial*, March 21, 1873; N. G. Gonzales to Emmie, February 19, 1882, Elliott-Gonzales MSS, SHC; Hiram J. Ramsdell to Whitelaw Reid, June 2, 1878, Reid MSS, LC. See also "An Interviewer Interviewed," 632; Sidney Andrews to Reid, July 30, December 26, 1870, Reid MSS. White would survive until 1889, but his retirement was only a matter of time, and he, like Ramsdell and H. V. Redfield, both of whom died in the following decade, succumbed at an unusually early age.

26. Hugh McCulloch to H. H. Van Dyke, April 6, 1866, McCulloch Letter-Books, LL/IU; New York *Sun*, December 31, 1871; House Report 799, 44th Cong., 1st sess., 314–16; B. Clower to William Henry Smith, February 9, 1871, W. H.

Smith MSS, ISL; William Dennison to Rutherford B. Hayes, November 13, 1876, Hayes MSS, HML.

27. Zebulon L. White to Whitelaw Reid, February 3, April 29, 1871, December 1, 1874, June 12, 1876, Reid MSS, LC; Lorenzo L. Crounse to George Sheppard, February 27–28, 1870, Garfield MSS, LC.

28. Hugh McCulloch to David A. Wells, December 17, 1866, McCulloch to Justin Morrill, December 20, 1866, McCulloch Letter-Books, LL/IU; House Report 799, 44th Cong., 1st sess., 327–28. For sources of information, see New York *Graphic*, March 20, 1876.

29. *Nation*, August 12, 1869; James Parton, "Falsehood in the Daily Press," *Harper's Magazine* 49 (July 1874): 273; New York *Graphic*, March 18, 1876. For Twain's quotation, see Cincinnati *Commercial*, September 22, 1869.

30. Parton, "Falsehood in the Daily Press," 273; New York *Times*, July 20, 1866.

31. Schuyler Colfax letter, Springfield *Republican*, January 3, 1871; Charleston *Daily Courier*, August 31, 1872; New York *Tribune*, May 1, 1867.

32. Frank Luther Mott, *American Journalism: A History of Newspapers in the United States through 260 Years*, rev. ed. (New York: Macmillan, 1950), 386. Credit often goes to J. B. McCullagh for his audience with Alexander Stephens in 1867 (though "Gath" claimed that it was he who did that interview; actually, the interview appeared in the New York *World* on August 17, 1866, while "Gath" was in Europe covering a war). Certainly, Andrew Johnson was the first president formally interviewed, in 1868. But Horace Greeley of the New York *Tribune* had elicited a string of remarks from Brigham Young in the summer of 1859, and this may have been the first actual interview given. See George S. Turnbull, "Some Notes on the History of the Interview," *Journalism Quarterly* 13 (September 1936): 272–79; Poore, "Washington News," 231; "An Interviewer Interviewed," 634.

33. For two "interviews" of Grant, see New York *World*, January 16, 1869; *Nation*, January 28, 1869; and New York *Times*, November 28, 1873. For a bogus interview with Senator Lyman Trumbull of Illinois, see Louisville *Courier-Journal*, December 4, 8, 1871. The Beveridge interview embarrassment is in Springfield *Illinois State Register*, February 4, 1874. For an interview that Congressman Robert Schenck never gave, see Springfield *Republican*, January 2–3, 1871.

34. New York *Graphic*, April 14, 1876.

35. Philadelphia *North American*, July 11, August 11, October 3, 1874; James P. Boyd to Butler, May 30, 1874, Butler MSS, LC.

36. Townsend, *Campaigns of a Non-Combatant*, 367.

37. Chauncey F. Black to Samuel J. Randall, May 3, 1877, Randall MSS, UP.

38. "Gideon," Chicago *Times*, March 11, 1874 (quotation); Memphis *Daily Appeal*, April 14, 1876; Zebulon L. White to Whitelaw Reid, January 27, 1873, Reid MSS, LC.

39. Frank B. Evans, *Pennsylvania Politics, 1872–1877: A Study in Political Leadership* (Harrisburg: Pennsylvania Historical and Museum Commission, 1966),

173–78, 188–92; New York *Sun,* September 1, 4, 8, October 9, 1875; A. M. Gibson to Samuel J. Randall, September 16, 21, October 7, 14, 1875, July 20, August 24, September 2, 1877, Randall MSS, UP.

40. The best brick in 1869 could withstand 2,000 pounds of pressure to the square inch. A common red brick would sustain 1,750 pounds. The university's brick at best could take 516 pounds, while the worst sample bore only 173 pounds; the average was 319 pounds, or 11 pounds to the square inch less than engineering authorities ascribed to chalk.

41. Cincinnati *Gazette,* January 9, 1869; George R. Bentley, *A History of the Freedmen's Bureau* (Philadelphia: University of Pennsylvania Press, 1955), 205–8.

42. House Report 121, "Charges Against General Howard," 41st Cong., 2d sess., 1–55, Testimony: 416–30; New York *Pomeroy's Democrat,* June 22, 1870.

43. Benjamin B. French to Pamela French, December 9, 1866, French MSS, LC; Bentley, *Freedmen's Bureau,* 206. Boynton actually lived with his father at the time of the conflict. See "Bueno Buro," New York *Citizen,* February 2, 1867.

44. "B. L.," Cincinnati *Commercial,* April 23, 1874; Cincinnati *Gazette,* February 22, 1878; N. G. Gonzales to Emmie, February 19, 1882, Elliott-Gonzales MSS, SHC (quotation).

45. "Henry V. Boynton," *Dictionary of American Biography,* 2:616–17; John F. Marszalek, *Sherman: A Soldier's Passion for Order* (New York: Free Press, 1993), 464–66; Jacob D. Cox, "Boynton's Review of Sherman," *Nation,* November 25, December 2, 1875.

46. One might cite, for example, any of Ames's columns, signed "M. C. A.," in the *Independent,* notably that on January 23, 1868.

47. "Van," Springfield *Republican,* December 14, 1871; *Ormsby v. Douglass,* 37 N.Y. 477 (1868); *John S. Holt v. Benjamin S. Parsons,* 23 Tex. 9, 76 Am. Dec. 49 (1859); Detroit *Free Press,* October 22, 1870; E. L. Godkin, "Libel and Its Legal Remedy," *Atlantic Monthly* 46 (December 1880): 734–35 (quotation).

CHAPTER SIX

1. Adrian Cook, *The Alabama Claims, American Politics, and Anglo-American Relations, 1865–1872* (Ithaca: Cornell University Press, 1975); New York *Tribune,* May 1, 9, 1871.

2. New York *Tribune,* May 4–5, 1871.

3. Ibid., May 11–13, 1871 (quotation, May 13).

4. Ibid., May 16–17, 19, 1871.

5. Zebulon L. White to Whitelaw Reid, May 21, 1871, Reid MSS, LC; New York *Times,* May 22, 1871.

6. New York *Tribune,* May 19, 1871 (quotation); Zebulon White to Whitelaw Reid, June 2, 1871, H. J. Ramsdell to Reid, October 3, 20, 1871, Reid MSS, LC. For President Grant's involvement, see Hamilton Fish Diary, May 16, 1871, Fish MSS, LC.

7. Zebulon L. White to Whitelaw Reid, November 21, 1874, Reid MSS, LC; Charles C. Clayton, *"Little Mack": Joseph B. McCullagh of the St. Louis Globe-Democrat* (Carbondale: Southern Illinois University Press, 1969), 66–67; Ben: Perley Poore to William W. Clapp, March 6, 1868, Clapp MSS, LC.

8. Poore to W. W. Clapp, March 2, 1876, Clapp MSS, LC. See also Zebulon L. White to Whitelaw Reid, January 16, 1873, Reid MSS, LC, and Washington *Evening Star*, November 23, December 6, 1870.

9. Chicago *Times*, March 18, 1876 (quotation); Joseph H. Barrett to William Henry Smith, January 17, April 1, 1868, R. W. Clarke to Smith, April 26, 1869, Smith MSS, OHS; Hiram J. Ramsdell to Whitelaw Reid, February 3, 1879, Reid MSS, LC; Washington *Chronicle*, February 16–17, 1875.

10. Clayton, *"Little Mack,"* 75–77 (quotation); Chicago *Times*, May 7, 1870; Charles A. Dana to J. Russell Young, August 18, 1870, Young MSS, LC.

11. Cincinnati *Enquirer*, April 1, 1875, April 16, 24, 1877; Cincinnati *Gazette*, May 5, 1869; Louisville *Courier-Journal*, September 2, 1875. For more malice, see *Nation*, January 2, 9, February 27, March 6, 1873.

12. Sidney Andrews to Whitelaw Reid, November 11, 1869, Ben C. Truman to Reid, April 30, 1879, Reid MSS, LC; "An Interviewer Interviewed: A Talk with 'Gath,'" *Lippincott's* 48 (November 1891): 635; Comparisons of *Congressional Directory*, 41st Cong., 1st sess., and 43d Cong., 1st sess.

13. Louis J. Jennings to Manton Marble, November 10, 1869, Henry J. Raymond to Marble [n.d.], Marble MSS, LC; Albert H. Tuttle to C. Willard, April 1, 1874, Willard MSS, Vermont Historical Society, Montpelier; James A. Garfield to Edward Atkinson, August 14, 1871, Eugene V. Smalley to Garfield, August 18, 1870, Garfield MSS, LC; Washington *Sunday Capital*, December 10, 1871; Cincinnati *Commercial*, April 1, 1869; Springfield *Republican*, January 2, 1871; "L.," Memphis *Daily Appeal*, August 28, 1873.

14. Donald A. Ritchie, *Press Gallery: Congress and the Washington Correspondents* (Cambridge: Harvard University Press, 1991), 87–89, 96; Cincinnati *Commercial*, November 30, 1869, May 29, September 24, 1874; Osman C. Hooper, *History of Ohio Journalism, 1793–1933* (Columbus: Spahr & Glenn, 1933), 166–70; "Junot," Chicago *Times*, January 22, February 12, 1876; "Carlfried," Springfield *Republican*, February 15, 1871.

15. Memphis *Daily Appeal*, August 9, 1873.

16. As, for example, New York *Times*, April 11, 1874.

17. Washington *Chronicle*, September 19, December 19, 1874; Topeka *Kansas State Record*, December 20, 1871; Cincinnati *Enquirer*, March 1, 1875; Memphis *Daily Appeal*, August 20, 1873; Omaha *Republican*, March 15, 1873.

18. Memphis *Daily Appeal*, August 27, 1873; George P. Rowell & Co., *American Newspaper Directory Containing Accurate Lists of All the Newspapers and Periodicals Published in the United States and Territories, and the Dominion of Canada and British Colonies of North America* (New York: Geo. P. Rowell & Co., 1873), 202.

19. Sam Acheson, *35,000 Days in Texas: A History of the Dallas News and*

Its Forbears (New York: Macmillan, 1938), 67; or see Hooper, *History of Ohio Journalism*, 170–71.

20. Senate Report 5, 42d Cong., special sess., 11; Ben: Perley Poore to William W. Clapp, November 30, 1868, Clapp MSS, LC; Chicago *Times*, May 21, June 5, 16, 1874; "D. P.," Cincinnati *Enquirer*, June 1, 1877 (White quotation).

21. Barton S. Jones to Samuel Bowles, May 23, 1877, Bowles MSS, SML/YU; Charles Nordhoff to Whitelaw Reid, January 13, 1875, Henry V. Boynton to Reid, October 26, 1874, Reid MSS, LC; House Report 799, 44th Cong., 1st sess., 295–99; "Laertes," New York *Graphic*, March 18, 1876 (quotation).

22. Charles Nordhoff to Whitelaw Reid, January 13, 1875, Henry V. Boynton to Reid, October 26, 1874, Reid MSS, LC; Charles Nordhoff to James A. Garfield, May 5, 1870, Garfield MSS, LC.

23. Whitelaw Reid to Richard Smith, December 9, 1865, Reid MSS, LC; Francis A. Richardson, "Recollections of a Washington Newspaper Correspondent," *Records of the Columbia Historical Society* 6 (Washington, 1903): 25; George Alfred Townsend, "Recollections and Reflections," *Lippincott's Magazine* 38 (November 1886): 522. The weekly salary rarely translated into $2,500 a year; editors paid only while there was material to report, generally that half year during which Congress was in session.

24. See press gallery list, *Congressional Directories*, 41st Cong., 1st sess. (1870), 43d Cong., 1st sess. (1874); "Bueno Buro," New York *Citizen*, April 20, 1867; Raleigh *Sentinel*, January 4, 1874; "Creighton," Washington *Chronicle*, April 26, 1875; "L. S.," Cincinnati *Commercial*, August 17, 1874. For salaries, see Townsend, "Recollections and Reflections," 522, and Richardson, "Recollections," 19–20.

25. Boynton to Whitelaw Reid, February 4, 1874, Reid MSS, LC.

26. Zebulon L. White to Whitelaw Reid, November 19, 26, 1870, October 23, 1874, Richard Smith to Reid, May 31, 1869, June 13, 1877, Reid MSS, LC.

27. Whitelaw Reid to William Henry Smith, July 28 [no year], Joseph Barrett to Smith, January 17, 1868, Smith MSS, OHS; Ben: Perley Poore to William W. Clapp, December 1, 1868, Clapp MSS, LC; John T. Morse, ed., *Diary of Gideon Welles* (Boston: Houghton Mifflin, 1910), 3:475 (December 5, 1868); Ritchie, *Press Gallery*, 80–81; Washington *Evening Star*, November 29, December 6, 1870.

28. Cincinnati *Commercial*, February 1, 1873 (quotation); Zebulon L. White to Whitelaw Reid, November 26, 1870, Reid MSS, LC; Harry J. Brown and Frederick D. Williams, eds., *Diary of James A. Garfield* (East Lansing: Michigan State University Press, 1973), 3:210 (January 4, 1876).

29. See New York *Tribune*, February 18, 1867; Sidney Andrews to Whitelaw Reid, November 11, 1869, Reid MSS, LC; Ben: Perley Poore to William Warland Clapp, March 2, 1876, Clapp MSS, LC; Ritchie, *Press Gallery*, 89–90.

30. See White's obituary, New York *Tribune*, January 12, 1889; "H. L. B.," Springfield *Republican*, May 25, 1871; "Creighton," Washington *Chronicle*, April 26, 1875.

31. Zebulon L. White to Whitelaw Reid, November 19, 26, 1870, Reid MSS, LC.

32. Ramsdell's obituary, New York *Tribune*, May 26, 1887; Washington *Post*, May 26, 1887; Zebulon L. White to Whitelaw Reid, March 6, 1873, Reid MSS, LC.

33. Zebulon L. White to Whitelaw Reid, November 19, 26, 1870, March 6, 1873, Hiram J. Ramsdell to Reid, March 16, 1873, Reid MSS, LC; Reid to Murat Halstead, May 9, 1872, Halstead MSS, CHS; "Creighton," Washington *Chronicle*, April 26, 1875 (quotation).

34. Dane to William Henry Smith, November 28, 1870, W. H. Smith MSS, ISL (first and second quotations); Hiram J. Ramsdell to Whitelaw Reid, December 28, 1870, September 21, 1872, Zebulon L. White to Reid, January 10, 1873 (third quotation), November 21, 1874, Reid MSS, LC.

35. White to Whitelaw Reid, May 11, 1871, Reid MSS, LC. Adams's account of the events on Monday night differ slightly. See Senate Report 5, "Treaty Investigation," 42d Cong., special sess., 12–13.

36. Ritchie, *Press Gallery*, 75–77, 90–91. For the illusion of further clarity on how the treaty was obtained, see Hamilton Fish Diary, May 13, 1871, Fish MSS, LC.

37. House Report 268, "Pacific Mail," 43d Cong., 2d sess., 12; Henry V. Boynton to Whitelaw Reid, February 4, 1874, Zebulon L. White to Reid, February 2, 1874, Reid MSS, LC.

38. Ben: Perley Poore to William W. Clapp, March 13, 1877, Clapp MSS, LC; "Laertes," New York *Graphic*, March 18, 1876; *Nation*, August 12, 1869.

39. James Parton, "Falsehood in the Daily Press," *Harper's Magazine*, July 1874, 277.

40. New York *Graphic*, February 25, 1876.

41. Charleston *Courier*, May 22, 1871; Henry V. Boynton to Whitelaw Reid, February 9, 1869, Reid MSS, LC; "D. P.," Cincinnati *Commercial*, November 8, 1869 (quotation).

CHAPTER SEVEN

1. Subsequent verses are from the same source. Townsend recalled writing the poem in 1869 or 1870.

2. "Bueno Buro," New York *Citizen*, February 2, 1867; Washington *Sunday Capital*, May 17, 1874; "Gath," Cincinnati *Enquirer*, April 27, 1877; Schuyler Colfax to J. Russell Young, April 29, 1868, Young MSS, LC.

3. S. M. Shoemaker to William E. Chandler, April 24, 1871, Grenville M. Dodge to Chandler, April 30, 1871, Jay Gould to Chandler, January 15, 1875, John Roach to Uriah H. Painter, February 1, 1875, Chandler MSS, NHHS; Thomas A. Scott to Painter, March 25, November 22–23, 1867, April 5, 1869, James F. Wilson to Painter, April 19, 1872, Painter Family MSS, HSP; "A Bedouin," Cincinnati *Commercial*, August 9, 1869 (quotation). For a fair summary of Painter's career, see Donald A. Ritchie, *Press Gallery: Congress and the Washington Correspondents* (Cambridge: Harvard University Press, 1991), 92–112.

4. Jay Cooke to Henry D. Cooke, December 15, 1870, December 18, 1871, Cooke MSS, HSP.

5. Cincinnati *Enquirer*, February 9, 1869, April 27, 1877; "A Bedouin," Cincinnati *Commercial*, August 9, 1869. For more on how that shakedown worked, see New York *Herald*, January 4, 1870.

6. New York *Sun*, November 30, December 9, 15, 1868; New York *Herald*, December 15, 24, 1868; Paul S. Holbo, *Tarnished Expansion: The Alaska Scandal, the Press, and Congress, 1867–1871* (Knoxville: University of Tennessee Press, 1983), 45–58 (quotation, p. 54).

7. Holbo, *Tarnished Expansion*, 41–47; House Report 35, "Alaska," 40th Cong., 3d sess., 39.

8. William W. Harding to Uriah H. Painter, May 11, July 9, 1868, Henry D. Cooke to Painter, March 21, 1868, Thomas A. Scott to Painter, April 7, May 11, 15, 19, 21, 1868, Painter Family MSS, HSP; Francis A. Richardson, "Recollections of a Washington Newspaper Correspondent," *Records of the Columbia Historical Society* 6 (Washington, 1903): 38.

9. New York *Times*, February 10, 1869; "Sigma," Cincinnati *Commercial*, August 9, 1869; Henry V. Boynton to Whitelaw Reid, February 9, 1869, Reid MSS, LC (quotation); "Gath," Chicago *Tribune*, February 6, 25, 1869.

10. Cincinnati *Gazette*, January 23, 1875.

11. James Parton, "The Pressure Upon Congress," *Atlantic Monthly* 25 (February 1870): 157; "A Bedouin" (quotation) and "Sigma," Cincinnati *Commercial*, August 9, 1869.

12. By implication, W. M. Grosvenor to Edward Atkinson, March 1, 1872, Atkinson MSS, MHS; New York *Tribune*, January 10, 1876.

13. H. V. Boynton to Whitelaw Reid, February 9, 1869, Reid MSS, LC; Richardson, "Recollections," 37–38; "Bueno Buro," New York *Citizen*, February 2, 1867; "A Bedouin," Cincinnati *Commercial*, August 9, 1869; Cincinnati *Commercial*, March 21, 1873.

14. Grenville M. Dodge to William E. Chandler, April 12, 1874, John Roach to Chandler, September 29, 1874, W. E. Chandler MSS, LC; W. B. Shaw testimony, House Report 248, "Pacific Mail," 43d Cong., 2d sess., 372.

15. Senate Miscellaneous Document 85, 45th Cong., 2d sess., 345, 376; H. C. Fahnestock to Jay Cooke, March 24, 1871, George B. Sargent to Jay Cooke, May 12, 1870, Henry D. Cooke to Jay Cooke, January 12, December 1, 19, 1871, Jay Cooke to Henry D. Cooke, March 3, 1866, Cooke MSS, HSP.

16. "Pickaway," Cincinnati *Enquirer*, February 8, 1875; Ben C. Truman to Whitelaw Reid, February 2, 1880, Reid MSS, LC.

17. Charleston *News and Courier*, October 16, 1869; Raleigh *Sentinel*, January 26, 1876.

18. T. C. Grey to Benjamin F. Butler, March 28, 1870, Butler MSS, LC (first quotation); Henry D. Cooke to Jay Cooke, February 14, 24, 1868, Cooke MSS, HSP; H. V. Boynton to Whitelaw Reid, February 9, 1869, Reid MSS, LC (second quotation).

19. "Creighton," Washington *Chronicle*, April 26, 1875 (residence); "Bueno Buro," New York *Citizen*, February 2, 1867 (looks and kindness); Henry D. Cooke to Jay Cooke, February 2, 1871, Cooke MSS, HSP; House Report 268, "Pacific Mail," 43d Cong., 2d sess., 371–75; T. C. Grey to Benjamin F. Butler, March 28, 1870, Butler MSS, LC; New York *Herald*, January 4, 1870 (Painter "fixed"). Shaw's explanation for the payment was unsatisfactory, but journalists offered another: it was widely believed that he had pretended to sell their friendship as well as his own. See "Gideon," Chicago *Times*, January 16, 1875.

20. Margaret A. Clapp, *Forgotten First Citizen: John Bigelow* (Boston: Little, Brown, 1947), 264; *Congressional Record*, 43d Cong., 1st sess. (March 20, 1874); H. C. Fahnestock to Jay Cooke, March 3, 1871, Cooke MSS, HSP (quotation). A similar practice existed in French journalism. See Theodore Zeldin, *France, 1848–1945: Taste & Corruption* (New York: Oxford University Press, 1980), 172–73.

21. J. S. Moore to Benjamin H. Bristow, 1875, Bristow MSS, LC; *Nation*, September 2, 1869 (quotation); H. C. Fahnestock to Jay Cooke, March 3, 1871, Schuyler Colfax to Jay Cooke, February 24, 1871, Cooke MSS, HSP.

22. Chicago *Tribune*, February 8, 1869; Senate Miscellaneous Document 85, 45th Cong., 2d sess., 344–45; Elizabeth Studley Nathans, *Losing the Peace: Georgia Republicans and Reconstruction, 1865–1871* (Baton Rouge: Louisiana State University Press, 1968), 188–89; "Dixon," Boston *Daily Advertiser*, April 19, May 20, 1870. For other suspicions of Forney, see New York *Herald*, January 5, 1869.

23. Candace Stone, *Dana and the Sun* (New York: Dodd, Mead, 1938), 390–91; "Iniquitous Journalism," Chicago *Times*, April 15, 1876.

24. "H. R.," Cincinnati *Gazette*, January 23, 1875; H. C. Fahnestock to Jay Cooke, June 4, 1870, March 3, 1871, Cooke MSS, HSP.

25. Jno. H. Bryant to Samuel J. Randall, October 2, 1875, Randall MSS, UP. The *Enquirer* had some justification in championing the Pennsylvania Railroad's interests. Its main rivals, the *Whig* and the *Dispatch*, spoke for Tom Scott's arch-enemies, William Mahone's railroad network and the Chesapeake & Ohio Railroad. For the railroad battles in Virginia politics, see Jack P. Maddex, Jr., *The Virginia Conservatives, 1867–1879: A Study in Reconstruction Politics* (Chapel Hill: University of North Carolina Press, 1970), 98, 150–60, and Nelson M. Blake, *William Mahone of Virginia: Soldier and Political Insurgent* (Richmond: Garrett & Massie, 1935), 112.

26. "Pickaway," Cincinnati *Enquirer*, February 23, 1875; Cincinnati *Gazette*, February 18, 1878; New York *Graphic*, October 12, 1874, June 5, 1875; George T. McJimsey, *Genteel Partisan: Manton Marble, 1834–1917* (Ames: Iowa State University Press, 1971), 180–81.

27. Henrietta Larson, *Jay Cooke: Private Banker* (Cambridge: Harvard University Press, 1936), 254–91; Eugene V. Smalley, *History of the Northern Pacific Railroad* (New York: G. P. Putnam's Sons, 1883), 204 (first quotation); John F.

Stover, *American Railroads* (Chicago: University of Chicago Press, 1961), 76 (second quotation).

28. H. C. Fahnestock to George C. Thomas, May 22, 1869, Jay Cooke MSS, HSP.

29. Henry D. Cooke to Jay Cooke, February 27, March 14, 24, 1870, Jay Cooke to Henry Cooke, March 12, April 23, 1870, Cooke MSS, HSP. For the persistent problem of the *Ledger*, see Ellis J. Oberholtzer, *Jay Cooke: Financier of the Civil War* (Philadelphia: G. W. Jacobs, 1907), 1:546–47, 2:189–92.

30. R. C. Mitchell to Jay Cooke, May 5, 1870, Sam Wilkeson to Cooke, November 2, 1870, A. B. Nettleton to Cooke, December 20, 1871 (quotation), Cooke MSS, HSP.

31. Oberholtzer, *Jay Cooke*, 584–85; H. C. Fahnestock to Jay Cooke, May 10, 1870, Cooke MSS, HSP.

32. H. C. Fahnestock to Jay Cooke, May 10, 1870, John Russell Young to Jay Cooke, February 17, 1871, Pitt Cooke to Jay Cooke, February 10, 1872, Cooke MSS, HSP.

33. Jay Cooke to Uriah H. Painter, March 25, 1869, Painter Family MSS, HSP; "Gath," Chicago *Tribune*, February 8, 1869 (quotation), March 15, 1872; Samuel Wilkeson to Jay Cooke, March 5, May 6, 1870, Cooke MSS, HSP.

34. J. T. Trowbridge to Whitelaw Reid, September 7, 1869, Sam Wilkeson to Reid, January 7, 11–12, 1870, Reid MSS, LC; Wilkeson to Jay Cooke, November 2, 1870, Jay Cooke to Henry D. Cooke, May 6, 1870 (quotation), William J. King to Sam Wilkeson, May 6, 1870, Cooke MSS, HSP; Jay Cooke to Uriah H. Painter, May 17, 1870, Painter Family MSS, HSP.

35. Samuel Wilkeson to Jay Cooke, March 3, 1869, March 5, 14, April 15, May 23–24, 28 (quotation), 1870, Cooke MSS, HSP.

36. John Russell Young to Jay Cooke, February 17, 1871, Sam Wilkeson to Cooke, March 22, 1870, Cooke MSS, HSP; Larson, *Jay Cooke*, 328–58.

37. Sam Wilkeson to Whitelaw Reid, December 6, 1870, Reid MSS, LC.

38. Larson, *Jay Cooke*, 343; New York *Independent*, April 6, May 4, 1871; New York *Graphic*, October 9, 1874; H. C. Fahnestock to Jay Cooke, June 4, 1870, Cooke MSS, HSP.

39. George B. Sargent to Jay Cooke, June 18, 20, 1870, H. C. Fahnestock to Cooke, June 17, 1870, A. B. Nettleton to Cooke, November 30, 1869, April 3, 1871, Henry D. Cooke to Jay Cooke, January 12, 1871 (quotation), Jay Cooke to Henry D. Cooke, December 14, 1871, Cooke MSS, HSP. On the campaign to win the *Herald*, see Pitt Cooke to Jay Cooke, February 1, 10, 1872, Henry D. Cooke to Jay Cooke, February 7, 1872, and H. B. Hanmore to Cooke, February 6, 1872, Cooke MSS. For the two references to Boynton, see A. B. Nettleton to Jay Cooke, December 13, 1871, and Henry D. Cooke to Jay Cooke, December 7, 1871, Cooke MSS.

40. Chicago *Times*, June 7, 10, 1870; Springfield *Republican*, January 31, February 1, April 18, 1871. See also New York *World*, February 8, 1871. An even more curious case of perfect bad timing was Sidney Andrews ("Dixon") of the Boston *Daily Advertiser*. Starting on May 30, 1870, he published three long, devastating

essays on the land grant mania, with particular attention to the Northern Pacific bill ("impudent . . . to the last degree," "a deliberate swindle on the public and the government, cloaked in speculation and conceived in fraudulent assumption," with one provision never before put into a land grant bill that was "such as the public ought never to let Congress put into another"). This was the first inkling readers would have of Andrews's distaste for the Northern Pacific bill, which until then was mentioned rarely, briefly, and in language oblique enough to mean one of two mutually exclusive things. The bill had had its final passage four days before.

41. Cincinnati *Gazette*, October 11, 14, 1873; Samuel Wilkeson to Whitelaw Reid, January 25, 27, 1873, Zebulon L. White to Reid, January 27, 1873, Reid MSS, LC.

42. Jay Cooke to Henry D. Cooke, February 1, 1872, H. B. Hanmore to Jay Cooke, February 6, 1872, Henry D. Cooke to Jay Cooke, February 7, 1872, Pitt Cooke to Jay Cooke, February 10, 1872, Cooke MSS, HSP.

43. Caleb Cushing to Hamilton Fish, November 26, 1875, Fish MSS, LC; Chicago *Times*, June 20, 1870; Sam Wilkeson to Jay Cooke, May 6, 1870, Cooke MSS, HSP.

44. *Nation*, September 2, 1869; Jno. M. Carmack to Andrew Johnson, September 26, 1874, Johnson MSS, LC. For other suspicions, see Hiram Calkins to Manton Marble, April 19, 1868, Marble MSS, LC.

45. *Tribune* quoted in New York *World*, January 21, 1869.

46. Cincinnati *Commercial*, March 21, 1873.

47. F. B. Marbut, *News from the Capital: The Story of Washington Reporting* (Carbondale: Southern Illinois University Press, 1971), 153–56; Ritchie, *Press Gallery*, 108–10. A similar certification process occurred simultaneously in Great Britain, but there it was used as the political means of controlling reporters' access to public figures. See Stephen Koss, *The Rise and Fall of the Political Press in Britain: The Nineteenth Century* (Chapel Hill: University of North Carolina Press, 1981), 238–39.

48. Ritchie, *Press Gallery*, 120–21, 145–46, 159–62; N. G. Gonzales to Emmie, February 19, 1882, Elliott-Gonzales MSS, SHC.

49. Marvin N. Olasky, "The Development of Corporate Public Relations, 1850–1930," *Journalism Monographs* 102 (April 1987): 4–15; Linda Lawson, "Advertisements Masquerading as News in Turn-of-the-Century American Periodicals," *American Journalism* 5 (1982): 81–96; Hugh McCulloch to H. H. Van Dyck, March 18, 1866, McCulloch Letter-Books, LL/IU. The "reading notice" was not uniquely American. See Zeldin, *France*, 164–70.

CHAPTER EIGHT

1. House Report 24, "William A. McGarrahan," 41st Cong., 3d sess.; "H. V. B.," Cincinnati *Gazette*, February 1, 1869.

2. New York *Times*, April 25, 1894.

3. Washington *Sunday Capital*, June 17, 1877, March 17, April 7, 14, 28, 1878; "D. P.," Cincinnati *Enquirer*, August 9, September 18, 1877; Donn Piatt in New York *Times*, March 10, 1879; Geoffrey Bret Harte, ed., *Letters of Bret Harte* (Boston: Houghton Mifflin, 1926), 55–59.

4. Cincinnati *Enquirer*, February 27, 1879; Washington *Post*, February 27–28, 1879.

5. Cincinnati *Enquirer*, February 28, 1879.

6. "H. C.," New York *Times*, March 9, 1879 (Cox's quotation); Donn Piatt in ibid., March 10, 1879; Washington *Sunday Capital*, March 2, 1879; Washington *Post*, February 28, 1879; Rollin H. Kirk, *Many Secrets Revealed; or, Ten Years Behind the Scenes at Washington City* (Washington, D.C.: N.p., 1885), 18–20.

7. Charles F. Wingate, *Views and Interviews on Journalism* (New York: F. B. Patterson, 1875), 20 (first quotation); "T. R.," Cincinnati *Commercial*, April 3, 1869 (second quotation); New York *Times*, November 16, 1891; Patrick D. Morrow, *Bret Harte: Literary Critic* (Bowling Green: State University Popular Press, 1979), 91; George R. Stewart, *Bret Harte: Argonaut and Exile* (New York: Houghton Mifflin, 1931), 239–41. The muddle of Piatts can be traced to Harte, *Letters of Bret Harte*, 55, which also assumes the *"Capitol"* to be a magazine just being founded in 1877.

8. Cincinnati *Enquirer*, July 30, 1876; "M. C. A.," New York *Independent*, January 4, 1872; Indianapolis *News*, July 4, 1874; "H. J. R.," Cincinnati *Commercial*, January 17, 1874.

9. Cincinnati *Enquirer*, July 30, 1876. For Piatt's immediate postwar career, see Piatt to William Henry Smith, January 17, July 13 [1867], October 28, 1867, January 9–10, 1868; Smith to Piatt, July 26, 1867, Smith MSS, OHS; Piatt to Robert C. Schenck, January 26, February 28, 1866, Schenck MSS, OHS; and Piatt to J. M. Comly, September 16, 1867, April 22, 1868, Comly MSS, OHS. The only life of Piatt remains Charles Grant Miller, *Donn Piatt: His Work and His Ways* (Cincinnati: Robert Clarke & Co., 1893).

10. Cincinnati *Enquirer*, July 30, 1876; "D. P.," ibid., August 20, 1876; Donn Piatt to Murat Halstead, November 23, 1869, December 10, 1878, Halstead MSS, CHS; Piatt to Whitelaw Reid, n.d. [probably 1870 or 1871], May 30, 1871, Reid MSS, LC; Piatt to James A. Garfield, June 18, 1869, Garfield MSS, LC.

11. "D. P.," Cincinnati *Commercial*, December 21–22, 1869.

12. "D. P.," ibid., January 17, February 4, 1870; Springfield *Republican*, January 3, 1871; Washington *Sunday Capital*, December 10, 1871, December 10, 1876, February 4, 1877. The frivolous style was not Piatt's invention, though he would be so credited. See Frank L. Mott, "Facetious News Writing, 1833–1883," *Mississippi Valley Historical Review* 29 (June 1942): 52–53.

13. "D. P.," Cincinnati *Commercial*, February 13, 1870; Washington *Sunday Capital*, December 7, 1873; Cincinnati *Enquirer*, August 5, 1876.

14. Piatt to Whitelaw Reid, n.d. [early 1871], Reid MSS, LC (first quota-

tion); Raleigh *Sentinel*, January 4, 1874; Cincinnati *Gazette*, March 4, 1878 (second quotation); Springfield *Republican*, June 15, 1871; "Gath," Chicago *Tribune*, March 15, 1872.

15. Donn Piatt to George Alfred Townsend, April 5, 1880, Piatt MSS, HML; Piatt to J. M. Comly, February 5, 1872, Comly MSS, OHS; Miller, *Donn Piatt*, 225–27. For the general level of journalistic dullness in Washington, see Washington *Post*, December 7, 1877—or, for that matter, any issue of the Washington *National Republican*.

16. Washington *Sunday Capital*, February 2, 1873; Chicago *Times*, April 26, 1876; Cincinnati *Enquirer*, March 10, 1877; *Harper's Weekly*, March 17, 1877, p. 201.

17. Miller, *Donn Piatt*, 263–64, 271–72; Cincinnati *Enquirer*, August 13, October 12, 1877; New York *Herald*, January 9, 1873. The Italian minister, Count Corti, denied that he had ever sent a formal challenge, though, said the *Herald*'s correspondent, Piatt bought himself an old muzzle-loading gun and practiced in the backyard, to the terror of his whole neighborhood.

18. Donn Piatt to George Alfred Townsend, April 5, 1880, Piatt MSS, HML; "D. P.," Cincinnati *Enquirer*, January 3, April 7, 1877 (Catacazy's quotation); Washington *Sunday Capital*, December 10, 1871. For the full story of the Cat-Fish War, see Allan Nevins, *Hamilton Fish: The Inner History of the Grant Administration* (New York: Dodd, Mead, 1935), 503–11.

19. Miller, *Donn Piatt*, 212–13, 217–23.

20. The quotation was an accusation from a Western newspaper that the *Capital* repudiated. See Washington *Sunday Capital*, August 16, 1874.

21. Washington *Sunday Capital*, June 18, 1871, March 16, 1873 (quotation).

22. "D. P.," Cincinnati *Enquirer*, August 20, 1876.

23. "D. P.," Cincinnati *Commercial*, January 28 (Dickey), February 14, 17, June 21 (Butler), 1870; Washington *Sunday Capital*, March 9, 1872 ("machine," committee quotations), March 2, 1873.

24. Washington *Sunday Capital*, November 28, 1875; or see ibid., February 2, 1873, July 30, 1876.

25. Washington *Sunday Capital*, May 17, 1874; New York *Herald*, February 8, 1875; Augusta *Constitutionalist*, March 29, 1876.

26. Washington *Sunday Capital*, December 20, 1874, July 18, 1875.

27. Ibid., January 31, 1875.

28. Ibid., August 16, 1874; Washington *Post*, January 8, 1878.

29. Washington *Sunday Capital*, September 6, October 11 (quotation), December 20, 1874.

30. F. A. Simkins to James A. Garfield, February 17, 1874, Garfield MSS, LC; Ari Hoogenboom, *Outlawing the Spoils: A History of the Civil Service Reform Movement, 1865–1883* (Urbana: University of Illinois Press, 1961), 102–5, 130–32; Morton Keller, *Affairs of State* (Cambridge: Belknap Press of Harvard University Press, 1977), 243–45.

31. On Dawes, see George F. Hoar, *Recollections of Seventy Years* (New York: Scribner, 1903), 232; *Nation*, July 2, 1874; "M. C. A.," New York *Independent*, February 25, 1869; and "D. P.," Cincinnati *Enquirer*, January 29, 1878. On Sherman, see H. Wayne Morgan, *From Hayes to McKinley: National Party Politics, 1877–1896* (Syracuse: Syracuse University Press, 1969), 40–43; Washington *Sunday Capital*, March 9, 1872; and "D. P.," Cincinnati *Enquirer*, March 9, December 26, 1877. On Foster, see "H. V. B.," Cincinnati *Gazette*, May 26, 1874, and "D. P.," Cincinnati *Enquirer*, March 24, 1877.

32. Cincinnati *Commercial*, March 14, 1870.

33. Washington *Sunday Capital*, July 30, 1876, March 4, 25, 1877; Washington *New National Era*, February 13, 1873, April 9, 1874. For the clearest expression of Piatt's own nostalgic views toward slavery, see *Capital*, December 22, 1878.

34. Miller, *Donn Piatt*, 260 (Kelley's response); William D. Kelley to William Cullen Bryant, February 11, 1873, Kelley MSS, HSP; Ira V. Brown, "William D. Kelley," *Pennsylvania Magazine of History and Biography* 85 (July 1961): 316–18. On Kelley's relationship with his daughter, see Ray Ginger, *Altgeld's America: The Lincoln Ideal Versus Changing Realities* (New York: Funk & Wagnalls, 1958), 113–16.

35. Cincinnati *Gazette*, January 29, 1870; "Van," Springfield *Republican*, December 14, 1871; "Gideon," Chicago *Times*, May 14, 1874.

36. Chicago *Times*, May 16, 1870; Donn Piatt to Whitelaw Reid, May 10, 1872, Reid MSS, LC.

37. Donn Piatt to Caleb B. Smith, June 9, 1861, Piatt MSS, OHS (quotation); "D. P.," Cincinnati *Commercial*, December 4, 1869, February 5, July 4, 1870; Piatt to Whitelaw Reid, April 1, 1871, Reid MSS, LC; Washington *Sunday Capital*, December 10, 1871; House Report 579, "Emma Mine Investigation," 44th Cong., 1st sess., i–xiii.

38. Peter J. Sullivan letter, Cincinnati *Commercial*, September 22, 1869; "Donn Felix," Cincinnati *Times*, June 12, 1858; Donn Piatt to William Henry Smith, August 5, 1867, December 25, 1868 (quotation), February 22, 1869, Whitelaw Reid to Smith, April 1, 1869, Smith MSS, OHS.

39. "G. G.," New York *Tribune*, April 9, 1870 (quotation); Washington *Sunday Capital*, March 15, 1874; Hans L. Trefousse, *Carl Schurz: A Biography* (Knoxville: University of Tennessee Press, 1982), 240–48.

40. Senate Miscellaneous Document 85, 45th Cong., 2d sess., 375, 377; "D. P.," Cincinnati *Commercial*, February 24, March 4, 17, 1871; Washington *Sunday Capital*, March 26, 1871; Eugene D. Schmiel, "The Career of Jacob Dolson Cox, 1828–1900: Soldier, Scholar, Statesman" (Ph.D. diss., Ohio State University, 1969), 266–67.

41. Washington *Daily Morning Chronicle*, January 27, 1875; Donn Piatt to James A. Garfield, January 12, 1871, Garfield MSS, LC; "D. P.," Cincinnati *Enquirer*, September 2, 1876; Harte, *Letters of Bret Harte*, 58–62.

42. Donn Piatt to James A. Garfield, July 20, 1872, August 4, 7, 29, 1874, Gar-

field MSS, LC; House Report 799, "Management of the War Department: Testimony Regarding the Contracts with Cowles and Brega," 44th Cong., 1st sess., 423, 433–35, 441–46, 454–55.

43. Donn Piatt to Alexander R. Shepherd, October 20, 1873, Shepherd MSS, LC; "H. R.," Cincinnati *Gazette*, January 11, 1875; Washington *Sunday Capital*, June 21, 1874; Whitelaw Reid to Zebulon L. White, April 9–10, 21, May 2, 1873, Reid MSS, LC.

44. Washington *Sunday Capital*, February 18, 1872. Quotation from *Congressional Globe*, appendix, 42d Cong., 3d sess., 71 (February 11, 1873).

45. New York *Times*, April 10, May 6, 1874.

46. N. G. Ordway to William E. Chandler, May 11, 1873, William E. Chandler MSS, NHHS; Washington *Post*, April 15, 1878. For similar allegations, see Washington *Chronicle*, November 24, 1875.

47. The most notable examples of word pictures are in "M. C. A.," New York *Independent*, March 29, 1866, March 26, 1868.

48. James L. Crouthamel, *Bennett's New York Herald and the Rise of the Popular Press* (Syracuse: Syracuse University Press, 1989), 28–32; George Juergens, *Joseph Pulitzer and the New York World* (Princeton: Princeton University Press, 1966), 43–92; Warren Francke, "Sensationalism and the Development of Nineteenth-Century Reporting: The Broom Sweeps Sensory Details," *Journalism History* 12 (Winter–Autumn 1985): 80–85.

49. Springfield *Republican*, January 11, 1862; "M. C. A.," New York *Independent*, June 18, 1868.

50. "G. G.," New York *Tribune*, January 20, 1870; "M. C. A.," New York *Independent*, May 3, 1866, April 2, 1868; "Gath," Chicago *Tribune*, February 15, 1869, February 14, 1870; Cincinnati *Enquirer*, January 14, March 15, 1878; Milwaukee *News*, April 7, 1874.

51. Thomas Nast to Orville E. Babcock, March 15, 1873, Babcock MSS, Newberry Library, Chicago; George P. Burnham to Benjamin F. Butler, April 7, 1874, Butler MSS, LC; Chicago *Times*, May 12, 1874. For contemporary discussion on the bounds within which caricature—Nast's in particular—ought to operate, see New York *Evening Post*, July 27, 1872; *Woman's Journal*, May 4, 1872; and New York *Tribune*, May 21, 1874. Morton Keller, *The Art and Politics of Thomas Nast* (New York: Oxford University Press, 1968), gives the best introduction to Nast's contribution.

52. "Gath," Chicago *Tribune*, January 29, June 7, December 3, 1870

53. "Gath," on Justin Morrill, Chicago *Tribune*, May 19, 1870.

54. "M. C. A.," New York *Independent*, May 3, 1866, January 23, 1868; "Gath," New York *Graphic*, February 26, 1876.

55. "Gath," Chicago *Tribune*, April 6, 1874; "H. V. B.," Cincinnati *Gazette*, April 3, 1869; "M. C. A.," New York *Independent*, April 25, 1872, June 18, 1874.

56. Donn Piatt to George Alfred Townsend, April 5, 1880, Piatt MSS, HML.

57. See, for example, Edward F. Noyes to William Henry Smith, March 2, 1867, Smith MSS, OHS.

CHAPTER NINE

1. Richard W. Thompson to his son, December 29, 1860, Thompson MSS, LL/ IU.

2. Glyndon G. Van Deusen, *Horace Greeley: Nineteenth-Century Crusader* (Philadelphia: University of Pennsylvania Press, 1953), 201; Richard Yates to John D. Strong, November 6, 1867, Strong MSS, ISHS. For other antebellum set-tos, see "Ezek Richards," Philadelphia *Press*, January 21, 1860; "Videx," Sacramento *Union*, February 9, 1860; William English letter, Washington *Union*, May 8, 1858.

3. "The End of Orator Mum," *Harper's Weekly*, February 14, 1874; Washington *Star*, March 14, 1875.

4. Washington *Chronicle*, January 21, 1876; "D. P.," Cincinnati *Enquirer*, June 1, 1877

5. Chicago *Times*, March 14 (quotation), 30, 1876; New York *Herald*, March 7, 9, 1876; New York *Tribune*, March 17, 20, 1876.

6. James G. Blaine to Murat Halstead, December 31, 1873, Halstead MSS, CHS.

7. On Wade, see "Gath," Chicago *Tribune*, February 9, 1869; on Julian, see George W. Julian to William Henry Smith, March 19, 1868, Smith MSS, OHS; Oliver P. Morton to Murat Halstead, March 10, 1867, Halstead MSS, CHS; James A. Garfield to Harmon Austin, February 23, 1871, Garfield MSS, LC; and "H. V. B.," Cincinnati *Gazette*, March 14, 1870.

8. *Nation*, January 28, 1869. Often, however, politicians botched the job. See "Earnest," Boston *Commonwealth*, March 28, 1868.

9. "D. P.," Cincinnati *Enquirer*, June 1, 1877; "H. V. B.," Cincinnati *Gazette*, December 1869–January 1870.

10. Cincinnati *Gazette*, April 28, 1869; Chicago *Times*, March 30–31, 1876.

11. Carl Schurz to Murat Halstead, September 29, 1866, Halstead MS, CHS; H. J. Ramsdell to Whitelaw Reid, December 28, 1870, Reid MSS, LC.

12. Peter Karberg to William Boyd Allison, February 20, 1874, Horace White to Allison, July 20, 1874, Allison MSS, ISDAH; George Bliss to Edwin D. Morgan, May 26, 1866, Morgan MSS, NYSL.

13. Archibald Gordon to Henry Clay Warmoth, March 8, 1873, Warmoth MSS, SHC; William Bross to Richard J. Oglesby, August 20, 1866, Oglesby MSS, ISHS.

14. James M. Ashley to William Henry Smith, March 21, 1868, Smith MSS, OHS; Springfield *Republican*, January 2, June 15, 1871; Henry V. Boynton to General A. H. Markland, July 25 [no year], July 2, 1874, Boynton MSS, OHS; Washington *Chronicle*, March 20, December 12, 1874, March 12, 1875.

15. Joseph P. McKerns, "Benjamin Perley Poore of the *Boston Journal*: His Life and Times as a Washington Correspondent, 1850–1887" (Ph.D. diss., University of Minnesota, 1979), 41, 138–41.

16. Ramsdell to Whitelaw Reid, August 28, 1877, Reid MSS, LC; Washington *Post*, October 31, 1881, May 26, 1887; Senate Executive Journal, October 27, 1881, 154, 157.

17. Washington *Chronicle*, January 10, 1876.

18. New York *Herald*, January 2, 1872; Springfield *Republican*, January 2, March 16, 1871.

19. Francis A. Richardson, "Recollections of a Washington Newspaper Correspondent," *Records of the Columbia Historical Society* 6 (Washington, 1903): 27.

20. "Laertes," New York *Graphic*, March 4, 1876; Ben: Perley Poore to R. G. Usher, September 1, 1873, Butler MSS, LC; *Nation*, July 29, 1869.

21. Ben: Perley Poore to R. G. Usher, September 1, 1873, Butler MSS, LC; McKerns, "Benjamin Perley Poore," 144–46; Springfield *Republican*, March 16, August 16, 1871; "Gideon," Chicago *Times*, March 6, 1874; Washington *Chronicle*, July 3, 1874; "Creighton," Washington *Chronicle*, April 26, 1875; Harry J. Brown and Frederick D. Williams, eds., *Diary of James A. Garfield* (East Lansing: Michigan State University Press, 1973), 2:65 (June 15, 1872); Ben: Perley Poore, "Washington News," *Harper's Magazine* 48 (January 1874): 230.

22. Henry Van Ness Boynton, "The Press and Public Men," *Century Magazine* (October 1891): 856.

23. "Gath," New York *Graphic*, December 27, 1876.

24. New York *Tribune*, May 10, 1867; "Mack," Cincinnati *Commercial*, January 19, 1866.

25. Cincinnati *Enquirer*, February 1, 4, 19, 1875.

26. Schuyler Colfax to ———, August 7, 1867, Colfax MSS, LL/IU; Colfax to Whitelaw Reid, September 9, 1870, July 13, 1871, Reid MSS, LC; Donald A. Ritchie, *Press Gallery: Congress and the Washington Correspondents* (Cambridge: Harvard University Press, 1991); "Earnest," Boston *Commonwealth*, April 4, 1868.

27. "M. C. A.," New York *Independent*, April 19, 1866, January 23, February 6, 1868; Schuyler Colfax to Murat Halstead, February 11, 1872, Halstead MSS, CHS; Colfax to Mary Clemmer Ames, June 24, 1872, October 30, 1872, Ames MSS, HML; Colfax to Edward McPherson, August 24, 1872, McPherson MSS, LC.

28. Richard H. Abbott, *Cobbler in Congress: The Life of Henry Wilson, 1812–1875* (Lexington: University Press of Kentucky, 1972), 241–42; "D. P.," Cincinnati *Enquirer*, June 1, 1877.

29. Grenville M. Dodge to William E. Chandler, January 11, 1872, W. E. Chandler MSS, LC; Schuyler Colfax to Mary Clemmer Ames, June 24, 1872, Ames MSS, HML; Blanche Ames Ames, ed., *Chronicles from the Nineteenth Century: Family Letters of Blanche Butler and Adelbert Ames* (Clinton, Mass.: Colonial Press, 1957), 1:361.

30. Mark W. Summers, *The Era of Good Stealings* (New York: Oxford University Press, 1992), 50–54.

31. Abbott, *Cobbler in Congress*, 247–48.

32. O. J. Hollister, *Life of Schuyler Colfax* (New York: Funk & Wagnalls, 1886), 404–6; Schuyler Colfax to Mary Clemmer Ames, October 30, 1874, Colfax to editor, Hartford *Post*, April 3, 1875, Ames MSS, HML; New York *Herald*, January 24–25, 1873.

33. For Blaine's cultivation of the press, see Ritchie, *Press Gallery*, 131–40; "M. C. A.," New York *Independent*, February 25, 1869; Zebulon L. White to Whitelaw Reid, January 7, 1873, Reid MSS, LC; "Gideon," Chicago *Times*, March 6, 1874; Eugene Casserly to Manton Marble, May 6, 1876, Marble MSS, LC; Carl Schurz to Samuel Bowles, January 4, 1876, Bowles MSS, SML/YU.

34. *Debates of the Convention to Award the Constitution of Pennsylvania*, 9 vols. (Harrisburg: B. Singerly, 1873), 8:319–25; New York *Herald*, September 17, 1871 (quotation).

35. Charles Grant Miller, *Donn Piatt: His Work and His Ways* (Cincinnati: Robert Clarke & Co., 1893), 337–39.

36. Roscoe Conkling to Edwards Pierrepont, December 12, 1871, Pierrepont MSS, SML/YU; Thomas F. Bayard to Manton Marble, August 24, 1875, Marble MSS, LC; William D. Kelley to Carrie Kelley, February 7, 1873, Kelley MSS, HSP; Hugh McCulloch to H. H. Van Dyck, May 25, June 16–17, 1868, McCulloch to George O. Glavis, July 30, 1868 (quotation), McCulloch to John M. McGinniss, June 26, 1868, McCulloch Letter-Books, LL/IU.

37. "Beadle," Cincinnati *Commercial*, February 16, 1874; Cincinnati *Commercial*, April 30, 1874.

38. Cincinnati *Enquirer*, February 12, 19, March 12, 1875; "H. V. B.," Cincinnati *Gazette*, November 1, 6, 1869; "D. P.," Cincinnati *Commercial*, November 8, 1869.

39. Cincinnati *Enquirer*, January 13, 16, 1877; "D. P.," ibid., March 9, 1877.

40. "Warrington," Springfield *Republican*, September 15, 1871; Boston *Commonwealth*, January 11, 1873; New York *Herald*, January 9, 1873; New York *Tribune*, February 11, 1874; Henry V. Boynton to Whitelaw Reid, February 9, 1869, Reid MSS, LC.

41. New York *Times*, April 8, 1874; New York *Graphic*, February 15, May 2, 1876.

42. New York *Graphic*, February 29 (quotation), March 11, 15, 1876; *R. H. Gove v. H. K. Blethen*, 21 Minn. 80, 18 Am. St. Rep. 380; *Talbutt v. Clark*, 2 Moody and Rob. 312; *Perrett v. New Orleans Times*, 25 La. An. 170; *Cass v. New Orleans Times*, 27 La. An. 214; *Castle v. Houston*, 17 Kan. 417; *Rearick v. Wilcox*, 81 Ill. 77. For a full discussion of the general trend and the cases following, see John Proffatt, "The Law of Newspaper Libel," *North American Review* 131 (January 1880): 109–27.

43. Pomeroy also published a booklet that had "a perfectly immense circulation" out West, accusing Butler, as general, of having arrested women and stripped them naked to see if they were secreting jewelry on or in their person. "The manner of conducting these examinations our pen cannot for shame record," the editor added. Perhaps the shame came from knowing that the charges were pure fiction. H. C. Martyn to Benjamin F. Butler, August 29, 1868 (quotation), Arthur D. Collins to Butler, August 13, 1868, Butler to Collins, August 15, 1868, Butler MSS, LC.

44. LaCrosse *Democrat*, September 8, 1866; H. C. Martyn to Benjamin F. Butler, August 29, 1868, Butler MSS, LC; William V. Crenshaw, "Benjamin F. Butler:

Philosophy and Politics, 1866–1879" (Ph.D. diss., University of Georgia, 1976), 203–5, 219–23; *Nation,* April 27, 1871.

45. Springfield *Republican,* August 25, 1871.

46. For the congressman's political career, see William D. Mallam, "General Benjamin Franklin Butler: A Critical Study" (Ph.D. diss., University of Minnesota, 1942)." But note, too, Summers, *Era of Good Stealings,* 6–7, 14–15, 174–77.

47. Springfield *Republican,* August 25, 1871. Butler's account was true but misleading in what it left out. See Stephen B. Oates, *To Purge This Land with Blood: A Biography of John Brown* (New York: Harper & Row, 1970), 181–87, 229–40, 314–16, 341.

48. New York *Herald,* August 25, 28, September 20, 1871; Mallam, "Benjamin Franklin Butler," 232–35.

49. Baltimore *Sun,* July 13, 1874; Chicago *Times,* July 10, 1870.

CHAPTER TEN

1. Donn Piatt to James A. Garfield, August 29, 1874, Garfield MSS, LC. A similar analysis appears in "M. C. A.," New York *Independent,* May 10, 1866.

2. For the definitive study of Garfield's character and life, see Allan Peskin, *Garfield* (Kent State: Kent State University Press, 1978).

3. James D. Norris and Arthur H. Shaffer, *Politics and Patronage in the Gilded Age: The Correspondence of James A. Garfield and Charles E. Henry* (Madison: State Historical Society of Wisconsin, 1970), 47 (quotation), 49, 64, 89, 230–32; Harry J. Brown and Frederick D. Williams, eds., *Diary of James A. Garfield* (East Lansing: Michigan State University Press, 1973), 2:165 (March 28, 1873).

4. Norris and Shaffer, *Politics and Patronage,* 71–72, 112, 230–32 (quotation, p. 230).

5. Ibid., 210, 212.

6. Ibid., 103, 211.

7. Norris and Shaffer, *Politics and Patronage,* 57, 62, 89, 105.

8. Ibid., 137–38; W. C. Howells to Garfield, February 18, 1874, Garfield MSS, LC.

9. Brown and Williams, *Diary of James A. Garfield,* 2:165 (March 28, 1873), 176 (May 7, 1873).

10. Garfield to F. H. Mason, March 2, 1871, Garfield MSS, LC; Brown and Williams, *Diary of James A. Garfield,* 2:65 (June 15, 1872), 234 (October 17, 1873), 235 (October 18, 1873), 3:29 (February 22, 1875), 32–33 (February 28, 1875), 56 (April 7, 1875), 123 (August 3, 1875), 241 (February 28, 1876), 340 (August 24, 1876), 400 (December 21, 1876), 425 (January 28, 1877), 508 (August 24, 1877), 549 (December 2, 1877).

11. Brown and Williams, *Diary of James A. Garfield,* 2:163 (March 23, 1873), 230 (October 7, 1873), 339 (June 21, 1874), 396 (November 30, 1874), 3:45 (March 22, 1875), 433 (February 18, 1877).

12. Ibid., 3:252 (March 13, 1876), 338 (August 23, 1876), 380–81 (November 12–13, 1876), 508 (August 24, 1877).

13. Garfield to New York *Tribune* editor, August 10, 1868, September 27, 1870, Garfield to *World* editor, August 10, 1868, Garfield to *Nation* editor, January 9, 11, February 22, 1871, Garfield MSS, LC.

14. Norris and Shaffer, *Politics and Patronage*, 30, 50, 89; Brown and Williams, *Diary of James A. Garfield*, 3:341 (August 29, 1876), 4:111 (September 1, 1878).

15. Garfield to Whitelaw Reid, June 16, 1869, April 4, 1870, Garfield to Joseph Medill, August 8, 1868, Garfield to Richard Smith, May 15, 1868, Garfield to James A. Briggs, July 29, 1870, Garfield to E. L. Godkin, January 16, 1871 (quotation), Garfield MSS, LC.

16. Garfield to Horace White, March 29, 1869, Garfield to John W. Forney, March 8, 1870, Garfield to Horace Greeley, July 16, 1868, A. W. Campbell to Garfield, January 26, 1874, W. P. Spencer to Garfield, February 6, 1874, Garfield MSS, LC; Brown and Williams, *Diary of James A. Garfield*, 2:260 (December 13, 1873), 3:549 (December 1, 1877).

17. Joseph Medill to Garfield, April 9, 1872, Frank H. Mason to Garfield, May 21, 1872, February 6, 1874, A. W. Campbell to Garfield, January 26, 1874, Richard Smith to Garfield, September 27, 1874, Garfield to Medill, January 11, 1870, Garfield to Charles Nordhoff, June 10, 1870, Garfield to Horace Greeley, March 14, 1871, Garfield MSS, LC.

18. Norris and Shaffer, *Politics and Patronage*, 65; Brown and Williams, *Diary of James A. Garfield*, 2:231 (October 10, 1873), 3:204 (December 20, 1875), 255 (March 18, 1876); James M. Comly to Garfield, January 18, December 31, 1872, Samuel Bowles to Garfield, March 23, 1873, E. L. Godkin to Garfield, January 9, 1877, Eugene V. Smalley to Garfield, February 21, 1872, Garfield MSS, LC.

19. Norris and Shaffer, *Politics and Patronage*, 213, 217.

20. Brown and Williams, *Diary of James A. Garfield*, 3:64 (April 21, 1875), 324 (July 14, 1876), 375 (November 3, 1876), 397 (December 18, 1876), 401 (January 3, 1877); Charles A. Dana to Garfield, January 24, 1870, Whitelaw Reid to Garfield, April 5, 1870, Halsey R. W. Hall to Garfield, June 7, 19, 1871, J. O. Converse to Garfield, January 20, 1874, J. Q. A. Campbell to Garfield, February 21, 1874, Garfield MSS, LC.

21. Garfield to Joseph Medill, December 29, 1869, June 28, 1870, December 9, 1871 (quotation), Garfield to Horace White, April 7, 1869, Medill to Garfield, March 1, 1870, Garfield to Charles Nordhoff, January 19, 1871, Nordhoff to Garfield, June 6, 1870, Garfield MSS, LC.

22. Brown and Williams, *Diary of James A. Garfield*, 2:96 (September 28, 1872), 3:138 (August 31, 1875), 380–81 (November 12, 1876); Norris and Shaffer, *Politics and Patronage*, 218.

23. James M. Comly to Garfield, February 12, 1874, Garfield MSS, LC; Cincinnati *Commercial*, April 19, 1874; Brown and Williams, *Diary of James A. Garfield*, 3:277 (April 23, 1876), 353 (September 18, 1876), 507 (August 20, 1877); Washington *Post*, March 23, 1878.

24. Norris and Shaffer, *Politics and Patronage*, 114, 116; Brown and Williams, *Diary of James A. Garfield*, 2:184 (May 23, 1873).

25. Brown and Williams, *Diary of James A. Garfield*, 2:27 (March 7, 1872), 40 (April 9, 1872), 43 (April 19, 1872), 120 (December 1, 1872), 132 (January 1, 1873), 153 (February 17, 1873), 158 (March 5, 1873), 177 (May 9, 1873), 178 (May 10, 1873), 190 (June 8, 1873), 306 (March 30, 1874), 247 (November 19, 1873), 249 (November 24, 1873), 280 (January 20, 1874), 316 (April 24, 1874), 336 (June 14, 1874), 398–99 (December 4, 1874), 401 (December 8, 1874), 404 (December 15, 1874), 411 (December 27, 30, 1874); 3:25 (February 14, 1875), 58 (April 11, 1875), 227 (February 3, 1876), 228 (February 6, 1876), 263 (March 31, 1876).

26. "D. P.," Cincinnati *Enquirer*, March 9, 1877; Washington *Sunday Capital*, February 25, 1877, March 17, 1878.

27. J. H. Scofield to Garfield, February 6, 1874, Garfield MSS, LC.

28. Brown and Williams, *Diary of James A. Garfield*, 4:80 (June 9, 1878); Mary Hinsdale, ed., *Correspondence between James Abram Garfield and Burke Hinsdale* (Ann Arbor: University of Michigan Press, 1949), 267, 294–95; Norris and Shaffer, *Politics and Patronage*, 121, 139, 233, 235; Garfield to F. H. Mason, February 23, 1871, Garfield to J. H. Rhodes, February 24, 28, 1871, Garfield to J. W. Mack, February 28, 1871, Rhodes to Garfield, December 7, 1871, Garfield MSS, LC.

29. "H. V. B.," Cincinnati *Gazette*, April 18, 1871; "Gath," Chicago *Tribune*, February 23, 1874; "Gath," New York *Graphic*, October 19, 1877; poem in Brown and Williams, *Diary of James A. Garfield*, 2:314 (April 18, 1874); Hinsdale, *Correspondence between James Abram Garfield and Burke Hinsdale*, 286–87.

30. Peskin, *Garfield*, 366–67.

31. Hinsdale, *Correspondence between James Abram Garfield and Burke Hinsdale*, 238–39, 243, 248–49, 252; Garfield to James M. Comly, May 20, 1873, Comly MSS, OHS; Norris and Shaffer, *Politics and Patronage*, 116, 213, 217; Henry to Garfield, January 19, 1874, Garfield MSS, LC (quotation).

32. Brown and Williams, *Diary of James A. Garfield*, 2:166–67 (April 2, 1873), 168 (April 6, 1873); Cincinnati *Commercial*, March 31, April 5, 1873; Washington *Sunday Capital*, January 25, 1873, August 30, 1874. For his private efforts with other journalists, see Piatt to Friedrich Hassaurek, February 8, 1873, Hassaurek MSS, OHS.

33. Norris and Shaffer, *Politics and Patronage*, 90, 92, 94, 103; W. C. Howells to Garfield, February 18, 1874, Garfield MSS, LC.

34. Henry V. Boynton to Garfield, June 7, 1873, Whitelaw Reid to Garfield, January 21, April 5, December 13, 16, 28, 1870, May 30, June 9, 1872, December 30, 1874, Garfield to Reid, June 16, November 12, 1869, April 4, July 9, December 15, 1870, Garfield MSS, LC; Brown and Williams, *Diary of James A. Garfield*, 4:42 (March 24, 1878).

35. Hinsdale, *Correspondence between James Abram Garfield and Burke Hinsdale*, 238; Whitelaw Reid to Garfield, March 11 (quotation), May 18, 20, 1873, Donn Piatt to Garfield, April 17, 1873, Garfield MSS, LC.

36. Peskin, *Garfield*, 370–71; Samuel Bowles to David A. Wells, November 3, 1873, Garfield MSS, LC (quotation); New York *Tribune*, December 1, 6, 1873; New York *Sun*, December 1, 1873; New York *Times*, December 1, 1873.

37. *Commercial* quoted in Washington *Post*, March 23, 1878.

CHAPTER ELEVEN

1. Springfield *Republican*, January 6–7, 14, 1871.

2. Charles A. Dana to Uriah H. Painter, February 5, 1870, March 3, 13, April 10, 1871, Painter Family MSS, HSP. Dana was right. See Hamilton Fish Diary, December 5, 20, 1870, May 29, 1871, Fish MSS, LC.

3. Henry Van Ness Boynton, "The Press and Public Men," *Contury Magazine* 42 (October 1891): 861; "H. J. R.," Cincinnati *Commercial*, 1871.

4. Springfield *Republican*, March 13, 1869; *Nation*, May 6, 1869; *Harper's Weekly*, March 20, 1869; New York *Tribune*, March 7, 8, 1869.

5. "H. V. R.," Cincinnati *Commercial*, September 30, December 18, 1871.

6. Amos Akerman to Scroggs, January 3, 1872, Amos Akerman Letter-Books, UV; John J. Creswell to Zachariah Chandler, September 9, 1869, Z. Chandler MSS, LC.

7. "D. P.," Cincinnati *Commercial*, March 17, July 13, 1870. For other slurs on Hoar, see "D. P.," Cincinnati *Enquirer*, August 20, 1876; "Cass," Charleston *Daily Republican*, January 17, 1870.

8. "M. C. A.," New York *Independent*, May 16, 1872; "D. P.," Cincinnati *Commercial*, March 14, 1870. See also Henry Adams, "The Session," *North American Review* 111 (July 1870): 32.

9. The best study of Grant's presidency remains William Hesseltine, *Ulysses S. Grant: Politician* (New York: Dodd, Mead, 1935), though see also William S. McFeely, *Grant* (New York: Norton, 1981). For an excellent study of his Southern policy, see William Gillette, *Retreat from Reconstruction, 1869–1879* (Baton Rouge: Louisiana State University, 1979). The ablest study of the British diplomacy is Adrian Cook, *The Alabama Claims, American Politics, and Anglo-American Relations, 1865–1872* (Ithaca: Cornell University Press, 1975). For an evaluation of Grant as politician and the role of corruption, see also Mark W. Summers, *The Era of Good Stealings* (New York: Oxford University Press, 1992), 180–99.

10. See, for example, Mobile *Register*, December 7, 1876.

11. "D. P.," Cincinnati *Enquirer*, January 13, 1877 (quotation); "Van," Springfield *Republican*, January 5, February 3, November 23, 1871.

12. Chicago *Tribune*, April 9, 1869, February 22, 1872; Hamilton Fish Diary, May 19, 1871, Fish MSS, LC; Portland *Eastern Argus*, May 16, 1874; Springfield *Republican*, April 21, 1874.

13. R. W. Clarke to William Henry Smith, July 6, 1869, William Henry Smith

to Richard Smith, December 23, 1871, Smith MSS, OHS; Springfield *Republican*, January 4, 1871; "Van," Springfield *Republican*, January 13, 1871.

14. Raleigh *Sentinel*, February 18, 1876; Peoria *Daily National Democrat*, January 3, 5, 1872; New York *Pomeroy's Democrat*, February 16, 1870. See also Concord *New Hampshire Patriot*, January 10, 1872, and Savannah *Morning News*, August 29, 1876.

15. New York *Herald*, January 28, 1869; Boston *Evening Transcript*, March 5, 1869; William M. Evarts to Edwards Pierrepont, February 7, 1869, Pierrepont MSS, SML/YU. In fact, Grant did leak his real intentions to the New York *Tribune*. See Whitelaw Reid to William Henry Smith, March 9, 1869, Smith MSS, OHS.

16. Harry J. Brown and Frederick D. Williams, eds., *Diary of James A. Garfield* (East Lansing: Michigan State University Press, 1973), 2:17 (February 10, 1872).

17. Irwin Unger, *The Inflation Era: A Social and Political History of American Finance* (Princeton, N.J.: Princeton University Press, 1964), 245–46; New York *Herald*, April 2–4, 23, June 6, 8, 1874.

18. "H. V. R.," Cincinnati *Commercial*, December 18, 1871.

19. "H. V. R.," ibid., December 18, 1871; "W. J. A.," ibid., October 25, 1869.

20. "Gath," Chicago *Tribune*, April 1, 1872; "Gath," New York *Graphic*, February 29, 1876.

21. Washington *Evening Star*, November 22, 1870; New York *Sun*, September 8, 1871. For Louisiana troubles, see Joseph G. Dawson III, *Army Generals and Reconstruction Louisiana, 1862–1877* (Baton Rouge: Louisiana State University, 1982), 108–12, and Henry Clay Warmoth, *War, Politics, and Reconstruction: Stormy Days in Louisiana* (New York: Macmillan, 1930), 112–25.

22. Amos Akerman to Atkins, December 12, 1871, Akerman Letter-Books, UV; Springfield *Republican*, January 3, 1876. For Akerman's dismissal, see Allan Nevins, *Hamilton Fish: The Inner History of the Grant Administration* (New York: Dodd, Mead, 1935), 591–92.

23. "Gideon," March 11, 26, 1874; "Magnificent Mistakes," *Harper's Weekly*, December 12, 1874; "H. J. R.," Cincinnati *Commercial*, August 28, 1871; "Carlos," Mobile *Register*, April 3, 1875.

24. Hamilton Fish to Whitelaw Reid, December 22, 1873, Charles Nordhoff to Fish, June 27, 1871, Fish to John W. Forney, October 16, 1869, Sidney Webster to Fish, December 6, 1871, Fish to L. A. Gobright, March 2, 1872, Fish to Jennings, November 19, 1872, March 3, 1875, Jennings to Fish, March 16, 1875, Fish MSS, LC. The sinister relationship of Webster, Fish, and the *World* gets unsettling ventilation in James Burke Chapin, "Hamilton Fish and American Expansion" (Ph.D. diss., Cornell University, 1971), 276–91.

25. H. J. Ramsdell to Whitelaw Reid, September 21, November 9, 1873, Zebulon L. White to Reid, November 21, 1874, Reid MSS, LC.

26. Henry Van Ness Boynton to Whitelaw Reid, October 26, 1874, Z. L. White to Reid, November 21, 1874, Reid MSS, LC; New York *Sun*, December 13, 1871;

"D. P.," Cincinnati *Commercial,* February 6, 1871; "Gath," Cincinnati *Enquirer,* May 10, 1877.

27. Nevins, *Hamilton Fish,* 587, 722–30.

28. Ben: Perley Poore, *Perley's Reminiscences of Sixty Years in the National Metropolis* (Philadelphia: Hubbard Brothers, 1886), 2:258; New York *World,* April 10, 1870; "H. V. R.," Cincinnati *Commercial,* December 18, 1871. "D. P.," in the Cincinnati *Commercial* of February 18, 1870, declared that Grant was allowed to see only the Washington *Chronicle* and Cincinnati *Chronicle,* though at some past time he had read the *World* as well. But his claim that the president was being kept from all reading matter by General Dent is as dubious as most of Donn Piatt's stories and should not be taken seriously. One paper that Grant did *not* read was the New York *Herald,* and he resented the leaks from cabinet members to it. See Ulysses S. Grant to Hamilton Fish, July 14, 1875, Fish MSS, LC.

29. James E. Pollard, *The Presidents and the Press* (New York: Macmillan, 1947), 444–45; New York *Times,* January 7, 1881; Cincinnati *Enquirer,* August 25, 1877 (quotation); New York *Sun,* September 8, 1871; Nevins, *Hamilton Fish,* 658.

30. Charles A. Dana to Uriah H. Painter, December 6, 1870, Painter Family MSS, HSP; New York *Times,* September 3, 1872.

31. "Gideon," Chicago *Times,* February 25, March 6, 1874; Chicago *Tribune,* March 4, 1874; "W. G. T.," Louisville *Courier-Journal,* April 18, 1874; New York *Sun,* April 12, 1875; Cincinnati *Enquirer,* December 1, 1876.

32. New York *Times,* August 8, 10, 1877; Henry V. Boynton to Benjamin H. Bristow, August 5, 1877, Bristow MSS, LC.

33. Washington *Sunday Capital,* March 16, 1873; "D. P.," Cincinnati *Enquirer,* August 13, October 12, 1877; Orville E. Babcock to Hamilton Fish, January 9, 1871, Fish MSS, LC.

34. Henry Van Ness Boynton to Whitelaw Reid, April 25, 1875, Reid MSS, LC; Nevins, *Hamilton Fish,* 2:773–76; Ulysses S. Grant to Hamilton Fish, September 10, 1875, Fish MSS, LC; "H. V. B.," Cincinnati *Gazette,* May 5, October 18, 1875.

35. Cincinnati *Commercial,* May 29, July 17, 1869, February 18, 1870 ("D. P."), January 3, 1874 (quotation); "M. C. A.," New York *Independent,* January 29, 1874.

36. Hamilton Fish Diary, January 13, 1871, Fish MSS, LC; Oliver P. Morton to Murat Halstead, January 15, 1871, Halstead MSS, CHS; Zebulon L. White to Whitelaw Reid, January 17, 1871, Reid MSS, LC; "D. P.," Cincinnati *Commercial,* January 19, 1871; Springfield *Republican,* January 16–17, 1871. Grant's annexation designs are in Charles C. Tansill, *The United States and Santo Domingo, 1789–1873: A Chapter in Caribbean Diplomacy* (Baltimore: Johns Hopkins, 1938), 338–464.

37. Zebulon L. White to Whitelaw Reid, November 28, 1871, Reid MSS, LC; "D. P.," Cincinnati *Commercial,* January 13, February 5, 1871. This does not mean that Fish never planned to retire and then reconsidered; the event simply happened months after Piatt reported it. See Nevins, *Hamilton Fish,* 494–97, 513–17.

38. New York *Times*, December 15, 1873.

39. Candace Stone, *Dana and the Sun* (New York: Dodd, Mead, 1938), 385–87; New York *Times*, December 8, 1871; John Russell Young to Hamilton Fish, November 14, 1870, Fish MSS, LC.

40. "Van," Springfield *Republican*, March 10, 1871; "D. P.," Cincinnati *Commercial*, March 8, 1871; Cleveland *Plain Dealer*, August 29, 1872; Washington *Sunday Capital*, March 12, 1871; Atlanta *Constitution*, January 6, 1875.

41. Benjamin B. French to Pamela French, October 29, 1867, French MSS, LC: Jay Cooke to Henry D. Cooke, April 27, 1871, Cooke MSS, HSP; House Report 502, "Freedman's Bank," 44th Cong., 1st sess., 24–29.

42. "Gath," Chicago *Tribune*, November 19, 1870; Eugene D. Schmiel, "The Career of Jacob Dolson Cox, 1828–1900: Soldier, Scholar, Statesman" (Ph.D. diss., Ohio State University, 1969), 269–83; H. B. Whipple to Jacob D. Cox, September 20, 1870, Manning F. Force to Cox, October 10, 1870, Cox MSS, Oberlin College; Cox to James A. Garfield, October 24, Garfield MSS, LC.

43. Summers, *Era of Good Stealings*, 194–96; *Nation*, October 20, 27, 1870; New York *Tribune*, October 15, 17, 1870; New York *Herald*, October 15, 1870; "Gath," Chicago *Tribune*, October 22, 1870; Horace Porter to Zachariah Chandler, October 13, 1870, Z. Chandler MSS, LC.

44. Crounse of the New York *Times* and J. Russell Young of the *Standard*. Memorandum in Henry Van Ness Boynton's handwriting, October 1870, Cox MSS, Oberlin College.

45. New York *Herald*, October 18, 26, 1870; William A. McGarrahan to F. Franck, October 28, 1870, in Senate Miscellaneous Document 85, "The McGarrahan Claim," 45th Cong., 2d sess., 373–74; Charles Cox to Jacob D. Cox, October 26, 1870, Cox MSS, Oberlin College; Cox to Garfield, December 6, 1870, Garfield MSS, LC.

46. Jacob D. Cox to James A. Garfield, December 9, 1870, Garfield MSS, LC; Charles Cox to Jacob D. Cox, November 1, 1870, Henry V. Boynton to Cox, November 1, 1870, Charles Nordhoff to Cox, November 3, 1870, Cox MSS, Oberlin College; "H. V. B.," Chicago *Tribune*, October 30–31, 1870; New York *Herald*, October 31, 1870; *Nation*, November 3, 1870.

47. New York *Herald*, November 1, 1870; Henry V. Boynton to Jacob D. Cox, November 4, 1870, Cox MSS, Oberlin College.

48. "Gath," Chicago *Tribune*, November 19, 1870; Donn Piatt to Whitelaw Reid, January 24, 1871, Reid MSS, LC; Charles Cox to Jacob D. Cox, November 1, 1870, Henry V. Boynton to Jacob D. Cox, November 2, 1870, Cox MSS, Oberlin College.

49. Boynton to Cox, November 15, 1870, Cox MSS, Oberlin College.

50. Boynton to Cox, November 4, 7, 1870, Cox MSS, Oberlin College.

51. New York *Tribune*, November 10, 1870; Henry V. Boynton to Jacob D. Cox, November 1–2, 4, 24 (quotations), 1870, Charles Cox to Jacob D. Cox, November 3, 1870, Francis A. Walker to Cox, November 3, 1870, Cox MSS, Oberlin College; William A. McGarrahan to F. Franck, November 6, 15, 1870, in Sen-

ate Miscellaneous Document 85, 45th Cong., 2d sess., 375–76; New York *Herald*, November 5, 1870.

52. Henry V. Boynton to Jacob D. Cox, November 7, 13, 15, 1870, Cox MSS, Oberlin College.

53. Charles Cox to Jacob D. Cox, November 1, 4–5, 1870, Cox MSS, Oberlin College. See also *Nation*, November 17, 24, 1870.

54. John M. Harlan to Benjamin H. Bristow, November 20, 1870, Bristow MSS, LC; Ebenezer R. Hoar to Jacob D. Cox, November 13, 1870, Boynton to Cox, November 1, 4, 1870, Charles Nordhoff to Cox, January 16, 1871, Cox MSS, Oberlin College.

55. Allan Nevins and Milton H. Thomas, eds., *The Diary of George Templeton Strong* (New York: Macmillan, 1952), 4:411 (January 25, 1872).

56. Daniel Manning to Nahum Capen, November 11, 1873, David B. Hill MSS, NYSL.

57. Henry V. Boynton to Jacob D. Cox, November 4, 15, 1870, Charles Cox to Jacob D. Cox, November 12, 1870, Cox MSS, Oberlin College; Cox to James A. Garfield, December 9, 1870, Garfield MSS, LC.

58. "Gath," Cincinnati *Enquirer*, March 5, 1877.

CHAPTER TWELVE

1. "H. V. R.," Cincinnati *Commercial*, March 6, 1871. For similar views on Clayton, see "Troy," Chicago *Tribune*, August 20, 1872; "Gath," Chicago *Tribune*, October 15, 1872.

2. Horace White to George A. Townsend, January 27, 1873, September 5, 1874, White MSS, ISHS; John Forsyth to Manton Marble, January 29, 1871, Marble MSS, LC; Henry F. Keenan to Whitelaw Reid, March 16, 1871, Reid MSS, LC; Charleston *Courier*, April 28, 29, May 4, 8, 17, 22, 1871; Memphis *Daily Avalanche*, October 13, 1874.

3. James Shepherd Pike, *The Prostrate State: South Carolina under Negro Government* (New York: D. Appleton & Co., 1874), 28–30.

4. Charles Nordhoff, *The Cotton States in the Spring and Summer of 1875* (New York: Appleton & Co., 1876), 41–63; Springfield *Republican*, April 5, 1871; "H. V. R.," Cincinnati *Commercial*, March 3, September 30, 1871; House Miscellaneous Report 211, 42d Cong., 2d sess., 368.

5. Springfield *Republican*, April 5, 1871; "Gath," Chicago *Tribune*, December 31, 1872; Richard Current, *Those Terrible Carpetbaggers* (New York: Oxford University Press, 1987), 243–44; Henry Clay Warmoth to J. Q. A. Fellows, May 9, 11, 1872, Fellows to Warmoth, May 10–11, 1872, Warmoth MSS, SHC; "H. V. R.," Cincinnati *Commercial*, November 9, 1871.

6. "E. K.," Springfield *Republican*, February 27, 1869; Forrest G. Wood, *Black Scare: The Racist Response to Emancipation and Reconstruction* (Berkeley: Uni-

versity of California Press, 1970), 133–35; Jean H. Baker, *Affairs of Party: The Political Culture of Northern Democrats in the Mid-Nineteenth Century* (Ithaca: Cornell University Press, 1983), 212–58.

7. New York *Times*, July 8, 1876; Springfield *Republican*, February 27, 1871; "Finch," Springfield *Republican*, January 4, April 18, 1871; New York *Tribune*, July 28, 1874; Nordhoff, *Cotton States*, 21–22, 97; "Gath," Chicago *Tribune*, January 2, 1872; Chicago *Tribune*, December 31, 1872.

8. "H. W. R.," New York *Times*, May 22, 1871; "H. V. R.," Cincinnati *Commercial*, July 27, 29 (quotation), 31, 1874. See also "Occasional," New York *Sun*, September 14, 1875.

9. See, for example, "H. V. R.," Cincinnati *Commercial*, July 31, 1874; "Z. L. W.," New York *Tribune*, October 15, November 14, 1874; Springfield *Republican*, September 1, 1871; "L. Q. W.," Chicago *Tribune*, July 25, 1872 (quotation); "H. C.," New York *Times*, November 4–5, 1874.

10. "H. V. R.," Cincinnati *Commercial*, September 18, 1871; "H. C.," New York *Times*, November 14, 1874; New York *Sun*, September 11, 1875; Washington *New National Era*, January 8, 1874; Nordhoff, *Cotton States*, 99.

11. House Report 262, "Affairs in Alabama," 43d Cong., 2d sess., minority rept., 56–57; Washington *Chronicle*, October 29, 1874 (*Times* quotation); Clipping from *Oregonian*, September 1, 1885, John Sherman MSS, LC.

12. New York *Times*, May 22, 1871; Springfield *Republican*, April 18, 1871; "L. Q. W.," Chicago *Tribune*, July 24, 1872; "H. V. R.," Cincinnati *Commercial*, January 2, 1873; "Z. L. W.," New York *Tribune*, November 7, 1874; Nordhoff, *Cotton States*, 92, 97, 100.

13. Robert F. Durden, *James Shepherd Pike: Republicanism and the American Negro, 1850–1882* (Durham: Duke University Press, 1957), 200–219; Pike, *Prostrate State*, 87–88. Pike's journey began in late January 1873. He remained in South Carolina until mid-March. The articles appeared in the *Tribune* on March 29, April 8, 10–12, 19, 1873. Pike's biographer suggests that in spite of their South Carolina dateline, Pike's letters were written only after his return to the North.

14. "L. Q. W.," Chicago *Tribune*, July 30, 1872; "Troy," ibid., August 20, 1872; George Alfred Townsend to Whitelaw Reid, May 14, 1872, James Redpath to Reid, March 24, 1877, Reid MSS, LC.

15. Charles Nordhoff to Whitelaw Reid, April 14, 1875, Reid MSS, LC; New York *Graphic*, April 10, 1875 (quotation); Washington *Chronicle*, May 26, June 2, 13, 1875. For Nordhoff's sources, see James B. Murphy, *Lucius Q. C. Lamar: Pragmatic Patriot* (Baton Rouge: Louisiana State University Press, 1973), 156; Nordhoff to Frederick G. Bromberg, January 9, April 27, 1875, Frederick G. Bromberg MSS, SHC.

16. "H. V. R.," Cincinnati *Commercial*, February 23, 1871.

17. Zebulon L. White to Whitelaw Reid, March 6, 1873, Reid MSS, LC.

18. "Burt," Cincinnati *Commercial*, January 30, 1871; "H. C.," New York *Times*, November 5, 1874.

19. Nordhoff, *Cotton States*, 68–73, 78, 107–10; "E. K.," Springfield *Republi-*

can, July 3, 1869, "J. P.," Springfield *Republican*, September 27, 1871; Chicago *Tribune*, August 6, 1872.

20. The standard study of the Radical experiment is Eric Foner, *Reconstruction: America's Unfinished Revolution, 1865–1877* (New York: Harper & Row, 1988), 346–411; but see also Michael Wayne, *The Reshaping of Plantation Society: The Natchez District, 1860–1880* (Baton Rouge: Louisiana State University Press, 1983), 110–40, and Loren Schweninger, "Black Economic Reconstruction in the South," in Eric Anderson and Alfred A. Moss, Jr., eds., *The Facts of Reconstruction: Essays in Honor of John Hope Franklin* (Baton Rouge: Louisiana State University Press, 1991), 167–88.

21. Warren A. Elem, "Who Were the Mississippi Scalawags?," *Journal of Southern History* 38 (May 1972): 217–40; William C. Harris, "A Reconsideration of the Mississippi Scalawag," *Journal of Mississippi History* 32 (February 1970): 3–42; Carl Degler, *The Other South: Southern Dissenters in the Nineteenth Century* (New York: Harper & Row, 1974), 191–229.

22. Charleston *Courier*, May 4, 1871; Chicago *Tribune*, July 24 ("diabolical teachings"), 25 ("reign of terror"), August 20 ("iron despotism"), 1872; "Gar.," New York *Times*, November 6, 9, 1874. For the facts on the Klan's suppression, see Allen W. Trelease, *White Terror: The Ku Klux Klan Conspiracy and Southern Reconstruction* (New York: Harper & Row, 1971), 155–74, 182–83, 215–22, 399–418.

23. "Z. L. W.," New York *Tribune*, October 27, 1874; Washington *Chronicle*, October 29, 1874.

24. See Baltimore *Sun*, October 20, 1874.

25. "Francis," Mobile *Register*, March 23, 1875.

26. John G. Hassard to Whitelaw Reid, September 1, 18, 1874, Reid MSS, LC; Washington *Chronicle*, October 29, 1874; House Report 262, 43d Cong., 2d sess., "Affairs in Alabama," 1081–83.

27. House Report 262, "Affairs in Alabama," 1082.

28. New York *Tribune*, October 15, 17, November 7, 1874.

29. Ibid., October 17, November 7, 14, 1874.

30. New York *Times*, January 17, 1889.

31. Zebulon L. White to Reid, October 9, 1874, Reid MSS, LC.

32. New York *Tribune*, October 14, November 21, 1874; Sarah Van Voorhis Woolfolk, "The Role of the Scalawag in Alabama Reconstruction" (Ph.D. diss., Louisiana State University, 1965), 259–60. Similar conclusions appear in New York *Times*, November 4, 14, 1874, which is not surprising: White shared his information with the *Times*'s reporter. For a sharp challenge to White's analysis, see Philadelphia *North American*, October 12, 1874.

33. New York *Tribune*, November 7, 14, 1874.

34. New York *Times*, April 4, 1874; Cincinnati *Commercial*, August 11, 1874.

CHAPTER THIRTEEN

1. "H. V. R.," Cincinnati *Commercial*, September 30, 1874.

2. Cincinnati *Gazette*, February 3, 1875. According to the Chicago *Tribune* (July 5, 1872), one editor's columns were widely prized because they could be used for paperweights.

3. "H. V. R.," Cincinnati *Commercial*, March 3, 1871; New Orleans *Picayune*, November 29, December 31, 1875.

4. Joseph Medill to William Henry Smith, March 16, 1871, Smith MSS, OHS.

5. *Congressional Directory*, 41st Cong. (Washington: Government Printing Office, 1870), 121–22; W. G. F. Shanks, "How We Get Our News," *Harper's Magazine* 34 (March 1867): 516.

6. Raleigh *Sentinel*, March 9, 1876; New Orleans *Picayune*, October 10, 1876; Savannah *Morning News*, March 1, 22, 1876; Augusta *Constitutionalist*, January 2, 5, 11, April 25, 1876.

7. Mobile *Register*, January 15, 1870, February 5, 17, 1875. For complaints about distorted news from the North, see T. P. Robb to John D. Strong, August 10, 1867, Strong MSS, ISHS.

8. J. M. Tomeny to William E. Chandler, April 4, 1868, W. E. Chandler MSS, LC: Willard Warner to William Henry Smith, December 12, 18, 1868, Smith MSS, OHS; Petition to Adelbert Ames, January 6, 1870, Ames Family MSS, SC; "Plato," Cincinnati *Commercial*, November 1, 1869.

9. Cincinnati *Commercial*, March 3, 1871; Henry Lewis Suggs, ed., *The Black Press in the South, 1865–1879* (Westport, Conn.: Greenwood Press, 1983), 159.

10. George P. Rowell & Co., *American Newspaper Directory Containing Accurate Lists of All the Newspapers and Periodicals Published in the United States and Territories, and the Dominion of Canada and British Colonies of North America* (New York: Geo. P. Rowell & Co., 1872), 496.

11. Ibid.

12. See, for example, N. G. Gill to Adelbert Ames, February 10, 1870, Ames Family MSS, SC.

13. Rowell & Co., *American Newspaper Directory*, 525; "Plato," Cincinnati *Commercial*, November 1, 1869, December 4, 1871; Atlanta *Constitution*, January 7, 20, 1875; Jackson *Clarion Ledger*, July 19, 1888; Crystal Springs *Monitor*, January 13, 1876; Washington *Chronicle*, December 10, 1874; *The Journalist*, February 21, 1891.

14. William C. Harris, *The Day of the Carpetbagger: Republican Reconstruction in Mississippi* (Baton Rouge: Louisiana State University, 1979), 414.

15. A. T. Morgan to Adelbert Ames, May 17, 1870, O. C. French to Ames, April 17, 1870, Charles W. Clarke to Ames, April 17, 1870, E. Hill to Ames, April 19, 1870, Ames Family MSS, SC.

16. M. B. Sullivan to Adelbert Ames, December 2, 1873, Petition to Ames, January 6, 1870, William J. Davis to Ames, April 8, 1872, C. W. Clarke to Ames, April 17, 1870, O. S. Lee to Ames, May 8, 1870, Ames Family MSS, SC; New

Orleans *Picayune*, January 13, 1876; Ted Tunnell, *Crucible of Reconstruction: War, Radicalism, and Race Relations in Louisiana, 1862–1877* (Baton Rouge: Louisiana State University, 1984), 23–24.

17. Suggs, *Black Press in the South*, 93–94, 160–61, 178–79, 294–95.

18. "H. V. R.," Cincinnati *Commercial*, November 9, 1871; Alan Conway, *The Reconstruction of Georgia* (Minneapolis: University of Minnesota Press, 1966), 185; Mobile *Register*, January 8, 1870.

19. House Miscellaneous Document 211, 42d Cong., 2d sess., 368; House Report 92, 42d Cong., 2d sess., 21; Ella Lonn, *Reconstruction in Louisiana after 1868* (New York: G. P. Putnam, 1918), 87; "H. V. R.," Cincinnati *Commercial*, September 30, 1871.

20. Montgomery *Alabama State Journal*, February 24, 1874; Port Royal *Commercial and Beaufort Republican*, December 11, 25, 1873; E. Culpeper Clark, *Francis Warrington Dawson and the Politics of Restoration: South Carolina, 1874–1889* (University: University of Alabama Press, 1980), 73–75; Robert H. Henry, *Editors I Have Known Since the Civil War* (New Orleans: E. S. Upton, 1922), 89–90.

21. Port Royal *Commercial*, January 8, 15, 22, 1874.

22. John S. Reynolds, *Reconstruction in South Carolina* (Columbia: The State Co., 1905), 473–76; Port Royal *Commercial*, January 22, 29, 1874.

23. A. T. Morgan to Adelbert Ames, April 6, 1872, Ames Family MSS, SC.

24. Raleigh *Sentinel*, January 9, 22, 1874.

25. Ethelbert Hubbs to Edward McPherson, December 5, 1874, R. H. Selman to McPherson, December 5, 1874, Thomas A. Davis to McPherson, November 28, 1874, Henry J. Ridley to McPherson, October 12, 1874, James H. Platt to McPherson, June 21, 1874, J. M. Hogan to McPherson, December 8, 1874, C. D. Darnall to F. Morey, December 10, 1872, S. M. Yost to McPherson, December 12, 1874, H. A. Pierce to McPherson, August 8, 1872, Horace J. Harrison to McPherson, May 6, 1873, McPherson MSS, LC.

26. Rowell & Co., *American Newspaper Directory*, 499; Memphis *Daily Appeal*, August 24, 1873; Natchez *Daily Democrat*, July 23, 1874.

27. J. L. Wofford to Adelbert Ames, February 4, 1872, Ames Family MSS, SC.

28. Rowell & Co., *American Newspaper Directory*, 90; Memphis *Daily Appeal*, October 1873; C. H. Kirkendall to Adelbert Ames, May 5, 1871, George R. Cannon to Ames, April 15, 1873 (quotation), Ames Family MSS, SC.

29. "H. V. R.," Cincinnati *Commercial*, September 30, 1871.

30. Rowell & Co., *American Newspaper Directory* (1872), 11–13; P. Smith to William E. Chandler, June 17, 1872, Chandler MSS, NHHS.

31. Rowell & Co., *American Newspaper Directory*, 23 (quotation), 89–91, 287–91; Suggs, *Black Press in the South*, 293; "H. V. R.," Cincinnati *Commercial*, September 30, 1871; Emerson Bentley to Henry Clay Warmoth, July 16, 1871, Warmoth MSS, SHC; Amos Akerman to Henry A. Turner, November 14, 1871, Akerman Letter-Books, UV.

32. Suggs, *Black Press in the South*, 317–18; Cincinnati *Commercial*, Novem-

ber 1, December 4, 18, 1869. For the disastrous switchover of two Radical Republican presses, the Nashville *Press and Times* and the Knoxville *Whig*, see Cincinnati *Gazette*, June 11, 15, 17, 1869.

33. Peter P. Bailey to Adelbert Ames, April 2–3, 6, 8, 1872, Albert T. Morgan to Ames, April 6, 1872, Ames Family MSS, SC.

34. *Pilot* quoted in Crystal Springs *Monitor*, August 5, 1875.

35. See Emerson Bentley to Henry Clay Warmoth, July 16, 1871, Warmoth MSS, SHC; Raleigh *Daily Standard*, January 27, 31, 1870.

36. The story has all the makings of bad farce and remains to be told. A good indication of its twists can be found in J. C. Webber to Adelbert Ames, March 12, 1870, O. C. French to Ames, April 28, 1870, Horatio N. Ballard to Ames, April 30, 1870, C. F. Norris to Ames, May 4, 1870, E. Hill to Ames, May 7, 1870, R. G. W. Jewell to Ames, May 8, 1870, O. H. Crandall to Ames, May 8, 11, 1870, J. Tarbell to Ames, May 9, 1870, Charles W. Clarke to Ames, May 9, 1870, Peter C. Bailey to Ames, May 9, 11, 1870, February 3, 19, April 2–3, 1872, A. T. Morgan to Ames, May 17, 28, July 1, 1870, D. L. Andon to Ames, May 28, 1870, N. G. Gill to Ames, March 13, 1871, A. Lovering to Ames, May 23, 1871, W. S. Stannard to Ames, February 19, 1872, A. R. Howe to Ames, February 16, 1873, Ames Family MSS, SC; and Harris, *Day of the Carpetbagger*, 414–17.

37. J. G. Patrick to Adelbert Ames, December 9, 1873, Ames Family MSS, SC.

38. Mark W. Summers, *Railroads, Reconstruction, and the Gospel of Prosperity: Aid under the Radical Republicans, 1865–1877* (Princeton: Princeton University Press, 1984), 238–39; John Tyler, Jr., to Benjamin H. Bristow, January 2, 1875, Isaac Caldwell to Bristow, October 30, 1871, Bristow MSS, LC; Charleston *Daily Republican*, March 19, 1870; San Antonio *Express*, June 28, August 11, 1870, May 26, 1873; Houston *Union*, August 3, 1870.

39. Edward McPherson to Richard Yates, September 6, 1867, T. P. Robb to John D. Strong, May 20, October 2, 1867 (quotation), Strong MSS, ISHS; San Antonio *Express*, June 16, 1870.

40. Chicago *Tribune*, October 12, 15, 17, 1872; Mobile *Register*, March 23, 1875; Natchez *Daily Democrat*, August 13, 1874; New Orleans *Republican*, September 2, 1875.

41. Rowell & Co., *American Newspaper Directory*, 26–27, 137.

42. Edwin Alden, *Edwin Alden's Catalogue of Legitimate American Newspapers, including All Daily, Weekly, and Monthly Newspapers and Magazines Published in the United States, Together with Population of City or Town in Which They Are Published, Their Politics, Class or Denomination, and Circulation* (Cincinnati: Edwin Alden's Advertising Agency, 1879), 5–37. See also J. L. Wofford to John Sherman, September 10, 13, 1885, Sherman MSS, LC.

43. Cincinnati *Commercial*, September 25, 1874 (quotation); "Plato," ibid., September 4, 1874; New Orleans *Republican*, September 5, 1875.

44. New York *Graphic*, January 14, 1875; New Orleans *Republican*, September 5, October 17, 1875; Bangor *Whig and Courier*, November 30, 1876. See also Washington *Chronicle*, September 25, October 18, 28, November 7, 1874.

45. *Congressional Record*, 44th Cong., 1st sess., 5308 (August 8, 1876).

46. Cincinnati *Commercial*, March 11, 1871; Chicago *Times*, May 9, 1874; Washington *Chronicle*, November 16, 18, 1874; House Report 2, "Affairs in Arkansas," 43d Cong., 2d sess., 513.

47. Summers, *Railroads, Reconstruction, and the Gospel of Prosperity*, 204–8; Powell Clayton, *Aftermath of the Civil War* (New York: Neale Publishing Co., 1915), 241–42.

48. New York *Graphic*, September 11, 1875; Washington *New National Era*, April 3, 1873.

49. Washington *Chronicle*, October 18, 28, 1874.

50. Suggs, *Black Press in the South*, 23–27, 65–68, 91–92, 151–62, 177–80, 257–64, 289–99, 313–20, 357–59, 379; Loren Schweninger, *James T. Rapier and Reconstruction* (Chicago: University of Chicago Press, 1978), 186; Charles W. Grose, "Black Newspapers in Texas, 1868–1970" (Ph.D. diss., University of Texas at Austin, 1972), 45–46, 55, 66.

51. See, for example, Suggs, *Black Press in the South*, 24–26, 67–68.

52. James A. Butler to Richard Yates, January 1, 1868, Yates MSS, ISHS.

CHAPTER FOURTEEN

1. New York *Times*, December 8, 1874; New York *Herald*, December 8, 1874; Vicksburg *Times and Republican*, December 7, 1874.

2. New York *Times*, *Herald*, December 8, 1874. A report soon contradicted. See New York *Tribune*, December 11, 1874.

3. New York *Times*, *Herald*, and *Tribune*, December 8, 1874; "C. W. B.," Louisville *Courier-Journal*, December 14, 1874.

4. New York *Times*, December 11, 1874; New York *Tribune*, December 11, 1874.

5. New York *Times*, December 11, 1874; "C. W. B.," Louisville *Courier-Journal*, December 14, 1874; New York *Herald* and Cincinnati *Enquirer*, December 10, 1874; New York *Tribune*, December 8, 11–12, 14, 1874; Charles Nordhoff, *The Cotton States in the Spring and Summer of 1875* (New York: Appleton & Co., 1876), 79.

6. New York *Tribune*, December 11, 1874; "C. W. B.," Louisville *Courier-Journal*, December 14, 1874.

7. New York *Tribune*, December 8, 1874.

8. "H. C.," New York *Times*, December 18, 1874. For the same argument, see New York *Herald*, December 10, 1874.

9. House Report 265, "Vicksburg Troubles," 43d Cong., 2d sess., minority rept., xxix; testimony, 9, 19, 52–53, 60–61, 76–78, 81–82, 106–09, 154, 196.

10. Vicksburg *Times and Republican*, July 16–17, 19–21, 24, 27, 31, August 22, 1874; House Report 265, "Vicksburg Troubles," testimony, 518; "Smoal," Cincinnati *Commercial*, August 12, 1874 (quotation).

11. House Report 265, "Vicksburg Troubles," testimony, 28, 313, 447, 449;

Blanche Ames Ames, ed., *Chronicles from the Nineteenth Century: Family Letters of Blanche Butler and Adelbert Ames* (Clinton, Mass.: Colonial Press, 1957), 2:73. See also Vicksburg *Times and Republican*, December 3, 1874.

12. Vicksburg *Times and Republican*, December 4, 1874; House Report 265, "Vicksburg Troubles," testimony, 505.

13. Ames impeachment testimony, 119–25, 148–51; Ames, *Chronicles from the Nineteenth Century*, 2:302; House Report 265, "Vicksburg Troubles," testimony, 538–39, 402–4.

14. House Report 265, "Vicksburg Troubles," testimony, 403, 516.

15. Vicksburg *Times and Republican*, December 5, 1874.

16. New York *Tribune*, December 19, 1874.

17. House Report 265, "Vicksburg Troubles," testimony, 109, 148 (second quotation), 151, 196 (first quotation), 523–24.

18. Ibid., 119.

19. Ibid., 80–81, 142–43.

20. Ibid., 109, 146–47.

21. Ibid., 208–10, 300–301.

22. Ibid., 490–93, 521.

23. New York *Tribune*, December 12, 1874; Cleveland *Plain Dealer*, December 8–9, 1874; Louisville *Courier-Journal*, December 8, 14, 1874; Cincinnati *Enquirer*, December 12, 1874; New York *Herald*, December 10, 1874.

24. New York *Times*, December 25, 1874.

25. Ibid., December 18, 23, 25, 1874. For the same disparagement of Republican officials' statements, see New York *Herald*, December 11, 17, 1874.

26. New York *Tribune*, December 8, 11, 1874; Cincinnati *Enquirer*, December 11, 1874.

27. William Gillette, *Retreat from Reconstruction, 1869–1879* (Baton Rouge: Louisiana State University, 1979), 226–35; George C. Rable, "But There Was No Peace: Violence and Reconstruction Politics" (Ph.D. diss., Louisiana State University, 1978), 126–40; Ted Tunnell, ed., *Carpetbagger from Vermont: The Autobiography of Marshall Harvey Twitchell* (Baton Rouge: Louisiana State University Press, 1989), 135–53. For the issues and general intimidation, see Shreveport *Times*, July 19, 21, August 2, 1874; Natchitoches *People's Vindicator*, June 20, 27, 1874; New York *Herald*, September 11, 1874.

28. "The Negro Hobgoblin," Chicago *Tribune*, December 12, 1874.

29. New York *Tribune*, November 14, 1874.

30. Melinda M. Hennessey, "To Live and Die in Dixie: Reconstruction Race Riots in the South" (Ph.D. diss., Kent State University, 1978), 248–62; Rable, "But There Was No Peace," 437–38.

31. Rable, "But There Was No Peace," 431–40; William Warren Rogers, "Reconstruction Journalism: The Hays-Hawley Letter," *American Journalism* 6 (Fall 1989): 235–44.

32. New York *Times*, December 19, 1874; New York *Tribune*, December 11, 1874. See also Nordhoff, *Cotton States*, 78–80.

CHAPTER FIFTEEN

1. Ernest Duvergier de Hauranne, *A Frenchman in Lincoln's America* (Chicago: Lakeside Press, 1974–75), 1:49; "D. P.," Cincinnati *Commercial*, January 17, 1870.

2. Louisville *Courier*, July 26, 1868; Springfield *Daily Republican*, April 21, 1871 (quotation); Therese Yelverton, *Teresina in America* (London: Richard Bentley & Son, 1875), 10; Henry Watterson, *"Marse Henry": An Autobiography* (New York: George H. Doran, 1919), 1:258–59; William Harlan Hale, *Horace Greeley, Voice of the People* (New York: Harper, 1950), 296–300. For the full details of Greeley's life, the best sources are Glyndon G. Van Deusen, *Horace Greeley: Nineteenth-century Crusader* (Philadelphia: University of Pennsylvania Press, 1953), and Hale, *Horace Greeley*.

3. "Gath," Chicago *Tribune*, December 14, 1872.

4. Allan Nevins, *The Evening Post: A Century of Journalism* (New York: Boni & Liveright, 1922), 395 (first quotation); *Nation*, June 10, 1869; Cincinnati *Enquirer*, June 1, 1877 (second quotation).

5. Benjamin F. Butler to J. Russell Young, April 3, 1869, Young MSS, LC; Charles A. Dana to Uriah H. Painter, April 24, 1869, Painter Family MSS, HSP.

6. Schuyler Colfax to Whitelaw Reid, August 19, 1870, Reid MSS, LC; P. H. Jones to John J. Creswell, December 27, 1870, Creswell MSS, LC.

7. Washington *Sunday Capital*, March 12, 1871; James A. Garfield to Samuel Bowles, March 31, 1871, Garfield MSS, LC; Francis E. Spinner to Edwin Morgan, February 2, 1872, Morgan MSS, NYSL.

8. *Nation*, June 15, 1871; Horace Greeley to Brockway, March 13, 1872, Greeley MSS, LC.

9. Charles A. Dana to Uriah H. Painter, April 8, July 21, 1869, Painter Family MSS, HSP; New York *Evening Post*, September 21, 1872.

10. New York *Sun*, December 5, 8, 11, 1871, January 22, 24, 1872; Charles A. Dana to Uriah H. Painter, April 8, July 21, 1869, Amos J. Cummings to Uriah H. Painter, January 30, 1871 (but clearly 1872), Painter Family MSS, HSP.

11. New York *Evening Post*, February 16, 1872; Joseph Medill to James A. Garfield, December 16, 1871, April 9, 17, 1872, Garfield MSS, LC; William Henry Smith to Whitelaw Reid, February 6, 1872, Reid MSS, LC. For the full story of the liberal Republican revolt, see Matthew T. Downey, "The Rebirth of Reform: A Study of Liberal Reform Movements, 1865–1872" (Ph.D diss., Princeton University, 1963); Richard A. Gerber, "The Liberal Republican Alliance of 1872" (Ph.D. diss., University of Michigan, 1967).

12. Charles A. Dana to Uriah H. Painter, February 20, 1870, Painter Family MSS, HSP; Springfield *Republican*, April 24, 1871; "Gath," Chicago *Tribune*, April 1, 1872.

13. Hale, *Horace Greeley*, 321–24; Van Deusen, *Horace Greeley*, 350–56.

14. Lyman Trumbull to Horace White, January 27, 1872, Trumbull MSS, LC; E. W. Rotterup to Edward Atkinson, April 1, 1872, David A. Wells to Atkinson,

April 7, 1872, Atkinson MSS, MHS; Eugene D. Schmiel, "The Career of Jacob Dolson Cox, 1828–1900: Soldier, Scholar, Statesman" (Ph.D. diss., Ohio State University, 1969), 330–31.

15. Gerber, "Liberal Republican Alliance," 153–54.

16. New York *Sun*, September 4, 1871; Cincinnati *Commercial*, July 10, 1871, "H. J. R.," April 15, 1872; Downey, "Rebirth of Reform," 415–22.

17. Roger Alan Cohen, "The Lost Jubilee: New York Republicans and the Politics of Reconstruction and Reform, 1867–1878" (Ph.D. diss., Columbia University, 1975), 174–80; Roscoe Conkling to Edwards Pierrepont, February 11, 1871, Pierrepont MSS, SML/YU; George William Curtis to Alonzo Cornell, September 12, 18, 1871, Cornell MSS, Cornell University, Ithaca; John Manley to Edwin D. Morgan, January 6, 1869, Morgan MSS, NYSL.

18. Charlton Lewis to Lyman Trumbull, February 26, 1872, Trumbull MSS, LC; Whitelaw Reid to James A. Garfield, November 2, 1870, July 17, 1871, April 11, 1872, Garfield MSS, LC.

19. Springfield *Republican*, January 1, 1874; Donn Piatt to James A. Garfield, December 4, 1871, Garfield MSS, LC; Gerber, "Liberal Republican Alliance," 160; Van Deusen, *Horace Greeley*, 281.

20. Jesse Moore to Richard J. Oglesby, December 11, 1869, H. Liebe to Oglesby, December 31, 1870, Oglesby to E. B. Lawrence, December 10, 1870, Oglesby MSS, ISHS.

21. Justin S. Morrill to Horace Greeley, March 11, 1872, Greeley MSS, LC; Francis E. Spinner to Edwin D. Morgan, February 11, 1872, Morgan MSS, NYSL.

22. Mark Krug, *Lyman Trumbull: Conservative Radical* (New York: Barnes, 1965), 325; Charlton Lewis to Lyman Trumbull, April 3, 1872, Horace White to Trumbull, March 24, April 3, May 8, 1872, Lyman Trumbull MSS, LC; L. G. Fisher to David Davis, January 3, 1872, Leonard Swett to Davis, February 25, March 4, 1872, David Davis MSS, Chicago Historical Society; Concord *New Hampshire Patriot*, May 1, 1872; Cincinnati *Commercial*, April 27, 1872; "Gath," New York *Graphic*, February 4, 1876.

23. H. F. Keenan to Whitelaw Reid, April 25, 27, 1872, Reid MSS, LC; "H. W.," Louisville *Courier-Journal*, May 1, 1872; Cincinnati *Enquirer*, April 29, May 1, 1872; Joseph Logsdon, *Horace White: Nineteenth-Century Liberal* (Westport, Conn.: Greenwood, 1971), 222; New York *Times*, May 1, 1872. Watterson's recollection, published years later, narrowed the conspiracy to Bowles, Halstead, Schurz, White, and himself. Like so much else he wrote, it failed to square entirely with contemporary accounts. Watterson, *"Marse Henry,"* 243–45.

24. Cincinnati *Enquirer*, May 1, 4, 1872.

25. Allan Nevins and Milton H. Thomas, eds., *The Diary of George Templeton Strong* (New York: Macmillan, 1952), 4:424 (May 3, 1872). For the editors' response, see New York *Times*, May 4, 1872; Watterson, *"Marse Henry,"* 257; Cincinnati *Enquirer*, May 4, 1872; and Cincinnati *Gazette*, May 7, 1872. Piatt did not disapprove of the nomination—only the delegates. See Piatt to Comly, May 12, 1872, Comly MSS, OHS.

26. Horace White, *The Life of Lyman Trumbull* (Boston: Houghton Mifflin, 1913), 385; Chicago *Tribune*, May 4, 1872; New York *Times*, May 4, 1872; George W. Julian, *Political Recollections, 1840 to 1872* (Chicago: Julian, McClurg & Co., 1884), 339–40.

27. "M. C. A.," New York *Independent*, May 16, 1872; James R. Doolittle to John H. Oberly, May 9, 1872, Doolittle MSS, Wisconsin State Historical Society, Madison; Cincinnati *Gazette*, May 7, 1872; Concord *New Hampshire Patriot*, May 8, 1872; "The Campaign of 1872, by a Veteran of It, in 1929," Cincinnati *Commercial*, July 10, 1871.

28. Cassius M. Clay to James S. Rollins, February 12, 1872, James S. Rollins MSS, State Historical Society of Missouri, Columbia; Gerber, "Liberal Republican Alliance," 455 (quotation); Nevins and Thomas, *Diary of George Templeton Strong*, 4:421 (April 10, 1872), 426 (May 17, 1872), 432 (July 8, 1872); Horace Greeley to J. Russell Young, July 28, 1872, Young MSS, LC.

29. Downey, "Rebirth of Reform," 583–84; Samuel Bowles to Henry L. Dawes, July 16, 1872, Dawes MSS, LC; George S. Merriam, *The Life and Times of Samuel Bowles* (New York: Appleton-Century-Crofts, 1885), 2:187; Horace White to David A. Wells, May 17, 1872, Wells MSS, LC; White to Lyman Trumbull, May 4, 1872, Trumbull MSS, LC.

30. Nevins, *New York Evening Post*, 395–96; Gerber, "Liberal Republican Alliance," 459–61; Chicago *Times*, August 13, September 24, October 7, 1872; Chicago *Tribune*, October 15, 1872.

31. J. Chamberlain to Manton Marble, May 3, 1872, John T. Bird to Marble, May 24, 1872, Marble MSS, LC; George T. McJimsey, *Genteel Partisan: Manton Marble, 1834–1917* (Ames: Iowa State University Press, 1971), 160–61.

32. Horace White to Whitelaw Reid, June 27, 1872, Reid MSS, LC; Michael C. Robinson, "Illinois Politics in the Post–Civil War Era: The Liberal Republican Movement, a Test Case" (Ph.D. diss., University of Wyoming, 1973), 204–6; H. A. Tilden to Francis Kernan, September 8, 1872, Kernan Family MSS, Cornell University, Ithaca; Cleveland *Plain Dealer*, August 29, 1872.

33. New York *Times*, August 25, 1872; Washington *Sunday Capital*, March 16, 1872; New York *Sun*, June 8, 10–11, September 2, 1872; Nevins and Thomas, *Diary of George Templeton Strong*, 4:442–43 (October 5, 1872); Cleveland *Plain Dealer*, September 7, 1872; Indianapolis *Journal*, October 1, 1872; Whitelaw Reid to James A. Garfield, May 30, June 9, July 25, 1872, Garfield MSS, LC.

34. Cleveland *Leader*, August 8, 1872; New York *Times*, August 24–25, 1872; Harrisburg *Patriot*, July 24, 1872; *Nation*, June 6, 1872.

35. *Nation*, October 31, 1872. See also New York *Evening Post*, October 1, 1872.

36. Charles Edgar Ames, *Pioneering the Union Pacific: A Reappraisal of the Builders of the Railroad* (New York: Appleton-Century-Crofts, 1969), 431–35. The circumstances of the discovery are explained by "Gath," Chicago *Tribune*, December 24, 1872. For "Gath's" own role, see Donald A. Ritchie, *Press Gallery: Congress and the Washington Correspondents* (Cambridge: Harvard University Press, 1991), 102–3.

37. Louisville *Courier-Journal*, October 29, 1872; Cleveland *Plain Dealer*, October 29, 1872; Cincinnati *Enquirer*, August 19, 1872; Topeka *Kansas State Record*, October 16, 1872; St. Paul *Pioneer*, November 1–2, 1872. For private echoes of alarm, see Richard Yates to L. U. Reavis, June 3, 1872, Reavis MSS, ISHS.

38. Cleveland *Plain Dealer*, September 9, 19–20, 1872; William Henry Smith to Schuyler Colfax, September 26, 1872, Smith MSS, OHS; Chicago *Times*, September 20, 26, 1872.

39. Clarkson Potter to Whitelaw Reid, November 1, 1872, Reid MSS, LC; James R. Randall to Alexander Stephens, November 10, 1872, Stephens MSS, Duke University, Durham; J. S. Moore to Carl Schurz, September 2, 1872, Schurz MSS, LC.

40. Charles F. Adams, Jr., to Murat Halstead, October 5, 1872, Halstead MSS, CHS; Richard Henry Dana to Samuel Bowles, March 16, 1876, Bowles MSS, SML/YU.

41. W. T. Hopkins to Richard Yates, May 3, 1872, Yates MSS, ISHS; Solomon Bulkely Griffin, *People and Politics Observed by a Massachusetts Editor* (Boston: Little, Brown, 1923), 132; Leon B. Richardson, *William E. Chandler: Republican* (New York: Dodd, Mead, 1940), 146; Keith Ian Polakoff, "The Disorganized Democracy: An Institutional Study of the Democratic Party, 1872–1880" (Ph.D. diss., Northwestern University), 121–22.

42. Harrisburg *Patriot*, July 23, 1872; Richardson, *William E. Chandler*, 146–49; Henry Clews to Edwin D. Morgan, July 31, 1872, Morgan to Governor Claflin, September 21, 1872, Morgan to Richard Smith, September 21, 1872, Morgan to Oliver P. Morton, September 25, 1872, Morgan MSS, NYSL; L. L. Cronisse to William E. Chandler, September 28, 1872, W. E. Chandler MSS, LC; Cincinnati *Gazette*, September 14, 30, October 2 (poem), 5, 1872.

43. Nevins and Thomas, *Diary of George Templeton Strong*, 4:409 (January 9, 1872), 422 (April 20, 1872),

44. Ibid., 4:411 (January 25, 1872), 417 (March 14, 1872), 424 (April 29, 1872), 429 (June 8, 1872), 436 (September 16, 1872).

45. Ibid., 4:420–21 (April 10, 1872), 424 (May 3, 1872), 427 (May 23, 1872), 429–30 (June 8, 1872), 444 (October 9, 1872).

46. New York *Tribune*, July 13, 1872; Topeka *State Record*, November 13, 1872; Logsdon, *Horace White*, 250; Horace Greeley to Mrs. Allen, September 6, 1872, Greeley MSS, LC; Horace White to Whitelaw Reid, September 15, 1872, George F. Pendleton to Reid, October 9, 1872, Reid MSS, LC; William Gillette, *Retreat from Reconstruction, 1869–1879* (Baton Rouge: Louisiana State University, 1979), 70, 391; Polakoff, "The Disorganized Democracy," 131; Nevins and Thomas, *Diary of George Templeton Strong*, 4:453 (November 6, 1872).

47. E. W. Alfreund to Alexander H. Stephens, November 10, 1872, Stephens MSS, Duke University, Durham; William R. Morrison to John F. Snyder, November 14, 1872, MSS, ISHS; Cincinnati *Commercial*, April 7, 1874 (Halstead's quotation).

48. Horace Greeley to Margaret Allen, November 4, 1872, Greeley to Mason W. Tappan, November 8, 1872, Greeley MSS, LC; Van Deusen, *Horace Greeley*, 414, 418–20.

49. Hale, *Horace Greeley*, 347–53.

50. Cincinnati *Gazette*, November 6, 1872; G. L. Fort to Richard Oglesby, November 9, 1872, Oglesby MSS, ISHS (quotation); *Journalist*, March 3, 1888; Springfield *Republican*, January 1, 1874.

CHAPTER SIXTEEN

1. Cincinnati *Commercial*, January 15, 1874.

2. Ibid., January 14, 17, 1874; Donn Piatt to Murat Halstead, January 23, [1874], Halstead MSS, CHS.

3. Washington *Sunday Capital*, January 4, 11, 1874; Donn Piatt to Murat Halstead, January 23, [1874], Halstead MSS, CHS; Cincinnati *Commercial*, January 18, 1874.

4. Rollin H. Kirk, *Many Secrets Revealed; or, Ten Years Behind the Scenes at Washington City* (Washington, D.C.: N.p., 1885), 26. For contemporary corroboration, see Henry D. Cooke to Jay Cooke, February 11, 1873, Jay Cooke to Henry Cooke, February 12, 1873, Cooke MSS, HSP; George Alfred Townsend, *Washington Outside and Inside: A Picture and a Narrative of the Origin, Growth, Excellencies, Abuses, Beauties, and Personages of Our Governing City* (Hartford: J. Betts, 1874), 229; H. Augusta Dodge, ed., *Gail Hamilton: Life in Letters*, 2 vols. (Boston: Lee & Shepard, 1901), 2:697–98; "Gath," Chicago *Tribune*, April 27, 1874.

5. For the poisonous response to press criticism of those implicated in both scandals, see George P. McLean to William D. Kelley, March 1, 1873, Kelley MSS, HSP; Henry Dawes to Mrs. Electa Dawes, January 10, February 20, 1873, Dawes MSS, LC; *Congressional Globe*, appendix, 42d Cong., 3d sess., 181 (February 26, 1873); Samuel Shellabarger to George F. Hoar, July 8, 1873, Hoar MSS, MHS.

6. E. Bruce Thompson, *Matthew Hale Carpenter: Webster of the West* (Madison: Wisconsin Historical Society, 1954), 196–202; H. J. Ramsdell to Whitelaw Reid, July 25, November 21, 1873, Reid MSS, LC; New York *Times*, December 2, 5, 1873.

7. Chicago *Tribune*, May 3, 1869; "Gath," ibid., June 7, 1870; Cincinnati *Enquirer*, October 7, 1873; Harrisburg *Patriot*, July 3, 1872.

8. Ben: Perley Poore, *Perley's Reminiscences of Sixty Years in the National Metropolis* (Philadelphia: Hubbard Brothers, 1886), 2:261–63; "H. V. B.," Cincinnati *Gazette*, October 26, 1875; "Eli Perkins," New York *Graphic*, January 28, 1874 (quotation).

9. Zebulon L. White to Whitelaw Reid, February 9, 1873, Reid MSS, LC; Henry D. Cooke to Jay Cooke, January 22, May 3, 1872, Cooke MSS, HSP; Milwaukee *News*, September 27, 1873; Portland *Eastern Argus*, May 2, 1874; New York

Herald, September 15, 17, 1873; Cincinnati *Gazette,* October 22, 1873; Edward Spencer to Manton Marble, January 28, February 2, 1874, Marble MSS, LC.

10. Crosby S. Noyes to Alexander R. Shepherd, September 18, 1868, Shepherd MSS, LC; Washington *Chronicle,* January 28, 30–31, February 13, May 26, 1874; Cincinnati *Commercial,* March 12, 1874; Chicago *Tribune,* April 4, 7, 10, May 6, 8, 19, 1874; Senate Report 453, "District of Columbia," 43d Cong., 1st sess., 717; "H. V. B.," Cincinnati *Gazette,* May 26, 1874.

11. Zebulon L. White to Whitelaw Reid, March 23, 1873, Reid to White, April 9, 21, May 2, 1873, Reid MSS, LC; New York *Sun,* November 2–3, 1874; "H. V. B.," Cincinnati *Gazette,* May 26, 1874 (first quotation); Chicago *Tribune,* April 14, 1874 (second quotation).

12. William M. Maury, "Alexander R. Shepherd and the Board of Public Works," *Records of the Columbian Society* 48 (1971–72): 394–410.

13. "M. C. A.," New York *Independent,* January 29, February 26, March 12, 26, 1874.

14. Marshall Jewell to Elihu Washburne, June 7, 1874, Washburne MSS, LC; New York *Herald,* June 9, 1874; *Harper's Weekly,* July 4, 1874, 554; Cincinnati *Commercial,* June 15, 18, 24, 1874.

15. New York *Tribune,* May 26, 1874; New York *World,* April 14, 1874; Chicago *Tribune,* April 6, 1874; House Report 559, "Discovery and Collection of Monies Withheld from the Government," 43d Cong., 1st sess., 8; "Sanborn and Other Matters," *Harper's Weekly,* June 13, 1874.

16. Cincinnati *Commercial,* January 30, April 30, 1874; New York *Tribune,* February 5, 13, 1874.

17. Cincinnati *Commercial,* June 16, 1874; New York *Sun,* August 10, 1874, October 8, 1875.

18. New York *Times,* April 4, 1874; "Senator Carpenter's Suit," *Harper's Weekly,* August 8, 1874.

19. Washington *Chronicle,* April 14, 1874; Washington *Sunday Capital,* April 12, 1874 (Hampden's quotation); Louisville *Courier-Journal,* April 16, 1874; Cincinnati *Commercial,* May 24, June 25, 1874; "Gideon," Chicago *Times,* May 27, 1874; Henry Boynton to Whitelaw Reid, April 25, 1875, Reid MSS, LC (Cartter's quotation).

20. Chicago *Tribune,* July 18, 1873; New York *Sun,* December 2, 1874.

21. Thompson, *Matthew Hale Carpenter,* 215–16; *Harper's Weekly,* July 4, 1874, 554.

22. *Congressional Record,* 43d Cong., 1st sess., 4978–88 (June 15, 1874).

23. Cincinnati *Commercial,* May 9, June 26 (quotation), 1874; *Harper's Weekly,* July 4 (p. 554), 11 (p. 574), 1874.

24. New York *Herald,* June 16–17, 1874; "Gideon," Chicago *Times,* June 20, 1874; Cincinnati *Commercial,* June 16–17, 1874.

25. Washington *Sunday Capital,* March 2, 1873; *Nation,* September 10, 1874.

26. New York *Tribune,* July 1, 1874; Baltimore *Sun,* July 1, 1874; New York *Sun,* December 2, 1874.

27. New York *Sun*, November 18, 1874; Cincinnati *Commercial*, July 28, 1874; *Harper's Weekly*, August 1, 1874, 630.

28. Baltimore *Sun*, July 9, 11, 1874; Henry V. Boynton to Whitelaw Reid, April 25, 1875, Reid MSS, LC; *Harper's Weekly*, July 25, 1874, 614.

29. *Harper's Weekly*, August 1 (p. 630), 8 (p. 650), 1874; "H. V. B.," Cincinnati *Gazette*, January 27, 1875.

30. Cincinnati *Commercial*, July 28, August 8, 1874.

31. Springfield *Republican*, February 17, March 2, 1874; New York *Tribune*, May 23, 1874; New York *Times*, April 13, 1874.

32. Morris S. Miller to Horatio Seymour, August 1, 1868, Seymour MSS, NYSL; Louisville *Courier*, August 6–7, September 6, 24, 1868; James R. Doolittle to Manton Marble, January 27, 1868, Marble MSS, LC; Cincinnati *Enquirer*, October 6, 9, 1868; Chicago *Times*, October 22, 30, 1868.

33. James R. Doolittle to Mrs. Doolittle, September 10, 1?, 1872, Doolittle MSS, Wisconsin State Historical Society, Madison; William B. Napton Diary, January 29, 1873, Missouri Historical Society, St. Louis.

34. Harrisburg *Patriot*, July 16, November 2, 1872. The link between Reconstruction's enforcement and Caesarism is suggested in Philadelphia *North American*, October 23, 1874.

35. A. J. P. Taylor, *Bismarck: The Man and the Statesman* (New York: Random House, 1955), 147–52; Daniel Halevy, *The End of the Notables* (Middletown, Conn.: Wesleyan University Press, 1974), 174–209. For explicit links to the Caesarism issue, see New York *Herald*, July 7–8, 10, 1873; for more implicit ones, see Chicago *Tribune*, July 15, 1873.

36. Richard Kluger, *The Paper: The Life and Death of the New York Herald Tribune* (New York: Knopf, 1986), 141–45. The best, if exceedingly dubious, biography of Bennett remains Richard O'Connor, *The Scandalous Mr. Bennett* (Garden City, N.Y.: Doubleday, 1962). For the *Herald*'s practice of defining issues (among them, Caesarism), see "Broadway," Cincinnati *Commercial*, September 14, 1874.

37. Jerome Mushkat, *The Reconstruction of the New York Democracy, 1861–1874* (Rutherford: Fairleigh Dickinson University Press, 1981), 219–20; J. C. Goldsmith to John Russell Young, September 15, 1873, Young MSS, LC.

38. New York *Herald*, July 7–10, 1873.

39. New York *Tribune*, July 12, 1873; Chicago *Tribune*, July 8–9, 20, August 19, 24, 1873. Lockport *Union*, Augusta *Chronicle*, New York *Express*, and Baltimore *Gazette* all quoted in New York *Herald*, July 14, 1873.

40. Woodbury *Constitution*, July 30, 1873; New York *Herald*, August 18, September 17, 1873. For that contempt, see New York *Herald*, November 7, 1874. See also John Y. Simon, ed., *Personal Memoirs of Julia Dent Grant* (New York: Putnam, 1975), 186. For one vice-president's and two cabinet members' suspicions that Grant himself wanted another term, see Hamilton Fish Diary, September 21, 1874, Fish MSS, LC; Harry J. Brown and Frederick D. Williams, eds., *Diary of James A. Garfield* (East Lansing: Michigan State University Press, 1973), 3:6 (January 7, 1875), 3:39 (March 9, 1875).

41. J. C. Goldsmith to John Russell Young, September 15, 1873, Young MSS, LC (quotation); Philadelphia *North American*, September 12, 1874; Cincinnati *Commercial*, July 3, 1874.

42. Wilmington *Morning Star*, July 11, 1874. See also Shreveport *Times*, June 19, 1874.

43. Chicago *Tribune*, July 8, 1873; "X. Y. Z.," Cincinnati *Commercial*, June 22, 1874; New York *Herald*, October 28, 1874; J. B. Kunkel to Lewis W. Wolfe, August 6, 1875, William Allen MSS, LC.

44. New York *Herald*, September 22, 1873; Indianapolis *News*, October 1, 1874. For Southern senators favoring the third term, see New York *Herald*, October 13, 1874.

45. New York *Herald*, July 2, 9, 16, August 26, October 12–13, 1874.

46. Cincinnati *Commercial*, May 9, July 17, 23–24, 1874.

47. New York *Times*, August 27, 1873; Cincinnati *Commercial*, June 16, 1874.

48. Cincinnati *Commercial*, July 15, 1874; Philadelphia *Evening Star*, August 21, 1874 (quotation); Philadelphia *North American*, October 24, 1874.

49. *Harper's Weekly*, November 14, 1874; "H. V. R.," Cincinnati *Commercial*, August 4, 7, 1874; New York *Herald*, August 18, 1874 (quoting Rome *Courier*); Baltimore *Sun*, July 2, 9–11, 1874.

50. Washington *Sunday Capital*, October 18, 1874; Springfield *Republican*, July 17, 1874; New York *Herald*, October 23, 1874; Royal Cortissoz, *The Life of Whitelaw Reid* (New York: Scribner, 1921), 1:284; *Nation*, October 8, 1874; Philadelphia *North American*, October 7, 1874.

51. *Harper's Weekly*, August 29, 1874; New York *Herald*, August 27, September 5, October 26, 1874; Thomas B. Keogh to Thomas Settle, September 8, 1874, Settle MSS, SHC (quotation); Baltimore *Sun*, October 12, 22, 1874; Cincinnati *Commercial*, July 24, 1874; Frank B. Evans, *Pennsylvania Politics, 1872–1877: A Study in Political Leadership* (Harrisburg: Pennsylvania Historical & Museum Commission, 1966), 247–49.

52. J. S. Moore to Manton Marble, October 17, 1874, Marble MSS, LC; John Bigelow, ed., *Letters and Literary Memorials of Samuel J. Tilden* (New York: Harper & Brothers, 1908), 1:333–34, 338–39; New York *Herald*, October 10, 12, 1874; Alexander C. Flick, *Samuel Jones Tilden: A Study in Political Sagacity* (New York: Dodd, Mead, 1939), 247; *Nation*, September 24, 1874.

53. New York *Tribune*, October 7, 1874; New York *Times*, October 31, 1874; New York *Sun*, November 2, 1874.

54. New York *Sun*, November 3, 1874; New York *Herald*, October 28, 31 (quotation), 1874.

55. Baltimore *Sun*, September 3–4, 1874; New York *Herald*, September 3, 1874; *Nation*, September 10, 1874. In fact, Poland's hold on his district had been shaky for some time, with Republican factionalism dating back some years. Luther O. Greene to Charles A. Willard, August 17, 1872, Willard MSS, Vermont Historical Society, Montpelier.

56. New York *Herald*, November 4, 1874; *Nation*, November 12, 1874; Cortissoz,

Whitelaw Reid, 292 (quotation); William Faxon to William E. Chandler, December 3, 1874, W. E. Chandler MSS, LC; Flick, *Samuel Jones Tilden,* 252. For those blaming the fall returns on Caesarism, see Indianapolis *News,* October 17, 23, 1874; Thurlow Weed in New York *Herald,* February 22, 1875; *Harper's Weekly,* November 14 (pp. 930–31), 28 (p. 970), 1874; Detroit *Free Press,* November 6, 1874; Eugene Casserly to Manton Marble, November 5, 1874, Marble MSS, LC; and, far more conditionally, Philadelphia *North American,* November 5, 1874.

57. New York *Sun,* April 5, 7, 1875; New York *Times,* April 6, 1875.

58. Hamilton Fish Diary, January 10, 1875, Fish MSS, LC; George M. Dallas to Samuel J. Randall, January 21, 1875, Alexander Long to Randall, January 26, 1875, Randall MSS, UP; Atlanta *Constitution,* February 20, 26, 1875; New York *Sun,* April 7, 12, 1875; New York *Herald,* February 16, April 14, 30, 1875.

59. New York *Pomeroy's Democrat,* February 21, 1875.

60. New York *Tribune,* December 8, 1874; New York *Graphic,* December 10, 1874, February 18, 1875; Chicago *Times,* December 21, 1874, February 17, 1875.

61. New York *Sun,* April 5, 22, 24, 1875; Cincinnati *Enquirer,* March 30, April 9, 1875; Washington *Chronicle,* February 2, April 4, 9, 22, May 12, 1875; Mobile *Register,* April 13, October 6, 1875; Chicago *Tribune,* February 26, 1875. For the Reid case, see Hiram J. Ramsdell to Whitelaw Reid, January 14, 1875, Henry V. Boynton to Reid, April 25, 1875, Reid MSS, LC; "Seymour," Mobile *Register,* January 26, 1875; "H. V. B.," Cincinnati *Gazette,* January 27, 1875; Washington *Chronicle,* March 23, 1875.

62. New York *Herald,* June 2–3, 5, 7, 1875; Mobile *Register,* July 21, December 12, 1876; William Penn Chandler to Samuel J. Randall, July 8, 1876, Randall MSS, UP; William B. Napton Diary, February 1, 1876, Napton MSS, Missouri Historical Society, St. Louis.

63. Frank L. Mott, "Facetious News Writing, 1833–1883," *Mississippi Valley Historical Review* 29 (June 1942), 48–49. The author was political correspondent Harry O'Connor. See *The Journalist,* August 20, 1892.

CHAPTER SEVENTEEN

1. E. Merton Coulter, "Amnesty for All Except Jefferson Davis: The Hill-Blaine Debate of 1876," *Georgia Historical Quarterly* 56 (Winter 1972): 453–57; *The Republic,* February 1876, 137; E. John Ellis to Tom Ellis, December 5, 1875, Ellis Family MSS, LSU.

2. "M. C. A.," New York *Independent,* March 25, 1869; "Gath," New York *Graphic,* January 10, April 20, 1876. See also "Gath," Chicago *Tribune,* March 11, 1871; Washington *Sunday Capital,* March 2, 16, 1873; and David Saville Muzzey, *James G. Blaine: A Political Idol of Other Days* (New York: Dodd, Mead, 1934).

3. Harry J. Brown and Frederick D. Williams, eds., *Diary of James A. Garfield* (East Lansing: Michigan State University Press, 1973), 3:195 (December 6, 1875); E. John Ellis to Tom Ellis, December 5, 1875, Ellis Family MSS, LSU; Burwell B.

Lewis to Robert McKee, December 10, 1875, McKee MSS, Alabama Department of Archives and History, Montgomery; New York *Tribune*, December 7–8, 1875.

4. New York *Herald*, January 11, 1876; *Congressional Record*, 44th Cong., 1st sess., 323–26 (January 10, 1876).

5. *Congressional Record*, 44th Cong., 1st sess., 326–30 (January 10, 1876), 345–51 (January 11, 1876); Coulter, "Amnesty for All Except Jefferson Davis," 460–94; David Lindsey, *"Sunset" Cox: Irrepressible Democrat* (Detroit: Wayne State University Press, 1959), 152–53; Chicago *Tribune*, January 17, 1876. For contemporary Democratic responses to Hill, see E. John Ellis to Tom Ellis, January 17, 1876, Ellis Family MSS, LSU; Eugene Casserly to Thomas F. Bayard, January 22, 1876, Bayard Family MSS, LC; Burwell B. Lewis to Robert McKee, January 19, 1876, McKee MSS, Alabama Department of Archives and History, Montgomery; "A. C. B.," Cincinnati *Enquirer*, March 29, 1876.

6. Thomas Ewing, Jr. to ———, March 28, 1876, Ewing Family MSS, LC; Charles Nordhoff to Rutherford B. Hayes, January 11, 1876, Hayes MSS, HML.

7. Ben: Perley Poore to William Warland Clapp, January 15, February 10, 1876, Clapp MSS, LC; Keith Ian Polakoff, *The Politics of Inertia: The Election of 1876 and the End of Reconstruction* (Baton Rouge: Louisiana State University, 1973), 16–44.

8. H. Wayne Morgan, *From Hayes to McKinley: National Party Politics, 1877–1896* (Syracuse: Syracuse University Press, 1969), 63–69, 281–84, 395–99, 401–3.

9. Charles Nordhoff to Whitelaw Reid, March 4, 1876, Reid MSS, LC; E. B. Wight to W. W. Clapp, February 29, 1876, Clapp MSS, LC.

10. Chicago *Times*, April 11, 1876.

11. Muzzey, *James G. Blaine*, 20, 299.

12. Portland *Eastern Argus*, September 9, 1874.

13. Chicago *Tribune*, January 1874; Zebulon L. White to Whitelaw Reid, January 29, 1874, Reid MSS, LC (quotation).

14. James G. Blaine to Jay Cooke, October 14, 1869, Jay Cooke to Henry D. Cooke, October 21, 1869, April 1, 1870, May 20, 1872, Henry D. Cooke to Jay Cooke, October 16, 18, November 1, 1869 (quotation), March 31, 1870, May 21, 1872, Cooke MSS, HSP.

15. Henry V. Boynton to Richard Smith, February 6, 1876, William Henry Smith MSS, OHS; A. M. Gibson to James G. Blaine, March 17, 1876, Blaine MSS, LC; Rollin H. Kirk, *Many Secrets Revealed; or, Ten Years Behind the Scenes at Washington City* (Washington, D.C.: N.p., 1885), 25.

16. Cincinnati *Commercial*, April 4, 1873. See also earlier versions of the charge in Chicago *Tribune*, October 14, 1872. On Stewart as lobbyist, see Kirk, *Many Secrets Revealed*, 25.

17. William Henry Smith to Rutherford B. Hayes, April 18, 1876, Hayes MSS, HML.

18. Charles Nordhoff to Whitelaw Reid, March 4, 1876, Reid MSS, LC; E. B. Wight to W. W. Clapp, February 29, 1876, Clapp MSS, LC.

19. Polakoff, *Politics of Inertia*, 44–45 (quotation); Henry V. Boynton, "The

Whiskey Ring," *North American Review* 123 (October 1876); Cincinnati *Gazette*, October 18, 1875.

20. Henry V. Boynton to William H. Smith, February 18, 1876, W. H. Smith Papers, ISL. See also Boynton to Smith, February 6, 17, 1876, Smith Papers, OHS.

21. Ross Webb, *Benjamin Helm Bristow: Border State Politician* (Lexington: University of Kentucky Press, 1969), 239–42; Henry Van Ness Boynton, "The Press and Public Men," *Century Magazine* 48 (October 1891): 856; W. R. Holloway to William Henry Smith, January 23, 1876, Smith MSS, OHS.

22. Whitelaw Reid to William Henry Smith, February 2, 1876, W. H. Smith to Richard Smith, February 22, 1876, Joseph Medill to W. H. Smith, February 21, 1876, Smith MSS, OHS.

23. Zebulon L. White to Whitelaw Reid, February 11, 1876, Reid MSS, LC; William H. Smith to Boynton, April 30, 1876, W. H. Smith Papers, ISL; E. B. Wight to William Warland Clapp, February 28–29, 1876, Clapp MSS, LC.

24. Richard Smith to William H. Smith, February 19, 1876, Delavan Smith MSS, ISL.

25. David M. Jordan, *Roscoe Conkling of New York: Voice in the Senate* (Ithaca: Cornell University Press, 1971), 234–36; Polakoff, *Politics of Inertia*, 48–49.

26. Henry V. Boynton to William Henry Smith, February 25, 1876, Smith MSS, OHS.

27. William Henry Smith to Rutherford B. Hayes, April 18, 1876, Hayes MSS, HML.

28. William Henry Smith to Richard Smith, February 22, 1876, James G. Blaine to Richard Smith (copy), February 11, 1876, Boynton to Richard Smith (copy), February 17, 1876, Joseph Medill to William Henry Smith, February 21, 1876, Smith MSS, OHS; William H. Smith to Henry V. Boynton, April 30, 1876, W. H. Smith MSS, ISL.

29. Richard Smith to William Henry Smith, April 1, 1876, Delavan Smith MSS, ISL; Statement of Joseph Medill, Cincinnati *Gazette*, April 17, 1876.

30. Chicago *Times*, April 15, 1876.

31. William Henry Smith to Henry V. Boynton, April 30, 1876, W. H. Smith Papers (ISL).

32. Chicago *Times*, April 13, 1876; Cincinnati *Enquirer*, April 12, 1876; Will Holloway to William Henry Smith, February 26, 28, March 1, 1876, W. H. Smith MSS, ISL. Harrison, on the contrary, claimed that Morton had known about the Blaine matter for many months.

33. Blaine's Catholic relations had been bruited about in the press. As Republicans, groping for a winning issue, had taken up that of protecting the public schools from the pope, and had used it to help them win the governorship of Ohio the year before, they could suffer an embarrassment from running a candidate whose sister had entered a convent or who, himself, was a secret Catholic. Blaine had heard the reports and arranged to have a reply leaked to the Pennsylvania press: that as a college student at a denominational institution, he had attended

Presbyterian services faithfully. See B. F. Potts to Rutherford B. Hayes, November 20, 1875, Hayes MSS, HML; James G. Blaine to Edward McPherson, January 1876, McPherson MSS, LC; Blaine to Samuel Bowles, January 22, 1876, Bowles MSS, SML/YU.

34. Charles Nordhoff to Whitelaw Reid, March 4, 1876, Reid MSS, LC.

35. Horace White to Carl Schurz, February 25, March 11, 1876, Schurz MSS, LC; C. B. Farwell to William Henry Smith, March 21, 1876, Smith MSS, OHS.

36. Chicago *Times*, April 13, 1876; Cincinnati *Enquirer*, April 14, 1876; Cincinnati *Gazette*, April 15, 1876; John Defrees to Samuel Bowles, June 4, 1876, Bowles MSS, SML/YU.

37. William Henry Smith to Henry V. Boynton, April 21, 1876, Smith MSS, OHS; New York *Graphic*, May 2, 1876. Information on John Fishback can be found in Cincinnati *Enquirer*, March 5, 1875. He bought in, in 1872, by selling his interest in a tanning yard. His brother, W. P. Fishback, was a successful journalist in Indianapolis.

38. Cincinnati *Gazette*, April 15, 1876. That some stories had reached the Chicago *Times* and been refused publication is clear from the *Times* of March 28 and April 12, 1876, though it insisted that Morton's friends were the ones peddling the allegations.

39. Cincinnati *Gazette*, April 15, 1876.

40. "Bully Blaine's Bosh," Chicago *Times*, April 25, 1876; New York *Herald*, April 25, 1876.

41. New York *Herald*, April 25, May 2, 1876; *Congressional Record*, 44th Cong., 1st sess., 2863–64 (May 1, 1876); Chicago *Times*, April 25, 1876.

42. James G. Blaine to Joseph Medill, February 29, 1876, Halstead MSS, CHS; *Congressional Record*, 44th Cong., 1st sess., 2864 (May 1, 1876); Cincinnati *Gazette*, April 12, 1876.

43. Sam Ward to Thomas F. Bayard, April 30, 1876, Bayard Family MSS, LC.

44. Edward Stanwood, *James Gillespie Blaine* (Boston: Houghton Mifflin, 1905), 149, 164; Cincinnati *Gazette*, June 1, 1876.

45. New York *Sun*, May 29, 1876; Cincinnati *Gazette*, May 30, 1876.

46. New York *Tribune*, June 2, 1876; Cincinnati *Gazette*, June 2, 1876.

47. Cincinnati *Gazette*, June 1, 1876. The charge of bias was made specifically in Cincinnati *Enquirer*, June 1, 1876.

48. New York *Tribune*, June 2, 1876.

49. Edward F. Noyes to Rutherford B. Hayes, June 3, 1876, Hayes MSS, HML; Zebulon L. White to Whitelaw Reid, June 3, 1876, Reid MSS, LC.

50. Cincinnati *Enquirer*, June 6, 1876.

51. *Congressional Record*, 44th Cong., 1st sess., 3602–9 (June 5, 1876); New York *Herald*, June 6, 1876; Muzzey, *James Gillespie Blaine*, 94–95.

52. *Congressional Record*, 44th Cong., 1st sess., 3616 (June 5, 1876); New York *Tribune*, June 6, 1876, New York *Herald*, June 6, 1876.

53. Charles Nordhoff to Whitelaw Reid, June 5, 1876, Zebulon L. White to Reid, June 8, 1876, Reid MSS, LC.

54. See Cincinnati *Enquirer*, June 6, 1876; Cincinnati *Gazette*, June 6–7, 1876.

55. Cincinnati *Gazette*, June 7, 1876; "Laertes," New York *Graphic*, June 8, 1876.

56. *Nation*, January 27, 1881; "A. C. B.," Washington *Sunday Capital*, March 11, 1877.

57. Harriet S. Blaine Beall, ed., *The Letters of Mrs. James G. Blaine* (New York: Duffield, 1908), 137; Webb, *Benjamin Helm Bristow*, 239–40; Henry L. Dawes to Mrs. Dawes, June 13–14, 1876, Dawes MSS, LC.

58. Carl Schurz to Rutherford B. Hayes, September 12, 1876, Hayes MSS, HML; Henry V. Boynton to Gen. A. H. Markland, June 29, September 3, 1884, Boynton MSS, OHS.

CHAPTER EIGHTEEN

1. Washington *Sunday Capital*, December 3, 1876. For the full story of the disputed election, see Keith Ian Polakoff, *The Politics of Inertia: The Election of 1876 and the End of Reconstruction* (Baton Rouge: Louisiana State University, 1973), 204–45.

2. Washington *Sunday Capital*, February 18, 1877.

3. "D. P.," Cincinnati *Enquirer*, February 22, 1877.

4. Cincinnati *Enquirer*, February 22–23, 25; "D. P.," ibid., February 28, March 9, 1877; Murat Halstead to Rutherford B. Hayes, February 21, 1877, Hayes MSS, HML.

5. *Nation*, September 4, 1879; "Caliban," Cincinnati *Enquirer*, July 29, 1876; "Creighton," New York *Graphic*, July 6, 1876, "Gath," New York *Graphic*, December 5, 1876.

6. G. W. Smith to Whitelaw Reid, January 26, 1873, July 29, 1874, Reid MSS, LC; New York *Graphic*, August 16, 1876; Royal Cortissoz, *The Life of Whitelaw Reid* (New York: Scribner, 1921), 1:290–300, 322–24.

7. Chauncey F. Black to Samuel J. Randall, July 5, 1876, Randall MSS, UP; Cincinnati *Enquirer*, April 7, 12, 1876; William F. Pelton to Manton Marble, March 28, 1876, W. M. Witmer to Marble, May 19, 1876, John P. Irish to Marble, May 19, 1876, Marble MSS, LC; John F. Norrish to Samuel J. Tilden, January 21, 1876, H. M. Alexander to Tilden, April 22, 1876, Tilden MSS, NYPL; A. J. Crawford to William Allen, June 19, 1876, Allen MSS, LC.

8. Henry Watterson, *"Marse Henry": An Autobiography* (New York: George H. Doran, 1919), 273–74 (quotation), 285, 288; Margaret A. Clapp, *Forgotten First Citizen: John Bigelow* (Boston: Little, Brown, 1947), 282–83; Polakoff, *Politics of Inertia*, 79–80; Henry Watterson to Samuel J. Tilden, February 16, May 25, 1876, Tilden MSS, NYPL; Cincinnati *Enquirer*, April 26, 1876.

9. Cincinnati *Enquirer*, April 18, 1876; Ravenna *Democratic Press*, April 20, May 18, 1876; Durbin Ward to Allen G. Thurman, May 21, 1876, Thurman MSS, OHS; H. M. Doak to Manton Marble, June 10, 1876, Marble to Samuel J. Tilden, June 18, 1879, Marble to George W. Smith, June 27, 1876, Marble MSS, LC.

10. Solomon Bulkely Griffin, *People and Politics Observed by a Massachusetts Editor* (Boston: Little, Brown, 1923), 165; Polakoff, *Politics of Inertia*, 126; Manton Marble to Dr. Mercer, November 5, 1876, Marble MSS, LC; James E. Harvey to Samuel J. Randall, September 5, 1876, Randall MSS, UP.

11. "Gath," Cincinnati *Enquirer*, September 20, 1876; James E. Harvey to Samuel J. Randall, September 5, 1876, Randall MSS, UP; Polakoff, *Politics of Inertia*, 125–26; Abram S. Hewitt to Thomas F. Bayard, September 20, 1876, Bayard Family MSS, LC.

12. Polakoff, *Politics of Inertia*, 116–18; August Belmont to Manton Marble, September 21, 1876, Marble to Dr. Mercer, November 5, 1876, Marble MSS, LC; Springfield *Republican*, October 25, 1876; Detroit *Free Press*, September 22, 1876.

13. Margaret A. Clapp, *Forgotten First Citizen: John Bigelow* (Boston: Little, Brown, 1947), 284.

14. Cincinnati *Enquirer*, April 12, 26, 1876; St. Paul *Pioneer-Press*, April 9, 1880.

15. See, for example, Rutherford B. Hayes to Clark Waggoner, April 20, 1870, in Charles Richard Williams, ed., *Diary and Letters of Rutherford Birchard Hayes, Nineteenth President of the United States* (Columbus: Ohio State Archaeological and Historical Society, 1922–26), 3:103–4; James M. Comly to Hayes, April 4, 1875, Hayes to W. D. Bickham, July 20, 1875, Bickham to Hayes, July 8, 1875, and Hayes Diary, October 17, 1875, Hayes MSS, HML.

16. Williams, *Rutherford B. Hayes*, 3:40, 42–43, 53, 55, 62, 310, 315–16, 322–23, 327; William Henry Smith to Rutherford B. Hayes, February 2, 1872, January 26, 1876, Smith MSS, OHS; Hayes to W. D. Bickham, July 10, 1875, Hayes MSS, HML; Cincinnati *Enquirer*, December 6, 1876.

17. Detroit *Free Press*, June 24, 1876; Cincinnati *Enquirer*, January 9–11, 18, 1877; Louisville *Courier-Journal*, January 10, 1877; Hayes to William D. Bickham, April 26, 1876, Hayes MSS, HML.

18. Williams, *Rutherford B. Hayes*, 4:125, 199, 214; Rutherford B. Hayes to Murat Halstead, February 2, 1866, Halstead MSS, CHS; William D. Bickham to Hayes, June 25, 1876, Halstead to Hayes, September 19, 1876, Hayes MSS, HML.

19. Edward F. Noyes to William Henry Smith, July 25, 1876, W. H. Smith MSS, ISL; Rutherford B. Hayes to Murat Halstead, September 18, October 14, 1876, Halstead MSS, CHS; Halstead to Hayes, September 19, 21, October 14–15, 23, 1876, Hayes MSS, HML; Springfield *Republican*, October 26–27, 30, 1876.

20. Murat Halstead to Rutherford B. Hayes, December 10, 21, 27, 1876, February 19, 1877, Hayes MSS, HML; Williams, *Rutherford B. Hayes*, 3:418.

21. William Dennison to Rutherford B. Hayes, December 13, 1876, James M. Comly to Hayes, January 8, 1877, James A. Garfield to Comly, January 24, 1877, Henry V. Boynton to Comly, January 25, 1877, Hayes MSS, HML; William Henry Smith to Hayes, December 7, 1876, Smith MSS, OHS.

22. Henry V. Boynton to William Henry Smith, February 18, 1878, Smith MSS, OHS; Andrew J. Kellar to Smith, December 10, 1876, W. H. Smith MSS, ISL. The full story is in C. Vann Woodward, *Reunion and Reaction: The Compro-*

mise of 1877 and the End of Reconstruction (Little, Brown, 1951), but see also Ari Hoogenboom, *The Presidency of Rutherford B. Hayes* (Lawrence: University Press of Kansas, 1988), 33–50.

23. Cincinnati *Enquirer*, May 19, 1877.

24. Allan Peskin, *Garfield* (Kent State: Kent State University Press, 1978), 422; Williams, *Rutherford B. Hayes*, 3:472, 538, 541, 548, 625; Hayes Diary, May 25, October 6, 1879, August 30, 1880, Hayes MSS, HML; William Henry Smith to E. Wight, August 8, 1877, Rutherford B. Hayes to Smith, [December] 1877, April 4, 1878, Emily Platt to Smith, January 15, 1878, Smith MSS, OHS; Smith to Whitelaw Reid, October 5, 1877, Reid MSS, LC.

25. Cincinnati *Enquirer*, March 1, 1879.

26. Williams, *Rutherford B. Hayes*, 431–32, 443. See also Rutherford B. Hayes to Murat Halstead, July 13, 1878, November 26, 1880, John Sherman to Halstead, November 24, 1879, Halstead MSS, CHS.

27. Rutherford B. Hayes to Samuel Bowles, June 7, 1877, Bowles MSS, SML/YU; Bowles to Murat Halstead, October 23, 1877, Halstead MSS, CHS.

28. Washington *Sunday Capital*, March 2, July 1, 1877; New York *Times*, April 8, 1877; Donn Piatt to Rutherford B. Hayes, January 3, 1878, June 4, 1881, November 9, 1882, Hayes MSS, HML.

29. Henry V. Boynton to William Henry Smith, May 30, 1877, Andrew Kellar to Smith, October 31, 1877, Smith to Stanley Matthews, February 6, 1878, W. H. Smith MSS, ISL; William Henry Smith to Rutherford B. Hayes, October 3, 1877, Stanley Matthews to Smith, February 11, 1878, Boynton to Smith, February 18, 1878, September 28 [1879], Richard Smith to W. H. Smith, March 22, 1878, Smith MSS, OHS; Williams, *Rutherford B. Hayes*, 445–47, 452, 594.

30. William H. Smith to Edward Noyes, October 6, 1877, Richard Smith to W. H. Smith, February 23, 1878, W. H. Smith MSS, ISL; Henry V. Boynton to W. H. Smith, February 18, 23, 1878, January 16, 1881, Smith MSS, OHS.

31. Rutherford B. Hayes to James M. Comly, October 29, 1878, Comly MSS, OHS; William H. Smith to John Sherman, September 27, 1879, Smith to Hayes, October 6, 1879, Smith MSS, OHS; Hayes Diary, March 12–13, 1878, July 3, 1879 (quotation), Hayes MSS, HML.

32. "An Interviewer Interviewed: A Talk with 'Gath,'" *Lippincott's* 48 (November 1891): 638; Hayes Diary, May 31, 1878, Hayes MSS, HML; Cortissoz, *Whitelaw Reid*, 1:392–424; Whitelaw Reid to William Henry Smith, October 24, 1878, Smith MSS, OHS.

33. Washington *Post*, January 28, 1878.

34. Cincinnati *Enquirer*, August 15, 1877. See also ibid., March 15, September 3, November 5, 1877.

35. George Alfred Townsend to Whitelaw Reid, December 23, 29, 1878, February 3, March 3, 1879, Reid MSS, LC; *The Journalist*, April 26, May 17, 31, 1884, September 8, 1888; Indianapolis *Daily Sentinel*, July 4, 1884 (first quotation); *Brann the Iconoclast*, 8:226 (second quotation).

36. "An Interviewer Interviewed," 632.

37. Obituaries, New York *Tribune*, May 26, 30, 1887, January 12, 1889; *Who Was Who in America, 1897–1942*, 1268.

38. *Dictionary of American Biography*, 1:298; Obituaries, New York *Tribune* (April 11, 1880), Cincinnati *Enquirer* (November 18, 1881), and Washington *Post* (November 19, 1881); Robert F. Durden, *James Shepherd Pike: Republicanism and the American Negro, 1850–1882* (Durham: Duke University Press, 1957), 222–29.

39. Indianapolis *News*, January 20, 1886; *The Journalist* March 22, 1884; House Report 1112, "H. V. Boynton and Others," 48th Cong., 1st sess., 198–99.

40. "Murray," Indianapolis *News*, January 20, 1886; *The Journalist*, December 8, 1888, October 24, 1891, April 16, 1892.

41. Thus, "Perley" did one of John A. Logan and Ramsdell one of Blaine in 1884 and "Gath" wrote one of vice-presidential nominee Levi P. Morton in 1888.

42. Indianapolis *News*, February 24, 1886; John A. Logan to William Henry Smith, January 20, 1881, Smith to Murat Halstead, January 25, 1881, Smith MSS, OHS; A. J. Ricks to John Sherman, October 12, 1885, Wilson J. Vance to Sherman, October 7, 10–11, 1888, Sherman MSS, LC.

43. Washington *Sunday Capital*, May 4, 1879; *The Journalist*, March 29, April 19, 1884, December 12, 1885, November 3, December 22, 1888, March 7, April 4, May 9, 1891; Henry Van Ness Boynton, "The Press and Public Men," *Century Magazine* (October 1891): 857. The process is well detailed into the twentieth century by Donald A. Ritchie, *Press Gallery: Congress and the Washington Correspondents* (Cambridge: Harvard University Press, 1991), 121–30, 163–94.

44. George T. McJimsey, *Genteel Partisan: Manton Marble, 1834–1917*, 143–44, 178–81; New York *Graphic*, May 26, 1876.

45. Springfield *Republican*, July 12, 1876; Donald W. Curl, *Murat Halstead and the Cincinnati Commercial* (Boca Raton: A Florida Atlantic University Book: University Presses of Florida, 1980), 73–78; Murat Halstead to Rutherford B. Hayes, September 19, 1876, Hayes MSS, HML; Richard Kluger, *The Paper: The Life and Death of the New York Herald Tribune* (New York: Knopf, 1986), 131–37; Cincinnati *Enquirer*, October 21, 1873; New York *Tribune*, July 28, August 29, September 20–21, 1876; Bingham Duncan, *Whitelaw Reid: Journalist, Politician, Diplomat* (Athens: University of Georgia Press, 1975), 67.

46. Washington *Chronicle*, November 12, 1874; Horace White to William Henry Smith, November 3, 1874, Smith MSS, OHS; Joseph Logsdon, *Horace White: Nineteenth-Century Liberal* (Westport, Conn.: Greenwood, 1971), 268–69; Lloyd Wendt, *Chicago Tribune: The Rise of a Great American Newspaper* (Chicago: Rand McNally, 1979), 242–49; Cincinnati *Enquirer*, March 15, 1877 (quotation). For the *Tribune*'s support for Hayes, see Robert L. Bishop and Stephen Friedman, "Campaign Coverage—1876 Style by the Chicago *Tribune*," *Journalism Quarterly* 45 (Autumn 1968): 481–86, 495.

47. Donn Piatt to Orville E. Babcock, October 7, 1876, Orville E. Babcock MSS, Newberry Library, Chicago; Charles Grant Miller, *Donn Piatt: His Work and His Ways* (Cincinnati: Robert Clarke & Co., 1893), 290, 299–306; New York *Times*,

October 14, 1882; Washington *Evening Star*, September 23, 1882; *The Journalist*, May 24, 1884, October 27, 1888, January 12, 1889.

48. Mark McGerr, *The Decline of Popular Politics: The North, 1860–1928* (New York: Oxford University Press, 1988), 118–19.

49. See, for example, *The Journalist*, February 28, 1891.

50. *The Journalist*, October 22, 1892.

EPILOGUE

1. "Mack," Washington *Chronicle*, August 15, 1875.

2. Mark W. Summers, *The Plundering Generation: Corruption and the Crisis of the Union, 1849–1861* (New York: Oxford University Press, 1987), 51–52.

3. *The Journalist*, July 28, 1888; New York *Times*, November 10, 1891.

Bibliography

Newspapers, Magazines, and Manuscript Collections

Newspapers and Magazines of Opinion Cited

Aiken (S.C.) *Tribune*
Atlanta *Constitution*
Atlanta *New Era*
Augusta *Constitutionalist*
Bangor *Whig and Courier*
Boston *Commonwealth*
Boston *Daily Advertiser*
Boston *Evening Transcript*
Boston *Morning Journal*
Bridgeport *Evening Standard*
Brooklyn *Daily Eagle*
Burlington (Vt.) *Times*
Charleston *Daily Republican*
Charleston *News and Courier* (*Courier*)
Chicago *Inter-Ocean*
Chicago *Times*
Chicago *Tribune*
Cincinnati *Commercial*
Cincinnati *Enquirer*
Cincinnati *Gazette*
Cleveland *Leader*
Cleveland *Plain Dealer*
Concord *New Hampshire Patriot*
Crystal Springs (Miss.) *Monitor*
Detroit *Free Press*
Harrisburg *Patriot and Union*
Indianapolis *Daily Sentinel*
Indianapolis *Journal*
Indianapolis *News*
Jackson *Pilot*
Jackson *Weekly Clarion* (*Clarion Ledger*)

Kansas City *Times*
LaCrosse *Democrat*
Little Rock *Arkansas Gazette*
Louisville *Courier-Journal (Courier)*
Marietta (Ohio) *Register*
Memphis *Daily Appeal*
Memphis *Daily Avalanche*
Milwaukee *Daily Wisconsin*
Milwaukee *News*
Milwaukee *Sentinel*
Mobile *Register*
Montgomery *Alabama State Journal*
Natchez *Daily Democrat*
Natchitoches (La.) *People's Vindicator*
Newport (R.I.) *Mercury*
New Orleans *Picayune*
New Orleans *Republican*
New Orleans *Times*
New York *Democrat (Pomeroy's Democrat)*
New York *Evening Post*
New York *Graphic*
New York *Herald*
New York *Independent*
New York *Nation*
New York *Sun*
New York *Times*
New York *Tribune*
New York *World*
Omaha *Republican*
Peoria *Daily National Democrat*
Philadelphia *Evening Star*
Philadelphia *North American*
Philadelphia *Press*
Portland *Eastern Argus*
Port Royal (S.C.) *Commercial and Beaufort Republican*
Providence *Journal*
Raleigh *Sentinel*
Raleigh *Standard*
Sacramento *Union*
St. Louis *Missouri Democrat*
St. Louis *Missouri Republican*
St. Louis *Post-Dispatch*
St. Louis *Times*
St. Paul *Pioneer*

St. Paul *Pioneer-Press*
San Antonio *Express*
Sandusky (Ohio) *Register*
Savannah *Morning News*
Shreveport *Times*
Springfield *Illinois State Journal*
Springfield *Illinois State Register*
Springfield *Republican*
Topeka *State Record*
Troy (N.Y.) *Weekly Times*
Vicksburg *Times*
Washington *Chronicle*
Washington *Evening Star*
Washington *New National Era*
Washington *Post*
Washington *Sunday Capital*
Washington *Union*
Wilmington (N.C.) *Morning Star*
Woodbury (Conn.) *Constitution*

Manuscript Collections Cited

Albany, New York
  New York State Library
    David Bennett Hill MSS
    Edwin D. Morgan MSS
    Horatio Seymour MSS
Baton Rouge, Louisiana
  Louisiana State University
    E. John Ellis MSS
    Ellis Family MSS
Bloomington, Indiana
  Lilly Library, Indiana University
    Schuyler Colfax MSS
    Henry S. Lane MSS
    Hugh McCulloch Letter-Books
    Richard W. Thompson MSS
Boston, Massachusetts
  Massachusetts Historical Society
    Edward Atkinson MSS
    George Frisbie Hoar MSS
Chapel Hill, North Carolina
  Southern Historical Collection,

University of North Carolina
    Frederick G. Bromberg MSS
    Elliott-Gonzales MSS
    Thomas Settle MSS
    Henry Clay Warmoth MSS
Charlottesville, Virginia
  University of Virginia
    Amos Akerman Letter-Books
Chicago, Illinois
  Chicago Historical Society
    David Davis MSS
  Newberry Library
    Orville E. Babcock MSS
Cincinnati, Ohio
  Cincinnati Historical Society
    Murat Halstead MSS
    Alexander Long MSS
Columbia, Missouri
  State Historical Society of Missouri
    James S. Rollins MSS

Columbus, Ohio
  Ohio Historical Society
    John A. Bingham MSS
    Henry Van Ness Boynton MSS
    James M. Comly MSS
    Friedrich Hassaurek MSS
    Donn Piatt MSS
    Robert C. Schenck MSS
    (microfilm copy)
    William Henry Smith MSS
    Allen Thurman MSS
Concord, New Hampshire
  New Hampshire Historical Society
    William E. Chandler MSS
Des Moines, Iowa
  Iowa State Department of Archives
  and History
    William Boyd Allison MSS
    Charles Mason MSS
Durham, North Carolina
  Duke University
    Francis Warrington Dawson MSS
    Alexander Stephens MSS
Fremont, Ohio
  Rutherford B. Hayes Memorial
  Library
    Mary Clemmer Ames MSS
    Henry Van Ness Boynton MSS
    Rutherford B. Hayes MSS
    Donn Piatt MSS
Indianapolis, Indiana
  Indiana Historical Society
    Delavan Smith MSS
    William Henry Smith MSS
  Indiana State Library
    John B. Stoll MSS
Ithaca, New York
  Cornell University
    Alonzo Cornell MSS
    Kernan Family MSS
Madison, Wisconsin
  Wisconsin State Historical Society
    James Rood Doolittle MSS

Montgomery, Alabama
  Alabama Department of History and
  Archives
    Robert McKee MSS
Montpelier, Vermont
  Vermont Historical Society
    Charles W. Willard MSS
New Haven, Connecticut
  Sterling Memorial Library, Yale
  University
    Samuel Bowles MSS
    Edwards Pierrepont MSS
New York, New York
  New York Public Library
    Bryant-Godwin MSS
    Horace Greeley MSS
    Samuel Jones Tilden MSS
Northampton, Massachusetts
  Smith College
    Ames Family MSS
Oberlin, Ohio
  Oberlin College
    Jacob Dolson Cox MSS
Philadelphia, Pennsylvania
  Historical Society of Pennsylvania
    Jay Cooke MSS
    William Darrah Kelley MSS
    Painter Family MSS
  University of Pennsylvania
    Samuel J. Randall MSS
Rochester, New York
  University of Rochester
    William Henry Seward MSS
St. Louis, Missouri
  Missouri Historical Society
    William H. Hatch MSS
    William B. Napton MSS
Springfield, Illinois
  Illinois State Historical Society
    Orville H. Browning
    Sylvanus Cadwallader MSS
    David Davis MSS
    Richard J. Oglesby MSS

L. U. Reavis MSS
John F. Snyder MSS
John D. Strong MSS
Horace White MSS
Richard Yates MSS
Washington, D.C.
  Library of Congress
    William Allen MSS
    Bayard Family MSS
    James G. Blaine MSS
    Benjamin Helm Bristow MSS
    Benjamin Franklin Butler MSS
    William E. Chandler MSS
    Zachariah Chandler MSS
    William Warland Clapp MSS
    John J. Creswell MSS
    Henry Laurens Dawes MSS
    Ewing Family MSS

    Hamilton Fish MSS
    John Wien Forney MSS
    Benjamin B. French MSS
    James A. Garfield MSS
    Horace Greeley MSS
    Thomas Jenckes MSS
    Andrew Johnson MSS
    Edward McPherson MSS
    Manton Marble MSS
    Whitelaw Reid MSS
    Carl Schurz MSS
    Alexander Robey Shepherd MSS
    John Sherman MSS
    WIlllam Henry Smith MSS
    Lyman Trumbull MSS
    Elihu Washburne MSS
    David A. Wells MSS
    John Russell Young MSS

Index

3 5282 00684 1269

LaVergne, TN USA
18 November 2009
164509LV00001B/82/A